A
Certain
Arrogance

The Sacrifice of Lee Harvey Oswald
and the Cold War Manipulation of
Religious Groups by US Intelligence

George Michael Evica

Introduction by Charles Robert Drago

A Certain Arrogance: The Sacrifice of Lee Harvey Oswald and the
Cold War Manipulation of Religious Groups by US Intelligence

Published by:
TrineDay LLC
PO Box 577
Walterville, OR 97489
1-800-556-2012
www.TrineDay.com
publisher@TrineDay.net

Library of Congress Control Number: 2010941378

Evica, George Michael — Author
A Certain Arrogance: The Sacrifice of Lee Harvey Oswald and the Cold
War Manipulation of Religious Groups by US Intelligence — 2nd ed.
p. cm.   (acid-free paper)
Epub (ISBN-13) 978-1-936296-63-7 (ISBN-10) 1-936296-63-2
Kindle (ISBN-13) 978-1-936296-64-4 (ISBN-10) 1-936296-64-0
Print (ISBN-13) 978-0-9841858-4-9 (ISBN-10) 0-9841858-4-4
1. Political corruption — United States — History — 20th century.
2. United States — Politics and government — 1945-1989. 3. I. Evica,
George Michael. II. Title

Second Edition
10 9 8 7 6 5 4 3 2 1

Printed in the USA
Distribution to the Trade by:
Independent Publishers Group (IPG)
814 North Franklin Street
Chicago, Illinois 60610
312.337.0747
www.ipgbook.com

"Foul deeds will rise, though all the earth o'erwhelm them, to mens' eyes."
Hamlet, Act I scene 2

Joseph Goebbels

Publisher's Foreword

If you tell a lie big enough and keep repeating it, people will eventually come to believe it. The lie can be maintained only for such time as the State can shield the people from the political, economic and/or military consequences of the lie. It thus becomes vitally important for the State to use all of its powers to repress dissent, for the truth is the mortal enemy of the lie, and thus by extension, the truth is the greatest enemy of the State.
— Joseph Goebbels

It is the emergence of mass media which makes possible the use of propaganda techniques on a societal scale.
— Jacques Ellul

What a life and what a riddle world.
— Louis Prima

"Well, I guess we are making romantic comedies," the senior vice president of creative affairs said humbly. It was out of his hands, and had gone way beyond his control. He had been harassed, bugged and chased. Wild rumors were spread in an attempt to get him fired, and when he persisted in advancing film projects of TrineDay's books, members of his family were threatened. Soon, a very capable company curtailed its pursuit to take several of our titles to the big screen. And this wasn't the first time, but that's another story.

The control and manipulation of our media has a long history. *A Certain Arrogance* gives us a look at some of the major players and how they played the game prior to, during and after World War II. Professor George Michael Evica deconstructs the webs of subterfuge surrounding Lee Harvey Oswald, and shows how private institutions get used and abused by our intelligence agencies ... and the spies who run them.

Today an aware person soon recognizes that America is acutely awash in propaganda, greed and corruption. This activity didn't begin with our most recent election cycle or latest war. We Americans are multi-generational sufferers of such psychological and fiscal abuse, which overwhelms any natural discourse or relations, leaving us twisted tattered pawns reacting to manufactured stimuli. This leads to division, distortion, dysfunction and eventually, disenfranchisement.

Most recently the "we can't say anything bad about the United States, our enemies will use it against us" excuse was trotted out as a perfunctory reason for the media's non-coverage of substantive issues presented in our books, and another day will surely bring a new excuse for such obfuscation. It appears that the creation of irrational fears trumps any semblance of honest journalism. Demonization, polarization, and continual crises appear to be the watchwords of the day. Yellow journalism rides triumphant, basking in its unholy light of deceit, while I.F. Stone, George Seldes, Ben Franklin and others must spin rapidly in their graves.

Here, the revered and renowned Professor Evica takes "history" to task and gives us a rigorous examination of many of the loose ends swept under the rug by official investigative bodies, especially focusing on many of the questions not asked about the activities of accused "lone-nut" Lee Oswald. Exposing the intelligence milieu swirling around the players, Evica shows how the actions fit within the arcane patterns of strategic espionage and the Machiavellian manipulations of psychological warfare.

The stage, script and players are engineered to influence different audiences, but mostly to mislead the general populace, who while being kept in the dark, foot the bill ... and pay the price. *A Certain Arrogance*, turns the house lights on and brings illumination into dark recesses, enriching our understanding of sordid deeds and sad days, and how they came about.

Why have there been so many books about the murder of John F. Kennedy? Was it simply because he was President of the United States? Or is it because we have been lied to about the evidence? There are those who say it doesn't matter, or that we will never know the truth – get on and get over it.

What can I say? Our republic, what's left of it, is dear to me. Our children are dear to me, and I strive with all of my heart and soul for a better world. We can change it. We need to recognize and excise the beast that cloaks itself within our national system: corruption running rampant that leaves us, the people, in despair, defilement and drudgery.

Let's talk and work with our friends, family and community, let's try to get beyond our differences, live up to America's destiny. Let's educate ourselves – not get lost in the invective rhetoric of right versus left, old versus young. We can revive the Republic for our children ... and theirs.

Onwards to the Utmost of Futures!
Peace,
Kris Millegan
Publisher
TrineDay
November 22, 2010

George Michael Evica
1927-2007

With love and great respect, this work is dedicated to the life and memory of Mary Ferrell.

Thanks

I thank: Ernest Cassara, former officer of Albert Schweitzer College; Professor Emeritus Paul Lacey; the clergy of all denominations who have given witness to the abuses of U.S. intelligence and who requested anonymity; the West Hartford Main Library and its departments of Reference and Interlibrary Loan; the University of Hartford Library and its departments of Reference and Interlibrary Loan; Tom Jones and Deborah Conway of JFKLANCER; the Rev. Leon Hopper, former director of Liberal Religious Youth; the Unitarian/ Universalist Association in Boston; the Unitarian Service Committee in Cambridge, Massachusetts; Frances O'Donnell, Archivist of the Andover-Harvard Theological Library, Harvard Divinity School; Ghanda Di Figlia, now at Harvard University, for her research, writing, and irreplaceable help; Alycia Brierley Evica for her patience and faith; and Charles Robert Drago for his wit, intelligence, and enduring friendship.

Reading Guidelines

The Epilogue may be the most useful place to begin this study of the abuse of religious individuals and groups by U.S. intelligence through two World Wars and the Cold War and the sacrificing of Lee Harvey Oswald. The endnotes for the prologue, the eight essays, and the epilogue are organic constituents of the book's argument and are extended analyses and documentation of the book's central thesis: see, for example, the endnotes' review of the families of Ruth and Michael Paine and their major U.S. government and intelligence connections. I strongly recommend the reader review each section's endnotes after having read that particular section.

Synopsis

A Certain Arrogance is a network of eight essays on the history of U.S. domestic and international intelligence, as developed in the early to mid-20th Century by Allen Dulles, John Foster Dulles and their many allies. Specifically:

[1] The manipulation and bankrolling of religious groups and individuals, especially well-meaning liberal Protestants, in establishing humanitarian front organizations to conceal clandestine political warfare operations (the destabilization of Communist Eastern Europe, South America, Southeast Asia, etc.).

[2] The development of psychological warfare operations (psyops/mass propaganda), from World War I through the Cold War, and its evolution into a finely tuned machine.

[3] The willing cooperation of "liberal" individuals on powerful administrative boards in illegally detaching the Central Intelligence Agency (CIA) and its sister organizations from any fiscal or operational accountability to Congress, elected Presidents, or the American Public.

[4] The strange history of Albert Schweitzer College.

[5] The mysterious journey of Lee Harvey Oswald, 1958-1963: from "Red" Marine to aspiring college student to Communist defector; then from re-defector to Castro-lover, and his diabolical apotheosis as a human sacrifice in the assassination of John F. Kennedy.

Introduction

To Withdraw From the Tumult of Cemeteries

> *...humankind*
> *Cannot bear very much reality*
> — T. S. Eliot, "Burnt Norton," Four Quartets

By Charles R. Drago

Let me be clear from the outset: *A Certain Arrogance* is no more or less "about" the assassination of John Fitzgerald Kennedy than cancer surgery is "about" the tumor. George Michael Evica, one of the preeminent prosectors of the malignant growth that disfigured the American body politic on November 22, 1963, for decades focused his intellect and intuition on the search for a cure for the underlying disease. In the course of forty-plus years of research, analysis, writing, broadcasting, and teaching, he followed its devastating metastasis through the vital organs of politics (deep and otherwise) to the extremities of business, culture, religion, and spirituality. All the while he cut away necrotic tissue and struggled valiantly, in the company of a surgical team as distinguished as it is obscure, to keep the patient alive.

Professor Evica, author of *And We Are All Mortal: New Evidence and Analysis in the Assassination of John F. Kennedy* (1975; University of Hartford), must be numbered among the most honored of the so-called second generation of Kennedy assassination researchers. Their labors to draw attention to, refine, expand upon, and add to the discoveries of their predecessors validate this direct statement of fact: Anyone with reasonable access to the evidence in the homicide of JFK who does not conclude that the act was the consequence of a criminal conspiracy is cognitively impaired and/or complicit in the crime. *A Certain Arrogance* stands as Professor Evica's final response to the unavoidable question: How do we define and effect justice in the wake of the world-historic tragedy in Dallas?

Clearly he understood that, at this late date, being content merely to identify and, if possible, prosecute the JFK conspiracy's sponsors, facilitators, and mechanics would be to endorse vengeance as a viable alternative to justice. Cleaning and closing the wound while leaving the disease to spread is simply not a survivable option.

With the nobility of knowledge comes obligation: How can we utilize all that has been learned from our post-Dallas investigations to heal and immunize the long-suffering victims of the malady of which the assassination of John F. Kennedy is but the most widely appreciated and putrescent manifestation?

The method by which Professor Evica, within *A Certain Arrogance*, honored his noblesse oblige is, at first blush, hardly novel. Like many other researchers, he chose to begin his exploration by focusing on a relatively simple-to-understand episode in the complex life of the lead character in the assassination drama, Lee Harvey Oswald. To carry the cancer metaphor forward: Think of the falsely accused killer as a tumor cell whose sojourn through the host organism in theory can be traced back to its source.

Oswald's movements, however, are not easily discerned. False trails and feints abound. Promising clues have been obscured by a host of ham-handed interlopers and sinister obfuscators.

Who was Lee Harvey Oswald? What was Lee Harvey Oswald? The best concise answer to those questions was provided by the novelist James Lee Burke – although he likely was not thinking of the accused assassin when he wrote, in Rain Gods, "If an individual, through either his own volition or events over which he had no control, found himself taking up residence in a country undefined by flags or physical borders, he could be assured of one immediate and abiding consequence: He was on his own, and solitude and loneliness would probably be his companions unto the grave."

Professor Evica's answers are directly responsive to the questions and, while informed by his ample creative gifts, rendered in the forms and language of historical inquiry.

Rather than traverse well-worn pathways, Professor Evica set out by following one of the few remaining under-examined passages of an otherwise over-mapped life. His uniquely painstaking investigation of Oswald's involvement with Albert Schweitzer College (hereinafter ASC), including the processes and implications of his application, acceptance, and nonattendance, led both to major discoveries and to significant refinements of previously developed hypotheses.

In the former category our attention is drawn to what Professor Evica termed "one of U.S. intelligence's last important secrets:" the infiltration and manipulation of student and youth organizations – especially those with religious affiliations – by the Central Intelligence Agency.

The U.S. government's faith-based initiatives, it seems, did not originate with George W. Bush's alleged presidency.

As he meticulously followed Oswald's ASC paper trail, Professor Evica was led not toward the Swiss campus, but rather into empty rooms and brick walls. A prime example: Oswald applied to ASC on March 19, 1959. Less than two months later, the chairman of ASC's American Admissions Committee (and, at the time, the pastor of the First Unitarian Church of Providence, Rhode Island) submitted to Switzerland the applications and related materials of prospective American students – including those collected in the Oswald folder.

Today the Oswald documents – evidence of inestimable value to the investigation of the crime of the 20th century – cannot be found in any official repository. Yet copies, or perhaps even originals, were in the Providence ASC file seized by the FBI shortly after the assassination. This deeply troubling disappearance, within a broader context fully substantiated in *A Certain Arrogance*, inevitably led the author to conclude that Oswald's application to ASC is "a still-protected American intelligence operation."

I do not wish to spoil the bittersweet joy of discovery to be experienced as readers accompany Professor Evica on what would be his final book-length tour through terra incognita. Yet the challenging methodology of *A Certain Arrogance* must be fully appreciated if the work's broader themes and implications are to be grasped, so I respectfully point to the following guideposts to help make the journey more fulfilling.

To discover the identities of Oswald's early manipulators is to be drawn into the necrotic nucleus of the disease. And so, thanks to the Evica investigation of the ASC set piece, we are left with a preliminary, inescapable conclusion regarding the "who" we seek.

"Whoever directed the Oswald [assassination] Game was thoroughly knowledgeable about both the OSS's and CIA's counterintelligence manipulations of Quakers, Unitarians, Lutherans, Dutch Reformed clerics and World Council of Churches officials as intelligence and espionage contacts, assets, and informants."

From the mountains and snowfields and quaint villages of Switzerland, Professor Evica would escort us through a darker, more hazardous landscape. Examinations of what he neatly summarizes as "U.S. covert intelligence operating under humanitarian cover" lead us to a confrontation with psychological operations – psyops and its propaganda, disinformation, and "morale operations" alter egos.

Professor Evica was the first to understand the Kennedy assassination and other intelligence operations as by-design theatrical constructs, replete with all the essential elements of drama – including both subtle and glaring manipulations of audiences' minds and emotions. Within the pages of *A Certain Arrogance* you will find additional support for and refinement of this hypothesis. For example:

"Psychological manipulations of individuals and groups, whatever the procedure may have been called in the 18th and 19th centuries, drew upon discoveries in anatomy, mesmerism, hypnotism, counseling, studies in hysteria, rhetorical theory, psychoanalysis, advertising, behavior modification, and psychiatry. In the same periods, the literary forms of irony, satire, and comedy and the less reputable verbal arts of slander, libel, and manufactured lies were applied."

Before we are tempted to argue that the realities of war often require an honorable combatant to mimic, for a limited period and with noble intent, the darker designs of an evil foe, let us heed Professor Evica's admonition: "Most of these genres and strategies were enlisted in the service of social, class, and political power." He went on to identify a likely director – or at the very least a prime facilitator – of the propaganda component of the aforementioned Oswald Game.

C. D. Jackson was "the psyops expert who organized and ran General Dwight David Eisenhower's Psychological Warfare Division at SHAEF ... an official of the Office of War Information ... [and] a veteran of the North African campaign."

Jackson's career and its impact upon American history, heretofore marginally understood at best (he is widely identified as the *Time-Life* editor who purchased the Zapruder film) comprise major areas of focus in *A Certain Arrogance*. In few places are both the validity of Albert Einstein's observation that "the distinction between past, present and future is only a stubbornly persistent illusion" and the contemporary relevance of Professor Evica's discoveries more clearly evident than in the author's exposition of Jackson's oeuvre. In particular we are drawn to the discussion of how mass media early on was identified as a key weapon in the mind control arsenal.

In a 1946 letter to Jackson, General Robert McClure, at one time Eisenhower's chief of intelligence for the European theater, boasted to his psyops counterpart of the scope of their manipulation.

"We now control 137 newspapers, 6 radio stations, 314 theaters, 642 movies, 101 magazines, 237 book publishers, 7,384 book dealers and printers, and conduct about 15 public opinion surveys a month, as well as publish one newspaper with 1,500,000 circulation ... run the AP of Germany, and operate 20 library centers."

Orwellian claims of fairness and balance, it seems, did not originate with promotions for the Fox News Network's alleged journalism.

****

Professor Evica and I, individually and collectively, for years struggled with the question of why so many honorable, gifted Kennedy assassination investigators decline to regard as established truth the conspiratorial nature of the scrutinized event and instead seem content to debate this long-settled issue ad infinitum with the cognitively impaired and/or accessories to murder.

Are these reluctant investigators' identities symbiotically linked to the high-profile roles they play as Kennedy assassination authorities to the degree that the termination of those roles – a certain consequence of universal acceptance of conspiracy truth – is perceived to be tantamount to the termination of the self? As sufferers of such a fear, they would be in exalted company.

Writing in *The End of Science* of what he perceives to be scientists' fear of reaching for absolute answers, John Horgan notes, "after one arrives at The Answer, what then? There is a kind of horror in thinking that our sense of wonder might be extinguished, once and for all time, by our knowledge. What, then, would be the purpose of existence? There would be none ... Many scientists harbor a profound ambivalence concerning the notion of absolute truth. Like Roger Penrose, who could not decide whether his belief in a final theory was optimistic or pessimistic. Or Steven Weinberg, who equated comprehensibility with pointlessness. Or David Bohm, who was compelled both to clarify reality and obscure it. Or Edmund Wilson, who lusted after a final theory of human nature and was chilled by the thought that it might be attained. Or Freeman Dyson, who insisted that anxiety and doubt are essential to existence ... "

And if not termination of the self, then what of that of the nation via the destruction of its fictive, dramaturgically rendered history?

The most effective psyop is the one that is self-imposed.

Haunting the pages of *A Certain Arrogance* in the company of the shades of John Fitzgerald Kennedy and Lee Harvey Oswald is a revelation so menacing in its assaults on convention and authority as to provoke a reflexive shielding of our eyes from its searing illumination. Yet Professor Evica could not spare us the psychic pain that is the unavoidable side effect of his scholarship, insofar as such suffering remains the sine qua non for the eradication of our common malady.

Within the nucleus of the disease, Professor Evica discovered "a treasonous cabal of hard-line American and Soviet intelligence agents whose masters were above Cold War differences."

In light of this truth, we are left with no choice but to embrace a new paradigm of world power.

Professor Evica revealed the universally accepted vertical, East v. West Cold War confrontation to be a sophistic construct, illusory in terms of its advertised raison d'etre but all too real in the bloody consequences of its staging, created by the powerful yet outnumbered manipulators of perception to protect what they recognized to be an all-too-fragile reality. The true division of power, he discovered, then as now is drawn on a horizontal axis.

Envision the earth so bifurcated, with the line drawn not at the equator, but rather at the Arctic Circle. Above the line are the powerful few – the "Haves." Below the line, in vastly superior numbers, are the powerless many – the "Have-Nots."

Can we bear so much reality?

While contemplating the implications of Professor Evica's research, I was reminded of how Francis Ford Coppola struggled to find the best thematic hook on which to hang the plot of *The Godfather, Part III*. It is said that he considered and ultimately rejected a treatment of the Kennedy assassination as the most cinematically viable expression of period systemic evil in full flower. Instead – perhaps wisely, perhaps not – he opted to dramatize the Vatican Bank scandal.

Upon initial examination, the conjoined stories of the looting of the Banco Ambrosiano, the perfidy of Roberto Calvi and P2, the assassination of John Paul I, and the corruption of the Roman Catholic Church at its highest levels present as the cellular components of yet another tumor, arguably the most horrific manifestation imaginable of the disease probed by Professor Evica.

We are incredulous. We are outraged.

Then reason returns.

The manipulations of religious institutions for unholy purposes by elements of the deep political structure should provoke neither surprise nor anger. For is not organized religion merely politics by other means? Are not the most power-hungry bishops – of the frocked, defrocked, wandering, and Maurice varieties, among others – all devoted to the same dark liturgy?

The assault on Albert Schweitzer, however, is another matter.

"The ethical spirit ... must be awakened anew," Dr. Schweitzer instructed at the height of the Cold War. The defiling of the name and the perversion of the mission of that saintly man no doubt provoked sweet satisfaction within the breasts of those for whom a universally held worldview informed by ethics is simply not a survivable option.

What then of justice? Have we any reason to expect the guilty to be punished, the disease to be eradicated? The novelist Jim Harrison, from Legends of the Fall:

"People finally don't have much affection for questions, especially one so leprous as the apparent lack of a fair system of rewards and punishments on earth ... We would like to think that the whole starry universe would curdle ... the conjunctions of Orion twisted askew, the arms of the Southern Cross drooping. Of course not; immutable is immutable and everyone in his own private manner dashes his brains against the long suffering question that is so luminously obvious. Even gods aren't exempt; note Jesus' howl of despair as he stepped rather tentatively into eternity."

It is for us to deliver justice and heal ourselves, to muster the courage to ask questions and the strength to endure answers.

Within the pages of *A Certain Arrogance*, George Michael Evica continues to lead by example.

****

Autumn Too Long: A Remembrance

November is a cruel month, and one that figures all too prominently in the life and times of George Michael Evica.

It was on a brilliant, unnaturally warm November morning in 2007 that loved ones laid to rest my friend and mentor, my confidante and comrade-in-arms, my spiritual guide and now my spirit guide.

As I carried the incongruously small urn that contained his physical remains, my thoughts drifted to another November day, when George Michael and I had found ourselves in Dealey Plaza at dusk, far from the madding crowd. Light was filtered thinly through brittle leaves and sorrow. And I asked if he too sensed the presence of unquiet spirits.

As usual, George Michael was years ahead of me. He said that he had experienced the same feelings on many occasions in that place. He spoke at length, his voice subdued yet redolent with conviction, about his certainty that the fight against the forces that struck John Fitzgerald Kennedy, the same forces that today prowl the killing fields of the Middle East and Africa and Asia and the Americas, endures into the next world.

The calm of Saint John's churchyard where he rests represents but a temporary respite.

Again I am drawn to the words of James Lee Burke, who showed us that he understands this immutable truth when he wrote the following ruminative passage for his fictional Cajun detective Dave Robicheaux:

> Down the canyon, smoke from meat fires drifted through the cedar and mesquite trees, and if I squinted my eyes in the sun's setting, I could almost pretend that Spanish soldiers in silver chest

armor and bladed helmets or a long-dead race of hunters were encamped on those hillsides. Or maybe even old compatriots in butternut brown wending their way in and out of history ... gallant, Arthurian, their canister-ripped colors unfurled in the roiling smoke, the fatal light in their faces a reminder that the contest is never quite over, the field never quite ours.

Charles Robert Drago
November, 2010

This is the Warren Commission. From the left: Rep. Gerald R. Ford, R-Mich.; Rep. Hale Boggs, D-La.; Sen. Richard B. Russell, D-Ga.; Chief Justice Earl Warren, the chairman; Sen. John Sherman Cooper, R-Ky.; John J. McCloy, New York banker; Allen W. Dulles, former Central Intelligence Agency director; and J. Lee Rankin of New York, general counsel.

Prologue

The "Dirty Rumor"

T he Warren Commission's first executive session on December 5, 1963 was quickly fouled by a dirty rumor: Lee Harvey Oswald had been a paid asset, an informer, for the Federal Bureau of Investigation (FBI). At least two later sessions were discomfited as well by the inconvenient subject.[1]

First on the list of distinguished witnesses was Alan Belmont, Assistant Director of the FBI.

The Belmont Ploy

A fter some preliminary questions and comments, Commission member Allen Dulles got serious, asking Belmont about teletype communications between FBI offices, specifically New Orleans and Dallas.

Commission member John J. McCloy asked about U.S. defectors to the Soviet Union. Both McCloy and Dulles wanted to know if the so-called Oswald file had been closed. Within half an hour, two important issues in the "dirty rumor" story had raised their thorny heads.

Then Samuel A. Stern, Warren Commission staff assistant counsel, brought up a report from the Bureau in response to a meeting on May 4, 1964 between Commission staff members and Belmont.

The Warren Commission had queried the FBI on March 26, 1964, with thirty questions about its knowledge of Oswald prior to November 22, 1963. Many of them related directly to Oswald's alleged covert status. The letter, prepared and reviewed by Belmont and signed by FBI Director Hoover, described 69 items contained in the FBI's Oswald file.

Without disclosing the actual contents, Belmont said the letter did indeed summarize the FBI's relationship with Lee Harvey Oswald, and answered "a number of questions which the Commission posed to the FBI." Earlier in the session, Assistant Counsel Stern had established the Commission's primary (and nearly exclusive) focus: Lee Harvey Oswald. Belmont had commented: "As the individual in charge of all investigative operations, [I am responsible for] the Lee Harvey Oswald investigation ... the same as any other investigative case in the Bureau."

Stern soon arrived at the hearing's crucial point: Belmont's "examination of the investigation... of the nature of the FBI interest in Oswald." Clearly, Stern wished to explore through Belmont the key issue of Oswald's rumored intelligence links. But Commission Chairman Earl Warren interrupted Stern twice, obviously attempting to shut him off early in the session. In this and later exchanges Rankin and Stern demonstrated quite different agendas from Warren concerning Oswald and U.S. Intelligence.

Ignoring Warren's objections, Stern queried Belmont about the FBI's domestic intelligence and identification divisions, including Oswald's defection, his Marine fingerprints, his correspondence, and the Albert Schweitzer College puzzle. Clearly, Stern was intent on examining the topic of false identity, a critical counter-intelligence area of great interest to both the CIA and the FBI. Stern elicited from Belmont that the FBI had set up certain "connections with the State Department passport file" on Oswald's activities and his dealings with the U.S. embassy in Moscow, but neither Stern nor anyone else pursued the matter any further.

Belmont asserted that the FBI had no interest in Oswald when he returned from the Soviet Union, and that he had no known connections with any FBI sources in New Orleans.

Despite Warren's interruptions and objections, Stern had managed to begin exploring the minefield of Oswald's possible American intelligence connections.

The FBI 'HQ' Oswald File

Stern then introduced the Belmont summary of the "HQ" FBI file on Oswald (CE 834.) Stern established that Belmont, as he sat before the Commission, was in possession of Oswald's actual file.

Stern asked Belmont about "materials in that file ... for security reasons you would prefer not to disclose...." Belmont responded by defining the file's security materials: "The file contains the identity of some of our informants in subversive movements." At the very least, Commissioners Warren, McCloy and Dulles, and counsels Stern and Rankin, must have understood that the names in the file had to include informants in New Orleans, and possibly Dallas, who had operated as double agents inside pro-Castro organizations. Their identities might have led directly to evidence establishing Oswald as a U.S. Intelligence agent or asset. Stern cautioned, "I think that is enough, Mr. Belmont, on that."

But it was not enough for Commissioner McCloy. His query of Belmont prompted Warren to attempt to cut off any further questioning on security matters in the Oswald file. Though he complimented Warren on his security-conscious behavior, Belmont reminded him that J. Edgar Hoover had insisted he be of "utmost help" to the Commission.

Warren's pre-emptive strike strongly suggests that he and the FBI had earlier scripted a dog-and-pony show in which the FBI's offer of the Oswald file to the Commission would be rejected on "security" grounds. Commission Counsels Stern and Rankin, not having attended rehearsals, were naively working to accept the FBI's seeming offer of the file.

After Stern elicited from Belmont that the FBI file was available to the Commission, Warren countered by establishing that the "security matter" involving FBI informers was contained in the allegedly complete file before them. Belmont verified that fact: "This file is as it is maintained at the Bureau with all information in it." Justice Warren responded: "With *all* information in it?" Belmont answered: 'Yes sir; this is the actual file." Warren: "I see."

Chief Counsel Rankin intervened, asking Belmont if he would leave the file in the Commission's possession so "any of the Commissioners [could] ... examine it personally."

Belmont agreed to leave the file, and Rankin was on the verge of appropriating the dossier for his Commission staff.

Warren immediately interrupted with a confused and obviously improvised statement about nonexistent "conditions" and not wanting "information that involves our security." Just *how* identifying a few FBI informants to the exalted Commission might compromise national security, the Chief Justice was not asked to explain.

Warren then pushed his argument further, refusing to accept any actual intelligence documents and opting for Belmont's vocal testimony alone. This firmly established Warren's antipathy toward *any* official paper trail concerning Oswald's suspected intelligence links.

Warren concluded with a muddled statement, supposedly in favor of "open" discussion as opposed to viewing sensitive documents "in privacy." This completed a perfect 'Catch-22': Exposing informants to public knowledge would compromise security, and sharing them *in camera* would be anti-democratic. Thus, forget about it, move on.

Apparently willing to give up almost all of his ground in exchange for access to the FBI file, Rankin then promised that "the staff will not examine it," a statement obviously directed at Warren rather than Belmont. But Warren countered that to read the FBI file was "one thing" (whatever that meant), but for him, Belmont's oral summary of the file was quite enough.

Finally, Warren defined his bottom-line position: "I really would prefer not to have a secret file… that contains [security] matters of that kind in our possession." Why did no one suggest a "sanitized" file, redacting the informants names?

Rankin now had little leverage except to air the vexing "dirty rumor" directly in his final argument for accepting the Oswald file. Though his impromptu statement was garbled, Rankin obviously wanted the file available so the Commission could "be satisfied that nothing was withheld from it in regard to this particular question. That was the purpose of the inquiry." This statement clearly pointed to the Commission's continuing problem: how to bury the rumor of Oswald's FBI link.

Allen Dulles followed Warren's lead, but McCloy, apparently looking directly at a copy of the file, interrupted, indicating that Belmont's summary was not "a complete description" of the contents.

Warren again tried to head off objections, but Rankin counterattacked, articulating the Commission's strongest argument for independent analysis of intelligence files, concluding: "we did want the record in such condition that the Commission could say in its report, 'We have seen everything that they have.' I think [this file]… is important to the case."

Commissioner McCloy suggested that the Commission might miss "the full impact of all the narrative." Both Belmont and Warren then argued with McCloy, telling him that the Commission already had possession of the reports to which he referred. But why not let

McCloy look at the reports, wherever they were? What difference did some duplication make?

This response was additional evidence of an earlier agreement to sabotage the "offer" of the file, giving Warren an excuse to reject it, and block any curious Commissioner from reading through actual files and documents. His justification seemed to be: Where will it all end? We shall see.

Rankin still persisted, trying to emphasize his and Stern's argument: that the Warren Commission would be in possession of "everything... the FBI had [on Oswald]... this is their total file ... so that ... nothing [would be] withheld from you as far as the FBI is concerned. That is ... what we are trying to develop this morning...." Obviously, the staff was concerned that if the file was rejected, the Commission could never assert that nothing had been withheld.

Former CIA Director Allen Dulles again supported Warren, speaking to a separate issue involving the staff, allowing Warren to close with his argument against sharing files with non-government investigators: "the same people who would demand that we see everything of this kind would also demand that they be entitled to see it, and [because] it is security matters [,] we can't let them see it. It has to go back to the FBI without their scrutiny."

Warren was clearly anticipating that people would argue for a more open investigation process.

Commissioner McCloy still persisted in opposing Warren, apparently examining Belmont's file summary on telegrams from "the Embassy" and "Mexico," key issues relevant to both the second Oswald mystery and the CIA's manipulation of the Oswald-in-Mexico story. Warren, however, triumphed: he and Stern finally moved to admit only the Belmont file "summary" into the official record. One last time, Warren emphasized his point with Belmont: "There are no security matter[s] in this?"

Belmont then continued his testimony, asserting that Oswald was neither an agent of, nor an informant for, the FBI. He spoke at length but to no productive purpose about the FBI, the Secret Service, cooperation, presidential security, Jack Ruby, Communism, and various minor matters.

After successfully burying the pesky FBI file, Warren blithely admitted without comment the unsupported testimony of U.S. Intelligence officers that Lee Oswald was not one of theirs.

In 1976, circumstantial evidence and some of the CIA's Oswald files were made available to the House Select Committee on Assassinations. These revelations strongly supported the argument that Oswald either thought he was, or indeed had been, an agent or asset of any of several U.S. Intelligence services.

Though transparently a ploy, the offer of the file raised significant issues, especially as Belmont's testimony is closely examined. Commission member John McCloy seemed genuinely interested in exploring the dirty rumor; Stern and Rankin, representing the Commission's staff, were obviously dedicated to opening up the topic. Allen Dulles made some shuffling noises with his Agency shoes but then supported Warren's rejection of the Bureau file.

Was the FBI Monitoring Oswald's Mail?

Standing against Belmont's testimony were two major questions that related directly to the dirty rumor: was the FBI monitoring Oswald's mail and, if so, did the Bureau know that a mail-order rifle was being delivered to Oswald's P.O. box? After four years of research and analysis, my conclusion remains yes, to both questions. This points directly to FBI manipulation of the mails (and Oswald) in a pre-assassination spy game. If so, then Sylvia Meagher was correct: the FBI knew about the mail-order weapon because the FBI itself had expedited both the purchase and delivery to their asset, Lee Oswald.

Belmont also spoke briefly about the Albert Schweitzer College puzzle. If Oswald was an intelligence asset or agent, or a lowlier pawn in their game, his strange Magical Mystery Tour which started at El Toro Naval Base in California and ended up in Moscow would make sense, especially after he became the object of an FBI False Identity/Illegals investigation.

Chief Justice Warren, in speciously rejecting the FBI Headquarters file, prevented exposure of the Bureau's mail intercept program directed at Oswald, and brushed aside the related Schweitzer College mini-circus. By so doing, he preserved the agreed-upon "lone gunman misfit/loser" mythos, scotched any real attempt to get at the truth behind the smoke-screen, and set course full-sail for Predetermined Island.

Afterward, having nearly been burned on this topic, the Commission (or at least its chairman Chief Justice Earl Warren) clearly decided to avoid any future back-draft as the Commission faced four months of testimony often touching on that same dirty rumor.

The fifth volume of the Warren Commission's twenty-six volumes of support materials is central to the topic of Oswald's possible participation in U.S. Intelligence activities, and contains a surprisingly rich collection of relevant testimony. In Washington, Dallas and elsewhere, from May 6th through September 6, 1964, the Commission listened to representatives of the FBI, including J. Edgar Hoover, the U.S. Army (on wound ballistics), CIA Director John McCone and his Deputy Director for Plans, the State Department with Secretary of State Robert MacNamara, the Secret Service and its Chief, James J. Rowley, the Treasury Department, including Treasury Secretary C. Douglas Dillon, and Texas law enforcement officers on state, county, and city levels. The Commission also took testimony from Mark Lane, asked by Oswald's mother to represent the dead and pre-convicted assassin, from new President Lyndon Baines Johnson and his wife; and several residents of Dallas, such as Jack Ruby, Marina Oswald, and her friends Ruth and Michael Paine.

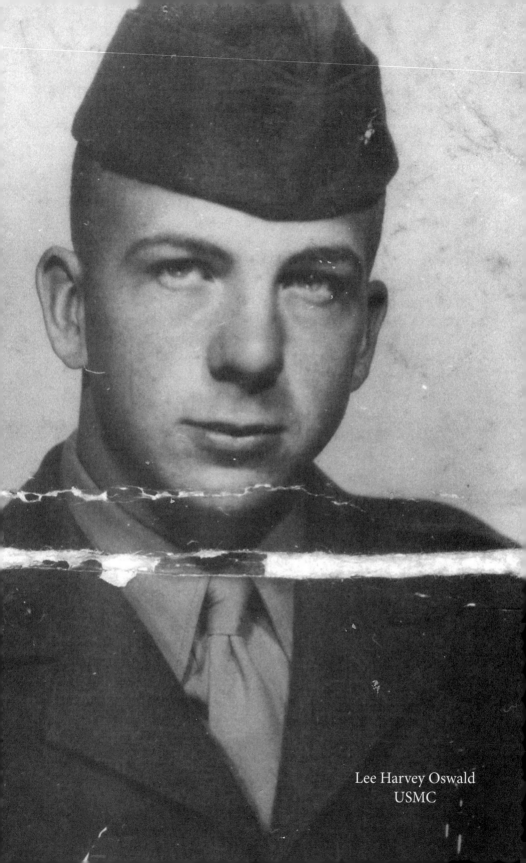

Lee Harvey Oswald
USMC

Essay One

A Friendly Interview with Mr. "Fannan"

It was February 1960. The FBI agent stared at the woman sitting before him. Just a moment before, her hands were crossed, their palms upward. Now they were flying. Finally they alighted on her lap, palms facing upward again. She examined them, as if she were reading some arcane communication in their lines and grooves.

She thought he had said his name was "Fannan."[1]

The translucent skin of her round and almost unlined face flushed briefly. Stacked on the small table next to her were three returned letters from the Soviet Union: a $20 money order with her son's scribbled note rejecting it as useless; another returned unopened, its $20 bill still inside; and a third, also unopened, with a $25 Foreign Money Transfer inside.

The agent carefully surveyed her corseted, rectangular body for some sign of stress. Her graying hair, almost white, had somehow begun to lift slightly, as if disturbed by a breeze blowing through her Fort Worth home.

For such a stout lady, Lee Oswald's mother seemed formed of very small bones.

"You understand, don't you?" she asked him.

He was passive. The Bureau had already intercepted her mail to the Soviet Union. Her foreign money transfer to Lee had been taken seriously by the Bureau's New York field office.

"Lee ending up in Russia, my letter unopened and returned. And you know, he took his birth certificate with him."

The agent stiffened. He was about to blurt out a question; then he caught himself, relaxed, and remained silent.

"My son has… completely disappeared. His brother Robert hasn't heard from him since the middle of December. I haven't heard from him since early January." He's just… gone."

The agent knew she was Lee's only living parent. He spoke carefully.

"It doesn't look good, ma'am. It looks like your son doesn't *want* to be found."

"Please help me," she implored.

He smiled.

"Of course. I'd say you ought to write directly to the Secretary of State, you know, at the State Department in Washington; and to Sam Rayburn and Jim Wright, your representatives? Ask all of them to assist you in any way possible."Her hands fluttered again, then dropped to her lap. "I will, I will," she promised.

He was pleased with his improvisation. While seeming to be helpful, he hoped it would be a major deflection that kept Lee's mother and the Washington bureaucracy busy for a while.

Long after the agent left, as the light faded in a clear Texas sky, Marguerite Oswald sat and brooded over the rejected funds she'd sent to her son at his Metropole Hotel address in Moscow. Now he was somewhere else in that vast and distant Soviet Union, refusing to make contact.

She loved her strange and wonderful Lee, though she often did not understand him. And she had begun to entertain a disturbing possibility: that her young son was some sort of secret agent for the American government.[2]

College Daze: The Missing Lee

Mrs. Oswald waited until April. She thought Lee had signed up for that oddly named college in Switzerland's fall session of 1959. But two months after her FBI visitor had been so helpful, after weeks of frustrating correspondence, Marguerite Oswald received some very bad news. Lee, who according to the letter was expected at Albert Schweitzer College for the *spring* session of 1960, had neither made an appearance nor informed the college he would not be attending.[3]

According to one knowledgeable CIA source, "Mail from Soviet agents in the United States would not have been sent directly to Moscow…" but through "neutral countries such as Switzerland…."

The same procedure would have been followed for clandestine mail from Moscow that was ultimately destined for the States. During the Cold War, Switzerland was a postal transfer for major espionage message exchanges, but its use by American intelligence dated back to the First World War.

Switzerland, as the most strategic neutral country, fulfilled its valuable function through World War II, when Allen Dulles, then director of the Office of Strategic Services (OSS) in Bern, controlled an intelligence network of Swiss civilians, military personnel, and American, British, and German agents, including doubled operatives out of Nazi intelligence. From his Swiss base, Allen Dulles operated a Europe-wide spy network in Switzerland, France, Germany, Hungary, Italy, and Yugoslavia.

Switzerland, covert operations, and mail intercepts were all significant elements of Lee Harvey Oswald's paper trail, made up almost entirely of his carefully monitored postal correspondence, including Oswald's letters to the American Embassy in Moscow and his family in the United States. Soviet intelligence also monitored that paper trail when Oswald was in the Soviet Union and, later, when he communicated with individuals in the Soviet Union after he returned to the U.S.

Oswald's Marine Documents: Whose I.D. Was This?

Oswald's Swiss connection became of intense interest to the FBI, specifically embodied in the suspicions of both Alan Belmont, the Bureau's number three officer, and the big cheese, J. Edgar Hoover himself.

That interest began when Oswald, still an active Marine, applied for his passport on September 4, 1959 and received it on September 10, out of Los Angeles. Though Oswald reportedly had possession of his birth certificate while in the Soviet Union, which was the usual identification when applying for a passport, he submitted a Department of Defense (DOD) I.D. Card.

But except for several crucial and undeniable reasons, Lee Harvey Oswald should never have had a DOD I.D. card on September 4, 1959: possibly on September 11th, but not on September 4th.

The Department of Defense card was allegedly found in a wallet belonging to Oswald just after his arrest at the Texas Theatre on November 22, 1963. The card clearly signaled to those who understood it that the bearer had some official connection to U.S. Intelligence, and the Marine Corps confirmed it had issued the card to Oswald before he was released from active duty. But the practice of issuing that type of card to Marine reservists ended officially as of July 1959. According to a Marine Corps public affairs officer, Oswald was probably issued the military I.D. card because he was about to fill a civilian position overseas which required it.

Was Oswald scheduled to begin a new job that would take him to Europe as an asset or agent of the CIA, or as a civilian employee of the Office of Naval Intelligence?

A helpful Marine Corps public affairs officer could not explain how on September 4, 1959, in Santa Ana, California, Oswald apparently submitted to the Clerk of the Superior Court, L.B. Wallace, an "MCR/INACTIVE I.D. CARD #N4, 271, 617," in his passport application. Officially, Oswald would not have been issued that card until September 11th, the day he was "released from Active Duty and transferred to the Marine Corps Reserve...."

Did someone other than Oswald have possession of that card before he did?

And whose photo was on the DOD card? Its image was the same as the one on the "fake" Selective Service card clumsily made out to "Hidell" and reportedly found in Oswald's wallet after his arrest. The card blatantly called attention to itself: its erasures were clearly visible, and Selective Service cards did not have photos.

But the problem did not end there. The photograph in question was a Warren Commission document, buried in the pile, without either its Defense Dept. I.D. card or "Hidell" Selective Service card contexts. According to the FBI, the picture was taken in Minsk and issued *before* Oswald went to the Soviet Union. It is identical to a fake Selective Service card photo "taken in Minsk" after Oswald defected to the Soviet Union.

The actual card is not available at the National Archives: Sue McDonough, of the Archives' Civil Reference Branch, said the FBI had effectively destroyed the card through "extensive chemical forensic testing." *Oops...*

The Oswald postal problem again presents itself. On the copy of Oswald's DOD card in the Dallas Police evidence files, one postmark, and possibly another, can be seen. The clearest is stamped October 23, 1963, but the card had officially expired over 10 months earlier on December 7, 1962. On the reverse side of the card were the instructions: "If found, drop in any mail box," and "Return to Department of Defense, Washington 25, D.C."

Is there any way to extract some sense from this postal noise?

The DOD card existed in someone's possession in Santa Ana, California, when it was used to obtain Oswald's passport in September 1959. But no official record of the card existed until it was supposedly found in Lee Oswald's wallet.

But someone also possessed the card after September 1959, and either "lost" it before October 23, 1963, or kept it until that day. The card entered U.S. Post Office records when it was delivered to the Department of Defense in Washington, D.C. Between October 23rd and November 22, 1963 the card must then have matriculated down to Dallas and into Oswald's wallet.

The card might have made one other appearance prior to November 22nd. Between August 21st and September 17, 1963, during a C.O.R.E voter registration drive in Clinton, Louisiana, a Navy I.D. card was used by a man who said he was Oswald. This may have been identical to Lee's Department of Defense card.

Even if we assume that Oswald retained possession of the DOD card until October 23, 1963, when he either lost the card or dropped it in a mail-box himself, how did it wind up in his confiscated wallet?

Did someone at the Department of Defense have possession of the card and assist in its migration back to Oswald's wallet when he was arrested?

In fact, after its use in obtaining Oswald's 1959 passport, the DOD identification card had no other verified function except to link Oswald to 'Hidell' and the rifle supposedly discovered at the Texas School Book Depository (TSBD).

The original DD Form 1173, "Uniformed Services and Identification and Privilege Card," had a very strained reality. Oswald submitted his passport application on September 4, 1959. His I.D. card established it had been issued on September 11, 1959, eight days after it had already been used as identification in Oswald's passport application. On the same day Oswald was placed on inactive status in the Corps, and signed a statement pledging not to "in any manner" give information that would negatively affect the national security of the United States, "which I gained during my employment..." by the US Marine Corps.

Could the DOD card have been issued to inactive Marine Oswald by American intelligence at the United States Embassy in Moscow? Though it is an attractive alternative theory, it is not really viable.

The card was purportedly signed on September 11, 1959, by Marine 1st Lt. A.G. Ayers Jr., in Santa Ana, California. According to available Marine records, Oswald then became an inactive Reservist "by reason of hardship," and the I.D. card was issued according to standard Marine Corps procedures.

But how did Marine Lt. Ayers sign both Oswald's I.D. card and "Separation Section" document without perceiving the contradictions between his "hardship" status and his simultaneous travel intentions?

The fact is, according to Warren Commission's records, Lt. Ayers did not actually sign the Separation papers. A Marine 1st Sergeant Stout signed for the apparently absent lieutenant. But this "Sergeant Stout" was a paper fiction. He did not actually exist. Oswald did have a close Marine buddy named Zack Stout: they had served together in Japan and the Philippines in 1957 and 1958. But the real Stout was not stationed at El Toro in 1959.

The overlaying of Oswald's Marine buddy with the fictional "Sgt. Stout" adds another whiff of covert ops to the paper trail.

These major contradictions between Oswald's separation date and his passport application date, along with his hardship status/ world travel plans, were blissfully (or willfully) ignored by American intelligence in 1959-60 and the Warren Commission in 1964.

Passport to...?

If the way in which Oswald obtained his passport were not suspicious enough, his stated travel plans were also provocative. Oswald listed Cuba, the Dominican Republic, England, "Turku," Finland, France, Germany, "Russia" and Switzerland. Turku refers to the University of Turku, which for some time had not been in the city of Turku, but in Helsinki. The incorrect location of the university is another in a series of "errors" concerning names, dates and places in the Oswald paper record.

An itinerary so ambitious for a man with few financial resources should have raised at least some eyebrows in American intelligence. How could Oswald pay for such a tour? Was he being underwritten, and if so, by whom? Was his trip an intelligence action? If so, it would not matter to the State Department, the FBI, the CIA, or the National Security Agency (NSA), unless they weren't in the loop. The excluded agencies would then take an immediate and fiercely territorial interest.

The travel list is provocative. It includes two nations in the troubled Caribbean, where reactionary repression and progressive revolution were vying for power, especially Cuba, the usual cultural stops in Europe (but, oddly, not Italy), Finland, the 'gateway' to the Soviet Union, and Russia. The omission of Italy may have been a variation on the Sherlock Holmes story of the dog that didn't bark, which would have alerted the CIA'S James Jesus Angleton, a veteran of the OSS Italian escapades in World War II: unless Angleton, as several researchers have suggested, sent Oswald to Europe himself as an espionage "dangle," hoping Soviet Intelligence would take the bait.

Finland and the Soviet Union were possibly the most provocative lures; the latter listed as "Russia," a word almost always preceded by "Communist."

Oswald named Albert Schweitzer College in Switzerland, handprinted on Oswald's passport application as "thE CollEGE of A. SchwETZER, CHUR SwiTZerlAnd." CHUR represents either Chur, or Churwalden, or both.

At the same time, Oswald also listed his intention to study at the University of Turku in Finland.

According to his application to the college, reportedly sent March 19, 1959, he intended to study in Switzerland from April 12 to June 27, 1960, the college's third term in its trimester schedule. His passport, however, listed "4 months" as his total length of stay outside the United States; enough time, but just enough, to attend the college's *fall* trimester. Attending the college's third trimester meant he would be in Europe for nine months, not four. But what about all those other stops on his itinerary?

Was any evidence found that clearly indicated Oswald would be attending the fall rather than the spring trimester? In 1995, the Assassination Records Review Board was able to force the release of a set of documents sent by the FBI *Legat* at the American Embassy in Paris to Bureau Director J. Edgar Hoover. Among those papers was a Swiss Federal Police memorandum from October 12, 1960, stating that Oswald indicated from Moscow he would be attending the fall trimester, 1959, *not* the third and last trimester.

But this police report, summarized in the first of four communications from the *Legat* to Director J. Edgar Hoover, was subsequently contradicted, without explanation, by the fourth and last *Legat* communication to Hoover, suspiciously anticipating the Warren Commission's conclusions about Oswald's intentions.

The Warren Report, based on Oswald's official college application sent from Santa Ana, California, had indeed stated Oswald expected to attend the college's third trimester. But Oswald's preparations for exiting the Marines and obtaining a passport all support the Swiss Federal Police's first conclusion: that Oswald was targeting the fall trimester at Albert Schweitzer College.

Since Oswald's active duty wasn't up until December 7th, 1959, he could not have made it to Schweitzer College for the fall trimester, unless he received an early discharge no later than the middle of September 1959. This was indeed the outcome of Oswald's hardship application in August. Supposedly, his mother had suffered a workplace accident and needed him to come home and care for her as quickly as possible. The evidence shows her doctor and other alleged witnesses falsely confirmed a non-existent injury.

The scheme also relied on the Marine Corps itself. It seems no one at El Toro was the least bit disturbed that Private Oswald wanted a passport for an extended tour of the Caribbean and Europe, while simultaneously going home to care for his invalid mother: certainly not 1st Lt. A.G. Ayers, Jr., whose phantom Sgt. Stout signed Oswald's "Separation Section" document on September 4, 1959, certifying he was to be released from active duty and transferred to the Marine Corps Reserve (Inactive) on September 11th.

In fact, the Marine Separation Section document itself was attached to Oswald's passport application and stamped (upside down):

Received Department of State
1959 SEP 9 AM 9 54
PASSPORT OFFICE LOS ANGELES

Oswald received his passport on September 10, 1959, while still on active duty in the Marine Corps, an unusual accommodation for a Private 1st Class with, at least officially, a less than distinguished service record.

Four days later, on September 14, 1959, Oswald was home in Fort Worth with his poor disabled mother. On September 19th, he was in New Orleans booking ship passage to Le Havre, France, and posting a goodbye letter to Mom. It seems Marguerite had made a miraculous recovery in just five days.

The Red Marine

In March 1959, when he allegedly applied to Schweitzer College for the spring trimester in 1960, Oswald was still a Marine on active duty. Despite his blemished military record, he had earlier been involved in a number of key Marine operations in the Pacific area; he was a player in the U-2 spy plane story. With his outspoken support of the Soviet Union, Oswald could have been called the 'Red Marine.' He received mail that provoked curiosity and comment: a newspaper printed suspiciously in Russian, but more than likely a White Russian newspaper, and virulently anti-Stalinist. He also subscribed to *The Worker*, the organ of the Socialist Workers Party, which also deplored Stalin's reign of terror. Oswald's 'leftist' mail ought to have been of interest to (if it wasn't directed by) American intelligence.

The framed image of Oswald the Red Marine, generated by a series of complacent researchers, has been accepted, passed on, and seldom challenged. There is, however, a contrary image based on primary evidence. U.S. Marines Nelson Delgado, Daniel Powers, Donald Peter Camarata, Peter Francis Connor, Allen D. Graf, John Rene Heindel, Mack Osborne, and Richard Dennis Call all gave sworn testimony in Warren Commission affidavits that they never perceived Oswald to be either Socialist or Communist.

Marine Kerry Thornley, testifying before the Warren Commission in person, maintained Oswald had shown a propensity for Marxism; but this claim was supported only by his casual observation of Oswald's mail.

Throughout his Marine career, Oswald maintained an active postal life. With the mail he reportedly received while still in the Corps, he would certainly have come to the attention of the Office of Naval Intelligence, especially when he announced an extensive tour of Europe and Cuba. But no military postal intercept records of Lee Harvey Oswald are available. Could they have been deliberately destroyed? Perish the thought.[4]

The FBI, the Office of Naval Intelligence, the CIA, the Warren Commission, the House Select Committee on Assassinations, and the Assassination Records Review Board never asked a series of obvious questions:

How did Oswald discover Schweitzer College?

Where was Oswald's initial letter of inquiry, posted from his Marine base in Santa Ana, California?

Was he, in fact, directed to request a domestic address for the college? Why is neither a catalogue nor any other Schweitzer College curriculum information available in any of the JFK assassination records on the college?

Where was, for example, the "brochure … from this college, dated 1960…" and apparently received through the U.S. mail by Lee's mother, who at one time had it in her possession?

And, finally, where were Oswald's three character references, with at least one from a chaplain, pastor or priest?

In 1975, this missing evidence concerned Paul L. Hoch, the most cautious of scholarly JFK assassination researchers. In one concentrated page, Hoch discussed the obvious need to explore both FBI and CIA knowledge of Oswald's relationship to the college. He pointed out that, "Oswald had… been accepted by that school, despite the apparent absence of the proper references and background." Hoch also questioned why no inter-agency communication between the FBI and the CIA concerning Oswald's non-appearance at Schweitzer College was "in the CIA file on Oswald, CD 692." Hoch further identified the central issue, which until now has not been explored: "The CIA, the FBI and the ONI [Office of Naval Intelligence] should … be asked if there was any intelligence interest in Schweitzer College, or any direct or indirect government support. That [support] might explain Oswald's peculiar contacts with the College."

Assume that Oswald did indeed somehow discover the college. Normally he would then have written to the college in order to receive the application materials that are now part of the Warren Commission's records. But no initial letter of inquiry exists in the public record. It is also not among the documents reportedly received from the college and delivered to the FBI by the Swiss Police.

Did Oswald's letter of inquiry ever exist, or did he receive the application materials from some helpful individual concerned with his continuing education? It's hard to believe the college would have arbitrarily sent an application halfway around the world to recruit Pfc. Lee Oswald. It is also unlikely a personal friend would have been the source of the material, which leaves the usual suspects. Did the CIA or the Office of Naval Intelligence provide the paperwork and prompt Oswald to apply? If so, why?

One program run by the Office of Naval Intelligence was the recruitment of soon-to-be discharged Navy and Marine servicemen as fake defectors to the Soviet Union. Was Lee Harvey Oswald one of the chosen? Certainly at least several U.S. double agent "dangle" operations were in progress during the Cold War, and the information and registration forms supplied to Oswald could have been part of that program. His actions in the U.S.S.R., his recantation and return to the U.S. fit this theory quite comfortably.

Since Oswald's non-appearance at Albert Schweitzer College provoked a major international 'search,' first called for by his mother and then by the FBI, these questions may go to the heart of Oswald's true mission in the Soviet Union.

They may also go to the heart of a Cold War black hole.

Whatever American intelligence's supposedly sketchy information about Albert Schweitzer College, the Warren Commission was concerned about the institution; but the interrogation of witnesses elicited nothing substantial about the college, and the Commission failed to explore the topic.

More Pulp Fiction

Oswald left for Fort Worth after his Marine discharge, arriving there on September 14, 1959. He then communicated a series of provocative half-truths, beginning by telling his mother he was in pursuit of shipboard employment and that he might go into the "import-export business." If, however, Mrs. Oswald's memory of her son's passport stamped IMPORT-EXPORT is correct, he had already had his passport so designated. Lee's brother Robert wrote in his own book of recollections that Lee "planned to go to New Orleans and work for an export firm...."

Promising his mother to make "big money," Oswald left for New Orleans, but not before he "had registered his dependency discharge and entry into the Marine Reserve at the Fort Worth Selective Service Board ... leaving behind one more entity, the Selective Service Administration, that would be officially interested in his ever-changing postal address.

In New Orleans, he established still another traceable paper link, by visiting a New Orleans travel agency, Travel Consultants, where he filed a "Passenger Immigration Questionnaire" and booked passage on a freighter to Le Havre. That immigration form allowed Oswald to continue to register his series of half-truths, listing his occupation as "shipping export agent," a variant of his passport "occupation." But he also recorded he would be staying in Europe for only two months, to complete a planned pleasure trip.

The immigration document flatly contradicts his passport application anticipating an extensive continental tour and studies at two European colleges. Further, Oswald's passport had listed four months as the length of his stay, but it was a time period almost as unrealistic as the immigration document's listing of two months; unless it implicitly referred to his attendance at Schweitzer College during the fall trimester.

Further, the handwritten "4 months" notation on Oswald's passport application differed significantly from Oswald's vagrant handwriting, although that variance may simply have meant that Oswald inadvertently left it blank, and a helpful clerk filled in the information after asking "How long will you be staying?"

But that benign version would not explain Oswald's unrealistic response, except as still another illogical element in the bizarre travel universe of Lee Harvey Oswald.

Oswald sailed from Le Havre on October 8th to England, arriving the next day. On board ship Oswald told his cabin companion, according to the Warren Report, "He intended to travel in Europe and possibly to attend school in Sweden or Switzerland if he had sufficient funds." Oswald did reportedly touch down in Sweden after entering Finland, at either the American or Soviet Embassy, and then returned to Finland. With his two other shipboard companions, Oswald was more specific: "he told them he planned to study in Switzerland ..."

Oswald told English customs officials in Southampton he intended to stay for one week, after which he would report to "a school in Switzerland."

Again, Oswald contradicted his stated plans. He went to Finland, possibly zig-zagged to Sweden, crossed into the Soviet Union and arrived in Moscow on October 16, 1959. Oswald's mode of transportation to Finland, his swift acquisition of a Soviet visa and defection was a highly questionable and suspicious process, apparently intended to call maximum attention to his movements. If he had wanted to, Oswald could still have contacted Schweitzer College and informed the school that he would be a bit late for the fall trimester, but was on his way.

Rather a long way 'round Red Robin's barn? Not for Oswald. According to the Swiss Federal Police, he indeed "had announced his planned attendance ... for the course beginning in the fall of 1959," and "had originally written a letter from Moscow indicating his intention to study ... at the College."

He, of course, never arrived. The Swiss Police, thinking they might have been investigating the wrong fall term, checked registration for the fall term of 1960, but found "no record of a person possibly identical with the subject... registered for the courses beginning October 2."

Oswald & Patrice Lumumba University

In 1960, Nikita Khrushchev announced the establishment of Patrice Lumumba Friendship University in Moscow, to reach the intellectually gifted of Asia, Africa, and Latin America, with a special mission: "To educate students from underdeveloped countries so they [can] ... return to their homelands to become the nucleus for pro-Soviet activities." The KGB actively participated in the university's origins: its "first vice rector ... Pavl Erzin, [was] a major general of the KGB." Faculty members were also drawn from the KGB, and students were reportedly accepted to Lumumba University "primarily on the basis of their potential usefulness to the KGB." The Soviet institution focused in particular on Mexico and other Latin countries, including Cuba, during the 1960s.[5]

According to author Gordon Thomas, the CIA was aware that Lumumba University was a center for psychological warfare, a training ground for behavior modification techniques and for "mind control" experiments.

While residing in the Soviet Union, Oswald reportedly applied to the new college. His letter has not been found in any American public record, though he did receive a rejection notice dated May 3, 1961 informing him that the school only accepted students from Third World countries.

Oswald's approach to Lumumba University, with the institution's concentration on Hispanic America, left a clear trail of Red pebbles back to his alleged Communist/Cuban interests. According to Edward Epstein, though his application was denied, Oswald was "friendly with several foreign students [at Lumumba U.], including Mary Louise Patterson, the daughter of William L. Patterson ... then serving on the executive committee of the [American] Communist Party ... and the wife of Roberto Camacho, one of the Cuban leaders then being trained in Moscow." What was American Mary Louise Patterson doing at a school which only accepted Third World students? Perhaps she had a special family membership.

Epstein's key contacts were William Sullivan of the FBI and James Angleton of the CIA, both senior counter-espionage officers, and Epstein gives a bizarre but telling source for the identity of the students Oswald reportedly contacted: "The information concerning Oswald's association with this group comes from a conversation among leaders of the Fair Play for Cuba Committee [FPCC] on a Cuban plane in 1964... electronically intercepted by the CIA."

One of the FPCC people on that flight had to have been a CIA asset wearing a wire.

Epstein added still more privileged CIA information: "A few weeks after Oswald decided to return to the United States, he received a letter from [Patrice Lumumba] ... university signed by 'Voloshin.'"

This letter is absent from the public record, and it cannot be the May 3, 1961 letter of rejection sent to him from the "University of the Friendship of Nations named for Patrice Lumumba": the letter was signed "P. Chikarev" (in Cyrillic), though the handwritten signature was "illegible." Epstein revealed "Pavel T. Voloshin ... was ... an administrator at Patrice Lumumba University ... [but he also had been] a KGB officer accompanying ... Russian dancers to Los Angeles in 1959 ... about the same time Oswald was making weekend trips ... [to Los Angeles] to get his passport ... for his trip to Moscow, according to the CIA." Epstein's "according to the CIA" suggests new and provocative information whose source was obviously Agency counter-intelligence. But why would Oswald make two (or more) weekend visits to Los Angeles for his trip to Moscow? Why not visit Los Angeles for his trip to Switzerland? Why more than one trip to Los Angeles?[6]

Corporal Nelson Delgado

The Oswald-Delgado story can be followed in Warren Commission materials, but Edward Epstein's take on it has an important CIA counter-intelligence perspective. In the summer of 1959, Oswald began to involve his Quonset hut cubicle partner, Cpl. Nelson Delgado, in his strange adventures. Delgado, a Puerto Rican, was allegedly as interested as Oswald in Fidel Castro and his Cuban revolution. In 1975, the Warren Commission's CIA liaison submitted a memo to the Rockefeller Commission's assassination review that was, in fact, a continuing part of the Agency's Delgado spin, calling in question the corporal's "credibility." What the CIA never mentioned (at least to the Warren Commission) was a series of co-incidences, beginning with Oswald and Delgado's shared interest in Castro and the Cuban revolution; an interest oddly expanded by the Commission's CIA source. The Agency officer told the Rockefeller Commission that "Delgado's testimony says a lot more of possible [intelligence] operational significance than ... the Warren Report...." This was apparently enough to scare off any snoopy investigators.

That "operational significance" included a shadowy, over-coated figure who visited Oswald before he left the Corps, Oswald's reported communications with the Cuban Consulate in Los Angeles, and his duffle bag stuffed with Intelligence photos. All of this was confided to Edward Epstein by James Angleton, the CIA's counter-intelligence chief. According to Angleton, Delgado suggested that Oswald contact the "Cuban Embassy" in L.A., and was the source of the story about the mysterious trip the two Marines took to Mexico, also stating that he and Oswald went to Los Angeles on several weekends to visit the Cuban Consulate.

The Warren Commission record gives a conflicting image of Nelson Delgado. According to his testimony, FBI interrogators treated him as if he were a suspected enemy spy. They badgered, intimidated and lied about him. Most importantly, Delgado denied under oath he had accompanied Oswald on his alleged L.A. excursions.

Why was Delgado treated so badly by the FBI? Was Oswald's Marine buddy actually an Office of Naval Intelligence or CIA plant? Did James Angleton know this? Angleton, using Delgado as his hook, clearly suggested to Epstein that in 1959 Oswald was holding a series of weekend meetings with a KGB officer in Los Angeles ("Voloshin"). Oswald would later make contact with Voloshin in Moscow, apparently regarding Patrice Lumumba University.

Oswald & the First Unitarian Church of Los Angeles

Lee Harvey Oswald's higher-education aspirations in the Soviet Union and Switzerland had Fair Play For Cuba Committee connections in Moscow and Los Angeles.

Oswald's trips to Los Angeles (beyond the intention of obtaining a passport) may have been his way of receiving information about Unitarian-supported Albert Schweitzer College. In 1958 and 1959, Lee Oswald, either alone or with his Marine buddy Nelson Delgado, visited Los Angeles. Kerry Thornley, another of Oswald's Marine friends, stated in his Warren Commission testimony that "[I] knew Oswald [at the same time] ... I had been going to the First Unitarian Church in Los Angeles." Thornley testified to the Commission that Fritchman's L.A. congregation was "a group of quite far left people politically."

Minister Stephen Fritchman had inspired his First Unitarian Church of Los Angeles to become a leading anti-war religious center in the United States: among Fritchman's parishioners were the distinguished U.S. scientist Linus Pauling and his wife, Ava Helen.

Concluding that the atomic bomb was fully capable of destroying humanity, the Paulings became anti-war, anti-racist, and civil rights activists. Establishing an ethical bond with Albert Einstein, Pauling openly rejected atmospheric weapons tests and the development of the hydrogen bomb.

Pauling's public appearances, petitions, and personal protests energized the FBI: the Bureau's files on the distinguished scientist filled up with reports of his arguments for unionization and "world government," and Pauling became the target of both U.S. Intelligence and a Red-hunting Congressional committee.

The Unitarians of Los Angeles and Pasadena rallied in support of the Pauling's, who gave anti-war speeches at several L.A. Unitarian churches. A thousand supporters crowded into Stephen Fritchman's First Unitarian Church of Los Angeles on April 15, 1954 to hear Pauling denounce the Bikini atoll atomic bomb test, with its immense and deadly fallout. Pauling and his wife became members of Stephen Fritchman's congregation, despite their lack of interest "in the mystical aspects of religion."

Pauling commented: "My wife and I joined ... because [Fritchman's church] ... accepts as members people who believe in trying to make the world a better place."

In 1958, when Lee Oswald was preparing to leave the Marines and travel to Europe, Linus Pauling authored a passionate attack on the hydrogen bomb and its chief Cold War enthusiast, Edward Teller. In that same year, the Soviets called for an immediate halt to atomic weapons testing, while Pauling brought suit against the Eisenhower administration for what he characterized as its flagrant assault on the "people's right to life through the release of radiation into the atmosphere."

Were there actual links between Kerry Thornley, Lee Oswald and Stephen Fritchman's "far left" First Unitarian Church? Apparently the FBI thought so: after the JFK assassination, a Bureau agent interrogating Kerry Thornley asked him "what Oswald's connection with the First Unitarian Church was, and I explained to him that there was none."

But Pastor Stephen Fritchman was enough a part of the Oswald story to be represented in the National Archives and Records Administration (NARA) Assassination files by a sixty-page FBI report (including one newspaper article, a photo, a "motion picture" film, and a Fritchman sermon.)

The FBI and the Warren Commission's curiosity about Oswald and Thornley's Unitarian link indicate both the Bureau and the Commission were interested in Oswald's unexplained ability to obtain information concerning Schweitzer College.

Did Kerry Thornley know about a possible Oswald tie to Fritchman's progressive parish? And did Thornley, the eccentric former Marine, withhold relevant facts from the JFK assassination investigation?[7]

Oswald's mysterious source of information about Albert Schweitzer College could be explained by Thornley's attendance at Fritchman's First Unitarian Church in Los Angeles: given Fritchman's progressive political and theological background, the pastor may well have possessed detailed information about the college, and copies of the college's registration forms. When Oswald visited L.A., he could have picked up the materials at the church. Alternatively,

Thornley, who admitted attending the church, could have picked them up and passed them on to Oswald.[8]

Oswald, the FPCC, the Unitarians & V.T. Lee

In the summer of 1963 Lee Harvey Oswald was arrested in a New Orleans street for disruptive political activity and interviewed by New Orleans police intelligence officer Francis L. Martello. Volunteering information about his one-person New Orleans branch of the Fair Play For Cuba Committee (hastily established and just as hastily abandoned), Oswald was asked by Martello how he became connected to the FPCC; he replied that, "he became interested in that committee in Los Angeles ... in 1958 while in the U.S. Marine Corps."

This was eighteen months too early: the national FPCC was established on April 6, 1960. But Oswald indicated he was visiting Los Angeles in 1958 when the same pro-Castro people who organized the FPCC's Los Angeles branch attended the progressive and radical Unitarian meetings in Los Angeles, including those held at Stephen Fritchman's First Unitarian Church.

The complexity of the story is apparent with Oswald's unprompted offer of FPCC information to New Orleans police officer Martello. Oswald had begun his correspondence with the New York FPCC office sometime between August 4th and October 8, 1962. V.T. Lee, actually Army veteran Vincent Tappin, had been an early Castro supporter, a frequent visitor to Cuba, and the chief of the FPCC's Tampa branch until he fled to New York City after he had been "hounded" (according to Lee) by the FBI. V. T. Lee became the FPCC's chairperson in New York, apparently arriving in time to receive Lee Oswald's letter.

No official postal record exists of another link between the two until April 16, 1963. But just two weeks earlier, on April 4th and 5th, V. T. Lee visited Los Angeles on a major speaking tour. The FPCC activist held a press conference, spoke at the Young Socialist Alliance of UCLA, and, most significantly, was the sponsored presentation guest of pastor Stephen Fritchman. "Reverend Fritchman was an FPCC sympathizer ... the public radical spokesman for the L.A. area with validity, because he was a minister."

Only twelve days later, Lee Oswald began corresponding regularly with V.T. Lee in New York. At the same time, the FBI "intensified its probe" of V.T. Lee and the FPCC. The Bureau's New York field office, utilizing its postal intercept machinery, maintained its awareness of Oswald's exchanges with V.T. Lee and the FPCC. When Oswald moved to New Orleans, he continued his postal connection to the FPCC, and this correspondence was also intercepted by the Bureau.

Richard Case Nagell, a reputed U.S. Intelligence officer, reportedly discovered at least one anti-JFK assassination plot that intended to use Lee Oswald as its primary patsy.[9] Whether or not any of his assertions concerning assassination planning, the CIA, the KGB, and organized crime have probity, among Nagell's counter-intelligence responsibilities were the Fair Play For Cuba Committee, the Los Angeles progressive and radical community, Stephen Fritchman, Kerry Thornley, and Lee Harvey Oswald; all of whom were carefully recorded in Nagell's investigative notebook.[10] Oswald had a propensity for association (at a very low degree of separation) with anti-nuclear activists in the 1950s, including U.S. Intelligence targets Fritchman and Pauling.

Patrice Lumumba University & Congo Uranium

Oswald's application to Patrice Lumumba University concerned the Warren Commission's staff: as American intelligence well knew, Lumumba University, though a legitimate educational institution, was also determined to propagandize its students in hopes of recruiting them as KGB assets or agents.

Lumumba University did not exist in 1959 when Oswald identified Schweitzer College and the University of Turku as overseas academic choices. His purported application to Lumumba U. was, therefore, an opportunistic add-on, either devised by Oswald himself (highly unlikely), by Soviet or American espionage entities, or some incestuous combination of the two.[11]

Why would Oswald apply to Lumumba University? His application fit perfectly with the Schweitzer College feint. In 1958 and 1959, a highly visible and articulate Patrice Lumumba became the Congo's leading spokesperson for political and economic freedom. His radical flamboyance was calculated to capture the attention of the thousands of abused and dispossessed Congolese, many of whom were seriously crippled by the terrible conditions in the Congolese mines and the regular practice of brutal whippings. Lumumba's mercurial outspokenness disturbed one official U.S. observer: "[Lumumba is] a spellbinding orator with the ability to stir masses of people to action...." That "action," of course, threatened Congolese stability and, therefore, Western profits. Without evidence, he was accused of being a Communist.

"His speeches set off immediate alarm signals in Western capitals. Belgian, British, and American corporations ... had vast investments in the Congo ... rich in copper, cobalt, diamonds, gold, tin, manganese, and zinc." And, of course, uranium. The corporations and the governments supporting them rightly feared Lumumba's political charisma: he clearly signaled that all of the African "continent must ... cease to be an economic colony of Europe."

The Soviet Union established Patrice Lumumba University in February 1960, to honor the Congolese independence leader.[12]

On June 24, 1960 Lumumba became the Congo's first democratically elected prime minister. On June 30, when Oswald was in Moscow, the Congo became officially independent of Belgium, and immediately went into chaotic spasms. Katanga province withdrew from the Union, taking with it the region's mineral riches. Both the United States and the United Nations "refused to supply [Lumumba] ... with transport for his troops to put down the secession in Katanga province, [so] Lumumba turned to the Soviet Union for aid..." ten Iluyshin troop transports landed at Leopoldville on August 26, with 100 Soviet technicians.

Belgium, Great Britain and the United States took immediate notice and targeted Lumumba for elimination. In August 1960, the Congo station of the Central Intelligence Agency sent a cable to Washington: "Embassy and station believe Congo experiencing classic communist effort [to] take over [the] government." Agency Director Dulles noted that a "communist takeover of the Congo [would have] ... disastrous consequences... for the interests of the free world...." Dulles' references to "consequences" meant an independent Congo (sympathetic to the Soviets or not) in control of its own highly valuable mineral resources.

Unfortunately for his future health, Lumumba could not be bought. Unlike the CIA's regularly bribed Congolese politicians, he was a real patriot. This the colonial powers could not abide, and they began their anti-Lumumba campaign. Allen Dulles met with key members of President Eisenhower's political and military intelligence staff and accepted "getting rid of Lumumba" as a viable next option. Dulles approved a $100,000 program whose goal was the elimination of Lumumba and his government, to be replaced by a "pro-western group."

Following intelligence, foreign affairs, and military analyses of the Congo, Eisenhower approved the shameful operation, and the CIA began its attack. Lumumba was deposed and imprisoned on September 14, 1960. His administration had lasted ten weeks. In September and October British and Belgian assassination plots were initiated, and, joined with the Americans, finally became a single conspiracy.

On January 17, 1961, only five days before John F. Kennedy's inauguration, Patrice Lumumba and two supporters were taken from their cells to a secluded place and executed by firing squad. The operation was commanded by two Belgian officers. A little last-minute housekeeping?

It is possible that this sordid episode was the last straw for Ike, and helped prompt the dire warning in his farewell address. Four months later, on May 3, 1961, Lee Oswald's application was rejected by Patrice Lumumba University.

Why the Oswald-Lumumba U. Connection?

Beginning in 1885, King Leopold II, sole proprietor of the Belgian Congo, was directly responsible for the deaths of no fewer than five million of his African subjects: victims of his highly profitable forced labor system. The Congo's mineral richness was, as always, the spur.

In 1913, cobalt and uranium were discovered, and in August 1915, Robert Rich Sharp found the Shinkolobwe deposit in Katanga province. It gave an astonishing yield of 68% uranium, the richest discovery in the history of mining, and it was all right on the earth's surface: a minimum of work would yield an enormous profit.

In the 1940s, the Congo's splendid uranium resources were crucial to both Belgium and the United States. On March 27, 1944, for $375,000,000, Belgium sold to the U.S. and England the absolute right of future, so-called prior, purchase for all uranium deposits in the Congo. British, American, and Belgian interests in Congolese uranium had been fused: the same three powers that, 16 years later, removed Patrice Lumumba when he threatened their nuclear monopoly.

The atomic bombs dropped on Hiroshima and Nagasaki were fueled by uranium from the Belgian Congo, and thereafter America "rewarded Belgium with its own [home] nuclear centre." The Belgians had become an atomic power. "In 1958, when Brussels thought it would hold onto its colony for many years, Belgium built the Kinshasa reactor, the first in Africa." The Kinshasa TRIGA reactor was "a part of President Eisenhower's Atoms for Peace Program."

In 1960, Belgium granted the Congo its supposed independence; an act clearly intended to initiate the major political instability that followed. The Congolese army, trained and dominated by the Belgians, mutinied after Lumumba refused to raise their wages. The province of Katanga, key to the West's mineral and pitchblende future, separated from the Congo. The leader of the secession, Belgian and CIA puppet Moise Tshombe, was happy to hand over control of both the Congo and its precious uranium to the colonialist anti-Lumumba forces.

Suppression of the Congolese working population, which in 1960 was on the edge of rebellion, had always been a primary corporate consideration. Patrice Lumumba was perceived to be unable or unwilling to contain that roiling mass, and after his murder Moise Tshombe helped block any progressive transformation of the Congo, which might have threatened the delivery of uranium ore to the Western powers.

Oswald's approach to Lumumba University dovetailed perfectly with his earlier application to Albert Schweitzer College. In fact, the two colleges shared a significant political context, just as Lumumba and Schweitzer themselves were, from the Eisenhower administration's point of view, politically linked.

Writer Dennis Bartholomew made as much sense as he could of the Oswald-Albert Schweitzer College postal maze, but all the stories lack sense except as provocative signs pointing to an American espionage operation involving Oswald (or a surrogate), the Soviet Union and Switzerland, in a Bermuda triangle of deception.

Oswald's Suspect College Records

This dark corner of the JFK assassination closet includes "Illegals" (espionage agents with false identities), mail drops, and, in the manipulation of Lee Harvey Oswald, a possible collaboration between elements of Soviet and U.S. Intelligence.[13]

The Albert Schweitzer College documents and letters in the Warren Report and the Commission Hearings volumes are in a haphazard and illogical order, exhibit suspicious gaps, have strange entries, and are missing crucial information: a typical footprint of the spook industry, strongly suggesting they were elements of a major American intelligence operation.

After the assassination, the fictionalized Oswald had to be dealt with, or hidden in plain sight. He was visible in his series of half-truths, all apparently intended to maximize suspicion concerning his trip to Europe and the Caribbean. The key falsehood was his proposed study in Switzerland: the Schweitzer College application was itself a fiction. How aware of all this was the Warren Commission?

According to fellow Marine and Warren Commission witness Richard Dennis Call, Lee Oswald told him he had received a scholarship to Albert Schweitzer College.

The Warren Commission's materials, the National Archives documents, the later Assassination Records Review Board discoveries, and the American Friends of Albert Schweitzer College files at Harvard Divinity School Library do not yield a single document referring to a scholarship for any American student in the late 1950s. Was Oswald the recipient of a non-existent scholarship for which he apparently never applied, or was this yet another in a series of red herrings?

Schweitzer College officers *had* proposed scholarships for students from the Iron Curtain countries, and the CIA had funded initiatives for American youth to attend educational and cultural events in Europe from 1959 through 1962.

According to his mother, Oswald was planning to "attend the short summer course of the University of Turku, Turku, Finland." Of course, the University was no longer in the city of Turku: it had long since returned to Helsinki. Oswald made the mistake, if indeed it was a mistake, on his Schweitzer College application, which his mother quoted exactly, but mistakenly assigned the "summer course" statement to Turku.

Did Oswald's long-form application go from the College to Texas Representative Jim Wright, then on to Mrs. Oswald? Did Mrs. Oswald then give the document to the Warren Commission staff? Almost certainly Schweitzer College Secretary Erika Weibel sent the college's Oswald file to Jim Wright, who in turn gave that file to the Warren Commission. Where, indeed, did Mrs. Oswald get that exact set of words?

Schweitzer College, the University of Turku, and Patrice Lumumba University were hotbeds of either liberal or outright Communist activity, and in the context of Oswald's paper trail would have alerted any competent counter-espionage analyst.

The FBI False Identity Case, Mail Intercepts & Illegals

In the first week of November 1959, following Oswald's announcement of his Soviet defection, the former Marine's FBI security file was opened. In itself, this file was important, but a related FBI action, largely overlooked, spoke directly to the "impostor" issue that would fuel the Bureau's inquiry: "A stop was placed in the files of the Identification Division of the FBI on November 10, 1959... to alert us in the event... [Oswald] returned under a different identity and his fingerprints were received."

Though garbled by typical Bureau-speak, the issue was clearly false identity. Either Oswald would return as someone else, or someone else would return as Oswald. But a third possibility was aired: "to evaluate him as a security risk in the event he returned [as himself], in view of the possibility of his recruitment by the Soviet intelligence services."

Lee's second-to-last letter to his brother Robert on November 8, 1959, covered Oswald's alleged interest in acquiring Soviet citizenship and living in the Soviet Union, his condemnation of the United States, and his intention to accept no further telephone calls.

Beyond the newspaper stories of Oswald's defection, that letter was probably the catalyst for the Bureau's identification stop.

Months before Lee's mother was urged to contact Secretary of State Christian Herter by Bureau Agent Fannan, Lee's brother Robert had wired him, but received no response. Fannan could have known about Robert Oswald's State Department query and indicated in his February 1960 interview with Mrs. Oswald that the communication line between the Oswald family and the State Department was now open.

Robert Oswald sent another letter to Lee, who wrote a long, well written, and positive response on November 26, 1959, which must have confirmed to both American and Soviet intelligence interceptors that he was serious about his new loyalties. No intervening letter from Robert to Lee has been found in the public record, but Lee's last letter to Robert was on December 17, 1959. No one but Lee's mother would hear from him for twenty months, and it would only be a short and questionable note.[14]

On December 18, 1959, Marguerite Oswald sent her son a $20 check addressed to his Moscow hotel. Lee returned it and asked for cash. On January 5, 1960, she sent him a $20 bill, but the apparently unopened envelope came back on February 25. Finally, Mrs. Oswald sent Lee a Foreign Money Transfer for $25.00.

The Warren Report stated that Lee's mother "sent him a money order for about $25.00." If we ignore that a money order is not the same as a bank transfer from one country to another, we can accept that the prevailing exchange rate between American and Soviet currency would make the transfer about $25. But sometimes accuracy only compounds confusion.

Mrs. Oswald had asked that an official receipt be returned to her bank. The bank never received the confirmation, so she assumed (correctly) that the transfer either was not received or had been rejected.

According to former Navy intelligence officer/historian John Newman, the Bureau never explained how it had acquired its information on Mrs. Oswald's attempted money transfer. But the buried record of the Warren Commission proved that the FBI monitored that most important transaction, and probably all three attempts by Marguerite Oswald to send money to her son. In fact, her mailings to Lee in the Soviet Union, and official Bureau memoranda in response strongly suggest constant postal monitoring.

Mrs. Oswald's December 18th mailing of the $20 check immediately followed Robert Oswald's letter of December 17th. Either Lee or someone else in the Soviet Union returned the check received by Mrs. Oswald on January 5, 1960, with Lee's scribbled request for cash. On January 18, 1960, the first in a series of Bureau memos was generated directly relating to the Oswald family's postal traffic between Texas and the Soviet Union. But the initiating FBI field office was neither Fort Worth nor Dallas; it was the New York field office, the Bureau site responsible for the FBI's Soviet mail interception program. That program, called Z Coverage, was one of several FBI mail intercept operations.

From 1940 through 1966, the Bureau ran its Z Coverage postal program against Soviet mail drops, monitoring and opening first-class mail between the United States and the Soviet Union. Z Coverage tracked suspected Illegals with false identities based on borrowed or stolen American birth certificates and passports. In 1958, FBI counter-intelligence (run by the Bureau's William Sullivan and Sam Papich) shared this information with the CIA's counter-intelligence chief James Angleton. HTLINGUAL, the Agency's own mail interception program, was functioning in New York at the same time, and the CIA would certainly have had an intense interest in mail going to a former Marine who had defected to the Soviet Union.

It's as if Oswald's defection was timed to intersect with the establishment of the combined FBI-CIA counter-intelligence program on false identity, postal interceptions, and Illegals.

Significantly, within that new joint enterprise, the FBI sent some Oswald material to the CIA in 1960, but the January 18th memo was withheld from the Agency.

On January 22, 1960, Mrs. Oswald sent Lee a $25 Foreign Money transfer. Three days later, the FBI knew of the transaction: "We determined on January 25, 1960, that Mrs. Marguerite Oswald had transmitted the sum of $25 to 'Lee Harvey Oswald.'"

Four days later, on January 29th, the Bureau's New York field office sent a memorandum to Washington, obviously responding to the intercept of Mrs. Oswald's attempted foreign money transfer. Another memo from the New York field office was sent to Bureau headquarters on February 2, 1960, probably confirming that Mrs. Oswald's bank had not received a receipt for the attempted transfer. Neither of these were shared with the CIA.

The three memos of January 18th, January 29th, and February 2nd were all cited in a 32-page memorandum on February 26, 1960.

Except for its first and last pages, the memo has remained classified. But the last page offers more evidence of the FBI's covert information techniques, citing "receipts and disbursements... in... bank accounts" held to be "strictly confidential" and attributed to a source whose identity was to be kept secret. That source was either a cooperating New York postal inspector, or an FBI agent working alongside the inspector.

The FBI's New York field office intercepted Mrs. Oswald's Foreign Money Transfer, traced it to her bank (First National in Fort Worth), and shared that information with Washington headquarters. In New York, the memo was placed in Oswald's counter-intelligence file. In Washington, however, it became part of his domestic security file. This difference in filing procedures only makes sense if the responsible FBI headquarters officer who filed the memo viewed Oswald's overseas disappearance as a False Identity case.

The February 26, 1960 memorandum was also not shared with the Agency; and later, it was withheld from the Warren Commission, since it would have confirmed that the FBI had been intercepting Oswald's mail as early as 1959, and no later than the first two months of 1960, and was taking quite seriously the possibility that a 'false identity' Oswald was already in the Soviet Union. When agent Fannan visited Marguerite in February 1960, the Bureau was already monitoring her mail.

Marguerite in the Maze

Mrs. Oswald's inquiries to her Texas representatives and Secretary of State Herter followed on March 7, 1960.

The resulting postal exchanges began March 7, 1960 and ended June 7, 1962: two years and three months of classic bureaucratic obfuscation. Once, very early in the interchange, a curious topic entered: on July 16, 1960, Mrs. Oswald asked in what city, state, and on what date her son received his passport. The answer was, of course, September 10, 1959, in Los Angeles.

Some odd things were happening at the State Department, and again the flow of mail was central. Texas Representative Jim Wright had written to the State Department, which in turn sent a query to the American Embassy in Moscow. Attached were the letters of both Marguerite Oswald and Representative Wright. The State Department responded to Wright, but virtually ignored Lee's mother. Further, Oswald's file now resided in the Department's passport office, suggesting that State was also aware of the false identity potential.

Tellingly, the passport office was run by two paranoid anti-Communists: Ms. Frances Knight and her key assistant, "the legendary red-hunter Otto Otepka." How did Oswald's suspicious application get past both Knight and Otepka in the first place? Or did it?

This passport office file ought to have existed when Oswald applied for a new passport in 1962, while still in the Soviet Union. Yet, despite Oswald's record, including an internationally reported defection, he received his new passport quickly and without a hitch. The Warren Commission, excepting former CIA Director Allen Dulles, was "highly suspicious." Dulles, who certainly knew better, asserted that neither the State Department nor its passport office was aware of Oswald's defection. He told his Commission associates (rather disjointedly): "I don't think the State Department or in... Passport... there was no record." He was immediately corrected by one of his fellow Commissioners: "The State Department knew he was a defector. They arranged for him to come back."

The Commission, however, was easily diverted, and its exploration of Oswald passport ended quickly.

But when it was happening, something was special about Oswald's defection and disappearance, and the entire Oswald case was handled in a special way, though not necessarily with efficiency. The American Embassy in Moscow recommended a plan that had been successful in the past. In order to elicit a current postal address, the inquiring mother would write a letter to her son, which would be forwarded to the Soviet Foreign Embassy.

Delaying its decision for almost two months, the State Department finally vetoed the Embassy plan. A year later, when Oswald's mother flew to Washington and confronted the State Department, it agreed to try the plan; but by March 22, 1961, State informed Mrs. Oswald that her son wanted to come home.

Back in 1960, Mrs. Oswald had heard nothing from either the Soviet Union or the State Department until March 30th, when she received a cool and wordy postal assurance that the American Embassy in Moscow had been asked to "obtain a report" about Lee's "present welfare" and communicate to him his mother's "continuing desire to help him." Was this Foreign Service message to Mrs. Oswald in some kind of obscure code? Or did it suggest that the State Department and its passport office did not really want to find Lee Harvey Oswald?

The Strange Schweitzer College Correspondence

Sometime before March 4, 1959, Oswald, or someone using his name, supposedly made an inquiry about Albert Schweitzer College seeking information and/or requesting application materials. No official record of it has ever been found. I have been informed by an extremely reliable source, however, that Oswald wrote a letter of inquiry to the "Chairman of the American Admissions Committee" in Providence, Rhode Island, in 1959. But if the person posting the letter of inquiry was Oswald, from where did he get the American Admissions Committee address and the name of its chief officer in Providence?

Before March 4, 1959, Oswald (or someone) was sent or given the short twelve-line Summer Study application form. Oswald apparently used it to apply for the spring trimester of the next school year, April 12 to June 27, 1960. The College then informed Oswald that he had used the wrong form.

The form as it appears in the Warren Commission documents is half of a standard sheet of paper, duplicated for distribution. The Warren Commission neglected to point out that it was, in fact, the bottom half of a full sheet, the top half of which gave a listing of the 1960 Summer courses. Sometime before March 4, 1959, Oswald (or someone) wrote on the application: "Please inform me of the amount of the deposit...." This application was then mailed to Switzerland. The major problem with this document was that the handwritten application date read March 19, 1959. The longer application form had a handwritten date of March 4, 1959; but that would mean Oswald received and returned the correct form *before* he sent the incorrect form. Since the College notified Oswald on March 27th that it had received an incorrect application, it could not have sent the proper form before that day. Still, Oswald may have written an incorrect date on one or both of the applications.

In a letter dated March 28, 1959, Erika Weibel, the Secretary of Albert Schweitzer College, wrote to Oswald at his Marine Corps address that the college had received his application but the short form he had sent was incorrect. The "proper forms," she wrote, were being sent to him: that is, two copies of the proper form, one to be completed and sent to Providence, the other to Switzerland.

Indeed, one copy was apparently returned to the College. The other copy was supposed to have been mailed to the Chairman of the American Admissions Committee, Dr. Robert H. Schacht, pastor of the Unitarian Church, Providence, Rhode Island, at 1 Benevolent Street, the Church's Parish House.

Unless Oswald's Benevolent St. file is retrieved from the FBI, no evidence is presently available that Dr. Schacht ever received the required form from Oswald, or any other material, including three required references.

That missing file might contain Schacht's attempts to contact Oswald's two personal references and/or the required "Minister who knows you." But those attempts would of course have failed, or faked responses would have been submitted, because the references, though reality-linked, were only partly true. Oswald's college application listed his personal references as "Mr. A. Botelho," a U.S. Marine with the "MCAF, MACS9 Santa Anna, Calif.", and "Mr. R. Calore," a Marine at the same location. The misspelling of "Santa Anna" for Santa Ana, California, was consistent with other misspellings in Oswald's College records. James A. Botelho (not "A. Botelho") and Anthony Calore (not "R. Calore"), were in the same military group as Oswald in El Toro, California; both knew Oswald, but neither could be called a friend close enough to qualify as a personal reference. Further, neither Botelho nor Calore is represented in any JFK/Oswald public record, though their 'references' (from whatever military or intelligence source) *could* have been in Reverend Robert Schacht's Oswald file in Providence, which was spirited away by FBI agents in December 1963.

Oswald's Personal "References"

The Warren Commission's photocopy of the application form reproduced the spaces for the two "References" and "a Minister who knows you," but its printed transcription, much easier to read than the faded original document, omitted (without explanation) both the "Name and Address" slots for the "Minister" reference and Oswald's handwritten entries at the bottom of the form.

Why? A readable application requiring a clerical reference would have strongly suggested the religious context of the college to which Oswald was applying. His handwritten ministerial reference was "Chaplin [sic] W. Waters, MCAF Chapel, MCAF, Santa Anna [sic], California" (CE 228). Like Oswald's two enlisted Marine references, his ministerial reference was at best a half-truth. No "W. Waters" counseled the Santa Ana servicemen, but Rev. Howard E. Waters, a Southern Baptist minister stationed at MACAF, Santa Ana, California, from 1947 through 1959, was available. I wrote to Rev. Waters, but he apparently decided not to respond to my queries concerning his Marine service (and his inclusion in CE 228).

Albert Schweitzer College never suggested to Oswald in any surviving correspondence that his acceptance was automatic. In the same paragraph of the letter dated March 28,1959, Erika Weibel wrote: "Upon [your] acceptance, a deposit... is required." Obviously some minimum evaluation process was to take place either in Switzerland, in Providence, or both (if both, more letters were therefore exchanged). Was an evaluation process carried out?

Dr. Robert Schacht was interviewed by the FBI on December 5, 1963; the Unitarian pastor "recalled Oswald had filled out an application ... in the spring of 1959 while still in the Marine Corps ... Because the Oswald application was approved, I [Dr. Schacht] am sure that he must have given three references and their reports must have appeared satisfactory. But I cannot recall now who they were."

Dr. Schacht's comments have always needed careful consideration. First, Schacht did not cite Oswald's letter of inquiry; rather, Schacht cited Oswald's March 1959 ASC application. Did Schacht indeed receive a copy of Oswald's longer, "correct" application form? Second, Schacht stated that Oswald's "application was approved...."

From where did Schacht get this information? Did the Swiss office of the college inform him of Oswald's acceptance? Did the FBI tell Schacht that Oswald had been accepted by the College? Or did his own Benevolent Street file contain that evidence? No existing documents support Dr. Schacht's statements.

Any relevant materials present in the Benevolent Street file would have been appropriated, and are apparently still being held by the Bureau.

Sometime between March 28th and June 19, 1959, PFC Oswald received his acceptance notice, requiring him to send "a deposit of $25.00 to Switzerland." That letter of acceptance has vanished from the public record, but must have existed, since he would not have sent his deposit until after he was accepted.

On June 19, 1959, Oswald did submit his required deposit with the standard formality, "I am very glad to have been accepted for the third term of your college next year." Curiously, he then added, "Any new information on the school or even the students who will attend next year will be appreciated."

Sometime in late June or early July 1959, Lee wrote his mother that he had been accepted by Schweitzer College, and sent a registration fee.

That letter is also not in the public record.

Oswald could not attend the fall term unless he received an early discharge, and after his acceptance letter arrived, he wrote to his brother: "Pretty soon I'll be getting out of the Corps and I know what I want to be and how I'm going to be it ..."

In one of those curious knots of events and postal communications in Oswald's story, Lee's mother had written reminding him of her long-standing insurance claim against a Fort Worth store. She alleged her nose had been severely injured when a candy jar fell on it. (Four doctors had found her to be perfectly healthy, but Mrs. Oswald insisted she was terribly disabled.) Lee wrote back in June 1959 that the Red Cross would be contacting her to validate his hardship request for early discharge, to care for and support the helpless Marguerite.

Oswald filed his documents in July 1959 with the Red Cross, and his mother sent him supporting correspondence from two friends, a lawyer and a doctor, along with her own. Had the Marine Corps conducted even a perfunctory investigation the transparent fraud would have quickly been exploded, and Oswald's request summarily denied.

In the event, his request was duly stamped "approved" on September 3, 1959, and Oswald was detached from duty. The next day he requested a passport, speedily granted on Sept. 10th.

Earlier, on July 10, 1959, Erika Weibel, the ASC Secretary, wrote to thank him for his letter of June 19th with its "enclosed deposit ... for the third term...."

After this series of odd, delayed, and now-missing postal responses, ASC expected Lee Harvey Oswald to attend its *spring 1960* program of instruction.

Then on March 22, 1960, Hans Casparis, the founder, director, and ultimately President of Albert Schweitzer College, wrote to Lee, apparently assuming he was still on active duty, and supposedly changed the schedule. The letter was posted to Lee's Marine Corps address, forwarded several times, and finally arrived in Marguerite Oswald's mail on April 6, 1960, just six days before the opening of the college's regular third term. This letter gave Lee's mother some hope that her missing son would soon resurface.

For Lee's Eyes Only? The ASC Schedule Change

Hans Casparis' letter has long awaited a careful evaluation. It was mailed to Oswald's correct former Marine address, though the city's name was misspelled: "Santa Anna" instead of

"Santa Ana." Oswald himself twice misspelled the name in his application forms. However, the heading of the letter was itself incorrect, listing the wrong California city: "Santa Barbara."[15]

According to Casparis, the college's first lecture would be held on April 19, 1960, rather than April 21st. This change meant that students would have to arrive either on the evening of Monday, the 18th, or before noon on April 19th, making it possible to end the term the weekend of July 2nd, instead of the 6th.

But this change did not match either the information Oswald apparently had available when he applied to the college or the official application form Oswald mailed (according to the Warren Commission) to the college. Spring trimester was to run from April 12th, 1960, to June 27th, 1960, the college's listed third term. Casparis's revised spring trimester was scheduled for April 19th through July 6th, according to his letter. Casparis's change for prospective student Lee Harvey Oswald constituted the *third* different spring trimester opening, but I have found no record in the available Schweitzer College documents at Harvard Divinity School Library supporting this schedule modification.

Casparis hoped that Oswald could "fit this change" into his "travel plans," but assured him that "we would understand" if he could not, and asked Oswald to "drop us a line so that we know." The casual tone of Casparis's letter, reporting a major change in the calendar while at least some of the students were already in transit, is disturbing. Even if fewer than fifty students were expected, a schedule change necessitating such last-minute personal travel adjustments should have provoked serious questions about the administration's competence.

But did it ever happen?

Dennis Bartholomew, a diligent JFK researcher, succeeded in finding a former Schweitzer College student who had attended the spring trimester in 1960 and confirmed Bartholomew's doubts, asserting that the delay never took place. According to this crucial witness, all went as scheduled for the opening of the spring trimester: all students arrived on time, and further, the witness did not recall seeing Lee Harvey Oswald's name on the student roster for that trimester.

Nevertheless, I discovered a Schweitzer College document verifying that the school was indeed expecting Oswald for the spring trimester: this according to a post-assassination review of the college's Oswald connection, which took place in Churwalden.

Still, the March 22, 1960, Casparis letter to Oswald announcing the college's schedule change must have given his mother's spirits a tremendous lift, as she was getting little or no support from the elusive State Department: Lee might still be on his way to Switzerland.

The letter's importance went far beyond the personal, as it initiated a series of postings, which helped to energize the FBI's Oswald investigation in Switzerland.

More Strange ASC Mailings

Lee's mother immediately responded to Casparis' letter. Written and (probably) mailed on April 6, 1960, the reply was as odd as the initial letter.

She wrote: "A few months ago he wrote me that he was accepted by your college and [he] had sent a registration fee [to you]."

On July 10, 1959, the college acknowledged receiving Oswald's deposit in a letter from Lee dated June 19, 1959. In this letter he was "very glad to be accepted," so he had to have received an acceptance letter prior to June 19th.

Sometime around June 19th, while still in the Marine Corps, Oswald must have informed his mother of his acceptance and that he was "looking forward to going there." Recall that on January 22, 1960, Mrs. Oswald had sent Lee a $25.00 Foreign Money Transfer that was returned to her; this transfer was monitored by the New York FBI office. The Bureau memo on that aborted transfer was one of four withheld from the CIA, along with the cover memo of February 26, 1960. The most crucial of the Bureau's counter-intelligence responses to Mrs. Oswald's Moscow mailings now occurred. The New York office requested that Mrs. Oswald be interviewed.

Mrs. O & the FBI's False Identity/Illegals Investigation

This was no ordinary interview. The FBI had probably been intercepting both Mrs. Oswald's and Robert Oswald's mail. Alan Belmont testified quietly to the Warren Commission that Oswald's "mother had sent... $25 to him in Moscow so we [the FBI] went to interview her in April 1960...." But two interviews were scheduled, apparently by Bureau counter-intelligence, originating either with Alan Belmont or William Sullivan in Washington. On March

9, 1960, an instruction memorandum from headquarters was sent to the New York field office and then relayed to the Bureau's Dallas field office. The New York Oswald file on the projected interviews was designated as a counter-intelligence concern. The subsequent FBI file covering these interviews was opened "under the Foreign Counter-intelligence Matters serial 105, file 976."

The local Bureau was given specific guidelines on how to interview Marguerite Oswald. Four full paragraphs of this memo remain censored by the FBI, but with what is left, the import of the interview and the guidelines governing it are measurable.

John Newman's observation on this Bureau memorandum was off the mark: "The instructions we are able to see appear to be general rules applicable to any interview... [in] what was apparently an FBI program for siphoning information from people's bank accounts." The siphoning of bank account information was indeed a part of the operation, but was not its ultimate goal.

Examine each of the uncensored lines in the instruction memo. First: "The Bureau has furnished the following instructions to be observed in this program." The phrase "this program," together with the specific history of Oswald's background, trip to Europe, and his subsequent disappearance, clearly points to a Bureau counter-espionage operation: interviewing people in the United States about material of value sent to family members in the Soviet Union, other Communist countries, or "neutral" countries (for example, Switzerland and Finland).

The rest of what has remained of the memo and the record of the FBI interview gives further evidence supporting this hypothesis.

The Bureau agents were urged to gain the cooperation of those interviewed: "the impression should not be created that the Bureau is investigating the persons being interviewed, or that their action is, in itself, derogatory as in regard to their loyalty to the U.S." The memorandum instructed interviewing agents to cover a specific series of topics: What were the reasons for the funds' transmittal? What was the identity of the purchaser of the transmittal document? What was the relationship between the purchaser and the payee? Further, and significantly, the individuals interviewed were to be questioned as to whether they had been asked "to furnish items of personal identification to their relatives abroad."

These questions were not intended to elicit information for the "FBI's bank-peeping project"; rather, the other way around. Foreign money transfers, especially to Communist countries or to ostensibly neutral countries such as Switzerland, were investigated as leads in the FBI's pursuit of espionage "illegals." The opening, doubling and hiding of counter-intelligence, internal security, New York, Dallas, and Bureau headquarters files on Lee Harvey Oswald from October 1959 through no later than May 1960, were all evidence Oswald constituted a major, troubling "Illegal" case. It was critical enough that the Bureau withheld everything from the Warren Commission except the thinnest version of the Oswald false identity problem.

But that FBI suspicion was also the basis for withholding both the Bureau's concern *and* the evidence for its false identity/illegal hypothesis from the CIA.

The "Oswald Challenge" Game

Imagine a multi-dimensional game board of intelligence and espionage activities stretching across the Eurasian mega-continent in its developmental mode for more than a century and, by the 1950s, being played with greater and greater sophistication. Among the many trained players, pawns, and ambiguous game pieces was Lee Harvey Oswald. Espionage game imagery has had a long and fascinating history, an especially relevant use being that of Flora Lewis in her well written, though not necessarily accurate, study of Noel Field.

Field's stepdaughter specifically rejected the "pawn" designation for her stepfather, insisting he was, in fact, a major piece or player. If so, he apparently was able to transform (or be transformed) from red to black and back to red again: but no version of chess has a piece capable of playing for both sides, though it is a fascinating possibility. Noel Field would certainly qualify.

Edward Epstein adopted the game-playing imagery (possibly influenced by James Angleton), specifically identifying Oswald as a minor piece offered up as a provocative and possibly entrapping sacrifice in his Chapter VIII title: "The Russian Gambit-Accepted." Epstein's Chapter XIII was also called "Oswald's Game." Finally, Jean Davison borrowed Epstein's exact phrase for the title of her own book.

But Oswald was more than either a pawn or game piece, no matter how complex: he himself was the center of "The Oswald Challenge" within the greater espionage contest. Other individuals, real or invented, have been similar in form or function.[16]

The Oswald Challenge was readily apparent in the 1959-61 period when, almost joyfully, FBI and CIA intelligence and counter-intelligence figures entered, using the real or the fictionalized Oswald (or both) in several espionage and counter-intelligence operations. The Soviet Union, Mexico City, and Dallas were three of the most important game board sites. In fact, John Newman caught some of the game-playing nuances when he observed how "Oswald-related information was handled [as]... part of an [Angleton/CIA counter-intelligence] operation to search out... [a] suspected [KGB] mole [in the CIA]." At the same time, Newman concluded that evidence also strongly suggested a second and separate Agency counter-intelligence action had made use of Oswald's alleged defection to the Soviet Union. If Newman is correct, Lee's trip to Europe itself would qualify as a separate sub-game, possibly run by the Office of Naval Intelligence, the CIA, or both.

Initially having nothing to do with the JFK assassination, but eventually used by the facilitators who ran the Dallas operation, the Oswald Challenge would account for a number of extraordinary complications and contradictions in the Oswald narrative. While some elements of the CIA and the FBI were complicit in the game, others (who were not players) were concerned.

The FBI's Stolen Identity Investigation

The Bureau's suspicion that Oswald had become part of, or fallen victim to, a stolen identity operation in the Soviet Union or Switzerland (or both) shaped the FBI's interviews of both Robert Oswald and Lee's mother. That same suspicion blocked the Bureau from sharing its intercept of Mrs. Oswald's mail material with the CIA and later accounted for the FBI withholding its false identity concerns from the Warren Commission (thereby protecting the Bureau's massive mail opening program).

When Mrs. Oswald was interviewed on April 28, 1960, she reviewed a number of significant topics. She reportedly spoke of her aborted foreign money transfer, gave a short history of the Oswald family, and reviewed Lee's Marine Corps experience. She also told Fain about her letters sent to Texas Representatives Rayburn and Wright and Secretary of State Christian Herter and reviewed the Hans Casparis letter from Albert Schweitzer College that, according to Agent Fain, "raised her hopes... [Lee] might actually be en route to... Switzerland...." Oddly enough, she told the FBI agent she intended to write a letter to the college inquiring whether it had "received any word from Lee." But she had already done so several weeks prior to her FBI interview. Why the (possible) deception? Or did Mrs. Oswald confuse the two ("Fannan" and Fain) interviews? She did indeed write Rayburn, Wright, and Herter after the earlier "Fannan" interview. The letters were sent out on March 7, 1960, more than a month before FBI Special Agent Fain saw her, who then reported on exactly those mailings.

Wouldn't a key event such as a Fort Worth FBI agent responding to a plea for help represent an important precedent for her Dallas Bureau interview? But either Mrs. Oswald withheld information about her earlier interview or, for whatever reason, Fain neglected to report the first visit by the alleged Bureau agent.

But Fain did ask Lee's mother one of the key questions relating to stolen personal identity: did she, he inquired, send "any items of personal identification" to her son?

No, Mrs. Oswald replied, though she reported that Lee had taken his birth certificate with him.

This information impressed agent Fain, precisely because an authentic birth certificate was a key document in false identity cases. His report was reviewed by the Bureau's New York field office, whose counter-intelligence intercept program – the FBI's "Z Coverage" – was responsible for monitoring all mail between the United States and the Soviet Union.

Agent John Fain submitted a report on May 12, 1960, summarizing his interview of Mrs. Oswald, but his 'case title' was "Funds Transmitted to Residents of Russia": the Fain document was an FBI domestic/internal security report (serial 105), and it became "the first external document [on Oswald] circulated within the Soviet Russia Division at the CIA."

A Freedom of Information Act (FOIA) search of the remaining Office of Security files might verify that the CIA's counter-intelligence staff, no later than June 1960, was deeply interested in the Oswald false identity story, especially as it involved Oswald's new passport and his birth certificate.[17] On May 23, 1960, the FBI's New York field office sent an air telegram to Washington headquarters, indicating the Bureau's New York counter-espionage unit considered that the information Fain gathered in his interview with Mrs. Oswald pointed to a major false identity case. Specifically, the New York field office targeted the evidence of the undelivered letters and the missing birth certificate, and recommended to Bureau headquarters "that a copy of [Mrs. Oswald's]... interview be furnished to the State Department...." On May 24, 1960, the Bureau forwarded the Fain report of that interview to the Department of State.

The "Oswald-impostor thesis" had now become a concern of both FBI headquarters and the State Department, though State, of course, had already been alerted to Oswald's apparent disappearance by his mother's letter to Secretary of State Christian Herter. Director Hoover wrote an official Bureau letter to the State Department's Office of Security on June 3, 1960, warning that an "impostor" might be using Oswald's birth certificate, asking State to supply the FBI with any information it had "concerning subject [Oswald]."

On June 6, 1960, Lee's mother finally replied to Casparis' April 26th response to her April 6th letter. Despite Mrs. Oswald's deep concern for her son's suspicious disappearance, she had allowed all of May to slip away before she wrote back. Where was Lee? Why had he disappeared?

J. Edgar Hoover

Essay Two

U.S. & Soviet False-Identity/ Illegal Programs

As the FBI mounted a major hunt for Lee Harvey Oswald, despite the supposed urgency, the pace of the inquiry and the reports were as slow as their earlier efforts on behalf of Mrs. Oswald.

The Bureau record of Oswald's (or someone else's) whereabouts at that time was heavily censored in available FBI documents for 35 years. But over Bureau objections, in December 1995, the Assassinations Record Review Board managed to flush out five crucial documents that were largely un-redacted. The documents proved that the FBI did much more than send an agent to talk to Oswald's brother and mother. Oswald's travels, his alleged defection, his non-response to his mother's postings, and his Schweitzer College application were apparently a red flag in the face of America's intrepid crime busters.

On June 3, 1960, FBI Director Hoover sent out two inquiries on the "missing" Lee Harvey Oswald. The first went to the Office of Security in the Department of State. The Bureau's false identity thesis was obvious in Hoover's request: "Since there is a possibility that an impostor is using Oswald's birth certificate, any current information the Department of State may have concerning subject [Oswald] will be appreciated." Hoover's memo, withheld from the Warren Commission, was finally released to the National Archives in 1975.

Richard A. Frank, the Department of State's legal liaison with the FBI, speculated that it was Hoover and his allies in State's Office of Security who effected the disappearance of the memorandum. But David Slawson, former Warren Commission counsel, suggested that if Hoover's inquiry had been about "something related to the CIA," the Agency might then have been able to push the always useful "national security" button and make it go away, at least until the dust had settled: especially since the Agency itself could have been the clandestine sponsor of Oswald's false identity operation.

Hoover's second communication concerning Oswald went to the Federal Police of Switzerland (SFP), that country's national intelligence agency, through the American Embassy in Paris. Why the State Department offices in Paris rather than Bern? The bypassing of the American Foreign Office in Bern, despite the fact that a Bureau Legat was stationed there, strongly suggests that the FBI still considered the Swiss location OSS/CIA territory, dating back to both World Wars when spymaster Allen Dulles ran American intelligence programs out of Bern. The Bern office, therefore, would have been suspect in any FBI false identity investigation that might involve CIA agents or assets.

Peter Dale Scott (former Canadian diplomat, retired professor of literature, investigative historian, and poet) in a private conversation with me in November 2000, found my theory without merit. He asserted the Legat in Paris was responsible for both France and Switzerland, since no American Embassy existed in Bern. But the fact that Schweitzer College attracted students who were philosophically or politically liberal, and therefore suspect in the overheated anti-Communist atmosphere of Cold War Washington, persuaded me that Bern was indeed deliberately bypassed.

False Conspiracy Stories

The afternoon of November 22, 1963, before any real evidence in the JFK assassination was thoroughly analyzed or even initially evaluated, "officials in Dallas and elsewhere were suggesting that Oswald was part of a Communist conspiracy, acting on orders out of Havana or Moscow. Worse yet, highly dubious reports, already in U.S. Intelligence files, provided some backing for these false conspiracy stories- which soon began to circulate about Jack Ruby as well." Both the FBI and the CIA promoted the Communist plot theory with the Red Marine Oswald as its hit man, what Peter Dale Scott called the "first-phase" explanation of the JFK murder. When the Communist conspiracy charges reached their peak, however, "phase two" kicked in, and both Oswald and Ruby became lone killers, with their alleged or actual connections to foreign agents, organized crime, and American intelligence suppressed by both the FBI and CIA and, later, the Warren Commission.

Both the phase one and phase two explanations were clearly well-coordinated public relations operations run both inside and outside the government, especially within the CIA and the FBI. Inside American intelligence the two phases were controlled by Agency legend James Angleton and Bureau officer William Sullivan, both frequent counter-intelligence collaborators.

J. Edgar Hoover had put his "anti-subversive specialists" to work early in the JFK investigation, including William Sullivan and William Branigan. Together they were responsible for counter-intelligence, espionage, the Socialist Workers Party, the Fair Play for Cuba Committee, and the FBI's mail intercept program (matched in the Agency by James Angleton and William King Harvey, Jr.), all areas that were and still remain relevant to the Oswald story.

The Kostikov, Cubela, Oswald Triangulation

"Angleton's pretext for [assuming command of the Agency's JFK inquiry]... was a cable from [Mexico City Station Chief] Win Scott, linking [reputed KGB agent Valery] Kostikov [in the Soviet's Mexico City consulate] to the CIA's... agent Rolando Cubela." Meetings between Kostikov and Cubela could indeed have occurred, especially if Kostikov himself was a double agent working for the CIA. CIA officers Scott and Angleton may have decided to use Kostikov opportunistically, to reinforce the reputed link between the designated assassin Oswald and both the Soviet Union and Cuba.

In effect, this would triangulate Kostikov, Cubela and Oswald.

In 1963, the CIA somehow listened in to a call from Oswald to the Soviet Consulate in Mexico City. The caller made an appointment with "Valery Kostikov," ostensibly a Soviet consular officer. In turn, the Agency reported the intercepted call to the FBI.[1]

Transmitting privileged CIA information, or guarding the CIA's Soviet Consulate secret, Epstein wrote that the FBI "knew through a double agent" that Kostikov was KGB. His source was, of course, James Angleton. Epstein was covering for the Agency when he stated that Kostikov's "Thirteenth Department of the KGB was in control of "saboteurs" based in North America. More importantly, that department was one of the two Soviet centers for civilian false identities, Illegals, and assassination; three areas significant to the reality or fiction of both Lee Harvey Oswald and Rolando Cubela.

J. Edgar Hoover himself had ample reasons to suppress the Bureau's knowledge of Kostikov as KGB, specifically his own survival. Withholding from the White House any information from the Bureau's security file on Oswald ensured that the FBI would not be accused of an enormous lapse in national security. Of course, this may have been precisely the CIA's intention when it sent the Mexico City report to the Bureau.

James Angleton had self-servingly informed Epstein that the CIA's "SAS Division," reportedly responsible for handling Rolando Cubela and the Agency's assassination plot against Fidel Castro, had withheld Cubela's operational files from Angleton and his staff. Thereby, according to Angleton, the Kostikov/Cubela association was effectively hidden first from Angleton and then from the Warren Commission for whom Angleton served as CIA liaison.

In fact, long before Mexico City and the JFK assassination, Rolando Cubela had been of intense operational interest to both the FBI and the CIA. Hence, it is extremely unlikely that CIA counter-intelligence, the Agency's Office of Security, and Angleton in particular lacked knowledge of Cabela.

Rolando Cubela

Rolando Cubela was one of the heroes of the anti-Batista uprising. He was part of a group of young Cuban students who fired on Batista police and Army officers as they left the Montmartre nightclub on October 28, 1956. One officer's wife and a military colonel were wounded, and the actual target, chief of military intelligence Colonel Blanco Rico, was killed. Rico was the only ranking Batista police officer who disapproved of torturing suspects and detainees, and rebel leader Fidel Castro publicly condemned the killing. Could the shooting, possibly organized by Cubela, have been a provocation?

Later, Cubela "led the Students' Revolutionary Directorate guerrilla forces in the mountains of central Cuba...." Cubela's patron was the exiled Carlos Prio, whose days in Batista's Cuba were marked by close relations with the casino and narcotics operations of Meyer Lansky and Santo Trafficante. Despite funding the yacht 'Granma' used by Castro to open his attack on Batista, Prio and his associates were ultimately unacceptable to Castro. Complicating the relationship was Cubela's reputed need for recognition: Cubela brought his Directorate into Havana and precipitated "a confrontation between Castro and [Cubela's] ... directorate that nearly led to an armed clash the first week after victory."

Cubela had probably been approached by, or was working with the CIA no later than 1959. Of the U.S. Intelligence documents on Cubela in the JFK Assassination Collection at NARA, 68 of them specifically CIA, the earliest is dated April 28, 1959. The Agency first approached Cubela after he was posted to Spain by Castro as a Military Attaché. Scores of FBI documents on Cubela from 1959 though 1963 clearly indicate that American intelligence was closely tracking him. His CIA operation was called AMLASH, and as an asset of the Agency, Cubela was code-named AMLASH-l. Given his involvement with the CIA through 1966, when Cuban counter-intelligence finally arrested and charged him, Cubela may have been an early asset of the CIA dedicated to bringing down Batista.

Cubela's role as Prio's agent and an Agency asset would explain Prio's support of Castro, Cubela's continuing contacts and meetings with representatives of the CIA in Europe, and Castro's willingness to allow Cubela to play a double (if not triple) espionage role through 1966. If Cubela's early anti-Batista actions were in the service of the CIA, it would also explain Cubela's supposed trial in Cuba, his "prison" interview, and, after his sentence was commuted by Castro, the help of agents or assets of the CIA in his exit from Cuba. In fact, Cubela may never have spent much time in a Cuban prison, except when he was interviewed by writer Anthony Summers. Peter Dale Scott observed: "After 18 years in prison, Cubela was released, and at last report had moved to Spain. Such a relocation seems difficult without Agency help."

The CIA knew about Cubela at the very moment of the JFK assassination, but chose not to reveal the Agency's covert relationship with him, since the whole story of CIA assassination attempts against foreign leaders would have been exposed, including the anti-Castro CIA/Organized Crime collaboration linked to the Kennedy killing, at least according to the House Select Committee on Assassinations. Had Cubela testified as late as 1975 to the Senate Intelligence Committee, he would have significantly contradicted the Agency's version of his AMLASH role, opening up still more unexplored dimensions of the plots against Castro and the CIA's duplicity.

After Cubela was interviewed by Anthony Summers in 1978, Summers concluded, somewhat awkwardly: "If Cubela's version is accepted as truthful, [then] several CIA officers are exposed as guilty not only of going along with a plan to kill Castro, without authorization, but of actually inciting Cubela to do it..."

Both the FBI and the CIA had information linking the Cubela/AMLASH plot directly to the 1960-62 attempts against Castro run by an Agency-Syndicate coalition that included organized crime boss Santo Trafficante and corrupt Florida Teamsters, established in testimony from a Cubela associate received by a U.S. Senate subcommittee.

But something more was withheld both in 1963-64 and in 1975. According to Castro biographer and journalist Tad Szulc, it was the Second Naval Guerrilla, a smaller but more secret version of the Bay of Pigs invasion. Planned for 1964, it reunited the CIA and its anti-Castro Cuban exiles with James McCord and E. Howard Hunt as Agency players in the action. Both were psychological warfare and CIA Office of Security operatives.

The invasion was to be energized by the killing of Fidel Castro, a CIA plan prepared in Paris and Madrid, with Rolando Cubela the designated assassin. Cubela's friend and associate, Manuel Artime, a CIA asset, was the leader of the Cuban exiles' second invasion. According to Tad Szulc, Second Naval Guerrilla was not abandoned until 1965. In 1966, Rolando Cubela was arrested in Cuba after Fidel Castro's counter-intelligence agents exposed the operation.

The Oswald-Cubela Intelligence Links

What do these assassination and invasion plans implicating Rolando Cubela have to do with Lee Harvey Oswald? Cubela was being tracked by FBI Legat communications originating in Madrid, Paris, and Bern from 1960 through 1966. Oswald was being tracked as well by the FBI in Paris and Bern from 1960 onward. In the same period, in France and Switzerland, from the same agents communicating with J. Edgar Hoover, identical intelligence topics were crossing, linked to either Cubela or Oswald. Both men were suspected by American intelligence of being fake defectors.

From 1959 through 1964, the CIA was monitoring Rolando Cubela, keeping tabs on the Fair Play for Cuba Committee, meeting with Cubela and planning to kill Fidel Castro. Through November '63 they were also intercepting Oswald's mail. At the moment of the JFK assassination and for some time beyond, the CIA was directly involved with Rolando Cubela.

James Angleton called AMLASH-1 "Cubella," apparently because a message he received from the CIA station chief in Mexico City said "Cubella" had been in contact with Valery Kostikov in the Soviet Union's Consulate office. But the CIA in Mexico City had also reported that Oswald (or, more likely, a double) met with Kostikov. Both the CIA and FBI apparently believed or knew that Kostikov was a KGB agent; therefore, American intelligence suspected that both Oswald and Cubela had a KGB association. Through Kostikov, Cubela and Oswald were linked.

The Kostikov connection is a clear signal that the two possibly fake defectors, one American, the other Cuban, had been involved in a Communist conspiracy directed against President Kennedy.

Only after both Oswald and Ruby became officially lone assassins were the ominous connections between Oswald, Kostikov, and Cubela muted and suppressed.[2]

In 1960, American intelligence concerns about Cubela and Oswald that registered when Oswald turned up "missing" in Switzerland were matched in 1963-64 when Oswald was charged with the murder of John F. Kennedy.

What should have been a straightforward investigation of the missing Oswald in 1960 was made darkly dense with American intelligence counter-espionage hocus-pocus: FBI and CIA messages from Bern, Paris, and Madrid, AMLASH, the Fair Play for Cuba Committee, and assassination plots against two heads of state in 1963-1964.

Both the FBI and the CIA veiled that dark density from a series of American presidents, and from the American people, for as long as possible.

The AMLASH/Cubela story has remained heavily censored by both the Agency and the Bureau. The CIA and the FBI had good reason to avoid tangling the story with Lee Harvey Oswald in 1960, and again in 1963-64. In 1960, the parallel tracks left by Cubela and Oswald led to Cuba, to liberal/left-wing student meetings and education overseas (Cubela frequently attended these conferences as Cuba's representative), to Switzerland, and to the Fair Play For Cuba Committee (in the United States and the Soviet Union). In 1963-64 the stops on the Cubela/Oswald tour also included Mexico City, the KGB and the CIA, and U.S. assassination plots against heads of state.

In sum, Rolando Cubela was a prominent Cuban presence in liberal and radical student meetings and conferences; U.S. Intelligence in Switzerland was aware of Cubela's operations. Cubela was tracked by the CIA, and may even have been an agent when he was involved in liberal student groups. Lee Harvey Oswald registered at a Swiss liberal college. Later, both Oswald and Cubela were reported to have been in close touch with KGB officer Kostikov in Mexico City.

If American intelligence wanted to pursue the Communist conspiracy hypothesis in 1963-64, the Oswald/Cubela confluence clearly was available. But the American power structure apparently opted for the lone assassin of phase two, and the Cubela/Oswald correspondences were quickly buried.

Was Bern bypassed in the 1960 inquiry regarding Oswald's no-show at Schweitzer College because of its association with Allen Dulles? The American intelligence cable traffic record now available from the National Archives strongly suggests so. Beginning in 1959, CIA messages on Cubela to and from Havana, Madrid and especially Paris were extremely heavy. In 1960, only three Bureau queries on Oswald went through Paris. No FBI Oswald traffic went through Bern and, of twenty Bern Legat messages, only one on Cubela (9/29/62) was sent.

The Bern FBI Legat line was always available, but FBI communications on Switzerland and Oswald in 1960 went through Paris. Communications on Oswald through Bern opened up only *after* the JFK assassination.

Despite Peter Dale Scott's argument, Bern was indeed bypassed during the 1960 FBI/Swiss Police investigation of Oswald, apparently for significant American intelligence reasons.

The Swiss Police Play Keystone Cops

The slow pace of the ostensibly urgent hunt for Oswald raises doubt about it's sincerity. Not until June 16, 1960, fully ten days after Hoover asked his agent in the Paris Embassy to institute an immediate search, did the Embassy communicate with the Swiss Federal Police. According to the Bureau Legat in the Paris Embassy, "pertinent information [on Oswald] was furnished... and... [the Swiss Federal Police] were requested to conduct [an] investigation...."

Remarkably, the Swiss Police said they could not *find* Albert Schweitzer College. According to the usually competent Helvetian authorities they did not locate it until September, because they "had no official records [of the college] on file...." This response is absurd. Students from the United States and Europe had been attending meetings in the Klosters since 1950, and the college opened officially in 1955. How could hundreds of prospective students with authentic passports and visas from dozens of U.S. states and other nations leave no traceable records with Swiss immigration, tourism, and education offices?

Further, because of its liberal-Protestant background, together with the freedoms it offered, the college had already been in trouble with the Swiss Federal Police concerning its students' use of recreational drugs. Rev. Richard Boeke, first President of the American chapter of the International Association for Religious Freedom, visited Albert Schweitzer College in 1964 and reported, "some of the Americans brought in marijuana, and the college was a bit in trouble with the Swiss."[3] Certainly, therefore, the Swiss had records that should have been available to the FBI. Apparently the Federal Police were either ordered, or made their own decision, to pretend ignorance of the college.

The Swiss Federal Police managed to squander three months conferring with the FBI, locating the elusive ASC campus, and then reporting back to the American Embassy in Paris. The embassy, in turn, sent the information on to the FBI in Washington.

The September 27th memorandum from Paris to FBI headquarters recorded a major intelligence effort by the Swiss: "considerable investigation had been conducted to locate the Albert Schweitzer College... since this college was previously unknown, and there was no official record of its existence in the [Swiss] Federal government records...." The college was, of course, not "previously unknown," but had been an official institution since 1955. Lee's mother had already been in touch with the college from Texas before the Swiss couldn't find it in their own country. The Swiss authorities were either enjoying some of the recreational drugs they confiscated from the Schweitzer College kids, or stalling: but at whose behest?

The FBI Paris Memoranda

On October 12, 1960, the Bureau's "Legat, Paris" sent the most relevant of the four memoranda to FBI Headquarters in Washington. Originally, this document was "exempted [censored] by the FBI because it contained foreign government information." Apparently reviewed in 1977 and "exempted," then reviewed again in 1992 and "severely redacted," the eviscerated "document was released in full" in December 1995, with three other documents in the 1960 series from the "Legat, Paris" to FBI Headquarters.

It is this memorandum of October 12, 1960, that is most significant. The original source was the Swiss Federal Police investigative report submitted to the American Embassy by October 1, 1960.

We will examine five excerpts from the Swiss report:

> Excerpt #1: "The investigation at the "Albert Schweitzer College" located at Churwalden, Switzerland, revealed that Oswald actually had announced his planned attendance at this ... school ... beginning in the fall of 1959."

Since the Swiss reported this announcement, they were most likely relying on a source, truthful or not, at the college. It may have been an outside source, and who knows if *that* information was truthful or not. If none of it were true, the College itself supplied the phony story, for whatever institutional reasons.

It would not take the most sensitive FBI counter-intelligence analyst to run through these alternatives and conclude that the Bureau's false identity hypothesis was alive and well, regardless of the original source.

> Excerpt #2: "He had originally written a letter from Moscow indicating his intention to attend there [at Churwalden]."

This followed hard on the fall trimester statement. Any FBI reader would logically assume the statement meant that Oswald meant to attend the college in the fall of 1960. Though this was old news, the phrase "from Moscow" was crucial new material.

> Excerpt #3: "A letter which was addressed to him at this address [in Moscow or Churwalden?] by his mother was returned to her since his whereabouts are unknown to the college."

This sentence strongly suggested that the letter was from Oswald in Moscow to his mother in Dallas, but no such letter has been found in the public record. In any event, how would the Swiss Federal Police have known about the letter? Could the college have informed them?

Even if the Swiss were repeating information received from the FBI, where is that letter now? And what letter was returned to Lee's mother? Was it originally delivered to the College? If so, where is *that* letter? The quirky shifting of tenses and modifying forms here only increases the murkiness of the memo: "A letter ... was returned to her since his whereabouts are unknown to the college."

> **Excerpt #4:** "The Swiss Federal Police advised that it is unlikely that he [Oswald] would have attended the course [assumed to be the fall trimester] under a different name."

> **Excerpt #5:** "At the present time there is no record of a person possibly identical with the subject [Oswald] who is registered for the [fall] courses beginning October 2."

The tenses and phrasings in these last two excerpts are again impossibly vague.

These five passages constitute the most important of the communications from the Swiss Federal Police to the Legat in Paris, which were then forwarded to Director Hoover.

The memorandum is headed "Subject": "LEE HARVEY OSWALD" and "INTERNAL SECURITY-R," on the missing Oswald, a domestic intelligence case relating to the Soviet Union. The entire communication hummed with ominous false identity signals, most if not all of them apparently generated by the FBI's initial queries to the Swiss Police.

Note that this communication focused entirely on Oswald's anticipated attendance at the fall trimester of the college. Some source, in Switzerland or the United States, made that presumption.

A quick reading of the communication by FBI headquarters could only have established a concern that its specific statements further reinforced. Remember, this investigation was not being run out of Moscow or Washington, but within Switzerland. If distortions or falsehoods entered the Bureau's communication pipeline and were subsequently recorded in this crucial memorandum, that false noise was most likely generated by the source in Switzerland, or, less likely, by the FBI legal attaché reporting to Hoover. It could have been the Swiss Federal Police, but one would have to assume that either former OSS, or acting CIA agents and assets, subverted some of Switzerland's finest to help strike terror into J. Edgar Hoover's cold, cold heart.

It is absolutely clear that the Swiss Federal Police ran a false identity investigation for the FBI. When no Oswald, real or fictional, ever showed up at Schweitzer College it increased the Bureau's fear that his passport, birth certificate, and persona were already part of Soviet intelligence's false identity machinery.

Through their Passport and Registration office, the Soviets knew that Oswald had entered the country carrying other important original documents. Interviewed by four unidentified Soviet Passport officials, he reportedly gave them his original "discharge papers from the Marine Corps." Those Marine Corps documents, had Lee Oswald not been a blinking "danger" sign, were of great value to the Soviet Union's ongoing Illegals operations.

The four memoranda from the Paris FBI Legat to Bureau HQ were dated July 27th, September 27th, October 12th, and November 3, 1960. The last was the strangest. It asserted that the Police had supplied "additional information on 10/24/60," which directly contradicts the memo of October 12th, without addressing the anomaly. This fourth memo, in fact, anticipated the conclusions of the Warren Report on Oswald's Schweitzer College adventure. As Dennis Bartholomew observed, the memorandum was apparently "one large quote, as if it were quoting some other [still unavailable] document."

The four memos were released by the Assassination Records Review Board in 1995, largely without redaction. Besides Bartholomew's two research articles, only two national publications have touched on disturbing aspects of the documents. The FBI itself has been silent about their puzzling contradictions.

The Bureau Retreats: State Holds the Line

On February 27, 1961, J. Edgar Hoover sent a communication to the State Department's Office of Security, announcing the FBI's "search for an Oswald impostor in Europe" was over. But the Passport Office was less willing to give up the investigation. One month later, on March 31, 1961, Edward J. Hickey wrote a memorandum to the Department of State's Consular division, directed to John T. White, clearly indicating the Passport Office still felt the false identity issue was very much alive. Hickey pointed to the returned Oswald letters, and Hoover's suspicion that an impostor might be using Oswald's papers. This constituted an espionage threat, especially if the suspected impostor gained possession of a "valid passport." Hickey cautioned the consular section to hand over that passport to Oswald only "on a personal basis" and only after the American Embassy in Moscow was "assured, to its complete satisfaction, that he [was]… returning to the United States."

Though the "Legat" at the American Embassy in Paris promised FBI headquarters that any "further information received [would]… be furnished to the Bureau," no such information has ever officially surfaced.

The FBI Connection at Albert Schweitzer College

What of the Bern connection? In a letter dated April 8, 1961, Schweitzer College secretary Erika Weibel replied to Representative Jim Wright's query on behalf of Mrs. Oswald. Weibel informed Wright that the college was sending him "the complete file on the [Oswald] matter…" The documents were not identified. How strange that an educational institution should strip its records rather than send copies of the requested material. Or did it really send the "complete file"? One month after the assassination, J. Edgar Hoover apparently sent a message to the Bureau's Legat in Bern, inquiring again about Oswald and ASC. On December 31, 1963, the Bern Legat sent a letter of transmittal together with seven Schweitzer College documents to FBI Director J. Edgar Hoover. According to NARA, the seven Oswald documents were obtained by the FBI from a "confidential" source at the College, whose name was included in the letter to Hoover but censored for security purposes.

Why did the FBI's "confidential" source at the college *after* the JFK assassination still need to be hidden in the late 1990s? Why, if Erika Weibel sent Jim Wright the complete file, were seven documents still at the college, to be shared with the FBI alone? Were those 1963 documents authentic? Could at least one of them have "been created… to provide more [fabricated] evidence of Oswald's intent to attend the third trimester… rather than the fall trimester as stated in the [crucial] Oct. 1960 memo…" [?]

Nothing has ever been clear concerning the origins of the documents (whether originals or copies) in the Warren Commission's
possession: Mrs. Oswald, Jim Wright, the Paris FBI Legat, and Erika Weibel all qualify as sources. But possibly the most crucial unexamined source is the Bureau Legat at Bern, who in 1963, just after
the murder of John F. Kennedy, was in touch with a most helpful
"confidential" FBI connection at Albert Schweitzer College. Who
was that Bureau source in Switzerland?

The bizarre record of Oswald's trip through the looking-glass
may well have accomplished its actual purpose, since it loaded the
FBI's files and those of the CIA, Naval Intelligence and the State
Dept.'s Office of Security with contradictory and suspicious data.

A Major Soviet Illegals Operation Suspected

Switzerland was a vortex of intelligence and espionage activity
from the First World War through the death of John F. Kennedy and beyond. Over the years, Allen Dulles and the OSS/CIA
used the Quakers, the Unitarians, the World Council of Churches
and other religious groups as sources of intelligence and information, and the Unitarian Church was the mainstay of Schweitzer
College. Oswald's trip to Europe and his hip-fake towards Churwalden followed by his defection are all signs of a major Soviet
"Illegals" operation.

American intelligence's dilemma was this: what seemed to have
been a faulty false identity operation might actually have succeeded, or been made to appear as if it had. The man who returned
from the Soviet Union may or may not have been a work of fiction, a "legend," who had replaced the real Lee Oswald. Thread-
ing through this complex story was the curious and suspect postal
trail Oswald laid down: first in the United States, then in Europe,
and then back home in America. It is a trail remarkably like the
tracks of an "Illegal."

The Illegals

What, in fact, *is* an Illegal, as opposed to a "legal" agent. The
KGB ran its overseas operations "chiefly through an extensive network of agents placed in its embassies, missions and official
agencies. These 'legal' KGB operators [had]... official cover and often diplomatic immunity."

Legal Soviet agents could hold high or low rank, anywhere from ambassador to embassy doorman. But the term itself is inaccurate. Though these agents were legitimate Soviet mission employees, espionage was of course highly *il*legal. To be a "legal" agent means only that one is protected from prosecution, usually by diplomatic immunity.

False identity Illegals living covertly in the U.S. had no such protection, and were dubbed "legends." They "established a life based on a false story," supported by "a completely false background or 'legend', complete with documentation…" To be an Illegal was to be a member of the most elite espionage group in the world, and to practice "perhaps the purest form of spying, and probably the most dangerous."

These Soviet agents were specially trained to become "average American citizens, usually very conservative politically and very anti-communist." Since Oswald was suspected of either participating in the creation of an Illegal (that is, a false identity) or himself an Illegal, what was American intelligence to make of the paradox who returned from the Soviet Union? Claiming to be a confirmed anti-Communist re-defector, he subsequently acted on occasion as an outspoken supporter of Communist Cuba and Fidel Castro.

The internal CIA conflict over the search for James Angleton's suspected mole was ultimately contained within the Agency's controversy over whether Yuriiy Nosenko was a legitimate defector, and the ultimate CIA take on Oswald was nested within *that* controversy.

Illegals and Legitimate Identity Documents

A Soviet Illegal did not adopt a completely fictional persona. He or she would co-opt the identity of a real person, with a birth certificate and passport or other *bona fide* papers.

How did the KGB gain access to these authentic documents? Some came from American tourists in the Soviet Union; for example, Lee Harvey Oswald. But why capture the identity of a real person? Why not just invent an identity? Quite simply, a real person has a valid historical record.

Clean identity papers were not easy to acquire. By 1954, Soviet intelligence had drawn up plans for "a network of 130 'documentation agents' whose sole responsibility was to obtain birth certificates, passports and other documents to support the illegals' legends." KGB officers who specialized in documentation for Illegals were sent to twenty-two countries to snare the valuable paper. A number of key agents were dispatched to collect birth certificates and passports in, among others, East and West Germany, France, Mexico, Turkey, and the United States: "Operations officers specializing in illegal documentation were posted to New York ... [and] Mexico City ...."

Intelligence Operations of Illegals

KGB Illegals in the United States used a variety of means to communicate with Moscow, including ordinary mail, but their letters were seldom if ever sent directly to the Soviet Union. They were transferred through "cover addresses in Western Europe," including Switzerland. "One FBI mail-intercept program, conducted between the 1940s and 1966... involved intercepting and opening letters to certain European addresses considered mail drops for Soviet intelligence. Bureau sources say that "[the] program helped expose several important illegals."

American citizens who established temporary residence in Switzerland were monitored by American intelligence, especially if they had already come to the attention of, for example, FBI counter-espionage. Though little known, the FBI actually had a physical presence overseas.

As part of KGB Illegals support operations, American citizens developed letter drops for either themselves or other U.S.-based Soviet agents. Letter drops were "innocent" intermediary addresses for intelligence mail transiting between the U.S. and the Soviet Union. The FBI may have suspected Schweitzer College was to be developed as, or had already become, an espionage letter drop. The Bureau's suspicion would therefore have seemed to be confirmed when Schweitzer College Director and founder Hans Casparis wrote to Lee Oswald about the strange switch in term start-dates.

"For the FBI, the [successful] search for an illegal [was]... the ultimate goal in counter-intelligence." William Sullivan and Sam Papich were the widely accepted false identity experts for the Bureau, working closely with CIA counterpart James Angleton, but occasionally a commentator with inside knowledge names a lesser-known FBI expert in false identity.

In January, 1963, "Anthony Litrento, a street-smart agent... was the bureau's leading expert on Soviet illegals." But when Don Moore, chief of the FBI's counter-espionage operations for seventeen years, wanted to meet with Anatoly Golitsin after Rudolph Abel was traded for captured U-2 pilot Gary Powers, he asked Sam Papich to accompany him.

Abel was a major figure in the history of Soviet Illegals. In May 1961, Abel's attorney James Donovan, who had major ties to U.S. Intelligence, received a letter from Leipzig supposedly written by "Hellen Abel," Rudolph's purported wife. An exchange of letters between the two resulted in the trade of Powers for Abel. But neither Donovan nor the possibly fictional "Hellen Abel" wrote the letters; they were manufactured by the CIA and the KGB in an early 1960s *détente noir.*

The Soviet "modern Illegal" had only one important category of activity: so-called wet affairs. Illegals infiltrated the United States primarily "to assist [in] and supervise assassination and sabotage." Little wonder, then, that the bundle of contradictions called Lee H. Oswald evoked such curiosity and suspicion in both the CIA and the FBI, or that his mail was monitored closely by both agencies. Accordingly, after the murder of President Kennedy, the CIA'S James Angleton insisted he and the FBI's William Sullivan, both deeply involved in mail interceptions and 'Illegals' investigations, should carefully coordinate their Warren Commission statements denying Oswald had been an American spy.

In 1963, Sullivan and Angleton had many things to hide from both the Warren Commission and J. Edgar Hoover. For example, beginning in 1961, Sullivan and Angleton ran "a highly secret international co-operative known as CAZAB, [including]... selected members of the security and intelligence agencies" of the British Commonwealth and the United States. CAZAB allowed Angleton and Sullivan to side-step Hoover's "malign influence over counter-intelligence liaison...."

What other joint FBI-CIA operations were then ongoing?

After he returned from the Soviet Union, Lee Oswald seemed to have an interest in microdots and cipher templates, both used by KGB Illegals. Microdots are specks of film read by microscope, and both GRU and KGB Illegals used miniature cipher pads as unbreakable code templates in seemingly innocuous communications.

The Directorate & The Superspy

Inside the KGB, the so-called First Chief (or "Main") Directorate was the operational home for all counter-intelligence operations, especially the aforementioned "wet work," which included assassinations and the running of Illegals. Officially designated the internal espionage network, it was considered "the keystone of the [Soviet] State Security." When Oswald was in Moscow, his Intourist guide was probably an active KGB agent of the Chief Directorate. 'S,' a KGB sub-directorate, "handled the recruitment, training, maintenance and support of an astonishing number of Illegals around the world." The majority of its teaching faculty were ex-Illegals or KGB spies, protected by diplomatic cover.

Another sub-directorate, designated "K" and run by Soviet counter-intelligence, was just as potent.

In 1958, fresh from the Soviet Union, twenty-three-year-old Oleg D. Kalugin was a Fulbright Scholar at Columbia. Difficult as it was for Soviet students to study in the United States, Kalugin accomplished that feat while serving as an undercover operative of the KGB. Kalugin apparently enjoyed his espionage days in the United States, working as "a Radio Moscow correspondent at the United Nations" after his Columbia campus experience. "He spied at the United Nations from 1960 to 1964...."

A rising Soviet counter-espionage star, Kalugin was a key officer in the KGB's New York operation, and U.S. counter-intelligence was well aware of Kalugin's spy activities, targeting him in "several FBI setups." Kalugin was "involved with some secret operations in New York," possibly intercepting postal communications, and described one of his operations as "penetrating anti-Castro Cuban groups;" but he did not explain the intent of this curious counter-intelligence, since the anti-Castro organizations were already heavily infiltrated by the CIA.

Kalugin's connections to the Kennedy assassination story and Lee Harvey Oswald are striking: Oleg Nechiporenko, a Soviet Consulate/KGB officer in Mexico City, who had met with Lee or his double, worked for Oleg Kalugin no later than the early 1970s. When word first spread around the world that a former defector to the Soviet Union had apparently murdered President Kennedy, Kalugin and his KGB crew in New York were immediately commissioned to spread the official Soviet word: "Oswald had lived in

Minsk, [but] ... he had never been trusted and was suspected of being a CIA agent..."

The late 1960s saw Kalugin in Washington, D.C., stationed at the Soviet Embassy. Each Embassy had a top 'resident' KGB officer who handled "Line PR (political intelligence)." Oleg Kalugin was the "youthful head of Line PR." He processed an extraordinary stream of U.S. Intelligence agents and government workers who were happy to supply the KGB with sensitive and classified documents, state secrets, and anything else Kalugin desired. These men collected thousands of dollars in return, living a life-style far beyond their federal pay grade, without registering a hint of suspicion inside the American intelligence community.[4]

This apparent non-interest was highlighted by Kalugin's involvement in dubious double-agent activities, as well as media and FBI disclosures of his operations, with no move made to expel him.

Oleg Kalugin was triumphantly hailed back to the Soviet Union and became the youngest KGB general in Soviet history, and the chief of the KGB's First/Major Directorate from 1973 to 1980. This gave him control of the KGB's Illegals and false identities files (the sub-Directorate "K" secrets).

Kalugin immigrated back to the United States in 1995, and became active in research, writing, teaching, and lecturing on espionage and counter-intelligence, sometimes in partnership with former CIA agents. On June 26, 2002, "Oleg D. Kalugin, a retired K.G.B. general... was convicted of treason in absentia... and sentenced to 15 years in prison for disclosing state secrets to the United States." When did Kalugin give up those State secrets?

From his 1958 espionage activity at Columbia University to his United Nations Intelligence operations, his Washington counter-intelligence work, and as head of the KGB's First Directorate, Oleg Kalugin was always directly involved both as an agent and an officer in Illegals and false identity operations. The KGB's First Directorate and its sub-directorate K had been responsible for monitoring Lee Harvey Oswald from his arrival in the Soviet Union in 1959 until he went home to the United States, and most certainly after.

Was Kalugin subverted by the CIA as early as 1958, over an icy-cold stein of beer in the Lion's Den at Columbia University? This could account for his remarkable success in signing up so many American traitors. Was Oleg Kalugin, in fact, a long-time member of a KGB/FBI/CIA double-agent operation during the Cold War? Was that why in June 2002, he was convicted of treason in *absentia* by a Russian court?

Kalugin was on a first-name basis with the best of Washington's mainstream journalists, such as Walter Lippmann, who could request and usually receive private meetings with sitting U.S. presidents. During the Cuban Missile Crisis, and JFK's subsequent moves toward peaceful reconciliation in the spring of 1963, diplomatic back channels were opened connecting Castro, the Soviet hierarchy, and the White House. In 1962 and 1963, a key communication line may indeed have run between an ostensible KGB operative and JFK's most trusted emissary, his brother Bobby: "One of Kalugin's most important contacts was Senator Robert Kennedy who, but for his assassination ... might have won the 1968 Democratic nomination. Before his death [Robert] Kennedy presented Kalugin with a tie-pin showing the PT-109 torpedo boat... his brother... captured during the war."[5]

Was Oleg Kalugin one of those back channel agents linking Moscow and Washington? Did he manage to betray both the Soviet Union and the United States?

When Kalugin was in Moscow in the 1970s he reportedly played a part in the assassination of Bulgarian dissident Georgi Markov, an operation that included an umbrella weapon with a poisoned dart. Kalugin has denied any direct involvement.

Might some of Oleg Kalugin's treasured American memories be of that strange American Marine suspected of being a U.S. Intelligence dangle, or was he himself Lee Oswald's manipulator in a false identity game?

Soviet GRU Control of Illegals

Most discussions of Soviet espionage Illegals have been about KGB "legends." But the military side of the Soviet Union's legend program was run initially by Soviet military Intelligence (GRU) rather than the KGB. A defecting Marine, for example, especially one who had made contact with the American Embassy in Moscow, would have been of great interest to the GRU's Illegals operations.

The GRU was technically the Chief Directorate of Intelligence of the General Staff of the Soviet. In the 1960s, the GRU had six interior operational directorates plus an information directorate. Though the 5th Directorate was specifically responsible for "Diversion and Sabotage," the GRU as a whole conducted "military, political, economic and scientific intelligence" as well as "propaganda activities, acts of provocation, blackmail, terrorism and sabotage." GRU Illegals could, therefore, be used in any one of these capacities.

The GRU's 1st Directorate was responsible for selecting and training prospective Illegals. Several GRU espionage schools both in and near Moscow prepared Illegals for overseas duty, and "each national or area desk [had] ... its own group of Illegals."

Illegals placed in the United States were especially prized. The crucial difference between the KGB and the GRU was the latter's "attention to collecting information on the armed forces and military installations of the Western countries..."[6]

The GRU ran a number of so-called "singles" and "doubles" throughout the United States. A double consisted of a man and woman living together as a wedded couple.

Throughout the Cold War, GRU was repeatedly compromised by the West. Penetrated by both British MI-6 and the CIA in the 1970s, military intelligence was finally placed under the complete control of the KGB.

Turning Soviet Illegals

Every Western counter-intelligence operation was interested in the Illegals from the East. Key Soviet Illegals in the United States were, in fact, periodically approached by the FBI, turned into double agents, and became players in that "most dangerous game in the world."

Though less publicized, the CIA also turned Soviet Illegals, and ran them as double agents. One especially crucial KGB Illegal in Helsinki, Finland was turned by the CIA, then betrayed to the South Africans by none other than James Angleton. In turn, the South Africans gave the man up to the Soviets, who then executed him. He was, of course, a loyal double agent of the CIA.

Both sides suspected the other of offering up false Illegals (dangles) who were booby traps. A Deputy FBI counter-intelligence Chief summarized several decades of Bureau experience in coping with false identity cases: "That's what the [Soviets] ... always threw out at you. They'd always dangle something ... [like] an Illegal ..." who would not be what he or she appeared to be. According to one former Navy Intelligence officer, when Lee Oswald went to the Soviet Union, he looked like an American dangle aimed precisely at the Soviets' false identity/Illegals programs; but when he came back out (according to James Angleton), Oswald resembled a Soviet-invented "legend."

Overlooked in the micro-analysis of Lee Harvey Oswald's life is his interview in June, 1962 with FBI agent Fain and his partner. In his report to the FBI's Dallas office, Fain recommended that Oswald be re-interviewed, and urged that his records at the Immigration and Naturalization Service be examined. Fain's suggestion clearly indicated that Oswald was still considered an Illegal/false identity suspect.

The Maestro of Masquerades

False identity/Illegal agents were a major part of Allen Dulles' massive spy operations throughout two World Wars and the subsequent Cold War. Dulles was a documented expert on false identity operations. He may even have invented them, at least for the Allies, in WW I. In 1917, after the American entry into the war, the Germans "stepped up their previously successful campaign to insert agents into the United States, and... specialized in forged or stolen documents to win the needed visas for entry from besieged legations such as the one at Bern." Dulles was at the time the "ad hoc intelligence officer for the US Legation in Switzerland."

Why then, during the Warren Commission inquiry in 1964, did Dulles, with his nearly fifty years of hands-on experience, have absolutely nothing to say about false identity cases and intelligence Illegals? When his fellow Commissioners began discussing possible links between American intelligence and Lee Harvey Oswald, Dulles might have said: "I have an idea or two on that topic."

His silence still echoes.

Albert Schweitzer

Essay Three

Schweitzer College: New Evidence and Analysis

Albert Schweitzer College was nurtured by the International Association for Religious Freedom (IARF), a world-wide liberal and progressive organization, backed by the IARF's liberal Swiss Protestant wing and, in the United States, energized by the Unitarian Church. In remarks celebrating the history of the IARF, the Reverend Maas ("Max") D. Gaebler identified Schweitzer College as "a project initiated and supported chiefly by our Swiss IARF member group... [that] served for several years [through the 1950s] as a magnet for our young people from our [IARF] affiliates in many countries. Its contributions to the experience of many young religious liberals... [were] significant." But Gaebler added: "Its subsequent history, however, was complex and unfortunate." He did not elaborate on that "subsequent" period. Though the college's later history was darkened, then largely redacted following the news of its link to Lee Harvey Oswald, its earliest days were highly romanticized. Richard Boeke, first president of the American chapter of the IARF, reviewing the Association's history, called Schweitzer College the "crown jewel" of all the IARF's associate religious centers. According to Boeke, the college had initially been "good for liberal Swiss Protestants."

By August 1958, ASC was registered as an "associate member" of the International Association of Religious Freedom, attaining that distinction just prior to Lee Harvey Oswald's application to the college.

The Founders

Beginning in 1950, Hans Casparis and his English wife Therese Casparis held summer conferences in Klosters, Switzerland, anticipating the establishment of the College. Hans and Therese were reportedly "the life and soul of the gathering[s]..." By 1955, the meetings developed into "an international center for the study of ethics, Christian morals and contemporary social, religious and political developments."

An enthusiastic Unitarian supporter summarized its origin: "In the summer of 1950, a group of progressive, international-minded citizens-all Swiss-started the ... College." But the college did not operate on a full-time basis until 1955: the first years were summer programs of study, group interaction, and fun, followed by more sober *curricula*. Though the founding "Swiss liberals" were "primarily ministers," they have not been identified except for Hans Casparis, earlier reported to be "a pastor like most of the founding fathers of Albert Schweitzer College...." These liberal pastors may have been linked to the college's first full-time faculty in 1955, or be identical to that initial college faculty, but no documentary evidence presently supports that possibility.

The new college "intended to help young people attain spiritual independence by developing a critical mind combined with clear moral and religious convictions." Beyond its liberal Protestant genesis, the College was declared to be "entirely free from denominational ties," welcoming students "of all faiths or those without [any] religious ties."

The Missing Records

How did those diverse students discover the college? On August 23, 2001, I visited the Unitarian/Universalist Association (UUA) headquarters at 25 Beacon Street, Boston. I fully expected to find published advertisements for Casparis' summer programs and later announcements on the development and final establishment of Schweitzer College. The key publication was the *Christian Unitarian Register*, first called the *Christian Register*, of which the UUA in Boston had a complete set. I had a second interest in the *Register*: its radical editor from 1943 through 1947 was Rev. Stephen Fritchman. Reportedly prodded by Quaker activist Noel Field, Fritchman supported the creation of the Unitarian Service Committee during World War II.

What I found at the Boston UUA, or rather what I did not find, was astonishing. Treated warmly by the staff, I carefully checked each glossy page of the monthly Register from 1948 through 1959. In those ten years, neither Casparis' summer programs nor Albert Schweitzer College received a single word of coverage: no announcements, no registration information, no news stories, despite a monthly section called "News of the Unitarian World." How did a college named after Albert Schweitzer, embodying his ideas and principles, with the full support of prominent Unitarians around the world, merit no mention in their signature publication?

Only in the June, 1959 edition of the *Register* did a short announcement appear at the bottom of a page about "summer study courses," but it gave no specific contact information, and left very little time to apply. In October 1961 the *Register* announced that, beginning on September 1, 1961, the college would have its first full-time director. This rather naked news story reported that the paid position was made possible by the "financial support" of unidentified American Unitarians. Since all the leading American Unitarians associated with ASC, including Robert Schacht, published regularly in the *Register*, the phrase "American Unitarians" is curious. The *Register* was published at the American Unitarian Association headquarters: 25 Beacon Street, Boston, a frequent address of letters exchanged concerning ASC, on Unitarian Association letterheads. How, then, did prominent Association officers become only unnamed "American Unitarians"?

I discovered one possible explanation for the absence of material in the *Register*, an undated but informative brochure on Schweitzer College in the files at Harvard Divinity School. An excellent photograph of the college was identified as appearing in the January edition of the *Christian Register*. Upon examination, the photo does not appear in any January edition. But in several volumes I noted that pictures and articles had been carefully but clearly excised. I reported the thefts to the Association staff. Did someone remove all notice, save for the two cryptic little articles, of Schweitzer College?

Was the college deliberately fenced off from other Unitarian activities? From 1948 through 1962 the *Register* had dozens of articles and reviews about young Unitarians and liberal religious youth and their programs: just the kind of students Hans Casparis wanted. Beyond any select excision of materials from the *Register*, why was not a single word published to link those American groups with ASC? I contacted still-existing liberal religious youth groups, who report absolutely no records of it. How were any American students ever recruited, let alone chosen? Perhaps, to fly under the anti-liberal reactionary radar, recruitment and registration information was quietly handled by Unitarian pastors like Stephen Fritchman.[1]

The institution was operated by the Albert Schweitzer College Association, a non-profit organization with its legal headquarters in the village of Churwalden, capital of the Grisons region, in eastern Switzerland. The largely Unitarian American Friends of Albert Schweitzer College, Inc., based in New York and Boston, was created as a "non-profit membership organization ... incorporated [in New York] to receive tax deductible contributions from United States citizens and corporations ..."

Despite Dr. Schweitzer's towering eminence, and his intimate relationship with the school named after him, nearly all historical records of Albert Schweitzer College have been lost, or more likely eliminated.

Liberal Protestant Support for Schweitzer College

Crucial to the college's history are the identities of the liberal American Protestant groups supporting the college. What, for example, were their financial and political connections? The Harvard documents supply some information: "The donations of churches ... [and] institutions, progressive, liberal, liberal-Christian, and free-thinking groups-mostly ... in Switzerland ... could not balance the [college] budget. A substantial contribution committed for several years was that of the Unitarian Universalist Association in Boston...."

This same document noted that two other "American groups" representing young liberal Protestants were in touch with ASC and bolstered the school's budget: the Student Religious Liberals and the Liberal Religious Youth (LRY), organizations attractive to young religious liberals and radicals interested in studying in Europe. Had these, like dozens of other religious and humanitarian groups, been penetrated by the CIA and co-opted with Agency money? Did CIA funding flow through young people's religious organizations into the founding of ASC? Unlike the Unitarian Service Committee (USC) and key members of the Friends of Albert Schweitzer College, the Liberal Religious Youth had no traceable U.S. Intelligence links. Reverend Leon Hopper, with whom I had a productive conversation in Boston in March 2003, was the LRY's director during the late 50s and early 60s. Earlier, Hans Casparis' elder son John Casparis had informed me that prospective students for the college were recruited through his father's international presentations, magazine advertisements, official contacts with "elite" U.S. colleges, and a network of personal contacts. But after several months of careful and persistent searching, I found no evidence of any such presentations, advertisements, or elite college arrangements.

Leon Hopper was not surprised. At our meeting, he confirmed that student recruitment was almost always through personal contacts. We agreed that Hans Casparis quite likely had a rich fantasy life and that Hans' son John may really have believed his father actually publicized the college. Hopper also confirmed that Stephen Fritchman could have been an information source, but did not think Fritchman received written material from Boston about the college, so only personal contact channels remain. Finally, Hopper confirmed that the LRY concentrated on the summer sessions of ASC, reaching prospective students through personal contacts.

Someone at El Toro Marine Corps station, or in Los Angeles, had supplied Lee Oswald with a summer session application form. That still-unidentified person is the major candidate for American intelligence manipulation of Oswald's Schweitzer college registration.

Eight faculty members were listed for the first full year of ASC's courses and lectures, including Hans Casparis, his English wife Therese, and Rev. Dr. Joachim Wolff, an "out-standing young German scholar ... [who had taken] a firm stand against Nazism, and had to flee to Switzerland ..." Both the faculty and the projected courses of study strongly supported the progressive direction planned for the new college. The college drew its sustenance from a close association with its namesake: "The most decisive reason for the College's initial growth was the profound interest taken by Dr. Schweitzer in the new enterprise. It is evidenced by several [personal] letters ... exchanged with ... Casparis and the other founders." Although a few letters from Schweitzer to Hans Casparis are present in the Harvard files, I found no Casparis letters to Schweitzer, nor any correspondence between the college's other "founders" and Albert Schweitzer.

Not only are the historical records in danger of disappearing, they have been almost completely lost to the educational, cultural, and memorial sites devoted to Albert Schweitzer. Though Schweitzer never visited the college dedicated to his life work, he kept in touch with Hans Casparis. In a rare surviving letter dated November 22, 1954, Schweitzer expressed his "great pleasure" at the "progress... our College in Churwalden has made [in two years]...." Schweitzer restated the college's cultural and moral goals: "The ethical spirit ... must be awakened anew..."

Edward Cahill was a member of the founding subscribers of the American Friends of Albert Schweitzer College and the Director of the American Unitarian Association's Department of World Churches. On April 27, 1956 Cahill wrote to Frederick May Eliot, another founding subscriber of the Friends, from Charlotte, North Carolina, using the letterhead of the AUA. The subject was the so-called Iron Curtain countries. The FBI and the CIA had been monitoring domestic and international mail since the late 1950s. To them, Schweitzer College must have been perceived as a radical hothouse, dedicated to nurturing pinko left-wing flora, especially with one prominent faculty member advertising his anti-fascist credentials. Any domestic and international postal traffic concerning the college would have been routinely intercepted by both the FBI and CIA. Cahill's letter to Eliot, therefore, must have immediately alerted the interceptors.

As the Director of the AUA's Department of World Churches, Cahill followed up his attendance at the department's most recent meeting in April 1956, initiating a "correspondence with Hans Casparis concerning the possibility of offering a scholarship for students from Iron Curtain countries."

Cahill also contacted a certain "Mrs. Robinson," thought by him to be the originator of "this idea." Though Cahill made a copy of his letter, none exists in the Harvard Divinity School Library. Cahill asked Eliot for his reactions to the scholarship idea, but again no record can be found.

The correspondence of ASC was being monitored by the FBI and the CIA no later than April of 1956, so they would have been prepared when Lee Oswald applied to the school in 1959, and for his disappearing act. The documented contradictions in his passport and college application would have put them on full alert.

Dr. Schweitzer, ASC, & U.S. Intelligence

Why did American intelligence track international activity involving Albert Schweitzer, either as a physical or ethical presence? In 1959, President Dwight David Eisenhower's intelligence analysts concluded that Schweitzer was under the influence of Soviet Communism. Four years earlier, Albert Schweitzer had been fifth among the "most admired [persons] ... in the world [according to a Gallup poll]. By 1956, Schweitzer had advanced to being the fourth "most admired" person in the world and both President Eisenhower and John Foster Dulles lavished high praise on the renowned musician, theologian, and ethicist. Yet within a few months, American support for Schweitzer had completely dissolved: "Secretly convinced that he was an adherent of 'the Communist line,' [Eisenhower and Dulles]... severed personal contacts with him... [and] ordered his domestic and foreign] activities investigated [and penetrated] by the FBI and the CIA, orchestrated rebuttals to his public statements, and discouraged his travel to the United States."

Why?

On April 23, 1957, Schweitzer began broadcasting to the world his "Declaration of Conscience," in opposition to all nuclear weapons.

Fifty countries heard his message, and planet-wide opposition to atomic weapons was registered in, among others, Norway, West Germany, Holland, Sweden, Great Britain, and the Soviet Union. In the United States, however, Schweitzer's plea was either ignored or belittled by the conservative *and* liberal media, including the *New York Times* and the *New York Daily News*. No American radio station carried his historic denunciation of nuclear madness.

Key elements of the American government moved against Schweitzer's ethical threat. The CIA monitored Schweitzer's first-class mail and intercepted no fewer than four personal letters he wrote to Gunnar Jahn and the director of Radio Oslo, Kaare Fostervoll.

The Agency then passed these intercepted communications to the U.S. State Department, who in turn shared the letters with anti-Schweitzer nuclear weapons advocates.[2]

Schweitzer's stand was a hindrance to the lucrative American-Belgian Congo uranium pipeline, and a few months later Patrice Lumumba rose to power, presenting a direct threat to that shower of gold. In 1958, Schweitzer again broadcast his opposition to nuclear arms, and people's movements supporting his stance were organized in Japan, Switzerland, England, New Zealand, and Ireland. Right on cue, American intelligence and the State Department launched new inquiries into Schweitzer's activities. On May 2, 1958, the FBI was commissioned to investigate the Schweitzer Fellowship, "the U.S.-based organization that had raised thousands of dollars to maintain Schweitzer's hospital at Lambarene."

In late May 1958, U.S. Consul General James Green informed the State Department he would be visiting Schweitzer in June. Despite being given specific warnings about Schweitzer's alleged adherence to the "Communist line" on nuclear testing, Green visited the renowned humanitarian in the Congo and reported on Schweitzer's mental alertness, eloquence, and sincerity. Green thought Schweitzer independent of the "Communist line." But the American government remained unconvinced (Wrong answer).

Ironically, though the Eisenhower administration finally came to agree with Schweitzer's anti-nuclear position, it never forgave him. (No good deed, etc.) When Schweitzer turned eighty-four, the United States refused to join in welcoming him to Princeton University. Instead, they attacked.

The anti-Schweitzer effort was led by key White House staffer, and crucial CIA connection, General Andrew Goodpaster. Bludgeoned by the American government's hostility, Schweitzer called off his projected visit. It was 1959, the year Lee Oswald decided to go to college.

He did not apply to any run-of-the-mill college program: he registered at ASC, an institution based on the moral principles of the most prominent international humanist critic of nuclear weapons. And, while in the Soviet Union, Oswald reportedly applied to Patrice Lumumba University, dedicated to still another adversary of Eisenhower and the Dulles brothers.

Oswald, ASC & Patrice Lumumba University

Both Albert Schweitzer and Patrice Lumumba were leading popular figures in Africa, a major Cold War hot spot. Schweitzer was a resident of Gabon, next door to Lumumba's Congo. One was white, one black, but both were people-oriented and focused on action. Lumumba called for the unity of the Congo and ultimately of all Africa. Schweitzer called for the unity of all mankind and abolishment of nuclear weapons, supported by millions around the world. Lumumba advocated the preservation and independent control of the Congo's natural resources, including the precious uranium. He also opposed the secession of Katanga province, which contained Africa's first atomic reactor: the result of Eisenhower's Atoms for Peace program. The two were therefore major threats to the on-going anti-Soviet nuclear program that sought total atomic hegemony. Assuming both Schweitzer and Lumumba were under Soviet influence, Allen Dulles designated them counter-intelligence targets. With Oswald's attempted registration at Patrice Lumumba University in Moscow, his earlier application to ASC was politically amplified. The institutions were a complementary pair: the Soviet school with its unabashed left-wing ambience and KGB connection, and the liberal Swiss school dedicated to bringing together citizens of nations that had fought one another in World War II.

Could Lee Oswald have chosen two schools more likely to attract maximum attention from the Security community? No institution comes to mind.

Waiting for Oswald, or Someone Like Him

Was Oswald ever really expected at ASC? Typically, the student lists for the academic year 1959-60 are missing from the records at Harvard Divinity School Library. As an accepted applicant, Oswald would have appeared on those lists. Existing records from the following year, the "Status of Student Applications for A.S.C.," list all students accepted for the 2nd and 3rd terms of 1960, and students accepted for academic year 1960-61, suggesting the college was thorough in its record-keeping. The second list was copied and sent to four people: Dr. Dana McLean Greeley, Dr. Ernest Kuebler, the Rev. Edward A. Cahill, and the Rev. Leon Hopper. This 1960-61 list may have been left in the Harvard Divinity School files to discourage future researchers: "See how disorganized and incomplete these records are?"

But two major sets of records were left at Harvard. Beginning in 1957, the Albert Schweitzer Alumni Association privately published and distributed a yearbook called *Das Ding An Sich*. Two of those publications are in the records at Harvard: in No. 3, published in December 1959, the last page was Year Course 1958-1959. Thirty students were listed for the three terms in 1958 and 1959. In No. 565, December 1960, the last page is "Year Course 1959-60," with thirty-nine students listed for the three terms. Some attended only one trimester, some two, and some all three. The "Year Course

1958-1959" list was accurate, confirmed to me by one of the students, Bjorn Ahlstedt of Sweden, who posted his experiences at the school for some years. He also posted a list of seventeen faculty and students, identifying the students only by their first names. With that information, I was able to identify fifteen of them. Only two are questionable: "George," whom I am certain was a faculty member, and "Pooh," whom I am certain was a student.

Any record of Lee Oswald as a prospective student is difficult to find. Regarding the schedule change supposedly sent to Oswald by Hans Casparis, nothing of the sort was ever received by Bjorn Ahlstedt.

It seems the revised schedule was for Lee's eyes only. Ahlstedt also says he was aware that Oswald was expected, but he never appeared.

On January 15, 1964, the Board of Albert Schweitzer College met in Churwalden, Switzerland. Nine board members and ASC President Hans Casparis attended. Also present were College Director Ernest Cassara and College Secretary Erika Weibel, acting as Dr. Cassara's interpreter. President Casparis opened the board meeting, welcoming the college's board members, and proceeded to give his "President's Report."

The first order of business was Lee Harvey Oswald, "the suspected murderer of President John F. Kennedy."

If any of the official line can be trusted, the Red Marine applied to the college on March 19, 1959. Fifty-five days later, Dr. Robert Schacht, the pastor of the First Unitarian Church of Providence, Rhode Island, submitted the names of American students who had applied for admission to Albert Schweitzer College for 1959-1960. According to Hans Casparis, "Lee H. Oswald was on the list of students who had applied from America, provided by Dr. Schacht on May 13, 1959." The Schacht document does not exist in any accessible repository, but either a copy or the original document was probably in Dr. Schacht's Benevolent Street file, which was whisked away by two FBI agents shortly after the JFK assassination.[3]

President Casparis' official review of the events subsequent to Oswald's defection to the Soviet Union closely anticipated the conclusions of the FBI and the Warren Commission: "He had applied for the 3rd term, the Spring term 1960. He then failed to appear. In fall 1960 we received an enquiry from the [Swiss Federal] Police in Graubunden, as to whether or not Lee Oswald had arrived. He had disappeared from the USA."

Casparis reported on Representative Jim Wright's investigation on behalf of Lee's mother and the resulting dispatch of the college's entire Oswald file: "We handed our material over to the Congressman." Casparis neglected to mention that college director Cassara disapproved of releasing the material. Secretary Erika Weibel had mailed the file to Wright on April 8, 1961, so presumably nothing pertaining to Oswald remained in the college's office in Churwalden: except, of course, the seven documents given to the FBI on December 31, 1963, just fourteen days before Casparis gave his "President's Report" to the board, including Director Cassara and Erika Weibel.

The FBI's Schweitzer College Source

The source had to have been someone with access to college records, who was present at Casparis' report presentation, and silent about their apparent special relationship with American intelligence on the subject of Lee Oswald. Only three people qualify: Ernest Cassara, Erika Weibel, and Hans Casparis. Cassara, who opposed the release of the file, is a highly unlikely choice. Though Casparis was no longer a resident of Churwalden, the trip from Flims to the college would have been short and easy, and he would certainly have had access to the college's records. Weibel, of course, was still in residence as the college's secretary. Casparis reported that, following the assassination, the Swiss Federal Police visited him on Monday, November 25, 1963. According to Casparis, "We had nothing to hide, as for us the matter was closed." Casparis did not indicate whether the Swiss Federal Police had represented the FBI, but someone, between November 22 and December 31, 1963, contacted the college in the name of the FBI, resulting in the delivery of seven documents to the Bureau.

Oddly enough, Director Cassara had been visited by a Swiss detective reportedly representing InterPol just after the Kennedy assassination, but at the meeting on January 16, 1964, neither Casparis nor Cassara gave the Board members this information. Of course, Cassara was listening to Erika Weibel's translation into English of Casparis' report and may have been distracted. The Swiss detective reportedly speaking for InterPol may, in turn, have represented InterPol's inquiry on behalf of the FBI.

Cassara already had more than enough to deal with: the college's environment was threatened by a meat-drying factory; the school needed a permanent director (Cassara had only agreed to be interim director, for 1963-64); a new scholarship program was being proposed; communications with the American Friends of ASC were not at their best, and Erika Weibel had handed in her resignation sometime between November 6, 1963, and January 15, 1964. The polyglot secretary/treasurer of seven years was leaving because she saw "no possibility of promotion." Later in the meeting, the "Board conveyed its profound gratitude to Frl. Weibel for her great and extraordinarily valuable service ... given to the college for the past 7 years." In his June 1964 Interim Director's Report, Cassara reported that Erika Weibel was leaving at the end of the trimester "for an extended holiday in the United States...."

The 1963 Annual Report of Schweitzer College was issued that same month, but it contained nothing on Oswald and the two international investigations involving the college. At the meeting on January 16, 1964, the Board did worry over the 1959 Oswald application. Member Reverend Amman asked: "Should the American Committee not have examined Lee Oswald's credentials more thoroughly?" President Casparis offered, "There must have been with him [Oswald] some irregularity of a psychological nature. This could not be deduced from the application form." Apparently Casparis had already admitted in private that the form may have been unable to detect possibly twisted backgrounds of prospective students, since Interim Director Cassara immediately added: "The application form has since then been revised and extended. Further, we now demand references. The applicant is also now required to state whether he has undergone psychiatric treatment, so that probably today a candidate like Lee Oswald would not be considered."

Since there is no public record of Oswald having undergone psychiatric treatment, both Casparis' and Dr. Cassara's statements are either uninformed or bureaucratic shuffling.

The sense of Amman's question still remains: how could Oswald have been placed on Schacht's anticipated student list when even a superficial check of his Marine references, especially his ministerial reference, would have raised immediate and serious questions about him. Were the phony references sent to Rev. Robert Schacht in Providence? If so, they should have been in the Benevolent Street file when it was confiscated by Bureau agents after the assassination. This action would have mopped up after Oswald's handlers if they had generated the fake references, whether the FBI boys were aware of it or not.

But what if the references had been sent directly to Schweitzer College, or indirectly by Robert Schacht? They would then have been in Oswald's college file until Erika Weibel sent them to Texas Representative Wright; or perhaps they were withheld from Wright by Weibel (for whatever reason) and then sent as part of the package of seven documents given to the FBI.

Whatever the true scenario, the documents have disappeared, and their absence from the public record exposes Oswald's college application as a still-protected American intelligence operation.

Hans Casparis

W as the college's founder, Hans Casparis, part of that operation? Who was Hans Casparis?

From 1950 through 1955, Casparis and his wife hosted student groups recruited out of liberal Protestantism in the United States and Europe, helping to establish ASC in 1955. Given all the suspicious circumstances surrounding Lee Oswald's application, Casparis' identity is critical. Born on September 2, 1901, Hans Casparis reported in various public and personal venues that between 1919 and 1934 he had graduated from three universities (including the University of Chicago), studied at a fourth, was the pastor of a local Swiss church, achieved the rank of Captain in the Swiss armed forces, met an English woman in Switzerland and married her in London, and was a full-time teacher in a Churwalden educational institution. His son John added still more academic achievements to his father's resume, but the official record does not support many of Hans Casparis' claims.

The Harvard Divinity School Library documents give more detail about ASC and its faculty, but those same documents invite serious questions about Hans Casparis. A four-page informational brochure introduced the college's first full-year faculty: Professor Dr. Victor Maag, Seminardirektor Dr. Conrad Buol, Rev. Dr. Joachim Wolff, Rev. Dr. Werner Niederer, Prof. Dr. Martin Schmid, David E. Clarke, Prof. Hans Casparis, and his wife, Therese Casparis.

Maag, Buol, Wolff, Niederer, Schmid, and Clarke all were resplendent with degrees: the first five all held doctorates, David Clarke held both a B.A. and an A.M., and Therese Casparis held a B.A.

Hans Casparis alone had no specific degrees listed, though his remarkable record of studies and teaching was summarized. According to the ASC brochure, Casparis listed himself as "Lecturer in German and Philosophy at Kantonsschule Chur." In other sources he was identified simply as the equivalent of a high school teacher. Casparis claimed he was a Lecturer in Education at the School of European Studies in the University of Zurich, but the university informed me that Casparis never lectured there.

Dr. Conrad Buol and Dr. Martin Schmid were listed as, respectively, the head and the "former rector" of the "Graubunden Teachers Training College," possibly accounting for the mistaken impression that Hans Casparis was an instructor there, rather than a Churwalden high school teacher.

Casparis listed himself as a "Graduate of Basel, Zurich and Chicago Universities [who] ... also studied at Tubingen," but he held no official diplomas or degrees from any of the three. Records indicate Casparis did attend the University of Chicago in 1946-1947, and the University of Tubingen from May 11, 1922, through March 1, 1923, but he received no degrees. He apparently never went near either the University of Basel or the University of Zurich.[4]

All three universities, of course, could be mistaken, but according to the official responses to all my inquiries, Hans Casparis never received a degree from any academic institution, either in Europe or the United States.

The Chicago Context

Hans Casparis lived in Chicago, the site of religious, political and social action, and anti-Communist psyops activity, from October 1, 1946 to June 13, 1947. One man who embodied that dichotomy was Paul H. Douglas, the famous senator from Illinois.

Douglas was a product of Bowdoin College, Harvard, and Columbia, receiving a Ph.D. from the latter institution in 1920. After teaching at the University of Illinois (1917-1918), Douglas began an extended relationship with the University of Chicago as a professor of economics. That same year, Douglas declared himself a Quaker.

Drawn to the Marxist/Leninist experiment in the Soviet Union, Douglas visited Russia in 1927 as a trade union representative, where his first-hand observations led him to reject Marxist economics. He remained, however, a Quaker socialist. As a political activist in the 1930's, moving in several socialist and some Democratic circles, he helped draft Illinois state legislation supporting the elderly, the unemployed, low-cost housing, and affordable utility rates. WWII transformed Paul Douglas from rebel anti-warrior to wartime patriot after he joined the Marine Corps as a private in 1942. He returned home a lieutenant colonel, having won a Bronze Star in the Pacific campaign.

Douglas rejoined the faculty of the University of Chicago late in 1946 (when Hans Casparis became a student) and was quickly recognized as a brilliant and inspiring professor, who emphasized the ethical link between intention and action. In 1947, Douglas was elected to the presidency of the American Economic Association, achieving the highest professional honor of his career. That same year, still liberal in his domestic orientation, Douglas declared himself a committed anti-communist, ultimately supporting the emerging Cold War operations of the newly created Central Intelligence Agency.

James Luther Adams

In 1937, Unitarian James Luther Adams, a Chicago political activist already recognized as an expert in religious social ethics, joined the faculty of the Meadville Theological School, a Unitarian seminary in Chicago. After the Unitarians and Universalists merged, the seminary became the Meadville/Lombard Theological School. By 1943, Adams was both a professor of the University of Chicago's Federated Theological Faculty and the Meadville/Lombard Theological School. In 1945, he earned a doctorate from the University of Chicago, studying with Paul Douglas, who became a close friend. In turn, Adams was a tireless worker for the Independent Voters of Illinois (the M), a liberal "grassroots" organization that aggressively supported Paul Douglas.

Both became prominent liberal Unitarians, and Douglas and his wife attended two prominent Unitarian churches, All Souls in Washington, D.C., and Cedar Lane Unitarian Church in Bethesda, Maryland. Forging a distinguished career as a U.S. senator, Douglas supported John F. Kennedy in his 1960 presidential campaign and championed Medicare, civil rights and Lyndon Johnson's Great Society program.

When it came to foreign policy, however, the Senator had moved to the hawk side of the aisle. He went from support of the Marshall

Plan to enthusiasm for the Truman Doctrine, anti-Soviet military alliances, and, after the onset of the Korean "Police Action," unqualified backing of South Korea. U.S. covert intelligence, operating under humanitarian cover, expressed interest in Paul Douglas, especially through its Operation Brotherhood, a program that ultimately enlisted Douglas as a member of its national committee. The Operation's reported intention was to bring "medical services to isolated regions [of the world]." But the International Rescue Committee (IRC), a long-time ally of and conduit for U.S. covert intelligence, was the sponsor of Operation Brotherhood, "a CIA operation from start to finish."

The Agency brought CIA agent Edward Lansdale to Vietnam, reputedly successful "in the Philippines, where, from 1950 through 1953, he had advised the [Filipino] government on a program of psychological warfare...." In Vietnam he drew heavily on his Filipino "counter-insurgency" plans and personnel. Lansdale's medical program, fronted by Oscar Arellano, Filipino Junior Chamber of Commerce vice-president for South East Asia, "proved to be an extremely effective cover for [CIA] intelligence gathering and psychological warfare throughout Southeast Asia." In February 1955, to legitimize its ostensibly humanitarian project in Vietnam, the IRC and the U.S. Junior Chamber of Commerce co-sponsored a fund-raiser for Operation Brotherhood, with Senator Douglas signed on as a national committee member.

After fifteen years of support for IRC/CIA psyops, Douglas returned to his populist roots. In 1970, he claimed the IRC's officers and sponsors had deceived and used him, but the senator's "long record as a staunch Cold Warrior negated his "professions of innocence." Whatever Paul Douglas' personal motives, he had obviously been manipulated by the IRC and the CIA in their pursuit of covert psyops goals.

James Luther Adams also moved in radical and progressive circles, in Chicago and beyond. After receiving his degree from Harvard Divinity School in preparation for the Unitarian ministry, Adams served as the pastor of two parishes in Massachusetts, earned a master's degree at Harvard in comparative literature, taught at Boston University from 1929 through 1932, and engaged in a number of progressive actions, including his public support of the Pequot textile mills strikers.

In 1935, Adams was invited to join the faculty at the Unitarian/Universalist Meadville/Lombard Theological School in Chicago. He accepted, only requesting a year of study in Western Europe before he took up his teaching tasks. Adams then spent an intense and defining year in Germany closely observing Nazi terrorism. Adams was introduced to the anti-totalitarian actions of "clandestine, church-related resistance groups," the offspring of the liberal Protestants who had collaborated with spymaster Allen Dulles in WWI, and would again be clandestine Allied assets in WWII.

James Luther Adams had, in fact, made direct contact with the Underground Church movement in Germany.

In a series of acts strongly resembling intelligence operations, Adams used a home-movie camera to film prominent anti-Nazi dissenters, including Albert Schweitzer, and pro-Nazi leaders of the so-called German Christian Church. Because of these "religious" activities, Adams was closely interrogated by the Gestapo and narrowly avoided imprisonment. Possibly because of this involvement with the Underground Church in Germany, Adams was made the subject of two FBI HQ (headquarters) files, HQ 1050002159 and HQ 1050105508, the initial "105" in both file numbers indicating that the Bureau's interest in Adams was "foreign counter-intelligence."

Adams did not escape charges from the paranoid anti-Communist right: Louis Budenz accused him of being an agent of a massive Communist plot to infiltrate and take over American education. From 1943 through 1967, the "Red Squad" of the Chicago Police Department maintained a file on Adams' civil rights activities; and in 1952 an Illinois legislator identified Adams as one of eleven top "subversives" in Illinois. Between 1927 and the late 30s, Adams had made a series of extended visits to Europe contacting liberal Protestant theologians and thinkers who were anti-Nazi, including Lutheran minister and teacher Peter Brunner, a friend of Adams from his Harvard days. Brunner had become a leading figure in the anti-Nazi Confessing Church, a group that a few years later would be called on for covert intelligence by Allen Dulles and the OSS.

Returning to Chicago after 1936, Adams was convinced liberal religious individuals and groups had to oppose "... the world's evils, and he stated his convictions loudly and clearly." Adams again visited Germany in 1938 and was involved in underground liberal church activity. A person of both action and ideas, Adams is recognized by Unitarians and Universalists as their leading theologian of the 20th century, and considered among the best of the century's liberal theological thinkers. In the 1950s, Adams became a commanding figure in the American Unitarian Association, closely associated with key Unitarians on the Unitarian Service Committee (USC), many of whom worked with the OSS. He was a key figure in the Unitarian mission to liberal religious youth, one of the earliest supporters of Hans Casparis and his vision of Albert Schweitzer College, and the first chairman of the American Admissions Committee of ASC.

Adams was also more than likely the source of Casparis' 1946-47 scholarship to Meadville/Lombard Theological School, and thereafter one of his professors. As one of Casparis' obituaries phrased it, "It was then that the thought ripened in him which would lead him to found the 'Albert Schweitzer College,' that is, an institution in which students from ... countries that used to be enemies could meet in an international free-religious setting...." Closely monitoring the college as the chair of its American Admissions Committee and, later, as a key member of the American Friends of ASC, James Luther Adams was most likely the source of Hans Casparis' dream.

If Lee Harvey Oswald's admission papers to ASC were sent anywhere besides Churwalden, Switzerland, they would have been sent to Adams, key officer of Schweitzer College's American Admissions Committee.

Therese Casparis

According to public documents in Switzerland, Hans Casparis married "Maud Therese Callie" in London on July 30, 1934. Born in London on May 21, 1909, her short resumé published in the Schweitzer College brochure listed a B.A. in Education from the University of London, and studies at Heidelberg and the Sorbonne. But up to 1934 she was officially a student at only one of these institutions.

According to Ms. Ali Burdon, Assistant Archivist, University of London Library, who checked the University of London student card index from 1900 through 1939, Maud Therese Callie was enrolled as a student at University College in October 1928, and passed the examination in the Intermediate Arts in that same year. Callie then studied for "the Honours degree in French, with German as her subsidiary subject. She passed her subsidiary subject examination in German in 1930, and then went on to receive a second class honours degree."

Ms. Burdon of the University of London also reported that in October 1931, Marie Therese Callie "enrolled at the London Day Training College to take a teacher's diploma." But Ms. Callie "left during the same academic session... without taking an examination [for her Teacher's Diploma]." Therefore, according to the University of London, Maud Therese Callie did not receive a "B.A. in Education from the University of London."

Why did both Hans and Therese Casparis find it necessary to inflate their academic records for the initial promotion of Albert Schweitzer College? From 1934 through 1948 Therese became the mother of five children, and had no further formal education during that period.

Hans was absent from Switzerland, September 1946, through June 1947, a registered theology student at the University of Chicago. The trip to the United States might have marked the end (or at least suspension) of Casparis' clerical connection, since he obviously could not attend to a parish's daily spiritual and administrative needs while living in Chicago. Yet the Casparis family apparently had sufficient income to support Hans' wife Therese and four children in Switzerland, and Hans himself in Chicago, for ten months. According to the public record, Hans did have a scholarship in Chicago, and it is entirely possible that either Therese or Hans (or both) had independent incomes, possibly from inherited family funds or gifts.

In response to my inquiries, no college in continental Europe or England had any record of Hans or Maud Therese having received a formal degree from 1934 through 1950. Further, no significant breaks occurred in either of their histories to allow for a sustained period of university study.

How then were these two young people, with seriously fraudulent academic credentials, able to raise five children over those fifteen years? How did they then establish an international college dedicated to Albert Schweitzer's moral and ethical values, with the backing of world-class Unitarians? Hans and Therese did precisely that, and the college was quickly penetrated and manipulated by the CIA both in Europe and the United States.

The Counter-intelligence Clue

The FBI's protection of its source for those seven documents sent from the college after the Kennedy assassination is a major counter-intelligence clue, especially if Albert Schweitzer College was in part or wholly a creation of U.S. Intelligence. It's subsequent decline and fall is revelatory.

Intriguingly, ASC never recovered from the FBI Oswald inquiries, ultimately expiring around 1968. Only the files at the Harvard Divinity School Library in Cambridge and the Unitarian Universalist Service Committee in Boston have preserved fragments of the college's curious past.

Allen Welsh Dulles

Essay Four

Allen Dulles & the Destabilization of Eastern Europe

In 1959, Lee Harvey Oswald failed to appear at Albert Schweitzer College, then "defected" to the Soviet Union. Allen Dulles' 40-year history of opportunistic espionage involving faith-based groups establishes the frame for that prologue to tragedy.

Through two World Wars and the ensuing Cold War, Allen Dulles manipulated key religious individuals and groups to achieve the economic and political goals of U.S. Intelligence and the American Establishment. In particular, the spymaster misused prominent Unitarians, American Unitarian Association officials, the Unitarian Service Committee, and board members of the Unitarian-supported Friends of Albert Schweitzer College.

CIA Director William Colby argued that his Agency's use of religious institutions and clerics did not damage either their moral integrity or their religious mission. With one word, Latin American historian Penny Lernoux responded: "Absurd."

The roots of the collaboration between religious institutions, anti-Communist political movements, and American Intelligence were planted and nourished early in the First World War, and the dark gardener was Allen Dulles.

The CIA's longtime abuse of religious organizations in Central and South America has been well documented, but the record of both OSS and CIA manipulation of European religious connections and assets has been carefully cloaked. Additionally, John Foster Dulles' misuse of religious groups for personal, political and corporate economic ends has been an untold story, closely paralleling his brother Allen's cynical intelligence activities.

Provocatively, but referring only to links between the Catholic Church in Latin America and the CIA, John D. Marks reported that at least 30 percent of the clergy he interviewed during his investigation into Intelligence abuse of religious groups were aware of an Agency-Church "connection."

Hinting at a documentary record of OSS and CIA misuse of American religious organizations, but offering no documentation, Christopher Simpson cited the CIA'S "penetration of the senior leadership of trade unions, corporations, religious groups, and even student organizations." In a study of the CIA and its culture, Frances Stoner Saunders ignored religion and religious institutions, though one of Saunders' chapters, "The Guardian Furies," seemed to promise an examination of the Agency's abuse of American church-related groups: "The religious imperative motivated Cold Warriors such as Allen Dulles who, brought up in the Presbyterian tradition, was fond of quoting from the Bible for [the Israelites']... use of spies...." Saunders pointed out that Reinhold Niebuhr, Henry Luce's favorite theologian, was the "honorary patron of the [CIA-sponsored and financed] Congress for Cultural Freedom...," and that Niebuhr was not highly thought of by Martin Luther King, Jr. It was a promising beginning, but after a few pages on Billy Graham, Joe McCarthy, Leslie Fiedler, Elia Kazan, and public confession, Saunders' otherwise splendid study offered no real enlightenment on the topic of religion and the Cold War. One other Cold War and culture study by Stephen J. Whitfield might have explored the topic, but did not.

Allen Dulles, 1917: Origins

Where did U.S. Intelligence's manipulation of liberal religion begin? Early in 1917 Allen Dulles joined the United States Foreign Service: the State Department's career staff. He was sent first to Vienna, then to Bern, Switzerland, where he became a junior intelligence officer, posted as the associate of Hugh Wilson, a senior Department of State official. By the end of 1918, Dulles and Wilson had "built up a network of European refugees and American expatriates who functioned... as intelligence agents for the American embassy [in Switzerland.]"

Bern was then a center of ethnic antagonists: "émigré insurrectionists" and elite businessmen, whose only limitation was the extent of their money's power. Allen Dulles "was assigned responsibility for liaison with representatives of... Central European liberal/nationalist groups... rebelling against the disintegrating Austro-Hungarian Empire."

A key contact in the Wilson/Dulles network was the eminent Dr. Herbert Haviland Field, a distinguished American scientist and patriarch of the Fields family of Boston. During World War I, he had resided in Zurich, Switzerland. A practicing Quaker, "pacifist and dedicated internationalist," Herbert Field impressed Dulles' associate Hugh Wilson as a gentle and candid man: "unsophisticated and lovable." But the seemingly child-like Quaker was also the distinguished graduate of a German university and a zoology scholar who had come to Zurich "to run the Concilium Bibliographicum, an international institute... [dedicated to compiling] a full bibliography of [worldwide] scientific research...." Further, Field spoke the German language flawlessly, and as a liberal had unique relationships with both the European academic community and anti-fascist individuals and groups throughout Germany. Field was, in fact, the reported source of a "mine of information" for the Wilson-Dulles intelligence operations.

The Lenin Link

Curiously, Herbert Field was later the target of an attack on his character and judgment involving Lenin's American Foreign Service connection in Switzerland. Since the ultimate source of the story was Allen Dulles himself, as reported by biographer Leonard Mosley and repeated a dozen times thereafter, the shape of the narrative speaks directly to Dulles' willingness to sacrifice his closest intelligence collaborators for purely personal goals. In this instance, the sacrifice was Herbert Field. Years later it would be Herbert Field's son, Noel.[1]

Lenin, living in exile in Switzerland, had been in periodic touch with James C. McNally, the American Consul General in Zurich, the German center of Switzerland and the neutral country's industrial and financial capital. This should have been of major value to the Allies: it was a direct line from Russia to Lenin and then to McNally. According to Mosley, Dulles said neither the Bern nor Washington brain trust found the intelligence significant: a highly doubtful claim.

McNally, though, had another important source of intelligence information: his daughter was married to an officer in the German Navy "who had argued against the Berlin decision to wage unrestricted submarine warfare [in the Atlantic], because he correctly predicted [it]... would bring the United States into the war." The couple was residing in Berlin and in touch with German refugees flowing into Switzerland. Reportedly unhappy with his government's aggressive U-Boat strategy, McNally's son-in-law alerted the American consul to "at least two major German offensives." Intelligence information on Germany therefore flowed from the McNally's through Switzerland into General Pershing's HQ in France.

McNally, however, had too many suspect German connections, so Herbert Field, Dulles' trusted Quaker connection residing in Zurich, passed on his negative judgment. Field accused McNally of consorting with the enemy, a charge that had some substance. How did Lenin get on that train to Finland Station in Petrograd? Leonard Mosley says Allen Dulles was Duty Officer at the Bern legation on Easter Sunday, 1917, apparently working alone.

The phone rang and Dulles answered. A man, reportedly speaking in German with a heavy accent, said he was Vladimir Ilyich Lenin, and that he would be in Bern later that day. "Lenin reportedly insisted on speaking to someone [in authority] who should take an important message and negotiate with him... [and] requested that the meeting be secret."

Lenin was already known as the leader of Russian exiles in Zurich. He was also a recognized intelligence source of the American consul in Zurich and had made no secret of his opposition to Russia's role in 'The Great War'.[2]

The story Dulles told Mosley included the transmission of Russian intelligence material from vague sources in Petrograd, some of which "Bern did not even bother to send on [to Washington]." Could those sources have actually sent the information through Lenin to McNally, or even directly to Allen Dulles?

The most authoritative version of the story is by Peter Grose, but it is also the most provocative; indeed, one of Grose's end notes calls attention to "the fun of this investigation," strongly suggesting a darker, less "delightful romp" was involved.

How dark? First, what was Allen Dulles doing in Bern, Switzerland? In March 1917 and presumably in April, Dulles was the third secretary at the American Embassy in Vienna. With Germany's submarine warfare as the final catalyst, the United States Congress declared war on Germany, April 6, 1917. The American Embassy in the Austrian capital was virtually emptied; nearly the entire staff boarded an evacuation train bound for Switzerland. According to biographer Peter Grose, Allen Dulles had given up celebrating his birthday that week because of the chaos in Vienna and his last-minute support of Red Cross evacuees from Austria.

Grose writes that Dulles got off the evacuation train at Bern, Switzerland, and began "retrieving his uprooted personal affairs at the United States Legation..."; certainly a most inelegant and strange turn of phrase. But why did Allen Dulles have "uprooted personal affairs" in Bern when he was officially working in Vienna?[3]

Is it possible that Dulles was periodically operating out of Bern on certain secret intelligence operations? Grose observed that Dulles was not officially posted to Bern until April 23rd, "but as we have seen, he was in Bern well before his official posting." Grose does not report this. Perhaps the information was carefully expunged from Grose's main text, while the revealing end note was accidentally retained.

Whatever Dulles did on Easter weekend could have been prepared beforehand in the Vienna embassy, and concluded at the Bern Legation offices on Sunday.

After the United States declared war on Germany and Austro-Hungary, "the U.S. Embassy packed up to leave Vienna, [but] Allen Dulles had already been posted to the American Legation in Berne..." Could Peter Grose have misread his sources? Could the posting date, in fact, have been March 23rd rather than April 23rd?

According to biographer Mosley, instead of arriving at a deserted Bern Legation office in early April, the spy-in-training joined the US Legation in Bern at the end of March 1917, when the legation was "a humming hive of activity."

Could both dates be correct? Could Dulles have been working in Bern as of March 23, 1917, but not officially posted until April 23rd? If so, what did the conflicting dates mean to hide?

Dulles' official title was 'political officer,' but with the Legation in near-total chaos, the harassed first secretary Hugh Wilson told Dulles: "I guess the best thing for you to do is take charge of intelligence."

How did Dulles perform last-minute duties in Vienna when he was already in Bern? Was Dulles, in fact, train-hopping between Vienna and Bern to accomplish an important clandestine mission? The evidence says yes.

During the war, newspapers, mail, and the all-important diplomatic pouches with sensitive letters, intelligence reports and coded messages had to go from Vienna to Berlin, then through a neutral Baltic port, before finally being sent to Bern and cabled to the United States. Adding to these delays, Germany held up communications in and out of Vienna for as long as a month.

Therefore, early in 1917, Allen Dulles constructed "a new transmittal route for the embassy's communications." Dulles assumed the role of hands-on communications officer, sometimes carrying "as many as two dozen of the bulky leather pouches."

Each week in 1917, Allen Dulles was absent from Vienna for at least two days, traveling to Zurich, to Bern, and then back to Vienna: Zurich, where Russian revolutionary exile Lenin lived; and Bern, where the German Legation made final plans for Lenin's sealed train trip to Petrograd.

Peter Grose's discoveries in both U.S. and Soviet sources have been extremely relevant, particularly Lenin's location in March and April 1917: "Lenin spent his years of exile in Zurich, not Bern, but the Leninist archives in Moscow showed that... Lenin and his common-law wife... went to [Bern]... that weekend to complete a still-unrevealed matter of intrigue." Grose clearly indicates it was Easter weekend, but does not reveal what he may have discovered concerning the matter. He does add that on this "crucial" Easter Sunday, Lenin had nothing scheduled.

Might Lenin, Grose speculated, have decided "to compare notes with a representative of the United States government," to establish "common cause" against Germany?

Grose's speculation, however interesting, lacks merit: Lenin clearly intended to close down the Eastern Front, which would free up many thousands of German troops to fight in France. This is why a far more important "matter of intrigue" was probably the issue in Bern.

According to Grose, because "no more senior officer at the Legation was available," Allen Dulles was asked to take an incoming phone call (despite not yet having been officially posted). It was from an "unknown foreigner" who was recognized by Dulles as "one of those Russian émigré agitators" in Swiss exile. According to Grose, just at that moment in history "the tsar had abdicated, and the revolutionaries were maneuvering to go home and take over."

In at least two versions, when the Lenin call came in, Dulles was about to leave on a date. In one, Allen and his "closest friend in Bern... Robert Craigie, a second secretary at the British Embassy..." had a weekend rendezvous at a country inn with two impressively endowed Swiss twins.[4]

In the other and more dignified version of the story, Dulles had a tennis date with a girlfriend who was, according to a knowledgeable source, "a young lady named Helene Herzog" (breast size not specified). Ms. Herzog was, in fact, "the daughter of a Swiss family he had met in his school years."

He reportedly dismissed Lenin, telling him to call back at ten the next morning (Monday), when the Bern Legation office was officially open.

Apparently sex and/or tennis trumped politics and intelligence. After the ensuing world-shaking events, Dulles "learned his lesson, and never neglected an émigré again."

On October 20, 1963, Allen Dulles told a final absurd version of the Lenin call: he said he had "received an invitation to a reception hosted by an eccentric Russian exile in Zurich. Dulles declined the offer... in favor of a tennis match with a young lady."

Why all these odd variations to the story?

Given his peripatetic train travels between Vienna, Bern and Zurich through March 1917, and the unsatisfactorily explained "matter of intrigue" on Easter Sunday, Allen Dulles may himself have sent Comrade Lenin to Russia. At the very least Dulles colluded with German military Intelligence in the Finland Station enterprise, afterwards trashing his close friend and intelligence source Herbert Field.

It is simply unbelievable that this budding spymaster passed up the opportunity to make direct contact with Lenin at the crucial moment of the Russian Revolution. According to Mosley, Dulles dismissed Lenin's call because: "What did it matter who was in power in Russia so long as they remained allies and went on fighting the Germans?"

Dulles would have been either stupid or obsessed with anticipated sex/tennis to believe such nonsense. Any powerful Red in exile who managed to get home would help to take Russia out of the war: precisely what the Germans wanted. And if Dulles were instrumental in sending Lenin to Russia, the intention would have been to further destabilize Russia, thereby taking the pressure off Germany's Eastern Front. After Lenin arrived in Moscow, the "winter of 1917-18 brought to Bern [a]... set of diplomatic newcomers... representatives of the Bolshevik government... who... demanded control of the old Czarist embassy." These men spoke for a Lenin government that had strongly hinted it "might... take the Russians out of the war...." Lenin, in fact, almost immediately directed that Russian-German peace negotiations be initiated.

Intelligence officer Dulles must have known this would happen.

Lenin went to Russia in a German train without reported Allied or American Foreign Service support, "in a sealed railway coach [chosen] by the German intelligence chief Colonel Walther Nicolai ..." Nicolai's intelligence group had secretly supported the Bolsheviks in their effort to take Czarist Russia out of the war, and Lenin accomplished exactly that goal.

Lenin's negotiations with the German government for passage through Switzerland, Germany, and the Scandinavian north were concluded the night of April 8th: "the German Legation in Bern signaled final departure for the next morning."

Within an incredibly short time, Lenin had transformed himself from a poverty-stricken "exiled head of a small extremist revolutionary party that had relatively little following even within Russia," into the leader of 160,000,000 people in Greater Russia. Michael Pearson's research, published in 1975, into British, German and Soviet sources established that Lenin had been supported and financed by the Imperial German government, not only in his sealed train ride to Finland Station but also in his successful takeover of the Russian Revolution. By supporting Lenin, Germany bought itself an assured withdrawal of Russian forces from the Eastern Front.

Allen Dulles was certainly no friend of Socialist or Communist reform. In an ironic conflict of interest, Dulles would have seen a total Allied victory as extremely dangerous to his corporate friends in German manufacturing, banking and commerce. Indeed, this proved to be the case after the war.

Was Dulles consorting with the enemy? Who, after all, *was* the enemy? In order to deflect charges against himself, Allen Dulles may have accused James C. McNally of consorting with the enemy, and boosted the charge through intelligence asset Herbert Field. His ludicrous versions of the Lenin story and the subsequent defamation of Herbert Field would have completed his series of defensive moves.

Whether or not he directly participated in Lenin's escape to Russia, Allen Dulles made certain he would not be accused either of collaborating with the Bolsheviks or of aiding the German war effort. In typical espionage fashion, he probably did both. Twenty-five years later during the Second World War, when he again became "the American intelligence chief in Switzerland, Allen Dulles's assignment was... to consort with the enemy." This observation was made by Peter Grose, Dulles' admiring biographer.

Allen Dulles, Herbert Field, & the Quakers

Allen Dulles' negative commentary on Herbert Field was far from the truth. According to the spymaster, he made contact with Field as a "fertile source of intelligence," but was rebuffed by Field. In truth, Dulles was a frequent visitor to the Field's family home, making valuable intelligence contacts. For Dulles' spy operations, Field and his powerful friends were "go-betweens." Dulles had cultivated these active and influential people first in Vienna, then in Bern. They were "individuals who happen to have access to different parties ... [and were] willing to make their access available." They were cutouts, connections between persons or groups who, for whatever reason, wished to avoid direct contact.

Herbert Field was one of those cutouts, making available "a wide range of intellectual associates across Europe." When the war first began, Field, reputedly an ardent pacifist, became "the head of a lively Quaker relief organization which ran food relief programs for the starving populations of war-torn Europe." But the Quaker program also serviced eminent émigrés with powerful political, economic, and intelligence links, and Dulles quickly learned how important it was to spend time "in the company of Czech, Slav, Moravian, Bothian ... Serbian [and other] groups operating on neutral Swiss ground...."

Dulles' use of the Quakers in no way detracts from the Friends' extraordinary program of care for the hungry, the sick and the imprisoned from the post-World War I period to the ascendance of Hitler, through World War II and beyond. But Allen Dulles did not forget the pragmatic utility of religious charity organizations like the Quakers as cover for intelligence activity. And he would not forget the Field family, especially one of Herbert Field's young sons, Noel Field, whom he first met in Zurich in 1918. Herbert Field's Quaker-based network in World War I became the foundation for Allen Dulles' Second World War spy operation, and Noel helped run it.

Allen Dulles: Elite American Agent

Just after World War One, Allen Dulles joined his brother John Foster Dulles, an assistant to the chief U.S. negotiator Norman Davis, at the Paris peace conference in 1919. Both were concentrated on German war reparations. In essence, the Dulles brothers' job was financial intelligence. At the same conference, Allen Dulles was attached to the "Czech Boundary Commission" as well as being "in charge of the U.S. delegation's political intelligence efforts in Central Europe."

Just as John Foster Dulles was always close to the centers of industrial and financial power in both Germany and the United States, so Allen Dulles was always available for American intelligence work, official or not. "In 1926, after service in Berlin, Constantinople, and Washington, Dulles left the diplomatic service to join his brother [Foster] in the ... firm of Sullivan and Cromwell, specialists in international law corporate practice." Dulles then worked for two decades through his legal, economic, and political connections to supply significant data to the elite of the United States.[5]

Officially, Dulles rejoined American intelligence with the Office of the Coordinator of Information (COI). In January 1942, he was made the chief of the COI's office in New York in Room 3663, International Building, Rockefeller Plaza.

Though Dulles' COI Manhattan staff had "projects" targeting the entire globe, Dulles, the ultimate espionage pragmatist, concentrated on Germany, including that nation's entire range of political entities.

Led by Arthur Goldberg, Dulles' "Special Activities desk in New York argued for the establishment of a German committee made up of anti-Hitler émigrés that "would act as a front for American [Intelligence] support of a ... resistance organization [in Germany]." Right, middle and left would, of course, be part of the operation in the plan closely anticipating Dulles' later OSS activities in Switzerland. Chosen to head the committee was Heinrich Bruening, a former Weimar Chancellor and a prominent "German Catholic."

Karl Frank, Alias Paul Hagen

The left was especially important: Dulles' operatives chose Austrian psychologist Dr. Karl Frank (alias "Paul Hagan," alias "Willi Mueller").

Beginning in 1935, Frank made several visits to the United States contacting leading socialists, including Reinhold Niebuhr, prominent Protestant minister, theologian, and active Socialist Party member. By the time Frank immigrated to the United States in December 1939, he had also cultivated key figures in U.S. intelligence. Frank/Hagen held credentials that linked him to influential anti-Nazi Socialist and Communist circles, vitally important for any resistance movement. In New York, his close connection with Dulles' operative Arthur Goldberg was ultimately established "through mutual friends in the Jewish Labor Committee and the Emergency Rescue Committee." Frank himself was a founder of the committee.

Unfortunately, charges based on Frank's "left-wing past" plagued Arthur Goldberg and his agent Karl Frank, threatening Dulles' All Germany project. Finally, the State Department, objecting to "Communists," reactionaries, and "Junkers" as members of Dulles' front committee in support of the German resistance, killed the program.

Dulles, however, never gave up his basic principle: to work with "the devil himself" to achieve his goal; a covert philosophy he carried out in Switzerland after he left New York.[6]

Dulles' allies in American intelligence remained busy with espionage activity. The American Friends of German Freedom organization was, for example, a U.S. Intelligence operation founded by Methodist minister and University of Newark president Frank Kingdon, theologian Reinhold Niebuhr, Karl Frank, who became its research director, and David Seiferheld, an OSS counter-intelligence officer who became secretary of the American Friends of German Freedom. Seiferheld worked with Secret Intelligence (SI) in its "Censor unit," maintaining a close connection with Karl Frank and his Arthur Goldberg/Labor Department associates. David Seiferheld was "an early recruit into the OSS and a confidant of its director, William Donovan."

Karl Frank, the OSS, & the CIA

Karl Frank worked closely with the American Friends of German Freedom and the OSS-supported Emergency Rescue Committee, just as, later, he would work with the CIA-supported International Rescue. With the help of Frank and his friends, key German refugees who had successfully entered the United States became employees of Shortwave Research, Inc., "a front organization for the COI Foreign Information Service ... interlocked with both the Emergency Rescue Committee (ERC) and the American Friends of German Freedom." Eventually most of the outstanding anti-Nazi refugees were hired by the OSS, finding jobs with its Research Branch.

In June 1940, the Emergency Rescue Committee was formed, following the eloquent argument for its creation by Thomas Mann's daughter at a fund-raising luncheon just three days after France surrendered to Germany. American Friends' Frank Kingdon became Chairman and David F. Seiferheld became Treasurer of the ERC. With support from Karl Frank, Frank Kingdon, and David Seiferheld, the ERC had major multiple links to U.S. Intelligence and its political goals.

Sharing Karl Frank's friendship with Reinhold Niebuhr was Joseph Buttinger, an Austrian underground activist and associate of Frank. Buttinger began as a social democrat but moved further and further to the right during his long association with the Emergency Rescue Committee and later International Rescue. In the 1930s, Buttinger had been a member of die Funke, a small Leninist group with ties to the underground German organization New Beginnings.

Buttinger and Frank served as the 'moving spirits' of the ERC during its first days. Frank could connect the new relief organization with New Beginning members in exile. And it was New Beginnings that figured importantly in the rescue and intelligence work of Varian Fry.

The Fight Against Fascism

When Varian Fry met Karl Frank, then known as "Paul Hagen," an extraordinary continental rescue operation was ultimately conceived that involved covert intelligence, radical dedication to the survival of contemporary European culture, and a major religious cover identity for its primary operative.[7]

Varian Fry was a liberal American journalist who had spent enough time in Germany to know and understand the country's most brutal and anti-cultural dimensions under the Nazis. As he had done when General Franco and his Italian and German allies attacked Spanish democracy, Fry volunteered his services in the fight against Fascism. When Fry joined the American Friends of German Freedom, he began his close connection to Karl Frank. The American Friends had split into two camps, activist and isolationist; though the factions agreed on the basic principle of rescue, their agreement ended there. Disturbed with the split, Fry and Frank-Hagen held an "emergency meeting" on May 16, 1940, at Child's restaurant in New York, and a plan developed that was carried over to a following fund-raising affair. The Emergency Rescue Committee was born, with its distinguished roster of board members and their major U.S. intelligence links.

The new organization was ready to help save German intellectuals and artists from the Nazis, but though the Emergency Rescue Committee had dedicated itself to saving European minds and talents, it also began collecting key intelligence data from its network of continental and stateside contacts and refugees.

Neither man held any office with the ERC, but Varian Fry has often been called a "founding father" of the Emergency Rescue Committee. And Fry had his own intelligence links: when the Committee needed an office, "Fry offered his [Horizon Books space] ... at the [American] Foreign Policy Association as a makeshift headquarters.... Three weeks later, the Committee had its 'permanent' office on East Forty-Second Street."

Someone from the Committee had to go to France to begin the ERC's work of rescue, and Fry volunteered. Fry's associate Frank-Hagen initially said no. But when no one else seemed suitable or available, Hagen agreed that Fry should go.[8]

Why did Hagen assent? According to him, Fry did not fit the Gestapo profile of someone who would be interested in spiriting away key cultural foes of the Nazi nation.

But just as Hagen had controlled the domestic options of the rescue effort, he now controlled the European option: ostensibly sending Fry to France.

In order to be effective in the Committee's planned rescue operations, Fry needed both a valid civilian passport and "some cover." His trip was "in essence a secret mission ... to appear transparent, innocent, and public." What the Emergency Rescue Committee found was the perfect cover. The YMCA agreed to give Fry false documentation as their representative.

Equipped with a passport and papers identifying Fry as a member of the YMCA, "a religious, politically neutral organization..." Varian Fry began an heroic operation that helped rescue, among others, Marcel Duchamp, Andre Masson, Marc Chagall, Max Ernst, Franz Werfel, Hans Habe, Victor Serge, Hannah Arendt, Andre Breton, and scores of scientists, intellectuals, and other artists, including Alma Mahler, herself an accomplished musician, who brought the precious musical scores of her first husband, Gustav Mahler, to America.

It was "Hagen [who] had decided Fry should head first to Marseille" in his search for refugees, and it was Hagen who directed Fry in his work from the moment the decision was made to send Fry to France as the covert agent of the "OSS-supported" Emergency Rescue Committee. But in August of 1940, just two days before Fry flew out of America on his way to France, a strange event occurred, pointing to an even deeper covert operation involving both Hagen and Fry.

Someone whom Fry knew quite well (but whom he never identified) visited him at his apartment and pleaded with Fry to let him go to France in his place. He noted they had similar physiques and were about the same height. He argued that he could get by Customs posing as Fry. Then the clandestine visitor attempted to frighten Fry, saying he had no idea with whom he would be dealing. The shadowy visitor warned that Fry's adversaries were extremely dangerous. Further, he argued, Fry had no experience whatsoever "in this kind of underground work, or what it really involved. He himself did... he could be far more effective."

Fry declined his friend's offer. We are told by Fry's biographer that Varian was "astounded at the [visitor's] insane proposal" and Fry "wouldn't break the laws of his country by this fraud." But Fry had already committed fraud in his untruthful passport application, falsely asserting he was an official of the YMCA.

Fry's chronicler concluded: "Logical deduction points to Paul Hagen as Fry's doppelganger. Hagen had the [necessary] experience...." Fry's biographer then supplied arguments for judging Hagen's offer as "rash and impractical."

The late night visitor was, of course, Karl Frank/Paul Hagen. But his proposal was neither rash nor impractical. Resembling Fry, Hagen would have entered Europe with a valid passport identifying the bearer as an American religious official. He would have been a convincing version of an American intelligence "Illegal," a covert entity bearing the name of "Varian Fry." Everything Fry's dark visitor said pointed to an operation much more secret and even more dangerous than the rescue of artists and intellectuals threatened by the Gestapo.

Varian Fry was always aware of his clandestine cloak, recording his debt to Hagen: "Paul Hagen and... others who've had experience with underground work told me you needed some sort of cover operations, something that would provide an innocent explanation for what you had to do on the surface."

Whether he fulfilled any of the goals Hagen would have attempted as his double, Fry's own subsequent actions in Europe have strongly suggested he, or at least his American handler, was aware of the connections between European relief/rescue work, dedicated religious groups, and productive intelligence sources. Those connections helped U.S. spymaster Allen Dulles with his grand plan for using both European and U.S. faith-based organizations.

Varian Fry, the Unitarians, the OSS & Covert Ops

Fry's intelligence history was dangerous: He was linked to President Roosevelt's private intelligence system through Frank Kingdon, the chief of the Emergency Rescue Committee, who, in turn, reported regularly to Adolph Berle, "assistant secretary of state and a key advisor to President Roosevelt on intelligence matters." Berle had long and close relationships with the Emergency Rescue Committee, the International Rescue Committee, and US covert operations.

From Karl Frank, Varian Fry accepted a "list of New Beginning members in exile who would be a focus for the efforts of the Marseille office. Frank was already working closely with government agencies, and New Beginning members were placed in key positions throughout the intelligence community during World War II, undertaking activities ranging from "black" propaganda to paramilitary operations. Contacting names on that list meant that, whatever his humanitarian and religious identities, Varian Fry was a spy.

Indeed, besides his double covert connection to US Intelligence through the Kingdon/Berle/Roosevelt and the Hagen/Frank Emergency Rescue Committee channels, Fry had a third and related clandestine link, established just after he arrived in France.

First, despite Fry's reported confusion in Lisbon, where a Unitarian Service Committee office was established, he was able to make extraordinary contacts throughout the religious relief community. Besides the YMCA, these included the American Jewish Joint Distribution Committee, and the Quaker Mission. Varian Fry entered Lisbon and went directly to the Hotel Metropole, where Dr. Charles Joy of the Unitarian Service Committee had an office.

Fry was sometimes "mistakenly" identified as a "Quaker," but his pragmatic approach to problem solving meant he was in frequent attendance at Quaker sites during his rescue work. The Quakers in Marseilles had, in fact, provided Fry with desperately needed food.

Rev. Waitstill Sharp, the director of the Unitarian Service Committee office in Lisbon, was asked by Varian Fry to be the representative of Fry's OSS-connected Emergency Rescue Committee in the Portuguese capital, and another link was forged uniting religious service groups with American intelligence. "Both organizations were interested in the rescue of... anti-Nazi political leaders, and the collaboration continued throughout the war...."

The Sharps were only able to reach Europe with the aid of Percival Flack Brundage, then a member of the governing Board of the American Unitarian Association (AUA). Brundage obtained air passage to Lisbon for the Sharps, though his motivation for getting the couple to Europe may have gone beyond humanitarian interests, given the AUA's wartime links to the OSS.

Having just arrived in France, Fry departed for a visit to Madrid, meeting the British ambassador to Spain and the embassy's military attaché (almost always an intelligence officer). Fry presented his packet of letters of reference that included "a letter of introduction from Sumner Welles, Under-Secretary of State, who wrote it at Eleanor Roosevelt's behest." The Roosevelt connection was an obvious "back channel" intelligence tie, though the president's wife was herself a devoted supporter of the Emergency Rescue Committee (and later the International Rescue Committee).

Fry and the British ambassador agreed on using the Emergency Rescue Committee to establish "escape routes for British soldiers trapped in occupied France, with the understanding that some of the political refugees [on the New Beginning underground list] stranded in Marseilles could exit by the same means." The British promised Fry ten thousand dollars, (in the early 1940s, a tidy sum) to be delivered to his Emergency Rescue Committee. Fry also brought to British intelligence a map of Mediterranean Nazi mine fields, given to him by an Italian Socialist in sanctuary in Marseilles.

By accepting the British agreement that included funding the Emergency Rescue Committee, Fry became "a British secret agent." But that dramatic designation was Varian Fry's, most likely a personal deflection from his two more serious intelligence credentials. Throughout his writing, Fry carefully bypassed his extensive relations with the Quakers and the Unitarians. He offered almost nothing about his relations with the Marseille Corsicans, and he never intimated that the Emergency Rescue Committee had OSS connections.

In Marseille, Fry contacted Dr. Donald Lowrie, a one-time officer of the International YMCA, a dedicated relief official, and an excellent source of information. Though Lowrie maintained connections to the YMCA, at the time Fry made contact he was associated with the international student colony at the University of Paris. With the help of the Lowrie contacts and others, Fry began a European Underground Railway for cultural refugees.

At the same time, Varian Fry became an important part of a network of relief organizations directly tied to the OSS and Allen Dulles. Included in that network was Dr. Charles Joy of the Lisbon Unitarian mission. Varian Fry and Joy were clearly partners in covert refugee work. Fry worked out of Joy's Lisbon headquarters for the Unitarian Service Committee at the Hotel Metropole. Joy, probably an OSS asset, was in communication with Robert Dexter, the Unitarian Service Committee executive director who, no later than June 17, 1942, was already an important Dulles OSS operative.

Four days earlier, on June 13, 1942, the Office of Coordinator of Information (OCI) had been transformed into the Office of Strategic Services. Elizabeth Dexter, Robert Dexter's wife, was also a member of the OSS-associated group, as was René Zimmer of the Marseille Unitarian medical program. Apparently another part of the network was Donald Lowrie himself: he had accepted Varian Fry's false YMCA identity (created by U.S. Intelligence in New York), and would recommend Unitarian Noel Field to Dr. Joy for a key Unitarian Service Committee position.

Robert Dexter had met with Allen Dulles in June 1942, accepting Dulles' commission of espionage, resulting in Dexter and other members of the Unitarian Service Committee delivering "large sums of money to resistance leaders in France." Dexter and his intelligence Unitarians made contact with "OSS agents in Madrid and in Marseilles ... [to gather] information."

In Marseilles, Varian Fry was in close touch with Corsican "gangster families," a pragmatic decision solving some of Fry's immediate refugee problems but helping to initiate troubling links between American religious service organizations, American intelligence and the European Mafia involved in narcotics traffic. Immediately after the war, American intelligence and organized crime in Marseille cooperatively blocked "anti-Communist" workers and Socialist activists, exchanged vital information, and partnered in narcotics trafficking that financed their operations. Wartime links between religious relief groups, American intelligence, and the Marseille mob had dark consequences: CIA assets Jay Lovestone and Irving Brown "of the AFL (later AFL-CIO) Free Trade Union Committee had passed [Agency] funds ... to French [anti-Communist] strong-arm gangs on the Marseille waterfront, which in turn worked with the Corsican heroin labs and trackers integrated by Meyer Lansky into the Luciane-Coppola-Gentile drug-trafficking network."

Varian Fry's clandestine bent was nowhere better illustrated than in his initial operations in Marseilles. Almost all of the twenty-eight refugees on Fry's first rescue list made it to Lisbon, and he had been in the city only two weeks. Suspected of cutting some questionable corners, Fry needed to assure local authority "that he would never countenance any illegality...." He therefore established "a proper office ... under the name of the Centre American de Secours (the American Relief Center)...." According to Fry, if an undercover operation with acceptable cover were to succeed, that action had to appear totally innocent.

Just as Allen Dulles and his operatives manipulated faith-based individuals and groups, Varian Fry also used people, including Unitarian minister Waitstill Sharp. Fry had already recruited Sharp to front for Fry's Emergency Rescue Committee in Lisbon in a hair-raising rescue mission, exposing the already heroic Sharp to mortal danger.

Ultimately, Varian Fry may have seriously upset his American intelligence handlers at the Emergency Rescue Committee. He certainly upset the State Department's Foreign Service, which was following its own German agenda. If Fry's daring rescues became for him more important than the intelligence information he sent to the Emergency Rescue Committee (and therefore to U.S. Intelligence), he would have become expendable. In fact, Fry was sent home in September 1941.

He tried to re-enter the exciting and productive wartime espionage world to which he had become accustomed. He applied to the Office of Strategic Services, "for which surely, of almost all Americans, he was uniquely qualified." But he was refused, probably because he had been compromised. All his efforts to rejoin the fight against Fascism were blocked by both the State Department and the FBI.

On April 12, 1967, Fry was awarded a major citation by the French government, but both his rescue work and his intelligence operations remained unrecognized by the United States. Near the end of his life, an FBI investigation accused Varian Fry of being a Communist. At the same time, he was an active member of several virulently anti-Communist organizations closely tied to the CIA. After Fry died in 1967, Israel honored him as a "righteous man." Fry would not, of course, be the only dedicated religious service person used and abused by American intelligence.

Paul Hagen/Karl Frank continued working with Allen Dulles' COI office in New York, and succeeded in persuading Dulles to support Hagen's plan for a collaboration between American intelligence and the anti-Nazi "Underground Movement" in Germany. In a memorandum to Allen Dulles dated April 10, 1942, Hagen argued for the establishment of a new "agency" that would link American intelligence with the German radical and labor underground, with technical and research staffs, with the "reorganization of contacts in Switzerland, Sweden, unoccupied France, maybe also Ankara [in Turkey]…" and tapping the refugee flow into the United States and Central and South America. On May 12, 1942, Dulles forwarded the Hagen report to Arthur Goldberg, the chief of the OSS's Labor Section in London.

Allen Dulles' Spy System: Dare One Call It Treason?

Coupled with the future work of Dulles operatives Emmy Rado and Noel Field in manipulating liberals, radicals, volunteer service and religious organizations, Paul Hagen's proposals had ably assisted Allen Dulles in structuring his Switzerland spy center. The American espionage system, fronted by faith-based groups, waited for lightning to strike.[9]

Six months after Pearl Harbor, the Office of the Coordinator of Information (OCI) became the Office of Strategic Services. By presidential order on June 13, 1942, the OSS was established "to collect and analyze strategic information" but also to "plan and operate… special services." The president and a few core intelligence people knew what the phrase "special services" meant: the emerging agency would not simply gather information; "OSS was to have charge of resistance, intelligence, and sabotage…." The Office of Strategic Services was a potential spymaster's dream-come-true.

In the fall of 1942, about to be shipped from New York to London to occupy an unexciting OSS desk job, Allen Dulles knew exactly where he really wanted to be. The center of war intelligence would be Bern, Switzerland, and he quickly petitioned for a transfer. He was off to Bern in early November 1942.[10]

Dulles had anticipated the Allied "penetration" of Nazi Germany, both in its short and long-term consequences: the first priority was the defeat of the Axis enemy. Possibly more important, however, was the post-war political and financial stability of Germany and the rest of Europe).

"He arrived [in Switzerland] carrying letters of introduction to the prominent [powers] in every important area of Swiss life. He also knew the anti-Nazi German politicians, labor leaders, religious figures, scientists, professors, diplomats, and businessmen [from all over Europe] living in exile in Switzerland."

Dulles came with both money and power, backed by Sullivan & Cromwell and the company's European officers, who were viciously anti-Bolshevik.

Allen Dulles had superior credentials for clandestine spying on Germany: "Dulles' chores with Sullivan and Cromwell [had] involved him intimately in the affairs of the elite among Germany's industry. He sat on the boards of directors of both the Schroeder Trust Company and the J. Henry Schroeder Corporation, American branches of Germany's great Schroeder international banking firm. The German firm was directed by Baron Kurt von Schroeder, at whose house in Cologne Adolf Hitler and von Papen negotiated their agreements for Hitler's rise to power."[11]

One of many possible treasonous actions by Allen Dulles was channeled through a Sullivan & Cromwell officer named Kurt Grimm. The law firm's "correspondent" in Vienna met Dulles when he arrived in Bern, bringing with him "a list of sympathetic [German] financiers and industrialists throughout the Nazi hegemony." But the Sullivan & Cromwell double agent asked for something in return, something, perhaps, on U.S. "aircraft production figures." Dulles dutifully supplied "projections" of U.S. production, which were then turned over to Nazi Intelligence, allegedly "to terrify the Luftwaffe." Whatever the alibi, by giving top-secret information on American aircraft, the spy chief had indeed consorted with the enemy.

Dulles' long-term plans for Germany meant he would have to court the leaders of the same middle and upper classes that had supported Hitler in his rise to power, and now realized the disastrous economic and political consequences of Germany's possible defeat. Dulles received "a flood of high-placed, right-wing Germans" eager to help Dulles reconstruct post-war Germany. Influential businessmen, bankers, and industrialists came to meet with Dulles, recognizing him as one of their own. With the help of old Sullivan and Cromwell hands, Dulles made contact with "Vichy" French who were ready to collaborate with the American OSS and the Gaullist resistance.

Dulles' imperial goals were now in the hands of the German elite, German industrialists, and the anti-Nazis.[12]

Dulles and the OSS spent a significant amount of time intercepting bank communications, following German and Swiss money trails left by a "malevolent old boys' network [that] stretched across wartime Europe." The interests of I.G. Farben, the Schroeder Bank, and Standard Oil of New Jersey were intimately linked, and Allen Dulles and John Foster Dulles were board members of Schroeder and I.G. Farben: those economic interests had to be protected through the end of the war.

First, however, Hitler's Germany had to be defeated. In Dulles' mind this must have been a distasteful necessity, to be dealt with as quickly and painlessly as possible. Meanwhile, how would the American spymaster deal with the coming waves of anti-fascist refugees ?

Spanish Republican Army veterans, anti-Franco groups, Free French, liberals, socialists, communists and other ostracized free-thinking people poured into neutral Switzerland's mountain haven throughout the first two years of the war. Dulles needed a key left-wing contact.

Allen Dulles & Noel Field

He found his conduit in Herbert Field's son, Noel. After Herbert died in 1921, the Field family returned to the United States and took up residence in Cambridge, Massachusetts. Noel Field's early career included stints with the State Department, where he met Allen Dulles for the second time, and the League of Nations. His activities prompted an undocumented accusation before a red-hunting Congressional committee in 1938: that Field was a card-carrying Communist.[13]

When it became apparent the Republican cause was lost, Noel Field went to Spain as a League of Nations commission representative. The mission was to evacuate the international brigades that had fought against Franco. Fields made contact with hundreds of anti-fascists from dozens of countries, managing "to meet scores of people whose names were destined to become symbols of power in [European] postwar communism." When the League declared 'mission accomplished' and pulled up stakes Field and his wife stayed on, delivering what relief their limited resources allowed.

Noel Field was a living example of Hans A. Schmitt's "Quaker portrait": "a personal relation with the Creator free from scriptural or hierarchic mediation, the advocacy of peaceful conflict resolution, and a commitment to abate human suffering wherever it may be found."[14]

After Noel Field resigned from the League, he was still paid by the declining international peace organization for over a year. He worked first in Prague on refugee relocation, then in France with the *Comite' pour le Refugees Anti-Fascistes*, linked to the U.S. Joint Anti-Fascist Refugee Committee, which in the U.S. was eventually labeled a Communist front.

Noel Field's organizational status was ambiguous. Some thought he was working with the Quakers, as his father did in the First World War. Others thought he was performing "some sort of survey" for the League of Nations, but he had no official backing.

Around the city of Marseilles huddled thousands of exhausted and hungry Spanish Republican refugees. The Emergency Relief Committee, the Quakers, the YMCA, the Scouts, and a dozen other groups did what they could. Prominent among these European relief organizations were the Unitarians who had "organized relief work in Czechoslovakia in 1938 and [then] in France...." Dr. Robert Dexter, in 1938 the Director of the American Unitarian Association's Department of Social Relations, had urged "Unitarians to organize relief for refugees from the Sudetenland..."

The Czechs held a special place in Unitarian consciousness, and their annexation by Germany "was a personal tragedy for the people whom we now regard as founders of the Unitarian Service Committee." As early as 1921, both the American and British Unitarians urged establishing a permanent center for the faith in Prague. Dr. Robert Dexter, who had been to Prague, joined other Unitarians in supporting the creation of a relief organization.

On October 5, 1938, the AUA Board of Directors announced the Unitarians would "explore the possibilities of a joint Unitarian-Quaker enterprise for the relief of refugees...." The Unitarian operation was, therefore, associated from its beginning with Quaker service activities. Robert Dexter, representing the Unitarians, and Richard Wood, the Quaker delegate, visited Europe on a fact-finding tour.

Commissioned by the AUA after it received an especially grave report from Dr. Dexter, Unitarian Rev. Waitstill Sharp and his wife Martha arrived in London the first week of February 1939, and began a series of meetings with Quakers, Unitarians, and British government groups that were bringing in relief to the Czechs and assisting some of them to get out of the country.

Dexter's report has needed perspective. He and other liberal, compassionate religious individuals saw the obvious problem: Fascism, whether in Spain, Italy, or Germany, destroyed democratic institutions and placed thousands of innocent people at risk. Inevitably, if Dexter had not yet approached Allied intelligence (or been approached by those services), the potential connection between refugee service operations and anti-Nazi activities would have been obvious. Dexter's report to the Unitarians became the basis for Unitarian medical and humanitarian services for the war's émigrés and internees.

The Sharps made contact with key people in Prague, including "Helen and Donald Lowrie, formerly with the International YMCA ... [who agreed] to be the Sharps' liaison in Paris." The Sharps then began an extraordinary series of relief actions in cooperation with a dozen international organizations.

But the Unitarian relief effort in Czechoslovakia came to an end, and the proposed project for Poland had to be abandoned. With the Unitarians still committed to "continued relief and emigration work," the need for an independent Unitarian service group became obvious; among the influential Unitarians supporting a continued European effort was John Howland Lathrop. Unitarian Frederick May Eliot and Boston businessman Seth Gano met to explore the founding of a Unitarian committee similar to the Quakers' American Friends Service Committee, and the Dexters were again commissioned to go to Europe "to conduct a four-month fact-finding tour ..."

In 1939, unhappy with the relatively conservative Quakers' program of relief, Noel Field met with Unitarian minister Stephen Fritchman. According to three well-placed Unitarian/Universalists, "Fritchman mobilized support for the idea of a separate Unitarian humanitarian relief agency, and succeeded a year later in persuading the General Assembly of the Unitarian Association to create a new agency..."

The OSS Co-opts the USC

The combined efforts of the AUA Refugee Committee, the Dexters, Stephen Fritchman, and others were probably responsible for the founding of the Unitarian Service Committee (USC) in early May 1940. Robert Dexter was appointed executive director, and the Sharps were asked to return to Europe as the Committee's "ambassadors extraordinary." From its beginning, then, the USC was directed by Robert Dexter, the man who no later than 1942 would be a key component in Allen Dulles' faith-based OSS intelligence operations.

In fact, the USC's "initial nature" was extremely close to that of the OSS-supported Emergency Rescue Committee: "the rescue of Europe's intellectual, academic and [anti-Nazi] political leaders..." The two groups collaborated, and the Sharps in Lisbon took messages from New York sent by the Emergency Rescue Committee or acted on cables from the Committee's Marseilles agent, Varian Fry. In its beginning, the USC was funded by the American Unitarian Association; later, it was additionally financed by Unitarians, Quakers, "other [unidentified] organizations" and the American "government-backed National War Fund."

By November 1945, the Unitarian Service Committee was registered with the War Relief Control Board and endorsed by the National War Fund (NDF) through "Refugee Relief Trustees, INC. Was the support of the Unitarian refugee effort by a "government-backed" fund suspect? Recall that by 1942, Unitarian Robert Dexter, executive director in Portugal of the Unitarian Service Committee, was a covert agent of the OSS, reporting directly to Allen Dulles. Was the USC even more closely linked to government funding of covert operations?

In 1942, the Emergency Rescue Committee and the International Relief Association merged, becoming the International Relief and Rescue Committee (IRRC), retaining both organizations' original radical orientation as well as their intelligence ties. Name changes later occurred: in 1949, the IRRC became International Rescue (Inc.), and it, in turn, became the International Rescue Committee (IRC).

In 1942, the U.S. War Relief Control Board began monitoring every relief agency, including the Unitarian Service Committee. In January 1943, the U.S. government centralized all refugee relief fund-raising in the National War Fund (NWF). With awesome economic clout, it became the only group designated to raise funds for "global war relief." In that same month of 1943, an extraordinary fusion of humanitarian, religious and political powers occurred: the OSS-supported International Rescue and Relief Committee (successor to the OSS-backed Emergency Rescue Committee), the American Churches Committee for Refugees, and the OSS-connected USC joined to establish the Refugees Relief Trustees. This coalition then allocated funds to the IRRC and the USC.

Attending the NWF budget meetings and assisting in the Fund's financial affairs was the influential David Seiferheld, American Friends of German Freedom officer, recently an Emergency Rescue Committee official, and covert OSS operative. Monitoring the USC/Refugees Relief Trustees linkage was Percival Flack Brundage, an American Unitarian Association officer.

On May 17, 1944, Brundage sent a memorandum to fellow board members of the Refugee Relief Trustees, titled "Statement Regarding Relation of Unitarian Service Committee to War Refugee Board." The memo concerned OSS-connected Unitarians and their involvement in government-sponsored refugee activity and intelligence gathering. The elaborate maze of government and 'private' rescue and relief operations had become even more complex when the new and powerful War Refugee Board was established.

To erase any doubts about the War Refugee Board's major U.S. Intelligence links, one need only consult the Board's 1,522 files at the FDR Library and Museum. Charles Joy, board member of both the USC and the Refugee Relief Trustees, responded to the new entity by writing to John J. Pehle, Executive Director of the War Refugee Board, expressing the concerns of the USC. Joy succeeded in meeting Pehle in both Washington and New York, resulting in the new Committee on Special Refugee Problems, a powerful advisory group to the War Refugees Board.

One key Unitarian was voted to chair the new oversight committee, and Charles Joy was elected the new committee's secretary. In Lisbon, USC officer Dexter was designated the official representative of the War Refugee Board, and an IRRC member with intelligence links became the board's Swiss representative.

The Refugee Relief Trustees and their intelligence-connected partners, the USC and the IRRC, had successfully moved to protect their government support through the War Refugee Board. Key Unitarians, including probable OSS asset Charles Joy, had been placed on its advisory committee to insure that protection.

In 1940 Joy, then the USC's Lisbon representative, enlisted the help of Donald Lowrie to find a Unitarian director for France. Lowrie recommended Noel Field. Joy met with Field, was immensely impressed, and hired both him and his wife. The couple moved to Marseilles in 1941.

Led by Noel Field, the USC in France took on a giant task, adding refugee camp infirmaries to the committee's relief work. The camps held at least 29,000 people from forty-four countries. When Field identified the camps he had examined as the responsibility of the USC, Boston headquarters sent Reverend Mr. Howard Brooks to evaluate the situation. But Brooks himself was a double agent: he was also on an intelligence mission for the Free French.

Still, Brooks fully supported Field, whose staff was much expanded, and Field's operation was heavily financed by a massive new American government fund that was intended "to enlarge the resources of the various private American relief groups working abroad."

Noel Field was eventually appointed "European director of the Boston-based Unitarian Service Committee [entering]... into an intense refugee rescue mission in both Marseilles and Geneva during the early 1940s..."

Field had placed exiled German Communists on his help list and, when one of his associates was questioned by Howard Brooks, she convinced the Reverend Brooks that the aid was humanely justified. The German leftists made Field a major part of their support and rescue system, and "thousands of dollars, in Swiss francs, were given to Noel from Communist funds in Switzerland for the use of the German Party in France." Utilizing a French underground established to effect secret crossings into Switzerland, Field sent German Communist refugees across the border. Eventually, Field had a network of anti-Fascist contacts, including "Polish, Hungarian, Yugoslav and Bulgarian communists in Switzerland."

In November 1942, anticipating the Allied invasion of Europe, the Nazis swept into previously unoccupied Vichy France. Facing internment, Field and his wife barely avoided the Gestapo and military border guards as they themselves crossed into Switzerland.

Robert Dexter, the USC's European Executive Director and key operative for the OSS, recognized the unique quality and utility of the information Field was capable of collecting, and the importance of the people with whom he was in contact. But Dexter reportedly did not know the extent of Field's Communist links. He brought Noel Field to Allen Dulles, who was now headquartered in Bern, and the old Field family connection to Dulles was re-established.

For Allen Dulles and the OSS, "Noel Field... presented opportunities for access to escapees from occupied France and to underground cells of the resistance working to obstruct the Nazi war effort." Field began his service as the crucial contact between the German Communists and the OSS. William Casey, OSS operative and future Reagan administration CIA chief, was involved in developing Illegals recruited from still other German Communist refugees in England.

When he brought Field into his Swiss fold, Dulles did so with full awareness of Noel's Communist connections. But was Field an actual spy? He was certainly an agent of Allen Dulles and the OSS. "Dulles regularly gave him money for the Communists," which Field passed on to the anti-Fascist refugees, but he apparently was not paid a regular OSS stipend or salary. "Dulles handed out $10,000 to Communist paymasters through Field, and afterward insisted privately that he got back more than his money's worth."

Noel Field & Alger Hiss

Whether Field was a 'commissioned' agent of the OSS (or later of the CIA) was far less important to certain U.S. researchers and writers than establishing Field's alleged earlier covert identity as a Communist. They were especially interested in Field's alleged attendance at a Communist "cell" in Washington and Alger Hiss's reported failure to recruit Field for his alleged spy group. These allegations were certainly intended to establish Alger Hiss as a Communist traitor guilty of espionage, but Hiss was never prosecuted on that charge.

From what innocent source might the story have originated of Alger Hiss and Noel Field attending a D.C. Communist "cell"? In the 1930s, Alger Hiss "had been a member of one of the study groups on foreign affairs... popular among Washington intellectuals, meeting once a month or so to talk about... Hitler... Italian aggression... and what could be done about them. There were... members of the Foreign Policy Association... and their wives... [and State Department people, including] Noel Field... and one or two others [attending]." Ideas, of course, can sometimes have dire consequences.

The earliest Eastern European accusation against Hiss was pushed by a Hungarian researcher and writer Maria Schmidt who "unearthed" the record of Noel Field's interrogation in Hungarian "secret police files" in 1993. These anti-Hiss conclusions were reported, not by Schmidt herself, but by Sam Tanenhaus, who was then writing a book on Whittaker Chambers. Tanenhaus announced Schmidt's alleged discoveries on the editorial page of the *New York Times* on October 15, 1993.

Why would Schmidt entrust the publication of such a significant finding to another writer? Apparently both Schmidt and Tanenhaus were members of a group of 'Conservative' writers whose principle goal was to paint Alger Hiss as a spy: "A little over a month later, [on] Nov. 18, 1993, Tanenhaus revealed in the *Wall Street Journal* that he had found significant documents regarding Alger Hiss... in the... National archives."Schmidt allegedly discovered a single document, ostensibly written by Noel Field, charging Hiss with being a Soviet agent in 1935. In their giddy delight with Field's accusations, none of the anti-Hiss fulminators seem to have noticed the obvious problem: if Field was correct about Hiss, then his other outlandish statements, used dramatically in the Stalin purge trials, might also be true. But if those statements were suspect, because they had been supplied under extreme stress, then his Alger Hiss testimony was also questionable.

A later use of the same questionable materials surfaced in 1996. In this manifestation, Noel Field was accused of being an NKVD operative, then a KGB agent, and identified as a personal friend and professional associate of Alger Hiss. The sources, authors Breindel and Romerstein, reported they had found a summary of the questioning of Noel Field by the "Ministry of National Security" in the Czech State archives. The alleged summary repeated the supposed charges against Hiss made by Noel Field, but it supplied no evidence that those charges should be taken any more seriously than the others.[15]

The anti-Hiss group continued to pound away. Allen Weinstein, author of *Perjury: The Hiss-Chambers Case,* and former Soviet KGB agent Alexander Vassiliev co-wrote *The Haunted Wood: Soviet Espionage in America-the Stalin Era.* Basing their charges on

KGB files in Moscow, Weinstein and Vassiliev asserted they had found extensive references to Noel Field and Hiss protected by a code name. But these references were, in fact, nothing more than reports on the communications of double agent Hede Massing to Soviet intelligence, and the only source Weinstein and Vassiliev had for their accusation.[16]

Significantly, Weinstein and Vassiliev referred to Massing as "Hedda Gumperz," and in only one of their references was she identified indirectly as Hede Massing: "Hedda Gumperz rejoined her husband and fellow agent Paul Massin...." Though they listed Massing's book in their bibliography, the authors were careful not to cite it when they examined the alleged relationships between Field, Hiss and Massing.

The authors also ignored Noel Field's relationship to OSS spy chief Allen Dulles, his willingness to use Communists as agents and assets, and Alger Hiss's personal, familial, and professional relationship to John Foster Dulles. Additionally, Weinstein and Vassiliev omitted any mention of the crucial role Noel Field played in the Stalinist purge trials, as well as the widely-held suspicion that Frank Wisner and Allen Dulles manipulated Noel Field in their successful plan to destabilize Communist Eastern Europe.

Finally, an extensive review of the alleged evidence against Hiss published in *The Nation* concluded that charges of treason and espionage could not be documented from any so-called "secret files."

The best defense of Alger Hiss was honed with the Occam's Razor of top-ranking KGB spymaster Pavel Sudoplatov. His narrative in 1994 anticipated later revelations about FDR's private presidential spy system. According to Sudoplatov, in the summer of 1941 President Roosevelt ordered trusted advisor Harry Hopkins to establish "confidential relations" with the Soviet ambassador's office in Washington, D.C. Sudoplatov and Soviet embassy officers connected productively with American Foreign Service and State Department officers, several of whom were part of President Roosevelt's personal intelligence operation.

The Yalta meeting was crucial for Sudoplatov, who was responsible "for preparing the psychological profiles of all the... [members of the] American delegation to Yalta ... and [whether] they were under our control as [KGB] agents."

The Soviet embassy in Washington had made crucial back-channel connections with several Yalta attendees, and one of them was Alger Hiss. Sudoplatov evaluated Hiss's relationship to the Soviets as a commission from FDR himself, "acting under the instructions of [Harry] Hopkins. On our list of [Yalta] psychological profiles, Hiss was identified as highly sympathetic to the interests of the Soviet Union and a strong supporter of postwar collaboration between American and Soviet institutions."

Was Alger Hiss a KGB agent, or a trusted member of FDR's covert intelligence corps?

According to Sudoplatov: "[The KGB had] no indication that he was a paid or controlled [KGB] agent, [of] which I would have known or would have been marked."

Sudoplatov, once a KGB spy chief, was in touch with an old Soviet intelligence friend, a "retired GRU officer" who told Sudoplatov that "Hiss was chosen by Hopkins and Roosevelt for confidential contacts with Soviet diplomats and intelligence officers, knowing that he had [such] contacts and was pro-Soviet."

Allegedly, Roosevelt's private intelligence network had been penetrated by the Soviets: "[Sudoplatov's] retired GRU officer remembers... a controlled agent source of information in Roosevelt's office. He was Roosevelt's assistant on intelligence affairs..." and on unfriendly terms with both the FBI and the OSS. But this negative attitude may have reflected his own superiors' judgment: both FDR and Harry Hopkins "were ill disposed toward the Office of Strategic Services and the Federal Bureau of Investigation. Soviet "GRU files reflect that Roosevelt set up his own informal intelligence network during the war, used by him for sensitive [back channel] missions." Sudoplatov reported that his old retired GRU friend was "certain that Alger Hiss, Harry Hopkins, and Averell Harriman were in this trusted group."

Though the statute of limitations had run out on Hiss's alleged espionage activity, he was still charged with perjury. But at least for a time he was surrounded by high-level protection emanating from both the Dulles family and FDR's successor, President Harry Truman. Foster Dulles so admired Alger Hiss that he had "recommended him to head the Carnegie Foundation after World War II."

Alger Hiss stood trial twice, and was finally found guilty only of perjury. "The mild sentence he received, the incoherent accusations against him, and the neutral stand of the [Truman] administration ... could indicate that he knew too much that was damaging to the prestige of both Roosevelt and Truman." With Joseph McCarthy, Richard Nixon and others bringing charges of Communism and even treason against New Dealers, liberals, and various State Department luminaries, those charges would have reached both past and present White Houses directly through Alger Hiss.

To use Hiss in that way may have been, in fact, part of the plan.

Sudoplatov's "old GRU veteran" surmised "the FBI had more material on Hiss than was revealed, and... perhaps there was a deal between Truman and Hoover... [to have] the charges be confined to perjury." The FBI's files on Alger Hiss need not have contained any direct evidence of espionage. They need only have contained information on Hiss's back channeling for FDR with Soviet officials from 1941 through 1945.

Given the multiple mail-opening operations by U.S. Intelligence in the 1940s and 50s, Alger Hiss's postal communications were probably part of the Bureau's priority reading list. His phone conversations were certainly treasured trophies: "In 1948, William Marbury, one of Hiss's lawyers, was told by an [unidentified] FBI agent that Hiss's phone had been tapped for years, and the FBI had three cabinets full of [phone] transcripts, but nothing derogatory or incriminating had been found."

"Some eighty percent of intelligence information on political matters comes not from agents but from confidential contacts." The Bureau's Hiss files would, therefore, have been stuffed with back-channel evidence from World War II, now embarrassing to the Roosevelt-Truman administrations in the new Cold War landscape.

Later charges concerning "Hiss's connections to Soviet military intelligence" surfaced only in those dubious Hungarian secret police files.

Playing the religion card, Hiss's major accuser performed a logical loop-the-loop: he charged that, since Communists could not belong to a Christian denomination, Alger Hiss "was forbidden to go to church." Hiss's response was that he and his wife regularly attended the nearby Episcopal Christ Church: "I have been a lifelong member of the Episcopal Church." Thus, the smear campaign against Alger Hiss, through Noel Field, ultimately tracks back to the Dulles brothers' manipulation of liberal Protestantism in their long-term crusade against all things Socialist.

Noel Field, The Unitarians & the OSS

After his recruitment by Allen Dulles, Noel Field worked simultaneously for the Unitarian Service Committee and the OSS in Switzerland. During the latter part of the war, in the midst of cooperative anti-Fascist and anti-German activity, Field carried out a number of important assignments, often at the same time, for the Communists, the USC and Allen Dulles; but Noel's overseas work with the OSS was never officially reported to the USC in the United States.

Field's liberal and radical connections were treasured by Allen Dulles, who quickly accepted "an offer by Noel Field to put him in contact with Julius Leber, the German Socialist leader, and other exiled union officials who kept open lines to potential saboteurs and spies in factories and on railroad lines." Two of Allen Dulles' labor union assets, Gerhard Van Arkel and John Clark, had been linked by Noel Field to his radical union associates. Erika Glaser, Field's foster daughter, "became secretary-interpreter to Van Arkel while still a member of the Swiss Communist underground youth movement." Van Arkel had been OSS officer Arthur Goldberg's delegate to anti-Nazi labor groups.

By 1945, the covert labor connections Noel Field (and Erika Glaser) made available to Allen Dulles meant "few trains moved within the German Reich that were not reported to Dulles within hour; the Rhine River bargemen had been organized into a network, and even the water levels of the Rhine itself were radioed to Eisenhower's Paris headquarters, lest the Germans open the floodgates during an Allied crossing." The U.S. Congressional Medal of Honor has sometimes been bestowed for less.

Despite his artfully muted self-praise and fellow OSS officers' support, the more material released from the OSS/CIA files, the less grand have become Allen Dulles' heavily promoted espionage triumphs. By January 1944, Washington was cabling Dulles in Bern about his shortcomings and inadequacies. Internal documents and other OSS sources further confirm that Dulles' intelligence was sometimes deficient.

Regardless of the quality of his espionage reports, Dulles' political-financial goals always remained primary: to defeat Germany with the least possible damage to the country's banking system, its industry, and its economy; to preserve the German economic elite as future political partners; and to oppose Socialism in all its forms everywhere, even if it meant the destruction of blossoming democratic movements. His brother John was in absolute agreement with these goals.

To those ends, Allen Dulles used religious individuals and groups. "Dr. Stewart W. Herman [a Lutheran minister] had been pastor of the American [Church] community in Berlin from 1936 to 1941. After... December 1941 he was interned ... before he could return to the United States. In 1942 he was drafted for the OSS." No later than 1943, Herman was an active OSS operative in London. After the war, Allen Dulles supplied Herman with "travel orders, transportation, and accommodations... and deployed him to the World Council of Churches staff in Geneva, where Herman was given the responsibility for helping rebuild the German Protestant churches." Herman had become the "Deputy Head of the Reconstruction branch of the World Council of Churches." By 1970, Herman was the President of the Chicago Lutheran School of Theology.

Swiss-born Emmy Crisler Rado was the wife of Sandor Rado, a psychiatrist who was an associate of Sigmund Freud. In the fall of 1941, she began work in New York for the Oral Intelligence Group of the Office of Coordinator of Information. Rado belonged to an OCI "nuclear intelligence net"; in a secret Manhattan office she interviewed refugee arrivals from eight European cities under siege or attack by the Nazis, culling valuable pieces of information from which she developed carefully wrought, insightful intelligence reports. When OCI was terminated, Emmy Rado joined the OSS as a German analyst. The information she began to accumulate suggested a productive pattern: "In mid-1943 Emmy Rado had started the so-called 'Biographical Records' project of the OSS." Rado then "proposed [in October 1944] that the Catholic and Protestant churches... be used as a base for German political reconstruction." "She felt the OSS could work effectively through the World Council of Churches to aid anti-Nazi German clergy of the 'Christian Socialist' variety."

Approving of Rado's plan, Dulles designated her coordinator of the program. Dulles then "met with a group of leaders in the religious field during a trip to New York." When the German church leaders returned to Europe, a World Council of Churches staff member from Geneva "was appointed to work through OSS underground sources to contact pastors inside Germany." Four months later, because Rado had been so successful, Dulles brought her to Switzerland, relying on Rado to draw up a list of the anticipated "Crown Jewels" of post-war Germany that included important religious figures "as clean of Nazi involvement as possible." The OSS assets in the German churches were then linked to anti-Nazi religious groups outside of Germany.

Fluent in German, French, Italian, Danish, and English, Rado became a distinguished multi-purpose operative for Dulles. "She assembled a checklist of all German Confessional churches and pastors in Germany who could be relied upon to influence public opinion. The new German Reformation was mapped out by her people in Switzerland... with substantial backing from the World Council of Churches." Rado's "German pastor contacts within Germany... sent out invaluable intelligence on conditions within the Reich."

Rado was remembered by her fellow officers as a remarkable combination of intelligence and beauty, who "loved to swim nude in the Danube."

Still active after the war, she personally chauffeured Bavarian Socialist leader Wilhelm Hoegner, an anti-Stalinist, from Switzerland to Germany. There he began his OSS-directed labors in the rehabilitation of his shattered country.

Emmy Rado was also granted an early SHAEF pass into defeated Germany, where she met many of her liberal "Crown Jewels" and received their promises to take part in the "spiritual rebirth of Germany." Those same religious individuals became key figures in supporting the anti-Communist agenda of John Foster Dulles, working through the same church groups exploited by his brother.

After Field and Rado, the wartime ties between Dutch Reformed churchman W.A.V. Hooft, General Secretary of the World Council of Churches, based in Geneva, and OSS spy chief Allen Dulles were next in importance. Hooft was so valuable an intelligence connection that the church official was given a personal OSS identity code: "474"

Extensive OSS records and documents made available in the early 1990s contain "a series of reports on the German church situation that ... Hooft ... forwarded to Allen W. Dulles on the latter's request." One of those confidential reports, in December 1943, extensively reviewed "The Situation of the Protestant Church in Germany." The documents were important in Dulles' mobilizing of religious groups for anti-Nazi activities. "Like his brother John, a leading member of the American Federal Council of the Churches of Christ, Allen was interested in strengthening the religious element in a post-war world, both as a stabilizing factor for... the German people, and as a stronghold against Bolshevism."

So commented the editors of the newly available OSS documents; other less spiritual goals were left unexplored.[17]

Reverend Visser't Hooft was personally connected to the so-called Kreisau plotters, alleged participants in the failed attempt to assassinate Hitler and depose the Nazi regime on July 20, 1944. Hooft had supplemented Dulles' alternate connection to the Kreisau Circle and its "reform program of Christian Socialism for postwar Germany." But Reverend Hooft also reportedly betrayed some of his anti-Hitler associates to Dulles when they attempted to negotiate a Nazi/Soviet armistice with Stalin: an interesting echo of Dulles and the closing of the Eastern Front in WWI.

In at least one instance, Dulles transmitted a long report from Hooft with an appended note to the American State Department indicating that the report had only "psychological warfare" value, and that no "serious organization of the opposition group in Germany" existed.[18]

In effect, Dulles had cut off the Kreisau group from any real Intelligence or covert support. The Kreisau Circle's involvement in the July 20th putsch was never completely proved, though vigorously alleged by the Nazi government.[19]

Though arraigned "before the Nazi people's court" the group was "comprised of men with deeply held Christian convictions... whose opposition to the Nazi regime was primarily based on moral aversion. Their concern was... with the fundamental problems that would confront Germany when the Nazi era was over." Still, the Circle's "highly placed members... were committed to killing Adolf Hitler and toppling his regime before Germany was destroyed."

Dulles's Swiss operatives connected to the anti-Hitler plots also reportedly communicated with Soviet Intelligence. Using a false name, Pavel Sudoplatov met with Averell Harriman, U.S. Ambassador to the Soviet Union. Sudoplatov had held a series of significant Intelligence positions from 1939 through 1946, and was instrumental in the 1940 assassination of Leon Trotsky in Mexico. Harriman clearly indicated he was interested in emerging business and investment opportunities following the defeat of Germany. Spymaster Sudoplatov apparently knew what Harriman wanted to hear: "I told him we were impressed by the information provided to us by American agents in Switzerland who had contacts with the German underground, in particular with the Halder and General Ludwig Beck's group[s], who had tried... to overthrow Hitler."

Less well known than the Kreisau Circle and its liberal Protestant supporters, these two groups had virtually the same political, economic and religious links as the better-known Dulles network.

Because Allen Dulles had long-standing business and personal ties to important members of the Kreisau Circle, the group's postwar recovery commitment gave it a part in America's European intelligence-gathering operation. The Circle had its own OSS code name: The Breakers.[20]

By early 1944, at the request of the U.S. War Department, the OSS' Research and Analysis Branch began close examination of the German churches for any military and political intelligence that might be gleaned from them. Research and Analysis prepared a confidential report, dated July 22, 1944. The OSS then tapped into the German liberal religious community.

But it was not only American espionage at work in the fields of the Lord: Soviet Intelligence had also infiltrated the World Council of Churches. At home, they penetrated and manipulated the patriarchal, hierarchical, and patriotic Russian Orthodox Church, directing its powerful prelates to join, and influence from within, a number of international religious bodies. The CIA had a reciprocal influence on the Russian Orthodox Church in America. This underground theological ping-pong match was definitively illustrated by the Dallas-area chapter. In the 1960s, the Dallas/Fort Worth White Russian community centered many of its "social activities" around the Church, which received CIA "philanthropy."

Martin Niemöller

Imprisoned by the Nazi's in Dachau from 1937 to 1945, German theologian Martin Niemöller somehow escaped execution and lived to become a determined pacifist and anti-nuclear advocate. After the war, Niemöller related a disquieting story: from his pulpit he had told his German congregation they bore a heavy responsibility for the horrors of Nazism. Their response was to "whistle, stamp, and even get up and leave the church..."[21]

Ironically, Reverend Niemöller related his discouraging experience to Mary Bancroft, OSS agent and mistress of Allen Dulles, just after he attended a 1945 international conference in Geneva of the World Council of Churches. The WCC had already been penetrated by the KGB and manipulated by Allen Dulles while he resided in Switzerland.

By 1960, any liberal Protestant or Quaker/Unitarian institutions in Europe, such as Albert Schweitzer College, was viewed with suspicion by both American and Soviet counter-intelligence.

In the Cold War years, sharing "the CIA's fear that Communism might be spreading, German church groups worked with... Christian and Social democrats" who in turn were supported by front organizations funded by the CIA.

Exit OSS, Enter CIA

On September 20, 1945, Truman abolished The Office of Strategic Services, but soon determined that the ensuing void had to be filled with a coordinating intelligence body. On January 22, 1946, the president "issued his Directive on Coordination of Foreign Intelligence Activities to the secretaries of state, war, and navy." Led by a "director of central intelligence" but subordinate to the National Intelligence Authority (NIA) was the Central Intelligence Group (CIG), created by the NIA on February 8, 1946. Though operational, "the Central Intelligence Group remained essentially a transitional organization pending the creation of a permanent organization through [Congressional] legislation...."

The CIG nevertheless quickly followed the game plans of World War's I & II, by tapping religious individuals and groups: CIG Directive No. 15, besides targeting business, scientific, and educational groups, established "Exploitation of American... Religious Organizations with Connections Abroad... as Sources of Foreign Intelligence Information." Cited as a victory for J. Edgar Hoover because the CIG had placated "the recalcitrant Hoover with promises to respect his domestic authority," Directive No. 15 was actually a coup for the CIG and the future CIA as the Agency inherited the Central Intelligence Group's prerogatives: "Under the directive the [DCI] ... was ... charged with coordinating the exploitation of such sources nationwide with other government agencies, particularly the armed services and the FBI."

The unit charged with implementing Directive No. 15's exploitation of "Religious Organizations with Connections Abroad" was the CIG's Domestic Contacts Service, a branch of intelligence the CIA absorbed in founding its own "program for domestic intelligence."

After being absorbed by the CIA, the unit became the Agency's Domestic Contacts Division. The Dallas office was headed by J. Walton Moore, an associate of Baron George de Mohrenschildt, Lee Harvey Oswald's odd friend in the Fort Worth/Dallas circle of anti-Communist Russians.

On September 18, 1947, the Central Intelligence Agency was created, and twenty-four hours later, "[DCI] Hillenkoetter submitted a... memo, requesting that the NSC [National Security Council] approve the continuance... of all NIA and CIG directives [including Directive No. 15...]." With the CIA Act of 1949 and, later, the collusion of George Kennan and Frank Wisner, NSC 10/2 was drafted, largely by Kennan. Following Kennan's recommendation, Wisner became director of the new Office of Policy Coordination (OPC). The Director of Central Intelligence would become the ultimate boss of the vastly improved CIA.

Directive No. 15, the Agency's *carte blanche* license to penetrate and exploit any religious organization it pleased, remained in operation, skewing elections in Europe and controlling missionaries and Catholic service groups in Central and South America.

Trouble in the Unitarian Service Committee

Earlier, a "bitter encounter" in 1944 had involved three key figures in the Unitarian Boston and Lisbon offices, all part of the Unitarian/OSS network. Elizabeth and Robert Dexter brought charges against Charles Joy for "incompetence and dishonesty."

What was the Dexters' "key issue"? Robert Dexter was both the Executive Director of the Unitarian Service Committee and its chief of European operations. The USC Board investigated, and concluded the Dexters' accusations were without merit. But the

Board also moved to split Dexter's jobs: Charles Joy would become Executive Director and Robert Dexter would be the European Director of the USC.

The decision was unacceptable to the Dexters, who both resigned. Charles Joy did accept the position of Executive Director in Boston, though his problems with American intelligence and the Unitarian hierarchy were far from over.

The OSS & Noel Field's Achievements

As the OSS' National Archives materials in Records Group (and others) are further explored, Noel Field's wartime achievements and Allen Dulles' pragmatic and unethical manipulation of Field's religious and radical contacts will be further proven. A first set of documents have now been analyzed relating to the OSS' work with the *Comite' Allemagne Libre Pour L'Ouest* (CALPO), whose origin can be traced to August 3, 1943, when a "Committee of German Exiles" was established that ultimately became CALPO. On August 1, 1943, a group of influential German exiles met and drafted its approval of an earlier Moscow-supported Free Germany Committee and its goals. The American committee requested that Thomas Mann be the leader of "a provisional Free Germany group in the United States." When Mann was warned off by the State Department (for whatever reason) and refused leadership, the New York group "invited Protestant theologian Paul Tillich to be their leader." Tillich accepted. The switch from Mann to Tillich looks very much like an Allen Dulles manipulation. First, the support for the new American-based committee had come from "the U.S. Communist Party and other anti-Nazi organizations, including the Joint Anti-Fascist Refugee Committee." Second, American intelligence tampering was evident when the Luce media empire, probably through Allen Dulles' associate C.D. Jackson at *Time/Life/Fortune*, at first openly supported the committee and then opposed it as "a Soviet attempt to lay the groundwork for a Communist government in postwar Germany."

Regardless of the patriot games being played by C.D. Jackson and Allen Dulles, CALPO's successes in resistance, counter-intelligence, penetration of the Wehrmacht, propaganda, and other intelligence actions were extraordinary, running from 1943 through 1945.

CALPO and Noel Field were major sources of "secret intelligence" for Allen Dulles and the OSS.

With the opening of the OSS' Record Group 226 files, a slanderous story, circulated in several published books, can now be refuted. Allied armies were advancing into Germany, and Field argued to Allen Dulles that an "orderly" administrative structure should be put in place in Germany for the moment when German field commanders realized it was politic to surrender before the American and British troops entered Berlin. The Germans could then capitulate to an already-established civil government.

"Field suggested that CALPO and its contacts be used for this task and that CALPO provide a steady stream of agents to be parachuted into Germany or inserted by some other means. Dulles thought the plan excellent and sent Field to the OSS in Paris, where CALPO was headquartered.

Young OSS officer Arthur Schlesinger, Jr. said he knew exactly who Noel Field really was: "A Quaker Communist" was the least offensive smear. Though Schlesinger never explained what Field's religious convictions or political beliefs had to do with the success of a covert Allied military operation, the Paris office disapproved the plan; but Allen Dulles prevailed in support of the infiltration scheme, "using people whom Field suggested."

Radicals chosen by Noel Field went into Yugoslavia, Hungary, Czechoslovakia, and Germany, helping to establish civil order where chaos could easily have prevailed. When the later Eastern European purge trials opened, these OSS-supported Socialists and Communists linked to Noel Field were presented as evidence of American intelligence's corruption of Eastern Europe.

According to author Stewart Steven, Noel Field had duped Allen Dulles, who was therefore eager for "revenge." But no other source has given so weak a motive for Dulles' betrayal of one of his key agents, especially since, according to actual OSS records, CALPO was clearly a major Allied triumph.

Noel Field had the reputation of knowing "almost everyone worth knowing in... Eastern Europe." An undocumented source (obviously referring to CALPO) stated that Field "established leading Communists in Poland, Czechoslovakia and Hungary as representatives for the Unitarians. One condition for this aid was... to... send reports concerning economic conditions... for which the aid was destined...." Those reports, flowing through Unitarian officials Charles Joy and Seth Gano were dispatched to Robert Dexter in Lisbon, and then on to Allen Dulles.

Documented in the OSS Records 226 files, all of CALPO's successful physical and intelligence operations supporting Allied efforts in Europe were dependent on "Communications... effected by two courier chains from within Germany, one reaching Paris via Switzerland and involving a Swiss representative of CALPO, the other controlled by the Swiss Free Germany Movement... in Germany."

A major figure "in this communication [network] was Noel H. Field, CALPO's representative in Marseilles ... who kept wires [open] to Swiss Communists and members of the Free Germany Committee and... to OSS representative Allen W. Dulles in Bern.

As more documents of Records Group 226 on the OSS become available to historians, the negative and self-serving comments of former OSS worker Arthur Schlesinger (and others) will be further exposed.

The Unitarians Investigate Noel Field

After the end of World War II, Noel Field continued his work in Europe as Director of the Unitarian Service Committee. Eventually a group of New York Unitarians led by the Reverend Mr. Donald Harrington decided to investigate reports concerning Herta ("Jo") Tempi, the volatile director of USC's Paris office, 1944-47. But Tempi, though "deeply entangled... all her life in both underground and open Communist organizations" and a close associate of Noel Field, was able to conceal her left-wing life from the Unitarians who visited her.

Tempi had been using the USC Paris office to rescue hundreds of threatened Christian and Jewish refugees, but she also allegedly promoted and supported Communism. Tempi's humanitarian and political balancing act was, in fact, supported by "an anonymous U.S. Intelligence report dated October 5, 1945... Jo Tempi was even-handed in her approach to clients." The Agency report concluded, "all of Mrs. Tempi's efforts were bent on carrying out objectively the aims of the Unitarian Committee."

But the rumors the Harrington group received ultimately meant Noel Field had to send Herta Tempi to the United States to repair her Unitarian fences. The outcome was a murky disaster, quite possibly orchestrated by the hostile FBI. Tempi was accused of sexual intimacies with a Unitarian minister on a train to New York. The "couple" was also accused of registering at a New York hotel as husband and wife. Apparently the Bureau had been monitoring Jo Tempi during her entire stay in the states. A Unitarian inquiry board found its suspect minister guilty, stripping him of his "offices and duties."[22]

Though the Unitarian official "steadfastly denied any impropriety between himself and Tempi, he was fired in August 1946...." It did not help that the Unitarian in question had earlier taken part in a serious quarrel with OSS agent Charles Dexter, and both internal politics and U.S. Intelligence concerns might have been involved.

The Harrington Unitarian group helped send the Reverend Ray Bragg to Paris, and with the power of the Boston Unitarian home office behind him, Bragg fired Jo Tempi. Noel Field, however, quite openly continued to support her. Bragg confronted Field on his close link to Tempi and the stories concerning Field's own alleged Communist bias in distributing Unitarian relief. Bragg urged Field to get out of Europe and come home to Unitarian Boston.

Herta Tempi sheltered many shattered veterans of the war and its aftermath, including anti-Nazi Helene Rado, the radical wife of Alexander Rado. Sentenced in absentia in Geneva to a year in prison and "expulsion from Switzerland... she escaped and came to France late in 1944." The Soviets so valued her extraordinary work they "continued to pay her for past services" through the end of 1945. What the French called a "burned" Soviet espionage agent, Helene Rado "obtained a position with the American Unitarian Service Committee in France [run by Herta Tempi]...." But by 1950, Rado was "tired, disillusioned, and gravely ill." Herta Tempi had done all she could for Ms. Rado.[23]

Despite the charges brought against her, Herta Tempi was a wondrous service worker. Few relief officials in the last one hundred years have been more dedicated.

Field's subsequent arguments mailed to the United States in support of Jo Tempi were judged to be inadequate, but Field still refused to return to Boston to deal with the charges against Tempi and himself. Further, the Unitarian Association was seriously divided on the "issue" of Communist "influence" within the USC.

The Unitarians & the FBI

The Association's efforts to establish the truth about Noel Field "repeatedly led to Unitarian inquiries to the FBI, and the FBI refused to open its files." One of those responsible for withholding information from the Unitarians was FBI Special Agent Robert J. Lamphere. In 1941, Lamphere had "joined a squad in the New York office working on Soviet espionage matters... [and] until 1955... [was] a specialist in counterintelligence and... spy cases of the Cold War era." Despite being part of the Bureau's unconstitutional mail intercept program, the same operation that intercepted Lee Oswald's mail, Lamphere wrote nothing on the subject in his memoir, *The FBI-KGB War: A Special Agent's Story*. His February 11, 2002, *New York Times* obituary also, predictably, failed to mention this unconstitutional action. It did, however, mention that Lamphere "was not as well known as his friend James J. Angleton, who headed counterintelligence operations" with whom Lamphere collaborated in counter-espionage activities.

Lamphere's achievements in spy code decryption have been recorded in the history of the so-called Venona case. Reportedly, the Army Signal Corps and Lamphere's Bureau team opened and decoded "thousands of enciphered telegrams sent by Soviet spies in the United States to Moscow...." KGB Spy Chief Pavel Sudoplatov, however, suggested delicately that the Lamphere narrative was exaggerated: "former FBI agent Robert Lamphere... presents a complicated story of how the FBI re-created our code books.... That may be true. I cannot absolutely exclude that code breaking might have played a role in exposing our agents.... But we have reason to believe that the FBI, wanting to hide its [double] agent source of information, invented the story of code breaking."

Lamphere was also close to Hede Massing, used by American intelligence to charge Noel Field with being an active Soviet agent whom she allegedly attempted to recruit. Massing said she failed because Alger Hiss told her Noel Field was already his agent. This was obviously a strategy to defame Alger Hiss and, except for Massing's personal assertions, has remained without documentation. Lacking actual proof, the Unitarian Association decided it could not move against Noel Field, but finessed the issue by informing Field of a reduction in its funding. His European Director's office, therefore, was to be closed. In 1947, the year that spawned the CIA, Noel Field was out of a job.

Destabilizing Eastern Europe

On May 5, 1949, still without work, Noel Field disappeared. Who was responsible? Why did Field vanish? And what did Field's disappearance and its consequences have to do with Allen Dulles and, finally, Lee Harvey Oswald?

Colonel Jozef Swiatlo was officially an officer of the Polish "Tenth Department, the secret section for important political matters in the secret police...." He was "the deputy director... at the time of his defection." Swiatlo may actually have been an Illegal invented by the CIA, inserted into Poland, and then run by American intelligence after World War II. Alternatively, he may have been an Illegal created by the KGB for penetration of the West, who was captured and turned by the Agency. These suspicions clung to Swiatlo, despite his official history.[24]

The story eventually involved an astonishing range of characters and organizations: the CIA, CBS, Solidarity and the Polish anti-Communist labor movement, CIA operative William King Harvey, Jr., the Vatican, and the Roman Catholic Church in Poland.

Swiatlo had attempted to defect to the British in 1948, but the Brits, "for various reasons," passed Swiatlo on to American intelligence. Captain Michael Sullivan, chief of British Secret Intelligence Service (SIS) operations in Poland, made the initial connection. Sullivan then sent a coded report to SIS in London that convincingly argued Swiatlo was an intelligence agent completely trusted by both the Poles and the Soviets, and that his material was "not only explosive but totally up-to-date."

British intelligence worried over the Swiatlo file until it was decided he was a "genuine defector." But why, they asked themselves, did he defect? Was it really disenchantment with Communism, as Swiatlo had stated? Michael Sullivan had another theory: Swiatlo was at odds with Jakub Berman, the second most powerful man in Poland, "responsible for security and party ideology." Berman had been a "United Press stringer in Warsaw" prior to World War II and his Western connection would only darken his image for Swiatlo, who "knew well that, because of the checkered history of Poland during the past few years, not everyone was who he seemed to be...." The comment, of course, applied to Swiatlo himself. But Sullivan argued that Swiatlo's offer to defect was impulsive, based principally on his antagonism for Berman, an argument that was reportedly accepted.

Even if the Sullivan memorandum was accurately presented, the suspicious nature of Swiatlo's defection story is still readily apparent. What followed did not enhance its credibility.

Suddenly, the British SIS gave Swiatlo a "grade-two defector" status because he "had made a few innocuous remarks to Sullivan about the high standard of living in the West...." The SIS then sent his name along with others to "Foreign Secretary Bevin, the nominal head of SIS." Bevin, reportedly scornful of British intelligence efforts in Eastern Europe, disapproved the entire list, and Swiatlo, "an invaluable find – an intelligence man's dream," was lost to SIS: *if* you believe the story.

SIS then decided Swiatlo should be given to the CIA. Sullivan informed Swiatlo, and the SIS called Allen Dulles.

Without any official intelligence status, Dulles requested that Swiatlo hold his Polish intelligence job until contacted further. At the time, Allen Dulles was "a close consultant to the Agency" but would not become the CIA'S Deputy Director until 1951.

The Dulles brothers had maintained their banking, business, intelligence and Protestant connections through the end of World War II. "From 1946 until 1948 [Allen] Dulles ran private intelligence operations inside Eastern Europe with funds collected from wealthy friends and companies. Like his brother, John Foster, [Allen Dulles]... was involved with a number of religious and charitable institutions, many with international connections... [offering] a useful cover."

In 1949, Dulles and his CIA allies opened up a two-front assault on radical and Communist parties and governments on both sides of the Iron Curtain. Dulles, George Kennan, DeWitt C. Poole, and the Council on Foreign Relations organized the attack's Western wing, run by the Committee for Free Europe. Characterized as a "private sector anti-Communist organization," the Committee had extraordinary establishment, government, and intelligence-connected luminaries as board members, including Poole, who had been chief of the Foreign Nationalities Branch of the OSS. The Branch's official duty was keeping track of the "political activities of... anti-Axis exile and immigrant groups in the United States.... But Poole ultimately commanded his own covert intelligence operation, including "surveillance of exile leaders by OSS officers" and the illegal opening of diplomatic mail pouches. With Dulles' blessing, Poole "served as president of the CIA-funded National Committee for a Free Europe, 1949-1951."

Also in 1949, the U.S. Congress passed the Central Intelligence Agency Act that "exempted the CIA from all federal laws requiring the CIA to disclose anything." That same act allowed the Director of Central Intelligence to plunder the U.S. Treasury for Agency operations, "without regard to... law and regulations relating to the expenditures of government funds...." At least a portion of those 'Black Budget' funds were channeled through compromised liberal organizations, secular and religious, in the war to destroy Communist Eastern Europe.

The covert campaign to destabilize the European Left was eventually a resounding success, and Jozef Swiatlo played a major part in Allen Dulles' Machiavellian spy circus.

After Noel Field lost his Unitarian Service Committee directorship, he was reluctant to return to the United States, with "Tailgunner Joe" McCarthy laying waste to the liberal establishment. The first Alger Hiss trial was scheduled to start on May 31, 1949, and Field's early association with Hiss was sure to be aired: he might even be called as a hostile witness.

In 1949, Field applied for a Czech visa, an action that reportedly "triggered [Soviet] surveillance of him...." A year earlier, Field had indicated he wished "to report on developments in Eastern Europe as an independent journalist," and develop his research into a book. But one source maintained that Noel Field went to Prague to visit a close friend of Jakub Berman, head of the Czech security services and supposed enemy of Colonel Jozef Swiatlo.[25]

Berman's secretary was Anna Duracz, who "had a distinguished record as a Communist activist before the war and had worked with [Noel] Field in Switzerland during the war. A third version claimed that Field went to Prague to inquire about a university teaching position. "... in October, 1948 Field asked for a Czech resident's permit... with the hope of getting a job as a lecturer at Charles University in Prague."

The most reliable evidence suggests that Noel Field was sent to Prague on May 5, 1949, either by Allen Dulles or his deputy Frank Wisner. He was then used by Jozef Swiatlo to begin the destabilization of Eastern Europe. Berton Hersh, relying on his extensive and knowledgeable intelligence sources, commented that "Colonel Swiatlo ... perhaps [more than] any individual ... helped break loose the anti-Communist tide that swamped Europe in 1956."

Earlier, Frank Wisner had quit the Department of Defense and moved into the State Department; with George Kennan's assistance, he had organized and run the Office of Policy Coordination (OPC), a largely unsupervised covert intelligence operation with its own secret budget. Allen Dulles recommended that OPC become an incorporated unit in the young Agency, and Wisner was appointed the CIA's "deputy director of Plans." Wisner had run anti-Communist Catholic political actions in Italy, ultimately crippling the democratic process. He also coordinated his anti-Communist counter-espionage in Europe with General Reinhard Gehlen's Nazi agents and military units in Germany, establishing "small private armies" of Rumanian, Hungarian, Ukrainian and Bulgarian reactionaries and dissidents, to be used in anticipated paramilitary "missions" in Europe. General Gehlen, Wisner's chief German collaborator, gained his reputation for accurate first-hand intelligence information through "the torture, interrogation, and murder by starvation of some 4 million Soviet prisoners of war."

Four million, tortured and murdered.

In brief, Wisner's CIA-within-the-CIA was the fastest growing, most powerful, utterly amoral, and absolutely arrogant clandestine cabal in the Agency. When Allen Dulles became the CIA's new "deputy director for Plans," he had the rabidly anti-Communist Frank Wisner and his OPC espionage network available for his own continuing dirty tricks and wet affairs.

Recall that, in the Jozef Swiatlo narrative, he attempted to defect to the British, who refused him their protection and shunted him on to U.S. intelligence. British SIS supposedly alerted Frank Wisner to Noel Field's alleged long-time Communist Party membership, and Field's trip to Prague to work with the Czech Communists. Finally, Wisner and Soviet double agent Kim Philby had worked closely on several intelligence programs when he was sent to London as CIA station chief.

Could one of the Wisner/Philby projects have been the use and abuse of Noel Field, a move benefiting both Philby's secret Soviet designs, and Wisner's intelligence associates, including Allen Dulles?

Of course, Field needed no Party card to collaborate with Communists. He had done so openly for years from his political, ethical and social convictions, and because Allen Dulles had instructed him to do so. Field was the OSS spymaster's key link to the European anti-Fascist organizations both during the Second World War and immediately after.

Further, Noel Field's stepdaughter Erika Glaser "remained convinced that Noel Field had been deliberately set up by Allen Dulles, who spooked him into making a break for Prague and then had him denounced through CIA channels [specifically Colonel Swiatlo] to his communist captors."[26]

Leonard Mosley, relying on his American and British intelligence sources, supported the set-up scenario: "The Wisner operation to 'blow' Noel Field to the Soviets is one of the black secrets of the CIA...." Dulles, aware of Frank Wisner's plan, if not the actual progenitor, gave his counter-intelligence chief the go-ahead. Wisner controlled Colonel Swiatlo, who "was in close touch with the KGB in Moscow and the security services of the other East European satellites." Wisner then reportedly instructed Swiatlo to contact all East European security and intelligence forces and inform them that Noel Field was actually a CIA agent on special assignment under the direct control of Allen Dulles. Later, the suspicion that Field was, in fact, "a double agent" for Dulles was not limited to the Communists. In the West, speculation circulated that Noel Field, "while appearing to defect to Communism ... was still following CIA orders."

Whether duped or doubled, witting or not, Noel Field fulfilled the destabilization goal advanced by Wisner and Dulles.

In the process, Noel Field, his wife Herta, his brother Hermann and stepdaughter Erica Glaser/Wallach were all arrested and imprisoned on espionage charges by the Communists.[27]

Noel Field was reportedly kidnapped in Prague by Hungarian Communist intelligence officers; his arrest and subsequent detention "released all the pent-up paranoia that ... began to surge through the corridors of Soviet power in eastern Europe."[28]

The arrests reached an estimated 200,000, with thousands executed. Noel Field and Allen Dulles were linked in hundreds of show trials, and, though Wisner commented with great satisfaction the Communists "were doing our dirty work for us in decimating the Eastern European Communist parties and governments," the operation also did the dirty work for Soviet dictator Josef Stalin, who now had the satisfaction of eliminating nationalists or reformers: "anyone in power in the new communist states" whom he intensely disliked, and whom he "thought would not toe the Moscow hard line." The trials and purges continued to grind away for three years until Stalin died in 1953.[29]

Erica Glaser considered the Communist political massacre "an enormous victory for Allen Dulles." The purges "devastated those [Eastern] governments for years afterward. Dulles had actually destroyed any chance of peaceful reformation in the Communist East: "no economic reform, no progress, and they never recovered from those purges, not ever."

Glaser commented further: "Would Allen Dulles do such a thing? Of course. It was his job. And it was easy enough to do. [The CIA] had contacts everywhere in those governments."

Operation X

How would Allen Dulles validate the Field revelations? John Foster Dulles, "in what appeared to be a monumental indiscretion, spoke of it in public-that Operation X had been mounted by the CIA." Truth had become fiction, and vice-versa. Allen Dulles, according to John Foster Dulles, was the author of Operation X, and created his own code name: "Operation Splinter Factor."

The documentary evidence is abundantly available: during the Second World War, "Soviet and American agents in Germany co-operated ... against Hitler's Germany." CALPO was one such extraordinary action, and two such "agents" were Noel Field and Allen Dulles. "The OSS had, through Field, subsidized and even relocated a number of Communist functionaries trapped in Western Europe by the eruption of war."

Erika Glaser added: "Evidence was easy to come by... many of those early party leaders had connections with the OSS during the war.... But what made it all work was having Noel Field there, still loyal to communism and willing to denounce anybody for anything."

Erika Glaser concluded that "Allen Dulles had a certain arrogance... he believed... he could work with the Devil ... [and, therefore, he] could work with Noel Field and betray him...."

Operation Splinter Factor was "probably the foremost intelligence battle of the Cold War, and set back the possibility of detente between East and West for a generation." The suspicion and fear of double agents lasted through the 1960s, a Communist bloc counterpart to the McCarthy period in the United States. Wisner and Dulles had been extraordinarily successful.

Further, Dulles and Wisner helped run the National Committee for a Free Europe (NCFE), the archetypal model for all future CIA corporations and proprietaries. What Swiatlo, Field, and the Eastern European show trials and purges did not accomplish, the NCFE successfully brought to Cold War closure.

Swiatlo in the U.S. & the JFK Assassination

In 1953, Swiatlo finally "defected" to the United States: his CIA mission to create political chaos in the Communist world was accomplished. A kind of inverted Agency Illegal, Swiatlo was given American citizenship and supplied with a new identity by the CIA. In late September, 1954, after a brightly-lit press conference in Washington devoted to anti-Communist revelations, Swiatlo officially disappeared into some dark corner of the United States.

Out of that dark corner, Swiatlo broadcast in Polish for Radio Free Europe/Radio Liberty (RFE/RL) between 1955 and 1983, a psychological warfare action run by Swiatlo's old handler, Frank Wisner. The overall psyops master responsible for RFE/RL was C.D. Jackson. Ominously, of the four Polish defectors who worked for RFE/RL, two re-defected to Poland: they were probably double or even triple-agents run by the KGB and the CIA. Swiatlo fed the paranoid fires: "Over Radio Free Europe, month after month, Swiatlo beamed into the East Bloc a smorgasbord of niceties about the apparatus he had served, every tidbit of corruption down to the identities of office snitches."

Immediately following the Kennedy assassination, and documented in a CIA memo buried in the National Archives, Jozef Swiatlo reportedly resurfaced, identified (or misidentified) as a Polish Illegal and, therefore, a suspected Communist espionage agent. The event apparently caused the CIA some anxiety, since the Agency might have recalled a radio broadcast in both Polish and English from Warsaw on October 25, 1954, in which Polish security forces accused Swiatlo of being a U.S. Illegal, "an agent provocateur ... who, with the aid of forged identity papers and disguising himself and taking advantage of defects in the exercise of control ... managed to infiltrate ... the [Polish] public security organization."

Why did the key agent in the CIA destabilization game pop up in the Kennedy assassination investigation? Why had Swiatlo been identified as an Illegal? Was the Agency, in fact, being haunted by the reappearance of its Oswald false identity problem?

No later than two months after the Communists declared Swiatlo a Western intelligence Illegal, the CIA was tracking Noel Field stories that implicated him, no matter how dubious the source, as "a convinced Communist and Soviet agent."

Counter-intelligence focused on Noel Field by the FBI and CIA was energized when Swiatlo surfaced. Dated December 20, 1954, an Agency document from its Deputy Director of Plans called attention to Field's USC "activity," and established that the CIA and FBI both had a continuing "interest in the case." It was routed to the Bureau's Sam Papich, an associate of William Sullivan. Papich and Sullivan were the FBI's top counter-espionage team concerned with both Illegals and U.S. citizens who might be working for the Soviets.

Broader and possibly more terrible in their consequences than Operation Splinter Factor were the Wisner/Dulles counter-espionage programs run by so-called diplomat George F. Kennan, who had a major planning, producing, and directing job "in the CIA-sponsored anti-Communist exile programs of the 1940s and 1950s, including those that employed Nazi collaborators." For Kennan, Wisner, and Dulles, the Cold War "was the means for tens of thousands of Nazi criminals to avoid responsibility for the murders they had committed."

Allen Dulles' Episcopalian Connection

Throughout his political life, Allen's brother John had close relations with the American Presbyterian Church, the Anglican Church of England and its spiritual offspring, the American Episcopal Church. An Internet search combining "OSS" or "Central Intelligence Agency" with "Episcopal Church" yields scores of obituaries of agents and officers who were faithful Episcopalians, often holding important positions in their local vestries. Through two world Wars and the subsequent Cold War, the ranks of the OSS and CIA were stuffed with top college graduates who were also active Episcopalians. To what extent they knowingly used their churchly clout, or whether were led down the rosy path by American intelligence, has not yet been documented.

After JFK accepted Allen Dulles' "resignation" as CIA Director in 1962, the spymaster had no visible links to any center of Protestant power. But Dulles generated a considerable hoard of documents ultimately preserved by his estate, and those materials cover the entire history of his tangos with liberal church individuals of many denominations in Europe and the United States.

Who, then, would be knowledgeable and discreet enough to organize, catalog, and if necessary sanitize the documents of Allen Dulles?

Enter Dr. F. Garner Ranney.

Ranney studied at London University, Cambridge University, and Harvard, earning an A.B. in 1942. During World War II, Ranney was "[the] Top Secret Officer on the staff of [the] Commander U.S. Naval Forces Europe." After the war, he was "a Desk Officer in the Department of State." It would be noteworthy if Ranney had indeed been a Foreign Service Officer: "In the late 1950s ... at least 75 percent of raw information came from people gathering intelligence around the world. At least two-thirds of that came from foreign service officers engaged in overt activities."

Ranney's postwar professional record included unspecified "library work in Baltimore ... at the Peabody Institute and... Maryland Historical Society." But from 1962 on, Ranney was involved in a serious bit of American intelligence housekeeping.

Ranney "served [1962-69] as archivist to... Allen W. Dulles." Ranney held that sensitive position throughout the former CIA director's stint as a member of the Warren Commission investigating the murder of John F. Kennedy.

Dulles died in 1969, and Ranney "was for twenty years a member of the committee of three administering the Allen Welsh Dulles Papers at Princeton University."

Beginning in 1960, F. Garner Ranney was also the chief archivist of the prestigious Maryland Episcopal Diocesan Center and the Diocesan historiographer from 1974 through 1995.

157

Over the years, Ranney has been an effective gatekeeper for American intelligence, the Maryland Episcopal diocesan records, and Allen Dulles' political/intelligence documents.

The boys in the back room could not have hand picked a more faithful spin doctor.

U.S. Intelligence Protects Its Unitarian Assets

Unitarian Service Committee officers collaborated in covert intelligence gathering with the OSS and the CIA through WWII and beyond. The American Unitarian Association also helped found the American Friends of Albert Schweitzer College, and actively supported the Swiss college. In 1978 the Unitarian Service Committee attempted to rediscover its own wartime history, and asked the CIA to release any pertinent files. Upon receiving a typical CIA mish-mash, the USC found that the Agency was still withholding the name of at least one intelligence source.

Who might that person have been?

In Frederick May Eliot, the American Unitarian Association, the Unitarian Service Committee, the American Friends of Albert Schweitzer College, and the OSS all came together. Eliot hoped to achieve a better world through religious, philosophical and cultural organizations, while the Spooks were working to accomplish their own political ends using those same groups. Was Frederick May Eliot manipulated by American intelligence?

Eliot died suddenly in 1958, then in 1960 Judge Lawrence G. Brooks, Chairman of the Board of Directors of the AUA, celebrated his life and works in the Proceedings of the Unitarian Historical Society. The following analysis of Eliot's activities draws upon the abridged version of Judge Brooks' opus: *Frederick May Eliot as I Knew Him.*

One in a procession of prominent Unitarian ministers, educators and poets from several interrelated and distinguished families, Eliot graduated from Harvard College in 1911 and Harvard Divinity School in 1915, ordained as a Unitarian minister. Most of America's liberal elite establishment counted Harvard as its leading educational institution. So did the CIA. No later than 1986, at least one out of four Company officers held a Harvard degree.

In 1934, seeking definitive answers to troubling questions about the decline of Unitarianism, the American Unitarian Association created a Commission of Appraisal and appointed Eliot as its chairperson. Challenged to effect a major change in American Unitarianism, Frederick May Eliot responded brilliantly. The Unitarian Church was revolutionized, with massive increases in its membership, scores of new churches, hundreds of fellowships, and the emergence of the American Unitarian Association as a leading humanitarian and cultural institution.

In 1938, significant Unitarian relief services began in Europe, with the Dexters as key Unitarian operatives. The effort was fully realized when the Unitarian Service Committee was established, with Frederick May Eliot as an influential member of the Executive Committee. The European networks created by Noel Field were in action.

Eliot, fearful of repressive Christian orthodoxy in Europe and the United States, explored "liberal religion," found it exciting, and joined what became the International Association of Religious Freedom, one of the earliest and most enthusiastic supporters of Schweitzer College. Eliot became a highly visible backer, and a founding member of the Board of Directors of the American Friends of Albert Schweitzer College. He and Hans Casparis exchanged letters throughout the college's first years, discussing shared educational and cultural concerns.

As President of the American Unitarian Association, Eliot had to withstand charges of radicalism, especially against Charles Joy, the Dexters, and Noel Field in Europe. The USC indeed supported Socialist and Communist refugees streaming out of Spain and France. Further, Eliot's defense of Rev. Stephen H. Fritchman, radical editor of the *Christian Register*, brought Eliot criticism from anti-Communist liberals in the Unitarians ranks that included the highly vocal A. Powell Davies and Donald Harrington.

Eliot felt Humanism was an important component of his religious and philosophical viewpoint, making him a target of outspoken Unitarian conservatives. Yet throughout his life, Frederick May Eliot moved within extremely powerful elitist circles which dominated American publishing, education, business, banking and government.

Those elitist links gave Eliot the leverage to perform humanitarian acts, but they also made him vulnerable to American intelligence abuse.

The OSS/CIA Files on the Unitarians

The American Unitarian Universalist Association (AUUA) used the Freedom of Information Act in 1978 to obtain covert intelligence files on officers of the wartime American Unitarian Association and the Unitarian Service Committee. Though the CIA sent 246 documents to the AUUA, most of the files were extensively sanitized.

The USC History Archives contain a "Guide to CIA papers in the UUSC file" entitled UUSC HISTORY PROJECT [:I CIA MATERIALS (in UUSC archives only). The UUSC project retained the CIA numbering system for the 246 "items" the Agency released to the UUSC, but the OSS material was reorganized chronologically by the UUSC into six file folders labeled I through VI.

Folder I holds the "Correspondence with Lisbon, 1942-1943 and other Lisbon business [of interest to the Office of Strategic Services]. The Folder I documents "include correspondence from Charles Joy and Seth Gano to the Dexters in Lisbon."

With the permission of Unitarian Service Committee officers in the field, the OSS had intercepted, photocopied and then sent on USC correspondence destined for its European headquarters in Lisbon, using the State Department's diplomatic pouch.

The Dexters in Lisbon and, most probably, Charles Joy were aware of the OSS use of the Unitarian Service Committee; but no available letters or memoirs record whether the USC fully recognized that exchanging the security of a diplomatic pouch for the integrity of the USC's humanitarian activity might have been an uneven and ultimately unethical trade.

In 1978, the Unitarian Universalist Service Committee established that the materials it entered in Folder I contained "only a small percentage of the mail that passed through the OSS on its way to Lisbon...." In Folder III the Committee placed other received documents, which proved the OSS had handled a significantly larger volume of USC mail than the CIA had indicated.

The UUSC organized the most important collection of covert U.S. intelligence material it received from the CIA in Folder II: "Business Between USC and the OSS." Here was the actual evidence of extensive OSS/USC wartime collaboration: "These papers relate to [1.] meetings between Service Committee personnel and OSS officers, [2.] financial dealings [between the two groups] [3.]

requests [by the USC] for facilitation of passports and other [identity and travel] matters, and [4.] the mail service provided [to the USC] by the OSS through the [State Department/Foreign Service] diplomatic pouch."

How did the Universalist Unitarian Service Committee know that wartime cooperation between the OSS and the Unitarian Service Committee was much larger than the highly restricted number of actual communications the CIA allowed the UUSC to see? UUSC's Folder III: the "Record of Correspondence sent to Lisbon but not included in CIA papers." "These letters provide an extensive-perhaps a complete-record of the mail... sent from USC headquarters or from the office of Seth Gano to Lisbon between 1942 and 1944."

Despite the CIA'S redaction of scores of documents, there remains a substantial case against American intelligence for manipulating religious individuals and groups. Specifically, there is much evidence of operational links between the OSS and the USC. The Administrative Records of the Executive Director of the USC, at Andover-Harvard Theological Library (bMS 16007), are preserved in 27 boxes of 10x12 files.

These files were apparently 'sanitized' at some earlier time: records from 1946 through 1957 are missing: the period when American intelligence manipulated religious groups and individuals. Other records from the 1950s (the early Cold War years) and for 1960-1962 are also missing. Since the OSS-CIA penetration of religious groups bears directly upon the history of Schweitzer College from 1959 through 1964, the nexus of AUA, OSS, ASC and Lee Oswald can easily account for the disappearance of the 1960-1962 records.

Combined with the OSS/CIA records now housed at the Unitarian Universalist Service Committee headquarters in Cambridge, the Andover-Harvard Theological Library files represent substantial evidence for [l.] the extensive relations between the OSS and the USC. [2.] a subsequent CIA cover-up to protect still-unidentified Unitarians. [3.] the redaction of OSS documents sent by the CIA to the Unitarian Universalist Service Committee in 1978, in addition to the apparent sanitizing of the Harvard files.

Beyond my suspicion that the CIA cleansed the OSS records in its possession and possibly the 27 boxes in the files at the Harvard Library, boxes 23 and 24 remain crucial. In the library finding-tool for bMS 16007, 23 and 24 are listed as simply containing "Cables" and "Letters" to and from "Geneva, Switzerland," 1945-1947. But 23 and 24 hold immense supportive evidence of the relations between Noel Field, Robert Dexter, Charles Joy, Herta Field and (implicitly) the OSS and Allen Dulles. Noel Field's hundreds of cables and letters are vital as substantive support for the OSS/USC intelligence collaboration (and as raw materials for a future history of Unitarian refugee work). Given the flow of information from Field and other on site refugee workers through the OSS/State Department pouch transmission line to USC headquarters in Lisbon, these communications define the significant intelligence value Allen Dulles and the OSS received from USC sources.

The CIA'S deliberate intent to withhold the truth from the Unitarian Universalist Service Committee in 1978 helps explain UUSC's awkward Folder III title. "This file consists of cover letters from various members of [the] USC enclosing letters to Lisbon and, in some cases, responses from the OSS indicating that the mail had been forwarded or internal memos with instructions for forwarding the letters to Lisbon." The CIA withheld the bulk of wartime OSS/USC correspondence from the Unitarian Universalist Service Committee, apparently protecting OSS agents or assets who in 1978 still had some continuing important relation to the Agency and/or whose revealed identity would compromise still-secret covert operations.

But the CIA may have had a more simple motive for sanitizing records that harkened back to the origins of modern American espionage: the identity of a World War II (or Cold War) agent or asset inside the Unitarian Church, whose exposure would prove embarrassing to a prominent Unitarian family.

The UUSC's Folder IV included whatever the CIA had sent the Committee on Noel Field.

"We [the UUSC] must assume that much of the material that the CIA refused to send ... pertained to Field." UUSC Folder VI held "two sets of papers originating with the State Department that were sent in a separate mailing. They deal with the closing of the [USC] Lisbon office in 1950 and the Noel Field trial."

The Unitarian Universalist Service Committee "received only one copy of all undeleted materials... but it was sent two copies of the OSS documents subjected to CIA deletions. The UUSC placed the second set of redacted OSS material in Folder V, "Expurgated Copies-2nd copy."

CIA Redaction of Unitarian OSS Files

All of the relevant OSS documents were heavily sanitized, clearly signaling that as late as 1978 the CIA had a significant stake in withholding certain information about links between the Office of Strategic Services (and possibly the CIA), the Unitarian Service Committee, and the Unitarian Church. In her excellent historical study of the Unitarian Service Committee, Ghanda Di Figlia discreetly described the working partnership between the USC and the OSS. But in a personal communication to me, Ms. Di Figlia stated: "I have no doubt that there are intelligence files on those members of USC who were involved with the Dexters, Charles Joy, possibly Howard Brooks, William Emerson... who was privy, I believe to the OSS involvement... [and] possibly Frederick May Eliot, president of the American Unitarian Association."

In fact, the close collaboration between the Dexters, Charles Joy, Noel Field and Allen Dulles could not have existed without the cooperation of Frederick May Eliot.

When Beacon Press came under attack and its editor Thomas Bledsoe was dismissed after a series of controversial book contracts in 1958, Frederick May Eliot planned to meet Unitarian Secretary Walter Donald Kring in New York in a move to support the publishing house. Eliot was scheduled to preach at the Unitarian All Souls Church, with a conference scheduled after the sermon. But a terrible snowstorm held up Kring's train outside of New York, and Eliot, on his way to speak, suddenly collapsed and died at the gate of the garden of All Souls.

Whatever the CIA kept secret concerning Unitarian cooperation with the OSS (and the U.S. Agency for International Development), the relationships between U.S. intelligence, the American Unitarian Association, the Unitarian Service Committee, and the Friends of Albert Schweitzer College had meshed together in the person of Frederick May Eliot.[30]

The Catchpool Connection

Corder Catchpool, born in 1883, was a practicing Quaker throughout his life. In January, 1917, he was jailed for refusing to serve in the British armed forces, though he had volunteered in the Allied ambulance service in France for twenty months. After three political trials and thirty-six months in prison, he was set free in April 1919, still defiant, pledging to destroy "Prussianism" the Quaker way. Later that same year Catchpool joined many other Quakers in Berlin, working inside "pacifist and ecumenical circles." With other religious individuals and groups in Germany, Catchpool and his fellow Quakers helped clothe and feed many victims of the recent apocalyptic war.

In the early 1930s, Catchpool was part of the movement to enlist Quakers and others in support of the German people and their "objections to the [WWI] peace. By 1932, Catchpool was one of many Quakers who supported general disarmament.

After the Nazi takeover, Catchpool moved "from spiritual messenger to activist defender of a new generation of victims." He became a close observer of the Nazis and the German people's support for what Catchpool characterized as the Nazi "uprising."

Accused by the Gestapo of being a Communist, consorting with suspicious "visiting foreigners," and of maintaining a file on mistreated anti-Nazis, Catchpool determined to be more even-handed; he joined those British citizens who viewed the Treaty of Versailles as the root cause of German mischief, advocating cooperation with Hitler's government to achieve peace and disarmament.

Catchpool's fellow Quakers, including several with impressive credentials, accused Catchpool of being "pro-Nazi" and an apologist for the dictator's suppression of German freedoms.[31]

By 1935, Catchpool was viewed by no less than British Foreign Secretary Anthony Eden as a pawn of Nazi propaganda. Catchpool, on the other hand, saw his own efforts as "bridge-building," necessary steps to be taken toward conciliation.

Still, that same year, Catchpool and his fellow Quakers in Berlin realized their "efforts on behalf of the politically persecuted... [had been] reduced to a kind of traffic control..."

Whatever the merits of Catchpool's work among the Germans, "Gestapo reports on [the] Friends for 1935 abound with speculations on Quaker conspiracies" that were never fully explained. But at least the "political police in Bavaria... claimed that members of Socialist organizations were receiving money, food, and shelter" from the quakers. The Gestapo was apparently assured by Catchpool that Quaker "work for political prisoners was the exclusive responsibility of British and American Friends" and did not involve Quakers who were German citizens. In turn, Nazi criticism of Quaker activities was muted by the Friends' willingness to help people whose welfare concerned the German government.

Tolerated by the Gestapo, the Quakers worked through the middle and late 1930s at "indiscriminate humanitarianism." But in a few short years, Germany became an "occupied country" with the Nazis in complete control of the nation's economic, political, and social life.

Anti-Nazi Religious Groups & Individuals

The religious life of Germany was deeply marked and often split on the question of Nazi tyranny. The German Confessional/Confessing Church, for example, inspired by the Protestant theologian Karl Barth, "resisted Nazi interference in church affairs." In opposition to the so-called "German Christian" movement, the Confessing Church attempted to preserve "the autonomy and integrity of the Christian church [in Germany]."[32] German Methodists, however, officially praised Hitler for his series of successful territorial acquisitions. Other religious groups, including priests and ministers, opposed Hitler's dictatorship and paid dearly for their spiritual principles. The ethical dilemma that faced the churches in Germany and throughout Europe elicited hundreds of heroic acts by Christian clerics.

In 1936, Catchpool and his wife returned to England, and the Berlin Quaker leadership posts were filled by Margaret B. Collyer from Great Britain and Americans Albert and Anne Martin.[33]

Catchpool continued to belong to a select group of so-called British appeasers of Nazi Germany, including "practicing Christians" who held high office in England. "All of them believed that the Nazi revolution was the product of the inequities of the [World War I] peace settlement … and were confident that by lending an ear to German grievances they were performing a major service for the cause of peace and justice." Members of the group traveled extensively, including the "peripatetic" Corder Catchpool, often between England and Germany. After leaving Berlin, Catchpool "continued to be involved in a variety of Quaker projects on the Continent and to pop in and out of the German capital until war actually broke out."

Catchpool worked for several years to preserve the shreds of peace, opposing Britain's entry into the war, justifying German absorption of European territory and hoping always to appeal to the so-called "better elements" in Nazi Germany. The ever-optimistic Quaker worked tirelessly with whatever friends of peace and conciliation he could contact in Germany, all the while engaging in his favorite pastime: "mountain climbing in Switzerland." Might Catchpool have visited Bern on one of his many pleasure trips to the Swiss mountains?

Catchpool's double character has been noted by his closest and most devoted friend: "During his last three years as the Quaker representative in Berlin[,] Corder had ... to walk very delicately. Attacked from one side as a Communist, from another as a pro-Nazi, with the German Quakers dreading that he might lead them into trouble, and his colleagues in the International [Quaker] Secretariat doubting the wisdom of some of his activities, with the secret police watching all his movements, and with fugitives from the same police coming to him for help, Corder went quietly on with his immensely varied work."

Catchpool's public record in England was largely a blank throughout the war, though at the end of the conflict Catchpool was again busy with "positive peace-making" when the bulging "displaced-person camps" taxed the laboring Friends' "emotional resources." Re-enlisting in Quaker humanitarian activity, Corder Catchpool and his wife then attempted "to get mutually hostile ethnic groups within camps to work with each other and with postwar German authorities whom inmates understandably resented...."[34]

Quaker Catchpool & Intelligence Gathering

Hans A. Schmitt, one of Catchpool's chroniclers, confirmed the Quaker's early intelligence role: "Shocked by the terrifying consequences of Hitler's investiture as head of the German government, Corder Catchpool instituted a network of agents who fed him eyewitness accounts of [Nazi] terrorist acts that he transmitted to Friends House in London."

London, site of the Quakers' British headquarters at "Friends House," was also the home of many highly-placed Nazi apologists, friends of Catchpool and Frank Wisner (who ran an extensive espionage operation in Germany using Nazis).[35]

Catchpool's curiously changing public stance toward Nazi Germany, his association with prominent British apologists for the German dictatorship, the suspicion that somehow he was a Communist, his frequent trips to Switzerland, and his postwar work with refugees (who were most attractive to both American and British intelligence) all suggest that Corder Catchpool might well have lived the life of a dedicated intelligence agent.[36]

On the other hand, he might just have been a complex and contradictory fellow.

John Foster Dulles

Essay Five

Slow Dance with the Devil

During John Foster Dulles' postgraduate year in Paris he adopted his trademark umbrella and bowler hat affectation, which convinced decades of observers that he was associated in some capacity with the English clergy. This perception spring-boarded Foster Dulles' manipulation of the liberal Protestant traditions in support of Foreign Service and State Department policy goals. Brother Allen manipulated those same traditions in support of American espionage and intelligence goals.

In a fusion of family, class, and financial clout, the Dulles brothers pursued their personal and political goals by co-opting the key institutions of the National Security State.

Elitist Religious Origins of the American Establishment

Despite the all-encompassing Presbyterian environment within which the Dulles brothers lived, the American Establishment they so zealously served had its origin in "a real religious establishment-the Unitarian church of Massachusetts." Outlasting the Anglican establishments of New York and the South and the Congregationalist establishments of New England, the Unitarians and their Liberal Christianity ultimately triumphed.

Harvard College was captured early by the Unitarians and became the "command center of the Unitarian wing of the church and part of the official apparatus of the Commonwealth of Massachusetts."

Contrary to received folklore about the American Republic, though the First Amendment prohibited a Federally established church, it left untouched the already established individual state churches. In fact, not until 1940 did the U.S. Supreme Court finally extend the ban to all the states.

Powerfully supported by its Board of Overseers, which included influential public officers, and richly supported by state-legislated tax revenues, Harvard became the training site of the Eastern Establishment Brahmins, both ministerial and secular.

Unitarianism, realized in Liberal Christianity, promoted tolerance, anti-sectarianism, and a warm regard for New England economic power, resident in "the merchants and businessmen of Boston."

Led by the "trinitarian Congregationalists" and other "non-established churches," the state legislature finally stripped the Unitarian Church of its special status in 1833. But the power of its ideas and "the ethos it had cultivated survived, passing from New England into the [national] Establishment...." And though secularized, that ethos was embodied in a social and political class, its generations made up of "lawyers, academics, businessmen"; the sons and grandsons of the earlier Brahmins who had been educated at Harvard in that same liberal tradition.

Walter Lippmann, a Harvard educated New Yorker, shaped the ethic of the modern Establishment in his 1929 book *A Preface* to *Morals*, prescribing a vision for the elite that included "a disinterested world view" to be imposed on the ordinary people from above by a "new class of moralists," the American Establishment, whose guiding principles were to be "disinterest and public morality-which is why... [that Establishment] resembles a state church. Biographers of the American "establishment" have distinguished it from business, whose aim was profit, and politics, whose aim was power. But it was precisely the triangulation of business, politics, and the Establishment (the ultimate trinity of profit, power, and public morality) that was the basis of the cynical manipulation of morality, especially as it was embodied in Liberal Christianity: that is, in the liberal Protestant churches that were taken advantage of by the Dulles brothers.

The Silks were witty chroniclers of the Establishment, which they defined as the "national force, outside government, dedicated to truth, liberty, and... the broad public interest." Ironically, they offered a definition of elitist behavior remarkably similar to the machinations of the Dulles brothers: "The Establishment is often vulnerable to the extremely serious charge of pursuing the private interests of its members behind a mask of disinterest." Indeed, and, more diabolically, behind a mask of sanctimonious morality.

The Silks also conveniently ignored Skull & Bones, a seminal training ground for the American Establishment from at least the 1870s through the present. Yale Skull & Bones members frequently moved to important positions at Harvard, verifying that the Cambridge school, as the Silks did observe, was the Establishment's official higher education institution.[1]

John Foster Dulles: Origins

A child of the American Establishment, John Foster Dulles (he preferred to be called "Foster Dulles") was named after his maternal grandfather, John Watson Foster, President Benjamin Harrison's Secretary of State during his last eight months in office. Earlier, Grandfather Foster had seen service in the Civil War and afterward was appointed Minister to Mexico, Russia, and Spain. Foster's Presbyterian ethic included "his moderate political liberalism," and though certainly not the Liberal Christianity of the New England Unitarians, it fused with other major influences.

Dulles' paternal grandfather was John Welsh Dulles, a zealous Presbyterian missionary. His father, Reverend Allen Macy Dulles, was a "liberal" who urged his lawyer son to enter the religious confrontation in the 1924 Presbyterian General Assembly, where William Jennings Bryan and the fundamentalists opposed Dr. Henry Emerson Fosdick, leading the "modernists," on the theological question of the Virgin Birth.

But that same liberal father required his children to attend all three of his weekly Sunday sermons, his Wednesday prayer meetings, take notes, memorize and recite hymns and biblical passages while Dr. Dulles presided.

Grandfather Foster also made certain that his grandson was inundated each summer with "talk about pioneering, war, diplomacy and the law."

With an undistinguished record at Princeton, Foster was reportedly examining future possibilities: his father urged him to become a minister, while his mother supported his interests in "more worldly prospects." But his maternal grandfather, John Foster, was apparently the major influence. As a representative of the Chinese Imperial Government, he took his nineteen-year-old grandson on a diplomatic trip to The Hague in 1907. Young Foster Dulles was then made the Chinese delegation's secretary, supposedly because he spoke French. Records, however, clearly indicate he was "competent only in English."

Barely one year after his strange experience at the Hague conference, he received a Sorbonne scholarship, suggesting a remarkable improvement in his French language proficiency. Reportedly focusing on philosophy, Dulles still "elected to take some courses in international law, [including]… lectures on international fishing rights."

Back from France, Dulles presented his new vision for his future at the new family home in Auburn, New York, where his father was a professor of apologetics at the Auburn Theological Seminary. Dulles argued for "a career that would combine the practice of law with dedicated lay service to the church." How he came to this union of secular law and Christianity has not been recorded, but his parents ultimately approved of his becoming "a Christian lawyer."

Dulles apparently made no attempt to find any such position, and Wall Street law firms he actually applied to found his credentials without merit. Foster's grandfather came to his rescue, and Dulles became a clerk at Sullivan & Cromwell, where he began his career combining law, commerce, Latin American investment, and covert political operations.

William Nelson Cromwell himself had been a key lobbyist in persuading America to build the Panama Canal, subsequently becoming the legal representative of the Panama Canal Company, the Panama Railway Company, and British, French and German investors in Central and South America.

Though he knew very little Spanish, Dulles was commissioned by Sullivan & Cromwell to handle the firm's Central American legal business. After a salary increase he married, and after five years with Sullivan & Cromwell, became a "respected associate." Dulles' first intelligence operation, in 1917, was "to gain assurances… Panama, Costa Rica, and Nicaragua would harmonize their policies toward Germany with that of the United States." In fact, Sullivan & Cromwell, speaking for the U.S. Government, demanded a simultaneous declaration of war on Germany from the three Latin countries.

The Secretary of State happened to be Dulles' uncle, Robert Lansing, so when Sullivan & Cromwell dispatched a lawyer to Central America, ostensibly on company business, John Foster was the obvious choice for the action.

In 1918, Dulles received an Army captain's commission and was attached to the War Trade Board, where his operations were both military and economic, including his service "as liaison between the War Trade Board and the War and Navy Departments..." Promoted to the rank of major by the end of the war, Dulles was held in high esteem by Vance McCormick, his boss on the War Trade Board, who was also the chairperson of the Democratic National Committee, and by Bernard Baruch, chief of the War Industries Board.

The complex wartime trade and shipping relations between the American government, the Netherlands, the Scandinavian nations and Germany had been successfully negotiated by Foster Dulles and his associates.

With the war ended, President Woodrow Wilson sent McCormick and Baruch to Versailles. Baruch, now on the "Reparations Commission," chose Dulles as his legal representative.

The British and French demanded that Germany pay through the nose for "war costs," but Foster Dulles and Baruch argued that Germany should not be pressed to pay "war damages" that would "sow bitter seeds of a new war." For Sullivan & Cromwell and the firm's investors, Germany was saved: Article 231 of the treaty accepted "Germany's finite capacity to pay war [damages and reparations]....'

Following his post-war service at Versailles, Dulles for twenty years "combined law with international finance and diplomacy" at Sullivan & Cromwell, handling a series of legal and financial assignments that involved oil, coal, and other lucrative commodities.

Foster Dulles Joins the International Power Structure

Germany's war debt occupied much of Dulles' attention through the 1920s until an odd series of deaths "catapulted [him] to the top of ... [his] large and famous law firm...." Dulles' desires could now be realized: his "special fondness for French wines, caviar, brandy and cigars, and... the diversions of European nightclubs." But he was without any interest in art or music, according to at least one source "a plain, rugged and rather gauche figure...."

According to a sympathetic biographer, like many successful over-achievers Dulles was a failure as a parent. Still, his son Avery ultimately reversed his own personal downward spiral. Responding to the claim that he had renounced the family's Presbyterian faith in 1939, Avery asserted "There was nothing there really to reject...." Coming to spiritual consciousness while a Harvard Law student, Avery chose to become a Roman Catholic. While a Naval Intelligence officer in World War II he was hospitalized with a bout of polio and, during his recovery period, decided to become a Jesuit priest.

Avery was "brilliant, gentle, and obviously well suited to the calling...." At the age of 82 he culminated his career as an eminent Roman Catholic theologian when he became a cardinal of the Catholic Church. He remained an important source on Foster Dulles' dubious religiosity until his death in 2008, aged 90.

Religion & Foster Dulles

In light of his supposed "Damascus Road" epiphany in 1937, John Foster Dulles' cynical manipulation of religious institutions seems counter-intuitive; but what, in fact, was his real relationship to the Almighty?

Thomas E. Dewey, who at one time was invited to join Sullivan & Cromwell met Dulles in 1937, and commented later: "I think he spent some years as an atheist." Indeed, as distinct from a practicing Christian, Dulles may have been of the lip-service variety: "his theology [was] ... a generalized faith in ... 'universal moral law' :[and] a belief that the church ... [had] a role to play in the political process...."

Despite valiant attempts by a half-dozen Dulles biographers to argue for some kind of continuity between the Dulles family's Presbyterian origins and his Christian "rediscovery" in 1937, Dulles, according to his son Avery, was not a religious person. Interviewed about his family's religious activities, Cardinal Avery commented: "My family had been very church committed, but then we got a country house out on Long Island, and [our] ... church practice [attendance] fell off. My father found his religion rather irrelevant to his life. He didn't have any particular connection to a church."

In February 2001, the Dulles Clan was characterized by a *New York Times Magazine* interviewer as "a family of agnostic Protestants." The newly appointed Cardinal Avery Dulles accepted the phrase without comment.

Despite attempts to spiritually justify his moral opportunism, Foster Dulles was precisely defined: "Jim Hagerty said he was a Roundhead, a Puritan," clearly suggesting Foster Dulles was the Protestant equivalent of a Spanish Inquisitor. Writing to Avery in 1949, Dulles clearly defined his own amoral ethic: "I know that you have contempt for 'expediency,' but that is what in fact determines most of people's conduct...."

In its last chapter, a 1962 "Reappraisal" of Dulles referred to him as a "Presbyterian elder" with a "deep Presbyterian sense of morality." Earlier, however, the same author went to considerable lengths to characterize Dulles as "devious," embodying "casuistry, ingenuity, intransigence, righteousness, ruthlessness, and inhumanity." Is this the portrait of a spiritual man?

In Dulles' writings and spoken words, "there was rarely any reference to sin, no admission ... [that] ethical decisions are fraught with moral ambiguity, and no evidence of an understanding that the dimension of self-interest, self-preservation and self-righteousness is implicit in every exercise of power."

Andrew H. Berding, who became Dulles' Assistant Secretary of State in March 1937, characterized his boss as "an intensely religious man." Yet Berding gave no evidence in support of this. Instead, Berding contradicted himself: "In my numerous conversations and meetings with him I recall no instance where he made a point of religion."

Still, according to several sources, Dulles acted as if he were either the right hand of God or the deity himself.

Foster Dulles' "Damascus Road" Moment

What really happened in 1937? Despite Tom Dewey's observation about Dulles' apparent atheism and Avery's statement about his father's non-involvement in church, Dulles "had remained a prominent Presbyterian layman." With his undocumented church attendance (unattested to by his son Avery), Dulles was supposed to have "taught a Sunday-school class at various [unidentified] periods." But Dulles felt in that fateful year of 1937 he had not given "enough attention to the possibilities of public service."

Were there political pressures in 1937 on John Foster Dulles that might have been a major factor in his alleged religious reconversion?

Powerful forces had indeed come together to enlist Dulles as a major player in the expected dark times. In 1938, John D. Rockefeller, Jr., had offered him the direction of a "task force" that would evaluate "missionary activities throughout the world." Given the historical connections between the Rockefeller family's goals in investment, politics, intelligence, and evangelistic religion, the offer to John Foster Dulles was anticipatory.

The Rockefeller clan and its missionary intelligence network had emulated other powerful families, including the historic Medici. For over a thousand years the Papacy, and later the Spanish Inquisition, used the Church's missionaries in Europe and the New World for intelligence collection. Their modern counterpart was the Rockefeller family, operating in the American West and, later, in Central and South America.

As early as 1883, the Rockefellers had "used missionaries to gather intelligence about [Native American] insurgencies in the West or to discourage them." The growth of the Rockefellers' wealth was exactly matched by the family's collaboration with Christian Fundamentalist missionary action.

By 1957, the Rockefellers had decided to support the Fundamentalist revivalism of Billy Graham, whose supporters included the ostensibly liberal Protestant Henry Pitriey Van Dusen, a Rockefeller Foundation trustee and editor of Foster Dulles' "spiritual legacy." The Establishment Protestant churches supported Graham, hoping to enlist converts, but the Rockefellers' allies in Fundamentalism ultimately triumphed.

Though Dulles was unable to join the Rockefeller missionary commission as its director, he did complete a part of his task, visiting Chinese General Chiang Kai-shek. Dulles assessed the Asian leader as a stalwart anti-Communist and "sincere Chinese patriot," who was the target of unfair Communist propaganda concerning the general's anti-democratic propensities. For Foster, the visit was the beginning of his long involvement in Sino-American politics. Dulles' appraisal of Chiang Kai-shek was an important illustration of the Rockefeller family's fusion of profit-seeking and Christian missionary work, Dulles maintained his relationship with Rockefeller interests throughout the rest of his life, eventually serving as chairman of the Rockefeller Foundation.

In 1937, just before his trip to China, Dulles accepted two invitations to a pair of major international gatherings later cited as catalysts for his religious "rediscovery." John Foster was invited to attend the "Conference on Intellectual Co-operation in Paris, under League of Nations auspices ... called to study the possibilities for peaceful change in a world ... moving inexorably toward war." Dulles' negative response to this political meeting was suspicious, dovetailing too neatly with his imminent return to Godliness.

The ensuing Conference on Church and State meeting in Oxford, England, had invited world-prominent clergy and secular leaders. According to one of his biographers, Dulles was most impressed "by the scope and range of the ideas the churchmen had to offer." But it was more likely that Dulles and his backers decided to revive Foster's dormant relation to the Divinity as a perfect tool of foreign policy and intelligence. His brother Allen's earlier success during World War I using the same tactic may, in fact, have been Foster's model.

Acutely aware of the economic and political importance of the world conflict that was to erupt, Dulles recognized the "moral dynamism potential" of the liberal Protestant tradition.

Foster Dulles' Epiphany: Spiritual or Political?

Dulles then supposedly experienced a religious revelation in July 1937. Yet "some [commentators] thought ... the more than casual effort to demonstrate a revival of his faith reflected an attempt to give himself a more appropriate 'image' for church work."

With Dulles' longtime commitment to German and Japanese economic and industrial development, his "reasons for moving deeply into church work at this time may have been complex." His "church work" after 1937 was, in fact, troubling to a number of observers.

Why? Both the secular Paris conference and the religious Oxford conference in 1937 had been organized by the same international elite establishment, and undoubtedly for the same purpose: to support an alliance of Western "Christian" power in opposition to the anticipated strength of the Communist East, led by the Soviet Union. Dulles' son Avery summarized his father's intention succinctly: "He began to be interested in using the churches [beginning in 1937] as a means ... to overcome ... nationalism and promote world peace." Not to mention, of course, nurturing a supranational capitalist world order engaged in a battle to the death against Stalin's USSR and labor organizations of any kind, anywhere.

Dulles' most intelligent and sympathetic critic could only conclude that he "experienced a limited and intellectual type of 'conversion' in the sense that he departed [the conference] with the impression that religion could serve as a significant social force" capable of supporting his political agenda.

Playing the Liberal Protestants

For ten years as the executive officer of Sullivan and Cromwell, whose European and Asian clients were among the wealthiest and most powerful supporters of the German and Japanese war efforts, Dulles was concerned about the real possibility the United States would enter the war and tip the balance in favor of the anti-Axis nations, resulting in the disastrous defeat of Japan and Germany and the decimation of their industrial strength.

How to justify, therefore, the saving of essentially tyrannical governments and economies?

John Foster Dulles' brilliant pragmatic choice was to argue his political goals through the media of the liberal Protestant churches. In his exhortations to both religious and secular audiences in the late 1930s, Dulles most often referred to an "undefined 'spiritual element' that was to bolster America's non-interventionist stance. After Pearl Harbor, this element was to direct the West's wartime activity with "humility and repentance." Neither humility nor repentance was defined in any real Christian sense.

In 1924, Dulles had tested the religious waters with his political toe. Appointed to the Presbyterian General Assembly's Committee on War by the New York Presbytery, Dulles authored an essay embodying one of his earliest political programs: though "worthy of the followers of Christ [it] did not necessarily proceed from a peculiarly Christian premise."

The 1924 essay anticipated all of Dulles' subsequent "spiritual" arguments: the content of those diplomatic, economic, or political arguments was always delivered in an empty rhetorical vehicle, whether the carrying cart was Christianity, Morality, or Righteousness.

Ultimately, whatever the ethical or even specifically Christian frame of Dulles's thesis, his major thematic concerns were always political: "the obsolescence of national sovereignty [and] the need for long-range national objectives." No matter that the two ideas contradicted each other; they became closely coupled with Dulles' Christian/anti-Communist "spiritual element."

As a certified delegate of the American Federal Council of Churches, Dulles began in 1938 to travel, write, and speak (ostensibly) in support of the Council "on the side of constructive efforts for peace." Dulles filled five intense years "making speeches in all parts of the country and taking part in study groups and public discussions." He reportedly felt this period of his life had been a part of a major "missionary movement." "He kept [dozens of] ... speaking engagements a year, talking [for example] to church [meetings] ... business groups ... [and] YMCA organizations ...."

But those five years were not a seamless stretch of moral arguments. For example, the word "peace," with all of its sympathetic connotations, was prominently displayed in Dulles' many presentations during the period. But before America's entry into the war, he clearly advocated non-intervention. Afterward, he argued for a peace that included the "rational" acceptance of Japanese and German economic needs. None of his definitions of peace was ever either spiritual *or* religious.

In the late 30s, Foster Dulles began to explore serious participation in international politics, and the World Council of Churches offered him a friendly forum at a number of WCC conferences.

In July and August of 1939, Dulles was in Geneva attending the small but grandly titled International Conference of Lay Experts and Ecumenical Leaders of the World Council of Churches where he reportedly helped shape "three principles ... [embodying] a Christian formula for world peace." But that formula was generic Dulles. It called for a "coextensive" exercise of world "political power and responsibility"; it affirmed that "all human beings [were] ... of equal worth in the eyes of [a presumably Christian] God; and it asserted that "[it was as necessary to effect changes [in the world order] in the interest of justice as to secure the protection of the status quo."

Aside from apparently voting in favor of the American Declaration of Independence and, by extension, its European philosophical origins, Dulles argued for a political world order that would support Japanese and German economic challenges (his idea of "changes in the interest of justice"), while strongly suggesting the Western powers were selfishly trying to preserve the status quo.

Dulles accused the United States, Britain, and France of post-war "blunders so colossal ... they must be paid for." Witting or not, Dulles applied "paid for" in both its religious and economic sense. In his uber-Capitalist view, the Allied powers and their abusive policies had "spawned forth" the "evil creatures" who had seized control of Germany and Japan.

Dulles was "much impressed ... by the effectiveness of the World Council as a platform for international pronouncements.... From that time onward his interest in and participation in the council's work never flagged."

On October 28, 1939, before the National Council of the YMCA in Detroit, Dulles made his position absolutely clear: the United States ought not to enter the European war. "I see neither in the underlying causes of the war, nor in its long range objectives, any reason for the United States becoming a participant in the war. Were we now to act, it would be to affirm an international order, which by its very nature is self-destructive and a breeder of violent revolt." When Dulles wrote for the Council on Foreign Relations' *Foreign Affairs,* and the journal of his suddenly renewed religiosity, *Presbyterian Life,* his focus was always political rather than spiritual. The engines of the Council on Foreign Relations and the Federal Council of Churches were running on the same fuel: Dulles' *Can We Be Neutral,* written for the Council on Foreign relations, was identical both in spirit and idea to his speaking and writing on behalf of the Federal Council of Churches. Because Dulles was the intellectual leader of both organizations, he had his own personal echo chamber. The Council on Foreign Relations was the creature of the American Establishment, particularly the Rockefeller family, with whom Dulles was closely allied, and it consistently anticipated or regurgitated the Federal Council of Churches' pronouncements.

In 1940, Dulles accepted the chairmanship of "the committee of direction" for the Federal Council of Churches' Commission on a Just and Durable Peace, an organization he had, in fact, helped to create. The Commission had "over a hundred representatives from all the Protestant communities making up the Federal Council of Churches, and thus [it] directly represented about twenty-five million people."

Probably the Commission's "best known achievement" was more political than religious: it published a booklet in 1941 embodying

Dulles' critique of Roosevelt and Churchill's Atlantic Charter, in which Dulles prophesied that the "end of the present war" would "find an overwhelming concentration of power in one or two nations."

Since, in his opinion, the Fascists were not to blame for their ruthless genocidal behavior, he had no interest in war crimes prosecution. Rather, he asked for "a beneficent reality." Dulles argued for a European human services operation that supplied "medicine, food, and clothing" to alleviate the anticipated post-war chaos; for a "federated commonwealth" and for "assurance to Japan of access to markets and raw materials...." Given the Japanese record of war crimes in Asia, this was a shockingly insensitive proposal. He also recommended that "all non-self-governing colonies" be placed under a European "international mandate."

Nothing in Foster Dulles' actual words or deeds ever seemed to support democracy, or the elimination of exploitation, bigotry, racism, and genocide. In fact, his Charter revisions look remarkably like an argument for sheltering Western and Japanese state-protected Capitalist economies. Dulles then came into direct conflict with dedicated Protestant church figures led by Henry Sloane Coffin, president of Union Theological Seminary, who argued that the European war indeed presented a "major moral issue," which supporters of Dulles were ignoring. The division between this ethical argument for joining the war against Germany and the Federal Council of Churches' interest in a cozy post-war reconciliation with the Axis Powers was clear: Dulles rejected any Christian church support for the anti-Nazi forces. He wrote to Henry Sloane Coffin that he "was distressed by the tendency to bestow a church sanction on the Allied war effort."

Friedrich Wilhelm Sollmann: A True Liberal Christian

John Foster Dulles' self-serving Christian morality can be most fully appreciated in contrast with the authentic spirituality in the service of peace practiced by Friedrich Wilhelm Sollmann. Born in Germany, Sollmann was a Christian journalist and editor targeted by the Kaiser as an enemy of the state during World War One, and he was one of the founders of the German Weimar Republic, subsequently becoming a member of its General Assembly. In 1933, Sollmann was "the first member of [the German] parliament attacked by Nazi storm troopers...." Severely wounded, Sollmann escaped to edit a Saar territory daily, then left the Saar when the Nazis entered, and eventually resided in Woodbrooke, Birmingham, England, where he made his first contact with Quakers. In 1937 Sollmann became a resident of the United States, lecturing throughout the country.

In America, he addressed almost one thousand audiences, and became a resident of the Quakers' Pendle Hill, where he made manifest his argument for "modern Christian democracy":

1. Work for all.
2. The highest development of useful production.
3. Just distribution of the wealth produced.
4. No economic monopolies by private corporations or governments.
5. Insurance for all needy citizens against private emergencies.
6. Mediation and arbitration between social groups in the nation.
7. Mediation and arbitration between nations.
8. A regional federation of free nations with the ultimate aim of a world federation of all nations.
9. Progressive limitation of armaments as gradual steps to disarmament. An international police force.
10. Education leading to voluntary national and international co-operation.
11. Emphasis on the supreme importance of liberty for the growth of the individual.
12. Fusion of individual liberty with a powerful leadership responsible to the people.
13. A new concept of the moral character of statecraft.
14. Strengthening of national and international solidarity.
15. Stress on the universal character of Christianity.

Sollman's Christian Democracy put Dulles' self-serving righteousness to shame.

Foster Dulles Goes To War

One month after Pearl Harbor, Dr. William Temple, the Archbishop of Canterbury, hosted an international Church of England conference at Oxford, reportedly "to define the spiritual bases of peace." Dulles and Dr. Walter Van Kirk, an officer of the Federal

Council of Churches, braved the perilous wartime skies over the Atlantic Ocean to attend the interfaith meeting. But it was a curious trip, suggesting that the British and American governments, now wartime allies, had co-sponsored the religious conference. Van Kirk and Dulles flew on a U.S. military aircraft into the blacked-out Limerick Airport in Ireland. There, the two boarded a British military plane and landed at Bristol, where an official car whisked them off to London, then on to Oxford.

Anticipating the coming push for an end to nation states, Dulles addressed the Oxford conference on the benefits of international economic agencies that transcended national boundaries. In effect, he called for globalization administered by a "supranational executive organ." Astonishingly, an unidentified "churchman" who attended the conference approved of Dulles' call to move beyond "abstract principles" (like, say, the Sermon on the Mount?) and to "get down into the gutter of international politics."

Dulles had no time for the Oxford conference's "Malvern Report," which called for European unity in a cooperative commonwealth, took a critical look at capitalism, and supported "social security."

A key officer, representative or delegate at more than a dozen national and international religious conferences and organizational meetings from 1937 through 1953, Dulles authored over "fifty addresses and articles concerned... [according to Henry P. Van Dusen] with the moral and spiritual foundations of world order, the significance of religion, and the role of the [Western Christian] churches."

By collecting twenty-two of those Dulles pieces, Van Dusen supplied a representative sampling of Dulles' "spiritual" work from 1937 through 1958.

In his introduction, Van Dusen summed up certain recurring themes and ideas embodied in Dulles' "Christian convictions": "moral law"; "human beings as children of God ... with certain inalienable rights"; the "teachings" of Jesus having "authority and practicability"; "faith" as necessary for a righteous life; and political "action" required to fulfill a Christian's commitment. But Dulles' citations of moral law and inalienable political rights in his works were not, in fact, specifically Christian; and though he was correct that Jesus' Gospel teachings apparently embodied "ethical principles" Dulles omitted any references to the Christian belief in

Christ's divinity save in passing, as in: "The church being a creation of God in Jesus Christ, in Jesus' death and resurrection; or in Jesus' defining act of sacrificial redemption."

Certainly these three convictions, central to Christianity, ought to have been part of the "faith in action" Dulles was so fond of featuring in his writing and speaking for twenty-one years. But they were not. Dulles did refer to Christians dedicating themselves to pursuing a "just and durable peace" and "seeking forgiveness for their sins," though the latter reference appeared in a conclusion to a proposal for the adoption of a "moral law" embodying "God's purpose for the world made known in Jesus Christ," a "law," Dulles argued, that both "Christians and non-Christians [could] ... accept." In 1939, however, Dulles defined Christian "sins" as political and economic, committed exclusively against Japan and Germany.[2]

One year after the United States entered World War II, Dulles set forth his "guiding [political] principles" in an address adopted by the Federal Council of the Churches as its own statement in December 1942. It would be the last time Dulles was so "Christian," despite his "spiritual legacy."

Foster Dulles as Hypocritical Opportunist

Even Reinhold Niebuhr, the favorite theologian of the governing American Establishment, had characterized Dulles' ostensible Christian ethic as "Self-righteousness ... the inevitable fruit of simple moral judgments."

Another source not especially friendly to Dulles reported the Presbyterian elder had commented to French Foreign Minister Christian Pineau: "For us[,] there are two sorts of people in the world: ... those who are Christians and support free enterprise and ... the others." Dulles had successfully launched the meme of Capitalism and Christianity united against all "the others" which has become Gospel for so many Americans.

In 1948, I.F. Stone brilliantly summarized Foster Dulles's hypocritical ethics, pinpointing an early "Dulles conversion" occurring during World War II, "when the fortunes of war had turned definitely against the Axis[:] ... Dulles [then] raised the slogan of 'a Christian peace.' He who had never risen to plead for the victims asked mercy in defeat for the oppressors. Stone cited Dulles' speech at the meeting of the World Council of Churches in Amsterdam: Dulles had presented Jesus as "a symbol to be drafted in the Cold War."

For Stone, "The man who keeps Mammon for a client shouldn't talk so much about God." To evaluate the Christian Dulles, Stone recommended reading Matthew 7:15-16. "Beware of false prophets who come to you in sheep's clothing but who are, inside, ravening wolves."

By 1950, Dulles saw the United States as a moral enclave in a "predominantly hostile world" destined to be destroyed if it did not take action against the Communists. For Dulles, "A United States which could be an inactive spectator while the barbarians overran and desecrated the cradle of our Christian civilization would not be the kind of a United States which could defend itself." Though President Eisenhower agreed that the United States was broadly "a product and representative of the Judaic-Christian civilization," he always chose "economic rather than moral considerations."

Dulles' evangelical anti-Communism generated his thesis supporting Western Christian exploitation of the Third World; he cited the "wise statesmanship" and "moderation" of the Western world that resulted in the "withering away of political rule by the West...." But Dulles' entire argument was bereft of evidence, suggesting, at best, self-deception: "We ... should not forget those spiritual leaders who in the past implanted in Western colonial policies the basic concept of human liberty so that, from the beginning, Western colonialism had a liberating quality."

In 1954, appearing before the Council on Foreign Relations, Dulles proposed his major foreign policy goal: "a maximum deterrent at a bearable cost," what the media dubbed "massive retaliation." Rather than ethical or moral, the policy looked like an amoral response to a perceived provocation, implying "that the [Eisenhower] administration would risk the incineration of tens of millions, Americans included, to prevent peripheral ["Communist"] aggression ..."

In 1956, Dulles spoke in Ames, Iowa, condemning "neutrality" as obsolete and almost always "immoral." Dulles arrived at this conclusion by contrasting the nonaligned "third world" with the United States in its epic battle with Communism: American foreign policy was dictated by what Dulles called "moral law." But the Secretary of State did not elaborate. What moral law? The Torah? The Gospels? Paul's epistles? The sayings of Henry Ford?

Dulles' "moral" arguments have most recently been characterized by a friendly commentator as "excessive," gratuitous," and full of "ethical posturing": a "smoke screen of ... provocative rhetoric." "Dulles' critics ... [have] pronounced him a hypocrite." Dulles' pragmatic diplomacy coupled with his self-serving moralistic language strongly suggested that Eisenhower's Secretary of State had his own psychological warfare agenda. A recent full and even-handed analysis of Dulles' political and religious proclamations characterized them as shallow, pretentious, and weak in vision with, at best, "a heavy dollop of religiosity."[3]

Foster Dulles & the Rhetoric of Prophetic Dualism

Though Foster Dulles did not invent the U.S. foreign policy trumpet of moral superiority, he certainly helped perfect it: comparing American rhetoric with American behavior through the 1950s, communications expert Justin Lewis concluded that "US foreign policy ... [had] little to do with moral or ethical imperatives," despite widespread assumptions to the contrary. Aristotelian logic in its simplest and most powerful manifestation, that something must either be A or null-A, has been critiqued by a dozen major logicians, philosophers, and semanticists: none more effectively than Alfred Korzybski, Kenneth Burke, Anatol Rapaport, and Wayne Brockriede, who have influenced communications theorists and rhetorical analysts who closely examine the fusion of symbolic act and persuasive rhetoric. With communicationist Martin Medhurst, a group of these academics have focused largely on American Cold War language.

Philip Wander has been interested in both foreign policy language and domestic political speech. In particular, he has concentrated on the linguistic strategies of the Eisenhower-Dulles administration, calling those strategies "prophetic dualism." Wander found that, to Foster Dulles, the world was a battlefield where two opponents were in absolute and irreconcilable conflict, one "act[ing] in accord with all that is good, decent and at one with God's will, the other act[ing] in direct opposition." For Foster Dulles, one side embodied the Divine Spirit, the other Evil Incarnate. No nation, no group, and no individual could stand outside this conflict: "neutrality [was] ... a delusion, compromise [was] appeasement, and negotiation a call for surrender."

Prophetic dualism, absolute good versus absolute evil, came to the New World with the Puritans in 1620, and in the 1950s was embodied by individuals who successfully melded this volatile theology into the sacred and patriotic American "mission." In the political usurpation of the sacred, "patriotism virtually became law, criticism of government policies grounds for censorship, [and] public protest evidence if not of treason then [of] some lesser form of Un-Americanism."

Prophetic dualism inhabited the inner circle of the American government in the 1950s, led by President Eisenhower and Secretary of State John Foster Dulles.

Though Wander does not speculate on who might have influenced Eisenhower to adopt prophetic dualism as a rhetorical strategy, from his time as Allied commander in the European Theatre through his successful campaign for the presidency, that individual would certainly have been deeply versed in psychological warfare: a brilliant wordsmith who could sway a whole nation.

Foster Dulles went far beyond Eisenhower's largely traditional morality, calling down Divine wrath on his Godless opponents, all in support of his own economic and political ends and American international hegemony. "One advantage of [Dulles'] prophetic dualism ... [was] that it stifle[d] ... debate; another... that it posit[ed] a life-and death struggle ... [and therefore] encourage[d] ... a heightened dependence on the established order. Conflict [was] inevitable between Good and Evil." Both of these advantages were embodied in Foster Dulles' twisted and spiritually empty morality.

Foster Dulles & His End Times Dualism

Nearing his death, Dulles apparently came to believe in the rhetorical split he had made between West and East, capitalism and Communism, God and the Devil. Dying of cancer, Dulles addressed the National Council of Churches (NCC) in Cleveland on November 18, 1958. For years, in press conferences, interviews, and addresses, Dulles had attacked the Godless Communists of the Soviet Union and the People's Republic of China. Though he now stressed the value of change and adapting to it, he still argued in his "morally righteous" mode for the continued exclusion of China from the United Nations.[4]

Friends and former allies who had worked with Dulles on the Federal Council of Churches' Commission for a Just and Durable Peace, from 1940 through 1948, were in his National Council of Churches' audience as he railed against the Reds. But the majority were no longer moved by Dulles' moral arguments. "Within a few hours of his talk they voted a resolution that put the National Council of Churches on record" backing China's bid for United Nations membership and calling for the United States to recognize China. Ironically, Allen Dulles' CIA secretly funded the National Council of Churches.

For Foster Dulles, the NCC vote was a "personal blow and repudiation." On December 4, 1958, he gave one more major address that again condemned Communist China; Then the Berlin Wall episode, his last major crisis, challenged his questionable moral authority. Dulles and his political agenda lost the support of the liberal Protestant churches, and his manipulation of those churches ceased.[5]

It was 1959.

C. D. Jackson

Essay Six

The Oswald Psyops Enigma

John Foster Dulles was only two months dead when, in the summer of 1959, Eisenhower made a startling change. He personally assumed the lead in U.S. foreign policy, overriding Christian Herter, Foster's anointed successor as Secretary of State. Eisenhower refused on many occasions to attribute his fresh approach to a rejection of Foster Dulles' "rigid negatives [that] ... had progressively isolated the United States from the sympathies and the aspirations of most of mankind."

Freed from Dulles' deadly domination of state affairs, which had closed down all reasonable dialogue between the American government and the Soviets, the president began asking himself how he could use his remaining time in office to avoid a nuclear cataclysm. His answer was to re-open the blocked channels of international communication.

Eisenhower Sans Dulles

Together with his White House advisor James Hagerty, Eisenhower constructed four major political trips to eleven allies on three continents: Europe, Latin America, and the Far East. In September 1959, Nikita Khrushchev visited the United States. "In effect, [Eisenhower] ... and Khrushchev tacitly agreed to work toward general detente." Despite setbacks in Latin America, Eisenhower's tour was largely successful. By May 1960, the president seemed to be the world's best hope for international peace.

On October 3, 1955, when Ike was seriously ill, I. F. Stone published an allegorical essay titled "The President's Illness." Identifying Eisenhower's backers as "the Eastern Seaboard moneyed interests standing in opposition to the Pentagon, swollen military expenditures, the aviation lobby," and the Democrats as "the cold war party," Stone characterized Eisenhower as a genuine "man of peace," someone willing to sit down with the Soviet leadership and negotiate.

What the hard-core Cold Warriors needed was an international incident to derail the US-Soviet peace talks: Say, the uncannily well-timed shoot-down of a U-2 flight over the Soviet Union. That is precisely what happened in May 1960, two weeks before the scheduled summit meeting in Paris. Another more recent event involving airplanes might cross one's mind.

Don't Bring Me Down: Lee Oswald & Gary Powers

For what purpose was Lee Oswald dropped into the unholy Cold War cauldron? The FBI and the CIA monitored Oswald's 1st-class mail from 1959 until his nationally televised rendezvous with death. During that highly unconstitutional process, both agencies were alerted to a strange and faulty version of the traditional intelligence Illegal, or "legend," upon his departure for Europe. But whose Illegal? Oswald's resumé looked remarkably like that of a "dangle" or "false defector." Whose false defector? Was Oswald a creature of the CIA, the FBI, the GRU, or the KGB? Perhaps he was an agent in the alliance of FBI and CIA officers who ran the pre-assassination shell game in Mexico City.

Attorney Bud Fensterwald once observed to me that all clandestine operations have at least two purposes. What might these have been *vis-à-vis* Oswald's skip-out to Moscow? One goal suggested by earlier analysts was to use Oswald in a plot to mangle President Eisenhower's credibility and sabotage the developing Soviet-American peace process.

What evidence supports that goal? Near the end of his Marine career, Oswald had apparently been prepped through a series of military adventures and defense secrets: "Lee Harvey Oswald's movements in the Far East ... dovetail[ed] with the salient points of the U-2's contribution to the [ongoing] strategic debate [on the so-called Soviet threat] in Washington." Oswald was at Atsugi from September through November 1957, when both Sputnik and early Soviet ICBM tests occurred. He was with Operation Strongback maneuvers from November 1957 through March 1958, and he was at Cubi Point in the beginning of 1958, tracking U-2 over-flights of China, which helped give the United States significant information about Chinese military movements, relations with the Soviet Union, and other important intelligence.

Oswald was in Taiwan in the fall of 1958, privy to American military intentions in the Taiwan Straits. From March through August 1958, when Oswald was back at Atsugi, the Soviets halted their testing of ballistic missiles, and the U-2 flights over Atsugi verified this information. After Taiwan, Oswald was at Atsugi again in October-November 1958. The U-2 flights he was monitoring confirmed that the Soviets still had not restarted their ballistic missile testing. At the very least, Oswald was loaded with U-2 information collected on both China and the Soviet Union, and the KGB would have been extremely interested in what the United States knew about Soviet strengths and weaknesses.

When the CIA opened its Oswald 201 file, however, it failed to "mention ... his [stated] threat to give up military secrets [to the Soviets]." This failure, historian John Newman remarked, was "extraordinary." Newman concluded that "circumstantial evidence [indicated] ... Oswald gave away something the Soviets used [to bring down Gary Powers' U-2 flight]." If this is true, it puts Lee Oswald in the middle of the secret campaign to scuttle Eisenhower's attempts at rational communication with the Socialist powers; nothing short of anathema to our permanent crypto-establishment.

In Newman's view, the CIA's so-called mole hunters deliberately failed to open a 201 file on Oswald in 1959 "when they knew ... Oswald had defected and offered to give up radar [and other] secrets ... a conspicuous breakdown of the Agency's security and counterintelligence functions." But for this theoretical construction, no real breakdown in Agency security need have occurred. Lee Harvey Oswald was deliberately stuffed with military secrets and sent to the Soviets and the KGB by elements of American intelligence, possibly in collusion with Richard Bissell. Bissell was the Agency man who authorized Gary Powers' fateful flight, contravening Ike's explicit ban on such flights. Were the Russians quietly given the time and place to lock onto the U-2? This is an all too familiar formula, which has been used many times over the years, in this case to sabotage Eisenhower and Kruschev's efforts to establish some degree of international sanity. The mission may very well have been run by a treasonous cabal of hard-line U.S. *and* Soviet Intelligence agents, who saw their mutual meal tickets in jeopardy.

The Original Oswald Scheme: Was Ike the Target?

Either the CIA'S Office of Security or its Counter-intelligence (or both) apparently piggy-backed a KGB mole hunt onto the original Lee Harvey Oswald operation, probably delighting those who had originally sent him to the Soviet Union instead of Switzerland. But the same CIA officers running the Agency's illegal HT/LIN-GUAL program had made their mail intercept program vulnerable to discovery by attaching an operation to the Red Marine, who was himself an HT/LINGUAL mail intercept target.

The Oswald overload may have been affected by a far darker espionage source, intent on ridding itself of a suddenly heretical president, and compromising the operations of those intelligence agents it had chosen as fall guys. If the National Security State decided Eisenhower had become a problem, and was ready to back Richard Nixon in 1960, what better false sponsor than Allen Dulles for the elimination of President Eisenhower? Was Oswald (or another of several defector/re-defectors) originally intended as the designated patsy in an attempt on Eisenhower? No known assassination attempt, however, was run against Eisenhower, and the leaders of the US Establishment apparently decided to let American politics take its course, at least for the moment.

At the same time Oswald was simultaneously picking up his intelligence credits throughout the Far East and developing his persona as the Red Marine, someone inside the intelligence complex was preparing him to apply for an early discharge, a new passport, and a suspicious tour of Europe.

The Perfect Illegal?

Oswald had been equipped with the necessary tools to create a perfect espionage Illegal, an authentic intelligence Legend. He reportedly brought with him to Europe a real birth certificate and a real passport. According to one author with excellent intelligence connections, Oswald even had his Marine discharge papers in his possession when he was in the Soviet Union. Yet everything he was before and after his defection signaled a spy disaster, an inverted Illegal who may have been created by American intelligence, was courted by Soviet intelligence, and mistrusted by everyone. Was he, in fact, a false defector being dangled before the suspicious Soviets?

His curiously faulty pedigree moved both American and Soviet intelligence to keep him under careful watch (especially through his first class mail) without closing him down.[1]

Almost immediately following his reported defection, Oswald was suspected by the FBI to be part of an Illegals operation. But whose operation? And why? Was anyone aware of the bizarre legend being built out of Oswald's Marine history and his trip to Europe, specifically with a new passport? At least one person was: Lee Harvey Oswald (or someone acting in his name).

On March 19, 1962, the Office of Naval Intelligence (ONI) prophetically re-opened Oswald's file because "Oswald might seek updating of his discharge in the near future." Oswald indeed made precisely that request in a letter from Minsk, postmarked March 21st but dated March 22nd, just three days between the ONI prophecy and its fulfillment.

As Robert Sam Anson noted, Warren Commission critics assumed Oswald was presenting an argument concerning his defection, wondering where in Minsk he had found a copy of the US Code to support his pleas. That in itself clearly signaled Oswald was being assisted either by the American State Department, American intelligence, or some Soviet entity friendly to Oswald. But Anson's correction of those critics focused on forged passports as intelligence artifacts and the possibility of an Oswald imposter in the Soviet Union.

Though that correction was relevant, the Oswald citation of the US Code had another major intention. The former Marine had argued that the Corps did not have the right to change his discharge to "undesirable" because he was not guilty of violating Title 18, section 1544 of the Code. What did that section of Code state? "Whoever willfully and knowingly uses or attempts to use any passport designed for the use of another" has broken the law. Oswald (or someone prompting Oswald) was specifically denying his passport had been misused in the making of an Illegal. That specific postal act constituted Oswald's "smoking letter," proving to anyone who checked the U.S. Code that Lee Harvey Oswald (or his Intelligence handler) was denying knowledge of a false identity/Illegals action for which he had never been charged. The signal had been sent, and the game was on.

Was the Oswald Game a KGB-CIA Collaboration?

Barely hinted at in surviving documents and illustrated by non-assassination incidents, the KGB and the CIA (that is, co-operating elements of the ostensibly competing agencies) may have run a 'joint operation' using Oswald, Marina Oswald, or both. Both the CIA and KGB had institutional value invested in the Cold War. Other potential origins for the Oswald Game were the CIA's Office of Security, the Office of Naval Intelligence, or a still undiscovered American business organization supplying cover for Department of Defense "civilian" operatives.

A False Defector?

Closely associated with the False Identity/Illegals programs of U.S. intelligence was its False Defectors operation. One American company that certainly qualified as a cover for U.S. false defectors to the Soviet Union was the Rand Development Corporation (RDC).[2]

Sometime between 1973 and 1975, two JFK assassination researchers, Michael Canfield and Alan J. Weberman, attempted to locate the New York headquarters of Rand Development Corporation. They called RDC's listed Manhattan phone number and instead reached the mega-corporation Martin-Marietta. Though the researchers had discovered that RDC was the "crushed foam" division of the conglomerate, Martin-Marietta's response (at the identical number for RDC) was "no one at Martin-Marietta [had] ever heard of Rand." Queried at its main office in Rockville, Maryland, Martin-Marietta (with a "large aerospace division") responded that "Martin-Marietta has a lot of things going on but Rand Development isn't one of them."

The curious ambivalences continued: Canfield and Weberman visited the address given in the New York phone book and found Rand Development was not listed in the building's register. A doorman at the address told them he had worked his post for thirty-four years, but, he said, "there's never been a Rand Development corporation in this building...." The doorman added: "Maybe you want the Rand Corporation-it's right across the street at 405 Lexington Avenue." The RAND Corporation's name has often appeared as "Rand." The two researchers discovered that Rand Development Corporation was first listed in the Manhattan telephone book in

1958, the year the False Defector/False Identity/Illegals programs of U.S. intelligence were revving up their engines. Oddly enough, the RAND Corporation was not listed until 1960, after which (except when the Rand Development Corporation disappeared from the phone book in 1971-1972) the two companies were both represented.

Though RDC was reportedly established by the Rand family and the "RAND" in RAND Corporation was reportedly an acronymic contraction of "Research and Development" (R+AND+D), proximity (and obfuscation) may have been the original motivitation. The physical closeness of the two companies was matched by their Intelligence connections. The RAND Corporation was a well-known think tank with excellent elitist connections, and first established for the U.S. Air Force and financed by the CIA. Daniel Ellsberg copied the Pentagon Papers while employed at RAND. In the 1950s and 60s, Allen Dulles counted on "former" CIA agents and officers who went into businesses associated with U.S. Intelligence and Defense, including RAND, which was so closely tied to the Agency that crucial CIA documents were often circulated "through other governmental organizations and extra-governmental organizations such as the Rand Corporation...."

Rand *Development* also had close ties to U.S. intelligence: RDC worked on a number of CIA contracts; its president, Dr. Henry J. Rand, and George Bookbinder, another officer of the company, were veterans of the OSS. In the late 1950s, "CIA agent Christopher Bird was Rand Development's Washington representative." The brother organizations were not only linked (at least indirectly) by their CIA contracts and contacts; they were also connected through their aerospace programs and the U.S. Air Force. One of the divisions of Martin-Marietta (despite its denials the parent company of Rand Development Corporation) was a leader in aerospace research and development. RAND, "formed by the Air Force" and ostensibly a creature of the Pentagon, was most probably a black budget CIA operation. A Pentagon/CIA insider described how the CIA used the U.S. government's offer of aircraft (and the indispensable airfield) to eager second and third world nations in order to establish CIA bases.

RAND gave important briefings to the CIA and the Pentagon in advanced military technology, including a major presentation on ballistic missiles. As early as April 1959, RAND was reporting on the development of camera lenses that would ultimately be used in the CIA's U-2 program. RAND, organized by the Air Force and ultimately funded by the CIA, was, according to one source, initially financed by Sperry-Rand, an aerospace corporation "working closely with the United States Air Force." The vice-chairman of the Sperry-Rand Corporation (the "Rand" in "Sperry-Rand") was the father of the president of the Rand Development Corporation.

This connection between the two "Rands" was, at best, indirect. RAND and Rand Development were directly linked through their Air Force/aerospace interests, but Sperry-Rand (with its provocative Rand family connection) did not midwife the Rand Development Corporation: RDC's actual initial sponsor was Douglas Aircraft. Still, links between RAND, aerospace companies and intelligence were relevant: for example, two former officers from RAND moved to Northrop Corporation and, in 1961, hired Bill Savey, "a French lawyer in Paris ... who ran several [informational] agencies.... [Savey] had been an intelligence officer, used for several [unidentified] investigations into the US aerospace industry." Both RAND and Rand Development Corporation had been part of an intelligence/military matrix especially attractive to the US false-defector program.

Robert Edward Webster

Robert Edward Webster, a Navy veteran, was employed by the Rand Development Corporation as a "plastics technician." Webster took part in an RDC "trade exhibition" in Moscow and chose to stay in the Soviet Union rather than return to the United States with the rest of Rand Development's exhibition group. Why was RDC in Moscow? It had been among the earliest U.S. corporations "to negotiate with the Soviet Union for the purchase of [US] technical products and information."

After announcing his decision to remain in the Soviet Union, Webster met with Rand Development Corporation officers Henry Rand and George Bookbinder and the US Embassy's Second Secretary Richard Edward Snyder, a Foreign Service officer (characterized in the Warren Report as a former Department of State intelligence official). Snyder had admitted to being a CIA agent for eleven months in 1949-50; the evidence on Snyder's career (collected and analyzed by Philip H. Melanson) supports the suspicion that Foreign Service Officer Snyder was, in fact, a CIA agent under diplomatic cover from 1959 through 1961, while he was stationed at the US Embassy in Moscow.

Relying apparently on James Jesus Angleton, his major CIA source, Edward Epstein stated that Snyder was a CIA agent when he interacted with both Lee Harvey Oswald and Robert Webster. The House Select Committee on Assassinations (HSCA) was more than curious about Snyder's CIA connections. The committee had discovered that Snyder worked for the CIA as a university campus "spotter" in 1956 and 1957, assigned to gain access to unidentified others who might be going to the Soviet Union.

The HSCA apparently had not realized that US students may have been recruited by the Agency's campus "spotters" to attend certain overseas educational institutions targeted by the CIA for penetration or observation, including Albert Schweitzer College. Not many U.S. students would have been planning to go the Soviet Union at the height of the Cold War. Could CIA spotters have been operating at California's El Toro Naval Base or at the First Unitarian Church in Los Angeles in 1958 and 1959, looking for likely recruits? Whatever Snyder, Rand, and Bookbinder, the trio of "former" U.S. intelligence agents who met with Robert Webster, said to him about his defection has not been made available.

Declaring he would not come home to the U.S., Webster obtained a technician's job in the Soviet Union, lived with his "Soviet common-law wife" (probably a KGB agent), despite having an American spouse, and, like Oswald, eventually registered his disappointment with the Soviet Union and asked for repatriation. Robert Edward Webster and Lee Harvey Oswald were on the same timeline: less than two weeks before Oswald announced his defection, Webster announced his; and Webster left the Soviet Union two weeks before Oswald. A handful of apparent U.S. defectors with suspicious credentials were in the Soviet Union at the same time as Webster and Oswald. The pattern of defection was provocative.[3]

Richard Edward Snyder: CIA Operative

The temporal confluence of Snyder, Webster, and Oswald in the Soviet Union strongly suggested Richard Edward Snyder, ostensibly a State Department Foreign Service officer, had been assigned by the CIA to monitor an experiment in U.S. Intelligence 'dangles' and double agents that included Webster, Oswald, and at least one other U.S. defector, still unidentified, who wound up in Minsk. All of the reputed defectors with whom Snyder had been in touch seemed to display a curious fusion of False Identity, False Defector, and Illegals indicators. And though Snyder was the most important witness of record, Snyder listed his monitoring of the U-2 episode in the Soviet Union as his one post-graduate accomplishment. Curious.

Webster and Oswald had a few strange post-Soviet connections. After the Oswald family returned to Texas, Lee's wife Marina told a Russian friend that her husband had worked at a U.S. "exhibition" in Moscow and had then defected to the Soviet Union. Marina Oswald was speaking, not about Lee, but another former Navy man and defector, Robert Webster, whose Leningrad apartment building address (without his name) had been entered into Marina Oswald's address book. Could Marina have been mistaken about who her husband was?

Lee Oswald, Marina's husband of record, also had an interest in fellow defector Webster: in 1961, while making arrangements for his family to return to the U.S., Oswald had "asked about the fate of … [Robert] Webster who had come to the Soviet Union shortly before he did…." Webster's re-defection was much more dramatic than Oswald's: Webster was "debriefed in great depth by CIA staff working in conjunction with Air Force representatives." Recall the weave of military (including the Air Force) and intelligence (including the CIA) between RAND and Rand Development, the employer of Robert Webster, who was then "brought to Washington and interrogated for two weeks."[4]

No record of any US Intelligence de-briefing of Lee Harvey Oswald has ever been made available, though tantalizing circumstantial evidence has pointed to such an event. Certainly Oswald was as important as Webster. Were Robert Webster and Lee Harvey Oswald ever mistaken for each other? "[In fact,] Robert Webster … looked rather like Oswald," and a CIA psychiatrist who had run a de-briefing of a "young American just back from Russia" thought he recognized photos of Lee Harvey Oswald as that "young American." Or was it the other way around? If the intention was to muddy the waters and heighten anxiety about Lee Harvey Oswald, the bizarre histories of Oswald and Marina and the Webster-Oswald interface were completely successful.

Oswald's Missions

What might have been Oswald's intelligence role beyond being offered up to the Soviets in the U-2 incident? Realistically, he looked like the point person in a dual secret mission: first, assisting in the search for Soviet intelligence Illegals, including their mail drops and accommodation addresses; second, helping to trace the double-agent "mole" links between the CIA and the KGB through religious and educational institutions in the United States, Switzerland, and the Soviet Union. Hence his application to Schweitzer College

That double covert intention would explain why a deliberately faulty False-Identity (and False-Defector) operation was carried out by American counter-intelligence utilizing Lee Harvey Oswald. Whoever directed the Oswald Game was thoroughly knowledgeable about both the OSS and the CIA's manipulation of Quakers, Unitarians, Lutherans, Dutch Reformed clerics, and World Council of Churches officials as intelligence and espionage contacts, assets and informants. Those directors were also aware of the FBI's responsibility in tracking down and identifying Soviet Illegals and double agents.

From the moment Oswald registered to attend Schweitzer College, and without ever setting foot in Switzerland, he moved to the center of a complex and dangerous double-agent operation. With so many suspicious flaws and so many obvious connections to American intelligence, Oswald was a "legend" begging to be exposed. Yet he was allowed to go largely unchallenged by American intelligence, compromising both the FBI and the CIA as apparent pre-assassination accessories.[5]

Oswald was the perfect patsy to be used in any way his creators saw fit. In the deadliest of all games, Lee Harvey Oswald was finally framed in the murder of John F. Kennedy.

The Illegals and False Defectors projects of Soviet and American intelligence were mutual reciprocals of each other. The U.S. Intelligence Illegals operation was a covert psychological warfare (psyops) program, and Oswald's suspicious Marine severance, his passport application, his Albert Schweitzer College application, his projected European trip, and his Soviet defection all look like a deliberately defective and therefore provocative psyops-illegals action. The U.S. Intelligence False Defectors program was also a covert psyops program, and again Oswald's resumé was a perfect fit. What psyops genius could have created this "Oswald"?

The American Psych-War Master

C.D. Jackson was the archetypal American establishment operator, yet he was nearly invisible as he stood at the elbow of political power: "although one of the most significant figures in U.S. Cold War history, [he] has remained strangely unknown, his activities largely unrecognized." Thoroughly upper class, Jackson was a member of the board of directors of the Boston Symphony, the Lincoln Center for the Performing Arts, the Metropolitan Opera Association, and Project HOPE; he was one of fourteen trustees of the Carnegie Corporation (among the oldest and most powerful philanthropic organizations), and a top executive of the Luce publishing empire. Before attending Princeton, Jackson traveled extensively, was educated in Switzerland, and spoke both Italian and French with great fluency.[6]

In the fall of 1931, C.D. Jackson visited "his good friend" Henry R. Luce (then *Time's* editor-in-chief) and, despite lacking any media experience, persuaded Luce to hire him, becoming "assistant to the president." When Luce introduced *Life* magazine six years later, Jackson was appointed its general manager. By 1940, Luce was the acknowledged master of American popular media, in touch with his enormous reading audience and, at the same time, shaping that audience's consciousness. His chief associate in that operation was C.D. Jackson.

In 1940, C.D. Jackson's ability to read attitude and ideology was already firmly established, and he was appointed an administrative vice president of Time, Inc., a position emphasizing "troubleshooting and public relations." Whether in advertising or propaganda, Jackson had become the master of the word.

That same year, Luce and Jackson decided to support the British war effort and overcome any remaining American isolationism, preparing *Time/Life* audiences for entry into the European conflict. Jackson and Luce established the Council for Democracy, characterized by an admiring biographer as "a committee of liberal and moderate journalists and academics ... to promote democracy in American society."

The Council was one of Jackson's earliest public explorations of psychological warfare activity, opposing all groups, "Nazi, Fascist, Communist, [and] pacific" committed to keeping the U.S. out of the war. The Council's greatest success was "to highlight Jackson's talents as a propagandist." More striking in its psyops dimension was another Jackson formulation in 1941: promoting the establishment of an American "institute for democratic leadership." Speaking at Princeton University, Jackson argued that the proposal was "not in slavish imitation of the Nazi idea": though, in fact, it was a version of the Reich's "Fuehrer Schule." Young Americans would be trained for two years as "pro-consuls of democracy" in a program that sounded remarkably like behavior modification.

Jackson, with Christian Herter, who later succeeded Foster Dulles' as Secretary of State, sponsored the Foreign Service Education Foundation, ultimately folded into Johns Hopkins University's School for Advanced International Studies. C. D. Jackson was a major organizer of Freedom House in 1942, dedicated "to mobilize public opinion" against America's wartime ally, the Soviet Union. In a propaganda pamphlet, Freedom House president Herbert Ager characterized the Soviet Union as a "slave system."

The argument was, of course, C.D. Jackson's. He had helped plant psyops seeds in 1940-42, which blossomed three years later into Cold War flora. In 1942, Jackson was called upon by the U.S. State Department's Bureau of Economic Warfare to run a "mission to Turkey." At risk was a British/U.S. contract to mine and buy precious Turkish chromium. The West's contract was vulnerable, and German agents were moving in. Jackson used his linguistic, public relations (read "psyops"), and covert operations skills to defeat the German attempt at co-opting the Allies' chromium source. The people who helped run the Cold War's psychological warfare operations gained their training and experience as agents in the OSS branch called "Morale Operations" (MO).

These veterans subsequently taught psyops students in the CIA. The work of Morale Operations was "disinformation" and "black" propaganda: "subversive, its sources [were] disguised and its products disowned by ... [the U.S.] government if an operation backfired." Among the MO officers was the influential Edmund Taylor, a former CBS newsman who had composed the basic book on psychological warfare, *The Strategy of Terror.* Much of what C.D. Jackson practiced was apparently absorbed from Taylor's published record of his own experience of German psychological warfare and, as an OSS officer, his subsequent psyops theory.

In Washington, representatives of the State Department, the Office of War Information, the Army and Navy, and the "Morale Operations" Branch of the OSS had met weekly as members of the Psychological Warfare Board coordinating information and disinformation as propaganda instruments.

London Calling

In London, at Supreme Headquarters Allied Expeditionary Forces (SHAEF) commanded by General Dwight David Eisenhower, the blackest psyops propaganda campaign of World War II was successfully run in 1944-45. Though it often appeared as if the OSS, created in June 1942, operated independently of U.S./Allied military command, it was officially a service of the American Joint Chiefs of Staff. On October 27, 1943, the JCS commissioned "Morale Operations" (created on January 3, 1943) to perform "all forms of morale subversion." The "psychological operations" against Germany, run out of Eisenhower's SHAEF, were driven by his Psychological Warfare Division controlling and directing the OSS's Morale Operations Branch using "dirty," fictional, and deceptive materials, including faked documents, radio transmissions, newspapers (real and fraudulent), and other media and communication devices to achieve the Division's psyops goals. The director of the Office of War Information (OWI) was Elmer Davis, who had rejected several attempts to convert the OWI to psyops. Bill Donovan argued for an American "black" propaganda intelligence capability, but Davis had successfully kept OWI out of the field. Donovan, however, held on, and with the birth of the OSS, followed by the jousting in early 1942 for influence over the new agency through the "Joint Psychological War Committee," the end of 1942 saw the OSS supposedly under the aegis of the Joint Chiefs of Staff.

Yet when the (noncombat) psyops program in London at SHAEF was fully operational, the expert who organized and ran General

Eisenhower's Psychological Warfare Division at SHAEF was C.D. Jackson, an official of the OWI and veteran of the North Africa campaign. The United States had rejected Charles De Gaulle as the leader of its French anti-German allies. Instead, FDR and Ike supported the representatives of the Vichy French government in North Africa, headed by Admiral Darlan, "a notorious Nazi collaborator." Public opinion in Great Britain and the United States fulminated against Eisenhower's apparent collaboration with these Franco-Nazis: the entire anti-Fascist world was outraged.

Eisenhower stubbornly maintained that all political problems were secondary to military decisions. Why? As early as February 1941, President Roosevelt used an "undercover emissary" to find an alternative to de Gaulle and close an important economic accord. He succeeded. North Africa, controlled by Nazi collaborators, was freed of an Allied blockade and opened to American "economic penetration." Oil was on the mind of the United States. But Great Britain, supporting De Gaulle and his commitment to maintaining the French colonial empire (implicitly backing British imperialism), found America's pragmatic conduct in North Africa intolerable. So did the OWI. The situation was "untenable." President Roosevelt sent Milton Eisenhower, the General's brother and the associate director of the OWI, to North Africa with four "specific assignments" in December 1942.

Most important for C.D. Jackson and the future of American psyops, the OWI associate director was "to study the work of the OWI in psychological warfare and make changes if they were needed." Milton Eisenhower, a convinced psyops advocate, found that "drastic action" was necessary; he began a systematic exclusion of Gaullist sympathizers, replacing them with OWI agents who arrived in North Africa with Patton. But the transformation was not complete. In the spring of 1943, C.D. Jackson was called from his *Time* magazine post to serve the American government, having already established his major psyops credentials.

As an OWI officer, Jackson was deployed to North Africa to be in "full charge of OWI operations"; he became "deputy chief' of the Psychological Warfare Branch (PWB) in Eisenhower's Headquarters. He was the civilian director of the PWB, given a challenging task: "to integrate psychological warfare into America's overall military policy." Arriving in North Africa, Jackson met and ultimately bonded with General Robert Alexis McClure, who would become his psyops associate and close friend.

Gen. R.A. McClure: Military Psyops & C.D. Jackson

McClure had spent time in the Philippines and "in a variety of infantry and service-school assignments...." A lieutenant colonel, he was sent to London in 1941 as an assistant military attaché. McClure's previous military career (from 1915 through 1941) qualified him for special intelligence duties: he became a brigadier general, then the American Embassy's military attaché in London, with special duty as the "military attaché to nine European governments in exile." In September 1942, General Eisenhower designated McClure as his "chief of intelligence for the European theater of operations."

Then in December, 1942, McClure was given a new assignment: he was designated the chief of the (North African) Allied Headquarters Information and Censorship Section (INC), fusing "public relations, censorship, and psychological warfare." McClure drew a number of separate Army functions into a single military command. With C.D. Jackson controlling the "civilian" side of psyops in the North African operation, Eisenhower had his psych-war team in place. In the spring of 1943, Milton Eisenhower made an address, "Psychological Warfare," to the Kansas Bankers' Association in Topeka, stressing that war was not simply physical but "a struggle for men's minds." Truth, the OWI associate director had asserted, was on the side of the Allies, or at least C.D. Jackson's version of the truth.

Milton Eisenhower put his seal of approval on Jackson's reorganizational job, and by October 1943, C.D. Jackson had General Eisenhower's complete "acceptance of the Psychological Warfare Board as a regular part of Allied Headquarters." It was "one of the earliest [headquarters] units to achieve a truly allied organization." Despite a common perception that General Eisenhower thought psyops a tactical war weapon rather than strategic, the North African invasion (Operation Torch) and subsequent events dictated that psychological warfare would ultimately take precedence over conventional military tactics: first in North Africa, then in Sicily and Italy, and, especially after the war, in Germany.

When Eisenhower established his Psychological Warfare Division at SHAEF in London, General McClure became its military director, again complementing C.D. Jackson as PWD's civilian director. McClure, "commander of all U.S. Army psychological warfare activities during World War II and much of the Cold War, called C.D. Jackson and William Paley of CBS his "right and left hands" during World War II, crediting the pair with a profound grasp of psyops policy and practice. All the techniques of behavior modification, false identity, deep deception, and fictional event-staging that became key elements of American espionage legends, Illegals, and false defectors were developed and practiced successfully under C.D. Jackson in SHAEF's Psychological Warfare Division.

Jackson had shuffled easily from an operation ostensibly dedicated to straight media communication at OWI to "black psy-ops" (SHAEF's Psychological Warfare Division), and he would dance from information to disinformation and back again throughout his relatively short but intense career. In July 1946, McClure wrote to Jackson, who had already returned to *Time/Life*, Inc., as its Vice President. He summarized for Jackson what it really meant to be the military director of the Psychological Warfare Division: "We now control 37 newspapers, 6 radio stations, 314 theatres, 642 movies, 101 magazines, 237 book publishers, 7,384 book dealers and printers, and conduct about 15 public opinion surveys a month, as well as publish one newspaper with 1,500,000 circulation, 3 magazines, run the Associated Press of Germany (DANA), and operate 20 library centers...."

Just one year after the end of World War II, the American Army was running the largest psychological warfare operation in history, with C D. Jackson's friend and psyops associate in charge. Though Jackson had returned to the Luce publishing empire, he continued his propaganda work: Henry Luce designated Jackson the developer of the new international editions of both *Time* and *Life*, and Jackson pushed "capitalism and its bourgeois values by disseminating as many copies of his magazines as possible [into Eastern Europe] ... before the Iron Curtain slammed down."

Psychological warfare during the Truman years remained on the shadowy edges of intelligence gathering and covert operations, the term "psychological warfare" was itself characterized as "an almost elastic perversion of language designed to prevent acceptance and responsibility for its implications."

From 1946 through the next four years, Robert McClure argued for a regular place in the Army's instructional and in-the-field plans for psyops training and strategy, writing to both influential military personnel and civilian government figures, including C.D. Jackson. In early 1946, McClure wrote the War Department, arguing that America's "military psychological warfare capability" was absolutely indispensable and should be rebuilt. On December 12th, 1946, the U.S. National Intelligence Authority was sent a psychological warfare report from the Coordinating Committee of the State Department, War Department, and the Navy (ultimately replaced by the National Security Council) establishing psyops as central to American "national aims and military objectives." McClure's persistence paid off: he was sent from Germany to the United States in the summer of 1948 as "Chief, New York Field Office, Civil Affairs Division, reporting to Chief of Civil Affairs, the Pentagon ... responsible for supporting U.S. reorientation and reeducation efforts in the occupied countries of Germany, Austria, Japan, and Korea."

McClure used his German organizational structure in the New York Field Office, with "sections for press, periodicals, motion pictures, radio, theatre, music, arts, exhibits, libraries and book rights." Now the pair of psyops masters who had shared psychological warfare duties during the North African and European campaigns were working in New York, in charge of the two largest producers of white, grey, and black pro-America propaganda: on the civilian side, C.D. Jackson at Time, Inc.; on the military side, Robert McClure.

In May, 1948, George Kennan, the State Department's chief of the new Policy Planning Staff, signed on to pysops, and with NSC 10/2, drafted by Kennan, an unofficial CIA was created: the Office of Special Projects,which later became the Office of Policy Coordination.

One year earlier, the CIA'S General Counsel had raised concerns about the legality of running psyops, "morale operations" and "black propaganda" without obtaining Congressional approval. But Kennan, his associate Frank Wisner and Jackson himself had no scruples about avoiding legalisms or collaborating with Nazi criminals in the service of psyops.

Just as the OSS and the CIA used religious groups and individuals, the Agency by 1948 was using the "Non-Communist Left," including intellectuals, artists, and former Party members in the fight against Communism, often with their knowledge, sometimes not.

One of the Agency's leaders in its anti-Communist pysops action enlisted the help of psyops hero C.D. Jackson, who gave enthusiastic support and advice.

America's Psyops Wizard

C.D. Jackson was an archetypal anti-Communist; just a few years before he became Eisenhower's "Psychological Warfare Director," Jackson planted his forward flag: "The ingredient that is going to make us win is fanaticism. Not only must we be fanatics ourselves, but, we have to instill fanaticism for our cause in a lot of doubtful friends and even more doubtful on-the-fencers." In May 1949, Jackson joined Allen Dulles in the founding of the National Committee for a Free Europe and, despite a clause in the Committee's "founding statute" to the contrary, dedicated it to Cold War propaganda. The group became the mother of all psyops, with its founding fathers including Dulles, Jackson, Lucius Clay, Francis Spellman, John C. Hughes, and Dwight Eisenhower, a veritable Who's Who of CIA psychological warfare innovators and supporters. The initial idea for the committee has been attributed to Allen Dulles, who in turn went to Frank Wisner and his backlist of hundreds, possibly thousands, of "dispossessed Eastern European notables fidgeting throughout the West...." Dulles then took Wisner to Eisenhower, then president of Columbia University and a dedicated psychological warrior. With "Eisenhower's prestige, Dulles picked up backers from everywhere in the Establishment." In 1949, as if to celebrate his pre-eminence among Establishment Cold Warriors, C.D. Jackson became the publisher of Luce's *Fortune* magazine.

Jackson Spreads His Wings Across America

Psychological manipulation of individuals and groups drew upon discoveries in the 18th and 19th centuries in anatomy, mesmerism, hypnotism, counseling, studies in hysteria, rhetorical theory, psychoanalysis, advertising, behavior modification, and psychiatry. In the same periods the literary forms of irony, satire, libel, farce, and the less reputable verbal arts of slander and manufactured lies were applied. Most of these strategies were enlisted in the service of social class and political power. Counterattacks by alternative and adversarial outlets were still available, but by the time the U.S. establishment declared a pysops war against Communism, the American media had been taken over almost completely by the crusade against perceived revolutionary movements, led by the Jackson/Luce *Time* machine: "The ninety-eight boxes of (Jackson's] ... correspondence in the Eisenhower Library ... reveal that the starting points for many of his views on foreign policy and international business were the conferences in *Time* offices with Luce and his associates. In the hierarchy of American Centurions, CDJ and Luce directed the hydra-headed media team."

The National Committee for a Free Europe expected "the voluntary silence of powerful media personalities ... to cloak its true operations in secrecy." In fact, influential popular media officers were some of the earliest members of the NCFE: DeWitt Wallace of Readers' Digest, Henry Luce and in 1951 the man who would run Radio Free Europe, C.D. Jackson, chief editor of *Fortune* magazine. Key members of the NCFE admitted that the organization's American intelligence links, government funding, and fundamental overt political and covert intentions would never surface, as they were protected by the union of psyops, media, and money dedicated to U.S. Cold War goals.

The corporate propaganda complex developed still further. Enlisting key elements of the American business/government collaboration, C.D. Jackson established "Enterprise America," an open psyops conspiracy of large dimensions: "Enterprise America was [intended] to transform private domestic business ... into a cooperative effort involving international expansion, government support, and interchangeable business-government personnel practices." What had been an ad hoc crossover of commercial and government people for at least one hundred years became public policy: Jackson had patented D.C.'s revolving door.

At an open and non-conspiratorial level, C. D. Jackson's plan for a fusion of American government and corporate power was an exact match for his in-place psyops conspiracy: "Through ECA, the Point Four Program, and participation at all levels of the Washington bureaucracy, business would merge with the State, and Enterprise America would be affirmed. As publisher of the *Fortune*, CDJ was in the unique position of being able to promote a new partnership between business and government among the very people who had opposed all New Deal policies and ... continued to oppose ... [the] reconstruction program for devastated Europe."

Cromwell and Sullivan, John Foster Dulles at State and Allen Dulles found Jackson's business/government/culture combination extremely appealing. Jackson promoted Enterprise America in a series of appearances and writings in 1949 and 1950, melding "free enterprise," anti-Communism and advertising, in a simmering psyops soup. And Jackson left no doubt that General Dwight David Eisenhower was the hero who would lead this revolutionary American transformation.

Jackson & McClure in Psyops Control

Enterprise America scored its first important victory in 1950: Jackson, as America's top psyops expert, was called upon to present "a list of psychological warfare personnel suitable for employment in sensitive posts ... submitted to the Office of the Secretary of the Army...." The Jackson list complemented an earlier memorandum of June 1947 that General McClure had sent to then Army Chief of Staff Eisenhower, giving "a list of former PWD/SHAEF members... [McClure] recommended for forming a psychological warfare reserve." In 1950, Eisenhower, Bedell Smith, Lucius Clay, and C.D. Jackson began developing "America's political-warfare strategies." Though three of the four had held generalships and Jackson had worked directly for Eisenhower, the four became the earliest directors of the United States' civilian presence on the "experimental battlegrounds" of psychological warfare.

Concurrently, almost immediately after hostilities broke out between South and North Korea, Robert McClure was asked to report to Major General Charles Bolte, Army Staff G3, in order to assist in preparing certain "organizational steps" to implement using psychological warfare in "the Korean situation or ... a general war." A psychological warfare division was established in G3 with McClure as its director, then a "special staff office reporting directly to the Army Chief of Staff," and finally, on January 15, 1951, the Office of the Chief Psychological Warfare (OCPW), with Robert McClure holding the Office title, was established.[7]

McClure was certain that "unconventional warfare" was the natural partner of psyops, and argued for its complementary development within his office. The Pentagon accepted McClure's argument, and he established three divisions for the OCPW: "Psychological Warfare, Requirements, and Special operations." Prototype psyops

A Certain Arrogance

field units out of Fort Riley were developed and dispatched to Korea and Europe "in the event of war with the Soviet Union." Hence, whatever positive motives McClure had for serving his nation and the American military, his OCPW became a part of the escalating Cold War.

C.D. Jackson, Allen Dulles & the CIA

By 1951, C.D. Jackson had unfurled the flag of the Crusade for Freedom, a CIA front veiled behind the ever-popular theo-political twins, God & Country. Jackson's associate retired General Lucius Clay was appointed chairman. Behind the Crusade for Freedom, a carefully crafted "spontaneous movement" to rid the world of the Red menace, mostly by raising funds for Radio Free Europe, was the National Committee for a Free Europe (NCFE). In February 1951, C.D. Jackson became president of the National Committee. The entire NCFE structure had "CIA officers in [all its] key positions," placed there by Jackson's partner, Allen Dulles. In Germany, Theodore Shackley, the CIA Station Chief in Berlin, "coordinated [his Agency] activities with Jackson's Radio Free Europe...."

The Crusade for Freedom also supported movie star Ronald Reagan, "a leading spokesman and publicist," and laundered funds for "the International Refugee Committee" in New York, run by ex-OSS agent and future CIA director Bill Casey. The IRC "allegedly coordinated the ex-filtration of Nazis from Germany to the States" where they joined Jackson's anti-Communist psyops campaign. Jackson's NCFE became a major educational psyops force, using European exiles recruited by American intelligence for anti-Soviet research and lectures. The NCFE created the Free University in Exile, based in Strasbourg and incorporated in 1951 as an educational institution under New York State law. The entire NCFE operation was a psychological warfare triumph for C.D. Jackson as he lied to the world and, treasonously, to the American people.

All the open and covert "bizarre activities," were provocations justified in the name of freeing the Central European countries under the heel of the Soviet Union. And the crown jewel of Jackson's NCFE was Radio Free Europe. Both RFE and Radio Liberty continued to operate with full CIA direction and support through June 30, 1971. Double agents like Josef Swiatlo, the Polish defector used by Allen Dulles against

Noel Field, worked for C.D. Jackson at Radio Free Europe, and Swiatlo surfaced alarmingly (for the CIA) in the JFK assassination inquiry.

"[Most of] America's cultural Cold Warriors found themselves caught in a dangerous paradox," arguing for "art and politics" to be totally separate when the Nazi connections of certain artists and writers were examined, but happily fusing the two in pursuit of prominent left-wing writers, such as Bertholt Brecht, and many others who had the effrontery to despise Corporate Capitalism.

Paradoxes, however, never bothered Jackson. In the name of psyops he manipulated American artists and writers, European émigrés, assorted poets, novelists, and literary critics, movie producers, directors, writers, actors and whole orchestras. In the early 1950s, as president of National Committee for a Free Europe, and later, special advisor to Eisenhower on psychological warfare, C.D. Jackson was one of the most influential covert strategists in America.

Propaganda techniques developed during World War II were tested and perfected in early Cold War newsreels and documentaries made for the United States Information Agency (USIA) and probably American intelligence by *Hearst-Metrotone News* in New York, recorded in dozens of languages for worldwide distribution. C.D. Jackson was active in cinema psyops, directing the National Security Agency's Operations Coordinating Board, he was able to "oversee the activities of [both] the CIA ... [and] the USIA...." In May 1952, C.D. Jackson was a bright star in the psyops firmament.[8]

Since he was first called to North Africa during the war to transform Eisenhower's psyops program, Jackson had worked to integrate all of the American civilian efforts in psychological warfare.

An important Jackson moment came at the historic Princeton meeting in May 1952. Representatives congregated from the State Department, the CIA, the Psychological Strategy Board, the CIA'S Center for International Studies (officially housed at M.I.T.), and the National Committee for a Free Europe and Radio Free Europe (RFE). Jackson's super psyops conference was to make a major statement on policy, a "blueprint" for anti-Soviet action. Jackson, his NCFE, and his RFE pushed hard for their crucial psychological warfare goals. Also in May of 1952, Robert McClure convinced General J. Lawton Collins, Army Chief of Staff, to fuse "the training activities for psychological warfare and Special Forces."

The Psychological Warfare and Special Forces Center at Fort Bragg, North Carolina, was initiated with "two instructional divisions," one for psyops, the other for Special Forces. C. D. Jackson participated as an idea generator and speech writer in Eisenhower's run for the presidency, with his and Emmet Hughes' salaries paid for by the Luce media empire. After Eisenhower was victorious, the team really got down to fine-tuning the intelligence/psyops engine.

Jackson, Eisenhower, & the Control of Psyops

The transformation of the State Department and CIA at the dawn of the Eisenhower era were executed with the approval of a powerful American establishment that controlled American spy-craft: "The choice of John Foster Dulles [as Secretary of State] was looked upon as a double plus by the intelligence community leaders ... Dulles ... [had] ties to military intelligence [that] went back to before World War I ... [as] an active member of the intelligence subculture fraternity, aiding an operation here and there with his legal and business connections as well as being himself a producer and consumer of intelligence information."

The development of psychological warfare, the designation of Allen Dulles as CIA Director, the reorganization of Eisenhower's National Security Council, and, finally, the actual control of the CIA were all placed in the hands of Robert Cutler, Brigadier General (ret.). His establishment credentials included Harvard College and Harvard Law School degrees, service in the American Expeditionary Force, 1917-19, a prestigious Massachusetts law practice, World War II military experience with significant "procurement" duties, and executive broadcasting experience. He was Truman's secretary of the Army, Atomic Energy Commission chairman (overseer of the H-bomb project), the Psychological Strategy Board's initial director, and president and director of Boston's prestigious Old Colony Trust Company Bank, which he left only when Eisenhower called him to presidential service.

As president-elect, Eisenhower informed the executive secretary of the NSC that, "Robert Cutler would be his administrative assistant with special responsibilities for the NSC." Cutler exhaustively reviewed the history and performance of the NSC and carefully codified its structure and operation, making sure that Council practice from 1947 through 1953 and the National Security Act of 1947 became the fused frame of future NSC actions and operations.

A few important modifications made C.D. Jackson, who was already Eisenhower's Cold War/psyops chief officer, a key facilitator of major CIA covert operations. Cutler's carefully prepared NSC reforms allowed Jackson to move in and out of crucial advisory capacities and other roles in the State Department, the NSC, the CIA, and the White House while simultaneously monitoring the power structure's disinformation and propaganda media operations, specifically at Time, Inc.

On March 17, 1953, Eisenhower accepted Cutler's report on the NSC and the CIA. Cutler (and probably Jackson) had anticipated the problem of controlling American psyops espionage activity. Cutler recommended that the director of the Psychological Strategy Board be dropped as an "observer" to the National Security Council and "the special assistant to the president for Cold War Planning ... [become] an advisor to the council...." The accepted recommendation seemed to eliminate psyops representation on the NSC, but it actually elevated C.D. Jackson to the White House's ad hoc director of national psychological warfare.

Almost immediately after taking over as Eisenhower's special assistant for National Security Affairs, Cutler perceived still more "problems" of NSC co-ordination. Relying on Cutler's judgment, On January 24, 1953, Eisenhower established the President's Committee on International Information Activities: its commission was (take a deep breath) "to make a survey and evaluation of the international information policies and activities of the executive branch and the policies and activities related thereto, with particular reference to the international relations and national security of the United States."

What kind of information (or disinformation)? Who would monitor and produce that information? The chairman of the committee was William H. Jackson (former deputy chief of the CIA). Many committees and commissions were identified by their chairperson's name, so the committee was known as the 'Jackson Committee.' Its seven members were all dedicated supporters of American intelligence, especially covert operations and psychological warfare, and the inclusion of Robert Cutler, Gordon Gray, and C.D. Jackson made its recommendations predictable.

In fact, Jackson's psyops influence during the group's deliberations resulted in the "Jackson Committee" often being attributed to

C.D. Jackson, who frequently wore several symbolic identification badges at Cold War intelligence gatherings, a technique he developed that blurred his actual role. At Jackson Committee meetings, for example, he "officially ... represented the State Department ... while informally he represented the president." John Foster Dulles would have been surprised that Jackson represented any part of the Secretary of State's Cold War strategy.

The Committee recommended that the NSC's Psychological Strategy Board, an offspring of Gordon Gray, be eliminated. Yet C.D. Jackson gained more psyops power because of that excision. How could less become more? The April 1951 NSC modifications established an important sub-committee, the Psychological Strategy Board (PSB). The specific revision, as it recognized the close fit between covert actions and psychological warfare operations, charged the PSB with examining all existing and proposed NSC/CIA covert projects and establishing their "desirability and feasibility."

Why, then, would Gordon Gray, the progenitor of the Psychological Strategy Board, vote for its abolition? The "state," "board," or "panel" that made the covert machinery run for the NSC, placed between it and the Psychological Strategy Board, rendered the effective control and direction of psyops cumbersome. The Jackson Committee had a crucial argument for eliminating the Psychological Strategy Board: according to the panel (led by Gordon Gray, Robert Cutler, and C.D. Jackson), "there is a 'psychological' aspect or implication to every diplomatic, economic, or military policy and action."

Every policy decision and every overt or covert operation had a psyops "aspect or implication." Therefore, in place of the PSB, the Jackson panel recommended that an "Operations Coordinating Board" (OCB) be established "to coordinate the detailed implementation of detailed operational plans developed ... to carry out approved NSC policies." Note the important redundancy: "detailed." The OCB had only five members: the undersecretary of state (the OCB's chair) ; the deputy Secretary of Defense; the director of the Foreign Operations Administration; the Director of the CIA; and "a representative of the president to be designated by the president."

Only two participants had any real American intelligence power, and both were dedicated psyops supporters: Allen Dulles, the Director of the CIA, and the president's "representative," C.D. Jackson. When the OCB was established, "the president designated his special assistant for Cold War Planning to serve as ... [Eisenhower's] representative on the OCB." Therefore, critical covert intelligence operations *and* psychological warfare operations were under the direct influence of C.D. Jackson for the first few years of the Eisenhower administration.

Even before the (William) Jackson Committee report was presented to the president, C.D. Jackson was running "psychological warfare operations" for the White House, according to Jackson himself, "constantly informing and persuading the members of the Government as to their Cold War responsibilities." When the Jackson Committee finally submitted its report to Eisenhower, the president was disturbed: what about the crucial "psychological factor"? Jackson gave the president his assurance that inside the Operations Coordinating Board (the OCB) was now a smaller "think tank" monitoring the "psychological dynamics" of all covert actions. This "think tank" was, in fact, the "Planning Board" (later called by a series of names and number combinations) inside the OCB, and dominated, of course, by C.D. Jackson.

C.D. Jackson & the Korean Brainwashing Problem

As Eisenhower's pysops chief, Jackson also had to deal with the even darker side of psychological warfare. During the "Korean Conflict," captured American servicemen had been ill-prepared for hostile interrogation and sometimes successful behavior modification: "Government officials had long known of the deplorable behavior of American POWS, but had worked fastidiously to conceal the facts from a wider audience."

On orders from C.D. Jackson, "indoctrinated Korean prisoners" (returned U.S. POWs who had been "brainwashed") were to be "kept in one place," segregated and under guard, until Jackson (or his designated psychological warfare spokesperson) could manufacture a cover story. What else was done with those segregated veterans may be an even more important story.

Many of the Korean War veterans who were not sequestered by Jackson were strongly suspected by the CIA of having been subjected to "mind control." Jackson was everywhere that psyops was a necessity: he "attended meetings of the Cabinet, the National Security Council, the Council on Foreign Economic Policy, and the ... Operations Coordinating Board ... to administer political and economic warfare ... and oversee the activities of the CIA, the USIA, and all Cabinet departments."

C. D. Jackson & the Cold War Psyops Fronts

When tensions mounted in the Cold War, President Eisenhower would call together a small, inner circle of psyops advisors: Allen Dulles, John Foster Dulles, and C.D. Jackson. Throughout his career, Jackson was supremely opportunistic, a function of his creative/situational responses to immediate political stimuli. Significantly, C.D. Jackson played a major part in the Eisenhower administration's response to Stalin's death in March 1953, developing it into a media-wide propaganda action that included Eisenhower's "Chance for Peace" speech on April 16, 1953.

In that same year, one of Jackson's OPC psyops consultants James Burnham estimated that more than one billion dollars a year was being allocated to "a wide variety of [unidentified] psychological warfare projects...." Having been given control of US covert operations, the National Security Council's 54/12 committee, the "inner circle" of power in the OCB (its five members including Allen Dulles and C.D. Jackson) made the decision in early August 1953, to overthrow the legal government of Guatemala, headed by Jacobo Arbenz. On September 4, 1953, the Eisenhower administration's in-house covert operations experts combined with the president's top psyops advisors led by C.D. Jackson to plan and execute the destruction of the Arbenz government.

Assembling material from Army G2 files and the FBI, CIA and State Department, C.D. Jackson's Special Staff at the OCB prepared a plan deliberately and falsely blackening President Arbenz's character and reputation; the material was then sent "to appropriate individuals throughout the Americas." A series of propaganda and terrorist actions followed, including unprecedented "search and seizure" of ships bound for Guatemala. "According to all U.S. conventions, the policy represented terrorism, illegal and belligerent action [that] ... was historically considered an act of war." The United States, with the president in full agreement, had decided to run a "secret" war against Guatemala, using black propaganda, bombers flown out of Honduras and Nicaragua dropping explosives on defenseless Guatemalan towns, fighter planes that strafed passenger trains and villages, and weapons delivered by airlift that armed the CIA-backed anti-Arbenz military forces. "The invasion of Guatemala was political warfare at its most detailed."

Running the operation was the US Government's "Guatemalan Group" consisting of representatives from the Defense Department, the USIA, and the CIA. Characterized as Eisenhower's "psych-war committee," the group enlisted the major talents of David Atlee Phillips and E. Howard Hunt. Phillips "had learned black propaganda techniques from a CIA specialist who had been in the Morale Operations branch of the OSS."

Phillips and Hunt were both assigned as psyops teachers of anti-Arbenz recruits trained in Miami. Both were cited as key psychological warfare agents by CIA Deputy Director Richard Bissell in his in-house review of the "Cuban Operation" (including the Bay of Pigs invasion). Phillips had at least an indirect link to C.D. Jackson through PBSUCCESS, the Agency's code name for covert psyops action monitored by C.D. Jackson's "Guatemalan group," but E. Howard Hunt worked directly as a writer and war correspondent for *Life* magazine in 1943, the same year he joined the OSS, ultimately becoming a close friend and working associate of Allen Dulles.

Later in 1943, C.D. Jackson left *Life* to join OWI and, eventually, Eisenhower in North Africa, running the General's psychological warfare program. With C.D. Jackson an early and continuing major force in the psyops dimensions of the plot against Arbenz, the ugly enterprise eventually succeeded, figuring prominently in the mistaken expectation of a similar coup against Fidel Castro.[9] The Bay of Pigs fiasco was the eventual result of this hubris.[10]

In 1953, Robert McClure was sent to Iran to head the U.S. Military Mission there, working closely with the Shah and "Iranian senior military." It was McClure's last intelligence assignment. Promoted to major general, McClure retired. Four years later, on his way to San Clemente, California, McClure became very ill, finally succumbing to a fatal heart attack at Fort Huachuca, Arizona, on January 1, 1957.

C.D. Jackson & the Control of Nuclear War

While McClure was in Iran, his friend C.D. Jackson was inventing one psyops action after another for the president.

219

On December 8, 1953, Eisenhower presented his historic Atoms for Peace speech to the General Assembly of the United Nations. The address has been almost universally accepted as a well-meant attempt to separate peaceful from military applications of nuclear energy. Virtually all discussions of the speech have argued for its basically positive thrust.

The truth emerged when the history of American nuclear policy during the Eisenhower administration was examined, and Martin J. Medhurst, the most reliable analyst of both the speech and the subsequent psyops campaign, summarized that truth: "Dwight Eisenhower's Atoms for Peace program, far from being idealistic, propaganda for the sake of propaganda, or an inconsistent and contradictory part of arms control policy, was, instead, a carefully designed and highly successful component of the basic defense and foreign policy stance of the Eisenhower administration. As part of a coordinated campaign to achieve national security goals, Atoms for Peace can be seen as the rhetorical counterpart to the New Look doctrine. By diverting audience attention, paving the way for the nuclearization of NATO forces, and serving as the rationale for export of nuclear technologies, Atoms for Peace was a central component of the administration's national security strategy."

The strategist who conceived that policy and wrote the substance of Eisenhower's speech was, once again, C.D. Jackson, chief propagandist and coordinator of Eisenhower's international nuclear strategy. Eisenhower's address, according to rhetorical analyst Medhurst, "marked the public commencement of a persuasive campaign the dimensions of which stagger the imagination." Medhurst persuasively analyzed the address and matched it to the resulting political and propaganda history of the Eisenhower administration: "Planned at the highest levels of government, shrouded in secrecy, aided by the military-industrial complex, and executed over the course of two decades," the speech was fashioned, written, and delivered in order to strike a psyops Cold War blow to cripple the Soviet Union; not as a legitimate disarmament proposal.

The entire campaign was chalk-boarded and successfully coached by C.D. Jackson. He supplied advance copies of the Eisenhower speech to *Newsweek*, the *New York Herald Tribune*, and, of course, *Time*. It was C.D. Jackson, in his capacity as a key intelligence psyops agent who directed the Operations Coordinating Board, the Voice of America, Radio Free Europe, the CIA, and other covert/cover venues in promoting his rhetorical and psychological "Atoms for Peace" strategy, as if the speech were "a serious peace proposal." As we have seen, two world leaders perceived as threatening to Eisenhower's nuclear policies became targets of American intelligence actions: Albert Schweitzer in Gabon and Patrice Lumumba of the Congo.

In January 1954, Jackson left his government psyops machinery in place and returned to the Luce media empire.[11] Several close friends in covert operations and psychological warfare followed C.D. as presidential representatives, including Jackson's immediate replacement, Nelson Rockefeller. Regardless of who held the position as White House psyops chief, C.D. Jackson had his hand on the throttle of American psychological warfare from 1954 through 1959, so frequently shuttling between his positions with Luce and Eisenhower's administration that Jackson's staff at *Time* created a party game out of his "send-offs and welcomes."

C.D. Jackson & the Elite's Psyops Programs

Later in 1954, Jackson wrote in support of Robert A. McClure, commander of the American Military Mission in Iran after the CIA coup. Analysts for the Agency regularly sent their reports to both the CIA and C.D. Jackson. He was able to bring his psychological warfare perspective to the United Nations in 1954 as the American delegate to the UN's Trusteeship Committee, but it was a troubling time as he tried to make political sense of the United States' ambiguous attitude toward colonialism...." Jackson felt "the Western World," outnumbered by "the swirling mass of emotionally Supercharged Africans and Asians and Arabs," would discover that this "much-needed world forum" would finally be witness to "putting white prestige on the skids." Notably absent from Jackson's concern for "white prestige" was any sense of either color-free justice or the truth. Jackson was a key member of the World Trade Foundation that "intensified the movement to globalize America's international business interests."

In 1953, C.D. Jackson became the acknowledged founder of the Bilderberg group in the United States, with President Eisenhower still an enthusiastic working partner of the new political and economic establishment. Jackson himself attended every Bilderberg meeting until he died in 1964. With the American branch of the Bilderberg Conference established, Jackson moved to develop an "economic expansion" project fusing potent symbols with powerful trade and commerce plans: images and actions were to be combined to "counter the lure of communism."

That project was established at the Princeton Conference for a World Economic Plan, held on May 15 and 16, 1954. Jackson shared his global vision with Allen Dulles. Jackson's careful selection of images and words, embodied in the Princeton Conference recommendations, "became the basis for ... a new world economic policy for the United States. Both the language and the actions of the trans-national corporations were created by the master of American psyops. Despite C.D. Jackson's "crisis-mongering," President Eisenhower realized how important propaganda was to the success of his "Foreign Economic Policy Battle plan." The Advertising Council of America was enlisted, a "private" Committee on Foreign Trade, Inc., was established, and through that front group Time, Inc., again commanded by Henry Luce and C.D. Jackson, "contributed expansively to [Eisenhower's] ... success."

By 1956, Eisenhower had captured significant support with his vigorous and creative word choice; Paul Hoffman praised the president, noting that 'Semantics are important....'" C.D. Jackson must have beamed. If a Third World War were to happen, President Eisenhower had reportedly confided to C.D. Jackson that it would be won by American psychological operations.[12]

Jackson continued to be called on by the president to brainstorm new intelligence ideas and operations. But those operations were frequently corrupt, and as a key agent of the US Power-elite C.D. Jackson was deeply involved in manipulating American social, educational, and cultural institutions. Just before Eisenhower called on him again to serve as the president's Cold War/psyops expert, Jackson attended a crucial academic meeting whose agenda was damage control from seven years of CIA collaboration.

Initiated in 1950, Project Troy, surely named for the famous Trojan Horse subterfuge, had collected a group of top-drawer Harvard faculty. The project ultimately morphed into the Center for International Studies (CENIS), responsible for key analyses of the Soviet Union, China, and nuclear weapons. Because Harvard banned on-campus classified research, Troy/CENIS had to meet at MIT.

The original Cambridge group had been given a typical C.D. Jackson psyops directive to solve a "specific [apparently technical] problem": How could the CIA overcome Soviet jamming of the CIA'S propaganda broadcasts to Eastern Europe? "Within one year, the Agency spent $300,000 so that CENIS could "research world-wide political, economic and social change ... in the interest of the entire intelligence community." Seven years after Troy/CENIS tackled its initial problem, a CENIS review board met to examine the difficult question of "academic integrity."

Despite the fundamental reality that the Cambridge faculty had been bought by the CIA, the reviewers worried over "corrosion" of the academic "channel," as if individual faculty members were somehow like mental tributaries through which classified analysis flowed into the main Agency pipeline. McGeorge Bundy, an intimate friend of the CIA who chaired the CENIS review, immediately saw the value of the metaphor. As he put it, "The channel is more important than that a lot of water should be running through it." There could be no doubt as to whose imagery had captured the flawed ethic of the Cambridge operation. Attendee C. D. Jackson observed that American intelligence "work has got to be done...." And, he added, "I have not noticed any visible corrosion." So much for the integrity of Harvard Yard's academic plumbing.

The program continued, and the initial intrusion of the CIA was almost immediately matched by the corruption of Harvard's Center for International Affairs, through at least 1957. In the summer of 1955, Nelson Rockefeller called a conference on "the psychological aspects of U.S. strategy" with key psyops stars from the Operations Research Office, Johns Hopkins University, including its School of Advanced International studies; the U.S. Military Academy; the director of CENIS, housed at M.I.T.; the director of the Council on Foreign Relations' "studies"; American air intelligence; the New England Electric System; and others, including Henry Kissinger, at the time hanging his hat at Harvard. The top U.S. psychological warfare veteran in attendance was, of course, C.D. Jackson.

Whatever moral rant John Foster Dulles was directing at that moment against Russia and China, Jackson and associates were running the American psyops show. On May 7, 1956, Jackson again met a powerhouse of "psych-war" people, including DeWitt C. Poole, A.A. Berle, Tom Braden, and Nelson Rockefeller, who were attempting to re-energize the OCB as Eisenhower was applying a brake to the government's psychological warfare engine. Whenever possible, psyops agents had been active outside the White House and the State Department.

Through 1955-56, Allen Dulles, Frank Wisner, the CIA, C.D. Jackson and his Radio Free Europe/Radio Liberty had cooperatively stirred the bubbling European pot of anti-Soviet revolution, hoping for American establishment and intelligence support. But President Eisenhower distanced himself from the more ferocious of the Cold War/psyops crusaders; the worst of a dangerous Cold War period was coming to a close, and C.D. Jackson apparently lost some power and influence. Yet Jackson still remained a key figure in the administration's "rollback programs, commanding the Operations Coordinating Board.

American covert actions had supported "fifty surviving garrisons of Eastern European paramilitaries [including old hands of the notorious General Gehlen] hanging on in Germany...." The "Hotspur" Colonel Philip Corso, C.D. Jackson's OCB agent, was given the job of "salvaging" and "reactivating" the rollback battalions. But C.D. Jackson was called to a meeting with the Secretary of Defense and the Secretary of State. Jackson's provocation, that might have led either to a major Soviet retreat or the opening of World War III, never went beyond the planning stage.

Eisenhower now had serious doubts about Foster Dulles' excessive anti-Communist denunciations, a rhetoric that was increasingly out of step with Eisenhower's enthusiasm for more subtle psychological warfare. The president met with the Secretary of State in 1957, asking Dulles about bringing in C.D. Jackson as Eisenhower's "advisor on Cold War matters." Dulles responded with an immediate and absolute "No": he saw clearly how much of a policy rival Jackson would be if he sat at a desk in the White House. But the president was still searching for a breakthrough, an alternative to Cold War confrontation.

In January 1958, Eisenhower contacted Jackson, asking him to meet with Foster Dulles and propose that Dulles become "Special Assistant and Advisor to the President" (a title conferring on its holder no foreign policy power), while Jackson would replace Dulles as Secretary of State.

C.D.'s Waning Power

After the Jackson-Dulles meeting, the psyops master wrote to the president, apparently hoping that his positive spin on the discussion with Dulles might move Eisenhower to effect what the meeting had not brought about. But Eisenhower's response was to offer Jackson the position of Under Secretary of State, running the nation's "Cold War effort."

Though it may have appeared that Jackson did not wish to serve under Dulles, only to be frustrated in his endeavors, the more likely sticking point was Eisenhower's desire for Jackson's psyops genius in support of "total" disarmament. For Jackson, that was completely unacceptable: a president who rejected "liberation," "intervention," and "political warfare" was someone for whom C.D. Jackson could not work.

One month later, in February 1958, Eisenhower proposed that ten thousand young Russians be invited to study in the United States on one-year government scholarships. The president's primary intent was to score a propaganda coup, though he was also "a great believer in promoting international understanding through [the] exchange of students...." Both Foster Dulles and the State Department argued vigorously against the idea, and Eisenhower eventually let the proposal quietly expire. Still, some Soviet students did arrive in 1958, including Soviet Fulbright scholar (and KGB agent) Oleg Kalugin, who ultimately became a master psyops warrior for Soviet intelligence.[13]

C.D. Jackson & the International Youth Movements

Reciprocally, C.D. Jackson was a prime mover in psyops actions targeting students visiting Europe in the late 1950s. Major student/youth festivals held in the Soviet Union and Eastern Europe were perceived by the CIA as significant Communist propaganda successes. The Soviets had funded, for example, the World Federation of Democratic Youth. A World Youth Festival was planned for Vienna in 1959, the first such event to be held in the West. C.D. Jackson conferred with CIA officer Cord Meyer and U.S. Establishment leader John J. McCloy, and the three organized a covertly funded "alternative" youth delegation to represent the United States.[14]

Jackson and Meyer hired the young Gloria Steinem as their Vienna Festival agent, who then established a CIA front in Cambridge, Massachusetts, eventually named the Independent Research Service. Steinem was able to get tax-exempt status for her group, and C.D. Jackson placed her in touch with several U.S. companies that provided her with some funding. Most of the operational cash, however, came from the Agency through Jackson, tucked inside a "special account."

The Free Europe Committee (earlier the Committee for a Free Europe) assisted the operation, setting up a CIA-financed Brass Plate operation called the Publications Development Corporation, with Samuel S. Walker, Jr. as its president. Walker, vice-president of the Free Europe Committee and a close associate of C.D. Jackson, functioned as Gloria Steinem's control in the CIA'S psyops action in Vienna: "Steinem ended up working closely with Samuel S. Walker, Jr." Steinem remained with the Independent Research Service, receiving CIA funds through 1962. Though she insisted the CIA never asked her to report on the students whom she encountered, she voluntarily wrote at least one extended political analysis of students. She submitted the report to C.D. Jackson, who actively planned and supported CIA penetration of youth and student groups traveling to Europe, including Finland, from 1959 through 1962.[15]

CIA funding also supported the World Assembly of Youth. The CIA/psyops involvement in student and youth organizations, especially those with religious affiliation, may be one of U.S. Intelligence's last important secrets. Though the Agency's success in controlling "the senior leadership of ... religious groups and even student organizations" has been recognized, the documentation is tantalizing but thin. Because C.D. Jackson's papers have been carefully sanitized, it may be some time before his complete psyops record in the manipulation of educational institutions is exposed.

Foster Dulles, seriously ill, went on leave in late February 1959. In mid-April, the dying Dulles resigned as Secretary of State. With the waning of Dulles' power, the president had begun making pacific moves in the face of Cold War antagonism generated by Time, Inc. In March 1959, the Berlin Crisis energized C.D. Jackson, who began to pound his war drum. But the president rejected the belligerent hysteria of America's conservative media.

In 1958, Jackson left Eisenhower's administration and returned to Time, Inc., where Luce and company "shifted allegiance and began to promote John F. Kennedy for the presidency ... Jackson and Luce now imaged Eisenhower as a "do-nothing president" who was worse than no president at all. After John Foster Dulles died on May 24, 1959, C.D. Jackson was one of his pall-bearers: certainly a heavy burden for the psyops master to have carried.

C.D.'s Sunset Years

Two months later, in July 1959, C.D. made his final attempt to reverse the Eisenhower administration's declining interest in psyops. Jackson convinced the White House staff to hold a so-called "stag party" for him attended by establishment and government luminaries. But the administration remained "profoundly hostile" to reenergizing psyops. On September 11, 1959, Jackson wrote to the one party attendee in sympathy with his psychological warfare argument: Vice President Richard Nixon. The word master, always alert to a psyops opportunity and mindful of America's probable political future, wrote to Nixon: "It is no exaggeration ... that with the possible exception of Allen Dulles, you [Richard Nixon] have a more experienced 'feel' for these [psyops] matters than any [other person] in the Government...."

While Eisenhower made overt moves toward peace in 1959 and 1960, C.D. Jackson still burned with anti-Communist fever, deeply disturbed that the president was apparently taking no aggressive actions in crucial hot-spots like Africa and Cuba. Ike appointed a propaganda committee on February 17, 1960, including C.D. Jackson, but the psych-sorcerer was mostly out of the inner White House loop, and Luce and Jackson were apparently not privy to the actual increase in the CIA'S covert operations in 1960. As Eisenhower moved to lessen international tension, the entire *Time/Life/ Fortune* media empire persistently and often viciously attacked the president, characterizing him as "tired" and "absurd."

On April 24, 1960, Jackson was appointed *Life* magazine publisher. On May 14, President Eisenhower called upon C.D. Jackson and his psyops magic for the last time in support of a government program. Faced with budget cut proposals that the president was certain would cripple American foreign policy and trade, Eisenhower urged Jackson to "suggest [again] a crusade for our country." But the engine of psychological warfare had, at least for a while, run out of fuel.

On January 17, 1961, Dwight David Eisenhower delivered his Farewell Address. His parting shot at the "military-industrial complex" he had helped to create was somewhat admirable, but it was too little, too late. Even as he spoke, the CIA and its psychological warfare agents cast giant shadows across his desk. One point in particular would have riled Allen Dulles and C.D. Jackson. Calling attention to the contemporary "conjunction of an immense military establishment and a large arms industry" in America, Eisenhower characterized that fusion as having a "total influence-economic, political, even spiritual" that was being felt at every level of American society.

According to Drew Pearson, "*Life* magazine [was] always pulling chestnuts out of the fire for the CIA," citing C.D. Jackson as a key chestnut-puller. Jackson has often been slighted in the annals of 20th century propaganda and psychological warfare, and he may have considered that a compliment. His major role in the creation of a rhetorical "reality," the "myth in media and public discourse" of the unquestionable righteousness of American foreign policy, coupled with the Cold War Bogeyman, is overwhelmingly evident.

Jackson & Lee Oswald: Degrees of Separation

One major link between the worlds of C.D. Jackson and Lee Harvey Oswald has remained unexplored. After two years in the USSR, Oswald wished to return to the United States with his new Russian wife. In January 1962, extremely impatient with the slow pace of his attempted exit from the Soviet Union, Oswald reportedly wrote two letters to the International Rescue Committee (IRC) "explaining his situation and requesting that it contact the American Embassy in Moscow in order to contribute financial assistance for his trip home."

The earlier version of the IRC, the Emergency Rescue Committee, was an OSS-supported operation, and in 1947 the IRC) was CIA-funded, engaging in, for example, ex-filtrating Nazis out of Europe and into the United States. A dozen documents relating to the International Rescue Committee are in the Warren Commission's records: one has immediate relevance. Dated May 1, 1964, a letter from the program director of the IRC to J. Lee Rankin, Warren Commission Special Council, described the Committee as "strongly anti-Communist" and gave details of the IRC's interaction with Lee Harvey Oswald. The story began in the Soviet Union.

In early January 1962, Oswald was attempting to leave the Soviet Union. Someone had given Lee information about the IRC and its supportive functions, and he had even been supplied with the committee's Manhattan address on Park Avenue. Oswald then sent a letter to his mother, dated January 2, 1962, urging her to contact the Red Cross in Vernon, Texas, so that it might intercede with (in Oswald's words) "a organization called 'International rescue committee' or any organizations which aids persons from abroad get settled.

The International Rescue Committee became the single-minded Mrs. Oswald's sole target. She contacted the State Department and asked for the address of the IRC. In a telegram Allyn Donaldson at State immediately responded on January 12, 1962. "Address [of] International Rescue Committee is 251 Park Avenue South, New York City." Marguerite then called on Helen Harwell, Executive Secretary of the Vernon, Texas, Red Cross, as Lee had directed. According to Oswald's mother, the contact was not a happy one.

Harwell refused to open the Red Cross office until Mrs. Oswald thoroughly badgered her. Then, in the Vernon office, the Red Cross officer proceeded to argue from a determined anti-Soviet position against assisting Lee Harvey Oswald. Marguerite would have none of that: Harwell and the Red Cross were there, she said, to help people in need: especially her son and his family. In the second week of January 1962, the Special Consular Service of the U.S. State Department telephoned the IRC and recommended they assist Oswald and his family in leaving the Soviet Union.

Given the International Rescue Committee's long history of close co-operation with the CIA, the Consular Service call must have sounded like a marching order. Less than two weeks later, the IRC received a missive dated January 14, 1962, from Mrs. Harwell in Vernon, Texas. According to the IRC, two letters were attached. The first was from Consul Norbury in the American Embassy in Moscow, apparently an iteration of the State Department's telephone pressure on the IRC to assist Oswald; the second letter was "addressed to the International Rescue Committee … and ostensibly written by Oswald…." The U.S. Embassy letter included a handwritten note: "Mrs. Helen Harwell, Executive Secretary, American Red Cross."

The IRC officer was apparently quite skittish: he compared the reputed Oswald letter with the Embassy letter and concluded that, "To a layman's eye it would appear that both copies were typed on the same typewriter." Sylvia Meagher asked: "Was it possible that the Embassy and the State Department, in their ardor to repatriate Oswald, had gone so far as to write letters in his name?" How did

Lee Harvey Oswald discover the International Rescue Committee while in the Soviet Union?

One curious piece of evidence is suggestive. In his so-called "Address Book, Oswald wrote in Cyrillic letters the equivalent of "INDEREDKO." Either the FBI or the Warren Commission staff had annotated this entry in the Warren Commission's records, suggesting Oswald's scribble might stand for an acronym of the International Rescue Committee. The IRC's two acronyms have been "IRC" and "INTRECOM." Charles Drago has commented that "Given the tendency of LHO (and/or his amanuensis) to misspell and mis-transcribe," the notation as a Cyrillic version of INTRECOM "makes sense." Though inconclusive, Oswald's note strongly suggests someone in the Soviet Union, possibly an official of the U.S. Embassy in Moscow or a cooperative CIA asset (or both) prompted Oswald to contact the IRC for exit support.

That query could only have rung more False Identity/Illegal alarm bells. The IRC was a major part of a Cold War network of religious and secular relief agencies and intelligence operators. In its earlier Emergency Rescue Committee/OSS manifestation, it included Varian Fry working with the Unitarian Service Committee and Paul Hagen-Karl Frank and his OSS/Dulles links. In the committee's Cold War period, the IRC was directed by Leo Cherne.

Throughout his life, Cherne was a major U.S. Intelligence player, at the table with Richard Nixon, Gerald Ford, George Bush Sr., and William Casey. After serving as a "consultant" to General Douglas MacArthur, Leo Cherne became an IRC Board member in 1946. In 1951, he was elected Chairman of the International Rescue Committee and held that office for forty years. When Lee Harvey Oswald applied to the International Rescue Committee, the Committee and its Chairman Leo Cherne were so deeply entwined in the web of Cold War black-ops that they were widely considered to be an appendage of the CIA.

Unitarian Percival Flack Brundage, close friend of both the U.S. military and the CIA and a major founder of the American Friends of Albert Schweitzer College, was a dedicated worker for the Unitarian Service Committee, laboring in the same refugee fields as, and often cooperating with, the IRC.

Lee Harvey Oswald had discovered a way to send at least one letter of appeal for financial support to the Committee while he was in the Soviet Union; yet Oswald (or someone) simultaneously raised a serious question about the authenticity of his application to that same CIA-funded organization. The International Rescue Committee was a major part of the refugee/religious/ intelligence operations run by Allen Dulles for half-a-century, until JFK showed him the door. It was also a major component of the international psyops network of C.D. Jackson.

The IRC's officers and board members, including Leo Cherne and William Casey, had State Department, military, U.S. Intelligence and, in particular, psychological warfare links. They were officers and board members of USIA, Radio Free Europe/Radio Liberty, the Research Institute of America, the National Endowment for Democracy (NED), Freedom House, and the Center For Strategic and International Studies (CSIS), the latter founded and run initially by Ray Cline, former deputy director of the CIA. These board members and officers were, in fact, a perfect fusion of intelligence gathering and C.D. Jackson's psyops techniques.

C.D. Does Dallas

The connection between C.D. Jackson and L.H. Oswald was not limited to his curious application for help to the International Rescue Committee. Time, Inc., C.D. Jackson, and his psychological warfare operations descended on Dallas immediately after the president's execution.

On November 22, 1963, Patsy Swank, a part-time *Life* Magazine asset, whispered into a closely held phone; around her, Dallas Police Headquarters was in chaos. A local clothing maker named Zapruder, she said, had reportedly shot film of the assassination. Swank was speaking to Richard Stolley, the Pacific Bureau Chief of *Life*, who had flown in to Dallas with Tommy Thompson and two photographers immediately upon hearing the terrible news from Texas.

As he sat in his hotel room, Stolley became very interested in what Swank had to say. He contacted Zapruder and, on November 23rd, reportedly viewed the film. Stolley then reached C.D. Jackson in New York, and, according to the West Coast bureau chief, followed Jackson's orders: he bought the original film and one or several copies, according to conflicting reports. Stolley recalled that the footage was delivered to Jackson, and after the psychological warfare chief looked at the film, Jackson "proposed the [Time, Inc.] company obtain all rights to the film and with-hold it from public viewing at least until emotions had calmed."

Among the many plots against Fidel Castro, "Operation Red-cross" had a direct *Life*/C.D. Jackson connection. Supported by William Pawley (a powerful China Lobbyist and friend of the CIA) and by Julien Sourwine, influential counsel for the Senate Internal Security Subcommittee, the operation had enlisted at least four important participants: Johnny Martino and Eddie Bayo, both organized crime figures; a representative of the CIA; and journalist Richard Billings, commissioned to write about and photograph the "rescue" raid on Cuba for *Life*. C. D. Jackson, who was, according to reporter/writer Carl Bernstein, "Henry Luce's personal emissary to the CIA," had reportedly allowed CIA assets and agents to carry Time, Inc., identification as cover, and the anti-Cuban Bayo/Martino/Pawley action was most likely funded (as were other attempted hits) by Henry Luce, through C.D. Jackson. Richard Billings, the *Life* journalist accompanying Operation Red-cross, was, at that moment, an in-law of C.D. Jackson.

Billings' connections to the Kennedy assassination story also included his authorship of a key article on the JFK murder for *Life* (for which he was an editor); after the assassination, he was Editorial Director for the House Select Committee on Assassinations that examined the Kennedy killing; and he co-authored (with G. Robert Blakey, the committee's chief counsel) a study of the assassination based largely on the Select Committee's materials.

His direct connection to an anti-Castro operation whose members included Organized Crime, the CIA, and Time, Inc., and the gaining of exclusive possession of the original Zapruder film (then suppressing it for over ten years) were not the only links C.D. Jackson had to the Kennedy assassination story. James Herbert Martin, former manager of Seven Flags in Arlington, Texas, had been Marina Oswald's business manager for a time; he arranged a sizeable amount of money to be paid to himself, to his lawyer, to Lee's brother Robert Oswald, and an advance of $25,000 to Marina from Meredith Press through Thomas Thompson or *Life* editor Edward K Thompson, Isaac Don Levine, Life's representative in Dallas (called "the dean of American anti-Communist writers"), and C.D. Jackson.[16] According to television newsperson Bob Schieffer (at the time of the Dealey Plaza murder, a *Fort Worth Star-Telegram* police reporter), a "New York-based *Life* magazine reporter named Thomas Thompson, also ... from Fort Worth ... managed to put the Oswald women [both Lee's wife and mother] under exclusive contract to his magazine and ... secreted them away in a Dallas motel."

Time, Inc., was well represented in the aftermath of the JFK assassination. C.D. Jackson (for *Life*) had directed the taping of Marina Oswald's personal story, scheduled to be transcribed by Ilya Mamantov. Mamantov was a close friend and associate of Peter Gregory, who had apparently controlled Marina's police testimony on the alleged JFK murder rifle. Earlier, Gregory and Mamantov helped organize a CIA-funded anti-Communist Orthodox parish for the White Russians of the Dallas-Fort Worth area supported by the CIA-financed Tolstoy Foundation. The Oswalds had been befriended by Paul M. Raigorodsky, a member of the White Russian Emigré community and on the Board of Directors of the Tolstoy Foundation. A Tolstoy family member had been a World War II OSS officer, and, later, "members of the [CIA-funded] Tolstoy family were in regular contact with ... [C.D. Jackson's] Psychological Strategy Board in the early 1950s...."

By 1953, Jackson was directly involved in obtaining funding for the Tolstoy Foundation. Isaac Don Levine, who at the time of the JFK assassination was a member of the Liberation Committee of the CIA, had been scheduled to ghost the Marina Oswald story; Levine was "a veteran China Lobbyist who had previously collaborated on anti-Soviet projects with the CIA and the CIA-subsidized Tolstoy Foundation." Levine reportedly spent a full week with Marina Oswald before her February 3, 1964, testimony to the Warren Commission, a period that has been characterized by one informed source as witness coaching.

In 1953, Allen Dulles, Isaac Don Levine, and C.D. Jackson had collaborated on the CIA/Eisenhower administration's major psyops response to Stalin's death. James Martin, part of the *Life*/Meredith Press publishing deal, had a relationship with Jack Ruby dating back to when Martin worked for the Statler-Hilton and, afterward, managed a Dallas "bottle club" similar to Ruby's Carousel. In addition to his involvement in the Time, Inc./Marina Oswald publishing scheme, Martin was responsible for the sale of the so-called "backyard rifle photo," allegedly of Lee Harvey Oswald, to *Life Mag-*

azine. C.D. Jackson made much of that photograph, an odd and tilted image that nevertheless helped to convince many Americans of Oswald's guilt. *Life's* cover of February 21, 1964, featuring the photo was an apt illustration of C.D. Jackson's psyops abilities, introducing Jackson's commissioned "psychoanalytic"'review of Oswald carried inside the magazine.

But Jackson and the photo editors of *Life* did have a major problem: the rifle being held by the man in the picture, presumed to be Oswald, did not match the "Mannlicher-Carcano" allegedly recovered at the Texas School Book Depository. The weapon's stock in the photo was altered, and the telescopic site was retouched, both transformations by *Life's* photo experts, *so* that the rifle in the cover photo looked more like the alleged murder weapon.

Jackson was reportedly responsible for selecting only thirty-one frames (in black and white) of the Zapruder film for the November 29, 1963, edition of *Life,* nine in color for *Life's* December 1963, edition, and, just before his death on September 18, 1964, selecting a limited number of frames for the *Life* edition of October 2, 1964, anticipating the unholy deed's first anniversary.

The several versions of the Zapruder film that have circulated for almost thirty years (including, most recently, marketed copies of the alleged original) have been subjected to close and critical analyses which raise serious questions about the film's authenticity. Those questions carry even greater weight given C.D. Jackson's lifelong history of using both words and images to manipulate and misinform the public.

Acting as *Life's* publisher, Jackson not only suppressed the Zapruder film; he converted it to a propaganda instrument supporting the government's dubious Lone Assassin theory. Jackson apparently allowed *Life* writer Paul Mandel to view an alleged copy of the film, then commissioned Mandel to describe what he saw. As Robert Sam Anson commented, Mandel's take on the film, published in the December 1963, edition of *Life,* was "totally fictitious."

Early in 1964, C.D. Jackson helped found the private International Executive Service Corps, becoming its board president. And on February 25, 1964, Jackson apparently allowed the members of the Warren Commission, the FBI, and the Secret Service to view a version of the Zapruder film in the possession of *Time/Life/Fortune*. On July 8, 1964, C.D. Jackson was appointed Senior Vice President of Time, Inc.

On September 18, 1964, less than one year after gaining control of the Zapruder assassination film, C.D. Jackson was dead, reportedly the victim of cancer. Writer and lone gunman die-hard Gerald Posner asserted that C.D. Jackson, who Posner stated died of a heart attack, had only one link to the Kennedy assassination. According to Posner, Jackson "was the *Life* magazine executive who decided to purchase the Zapruder film." So much for the journalistic credibility of a would-be Pulitzer Prize winner.

Who Was Oswald's Puppet Master?

From 1959 through his death in 1963 (and even beyond), Lee Harvey Oswald was a classic psychological warfare principal. The U.S. Intelligence programs in Illegals, False Identities, and False Defectors were psyops; the Dulles brothers' manipulations of religious individuals and groups were psychological warfare operations. C.D. Jackson's entire career in publishing, advertising, fund-raising, public opinion shaping, wartime propaganda, black operations, political campaigns, and economic global planning was a lifetime of pure psyops.

Only someone with extraordinary psychological warfare abilities could have created the "Red Marine," Lee Harvey Oswald, quickly silenced by Jack Ruby on November 24, 1963 after vehemently stating his innocence: "I am just a patsy."[17]

Percival Brundage

Essay Seven

Percival Brundage & The Bureau of the Budget

Working in less than mysterious ways, the U.S. National Security State in its earliest manifestations controlled the White House, its legislative and budgetary operations, and its military and intelligence activities. Chief among those controls were the Bureau of the Budget (BOB), James R. Killian Jr., Lyndon Baines Johnson, and key Unitarians and their partners in U.S. covert intelligence. Among the most important of those budgetary and religious assets was Percy Brundage.

Percival Flack Brundage

Percival was born on April 2, 1892, the son of Charlotte Flack Brundage and William Brundage, a Methodist cleric who became a Unitarian minister.

Receiving his Harvard undergraduate degree ("cum laude") in 1914, Percival Brundage joined the New York accounting firm of Patterson & Ridgeway and rose from office boy to senior accountant in two years. Brundage resigned in 1916 to take a wartime civilian position with the Material Accounting Section of the War Department's Quartermaster Depot Office in New York, a job combining extensive and confidential record keeping with major military procurement operations. Brundage held that crucial position through the Armistice of 1918.

In just five years, Percival Brundage had distinguished himself as a major accounting mind.

From 1919 (when he became a CPA in New Jersey) through 1954, Brundage reportedly established an unequaled record in accounting, business, business law, and commerce, holding national offices in the AICPA, the National Conference of Lawyers and CPM, the Massachusetts Society of CPA's, the New York State Society of CPA's, the New York Chamber of Commerce, the Society of Business Advisory Professions, the National Bureau of Economic Research, and lectureships at both Oxford and Harvard.

When he was not a major public service official or a full-time National Security Council or Cabinet member of the U.S. government, Brundage was a senior partner at Price-Waterhouse (not unlike his friends at Sullivan and Cromwell, Allen and John Foster Dulles). Percival Brundage's global concerns were, in fact, identical to those of the Dulles brothers: Brundage was the director (1940-54) and chairman (1951-54) of the Federal Union that argued for "federation of the Atlantic democracies." He was the treasurer of the International Movement for Atlantic Union, an affiliation of the Federal Union, and the treasurer and director of the Atlantic Council of the United States.

In 1954, at the height of his global activity and while an active member of the Council on Foreign Relations, Percival Brundage accepted the position of Deputy Director of the BOB in Eisenhower's first administration.

In 1956, the master accountant of America became the Director of the Bureau of the Budget, monitoring the debits and credits of the Eisenhower government, an office he held until 1958. After his official retirement from government service, he signed on with the BOB for two more years as the Bureau's key "consultant."

From 1954 through 1960, Percival Brundage kept close watch on the national budget of the United States; and for those six years was obviously comfortable with the fact that the Department of Defense and CIA "black budget" operations were hidden in the accounts of the Pentagon and other departments and divisions of the U.S. government, and would never be critically reviewed by his Bureau of the Budget. Neither was subject to the ordinary government-wide funding and spending surveys performed by the BOB. The Bureau, in fact, happily participated in promoting and maintaining both intelligence and military budgets.

The Rise of Brundage's Budget Bureau

As mandated by the Constitution of the United States, every chief officer of every division and department of the U.S. Government is required to submit a budget for close analysis by the executive branch and, after 1920, the Director of the Bureau of the Budget.

Profiteering by contractors in World War I reached so gluttonous a level "a public cry of outrage against them ... reverberated for two decades." Despite that rush of citizen anger, the government's wartime accommodation with the profiteers was institutionalized in 1921, when the Bureau of the Budget was created, a signal agency "in increasing the power of the President."

The Budget and Accounting Act of June 10, 1921, established that the new Bureau would function "under a Director appointed by and accountable to the President [alone] ... created ... to carry out the task of budget preparation." With the recognition of fiscal responsibility also came recognition of the president's further responsibility to initiate legislation, therefore the necessity to create "machinery [within the executive branch] for central clearance of legislative proposals from the executive branch." The Bureau was, in fact, that legislative machinery. The double power of initiating legislation and monitoring expenditures meant that the BOB could effectively control and conceal the distribution of key military and intelligence funds.

The BOB, U.S. Intelligence & the Military

After FDR expanded his legislative/budgetary powers, Truman and Eisenhower further enhanced those powers. Congress did little to check this growth of executive clout, and though the Department of Defense and the U.S. Intelligence community eventually freed themselves of any Bureau of the Budget control, the Bureau remained a powerful executive instrument through the 1960s, called upon for support by Congressional leaders like Lyndon Johnson and power players like James Killian, Jr.

The strength of the BOB and the secret funding of covert operations had an almost identical history. When, for example, the ear-

239

lier version of the OSS was inaugurated as the office of the Coordinator of Information (COI), President Roosevelt sent a note (on June 18, 1941) "to officials of the Bureau of the Budget to set up the [COI] office ... and to fund it initially out of the $100 million in secret, un-vouchered funds that Congress had [previously] appropriated...." Presidents both before and after Roosevelt had called on the Bureau to develop new agencies, prepare the initiating legislation, fund their operations, and on occasion direct the dismantling of existing offices. The BOB was instrumental in setting up the COI and decommissioning its later manifestation, the OSS, to prepare the way for the CIA.

Roosevelt operated his Bureau of the Budget as a presidential 'secretariat' for monitoring the activities of the entire executive establishment. On September 8, 1939, President Roosevelt had declared a "Limited Emergency" following Nazi Germany's successful penetration of Poland. His Reorganization Act then reconstructed the Executive Office of the President: its key provision transferred the BOB from the Treasury Department to Roosevelt's Executive Office, ensuring that the massive military procurements sure to come when America joined the war would be monitored by friendly bookkeepers in the Bureau.

That reorganization also ensured that Roosevelt's private intelligence operations would be protected on both the domestic and foreign fronts. For international connections, the president's agents included Averell Harriman and Harry Hopkins. The Bureau became a powerful wing of FDR's personal intelligence apparatus, in control of the budget but also commissioned by the president to make major evaluations of the nation's intelligence agencies throughout World War II.

To guarantee his domestic information was unfiltered and completely trustworthy, Roosevelt sent his Bureau of the Budget agents "into every branch of the government, and their reports came directly back to the President."

Later, in 1953, when the Eisenhower administration was interested in paring down its national debit column, it suddenly discovered what the government spent was largely protected as "built-in costs." President Eisenhower (reportedly with reluctance) therefore opposed any significant reductions in the only areas where cuts could have been made, i.e. the military and "other national security needs." The "National Security" card, developing at least since the days of World War I, became a Cold War ace of spades.

Ultimately the most sensitive, illegal, and unconstitutional military, intelligence, and psyops programs, costing billions of dollars, were not only freed of BOB oversight but were actively promoted by the Bureau, which either ignored buried expenditures or supported those outlays, approving or overlooking fund transfers from other cooperating government departments and agencies. In available Bureau of the Budget documents, those funding transfers were most often called "arrangements." In fact, the Central Intelligence Act of 1949 authorized the Agency to "transfer to and receive from other government agencies such sums ... approved by ... [the Bureau of Budget] for the performance of any functions or activities authorized ... without regard to any provisions of law limiting or prohibiting transfers between appropriations."

From Roosevelt through Eisenhower, the budget machinery developed by the Bureau of the Budget transferred actual spending power from Congress to the Office of the President, from which military and covert operations funding was ultimately handed over to the National Security Council, the Department of Defense, and the CIA. That transformation was "the result of struggle, usurpation, delegation, abandonment, abduction, and atrophy." Howard E. Shuman succinctly summarized the context of that transference: "Each act and each transfer of [budget] power was preceded by economic problems, panics, wars, depression, or constitutional crisis."

At every instance of that budgetary transference, powerful individuals and groups associated with the Federal Reserve, the Treasury, the American banking industry, and the Bureau of the Budget were present as midwives. Shuman correctly diagnosed the unconstitutional takeover of the budgeting function from Congress by agents and assets of a series of presidents, but he did not fully appreciate how the Bureau of the Budget created a phony "review" of a joint meeting of the Bureau, Defense, and the sitting president over a period of years from 1947 through 1960, then assisted in transforming the military, industrial and intelligence complexes into pan-federal operations.

Walter L. Pforzheimer helped direct the U.S. Intelligence community through World War II and the Cold War that followed, as the CIA achieved maximum power, and his abiding concern was

241

concealment of the funding for covert operations of both the OSS and the CIA. Appropriately, Pforzheimer was the CIA'S liaison to the US Congress when the Agency operated without any "legislative charter ... running covert operations around the world before it had the slightest legal authority to do so." He recalled that in 1949 the U.S. Congress "passed legislation authorizing the agency's secret [and, therefore, unmonitored] budget ..."

The William T. Golden Operation

In the fall of 1950, during the Korean "police action," a major step was taken in the nexus of Bureau of the Budget and U.S. Intelligence interests. The director of the BOB and his senior staff were apparently alerted by their military and intelligence friends that crucial policy decisions bearing on spending for "defense" and covert operations ought to be anticipated. Senior members of Budget Director Frederick J. Lawton's staff, without prior presidential direction, contacted William T. Golden about exploring certain important policy issues and then writing a report for the president under the auspices of the Bureau of the Budget.

Golden was then a Manhattan investment banker, but earlier he had been with the U.S. Navy in World War II, probably in technological intelligence, and in 1946 helped establish the Atomic Energy Commission. Golden "knew, or had access to, most of the principal civilian and military officials in the government, as well as many of the most influential scientists...." Golden's resumé was powerful.

Without either presidential direction or authority, BOB consultant Golden proceeded to meet with key American scientific individuals possessing high academic, military, and Congressional connections. On October 20th, one day after the Bureau of the Budget submitted a memorandum to President Truman proposing what Golden was already deeply engaged in, Golden met with Herman A. Spoehr, the new science advisor to Undersecretary of State James Webb. Both Spoehr and Webb were quite comfortable with State Department intelligence and the CIA.

Golden had begun his scientific intelligence survey early in September, 1950; after a short series of meetings with scientific and political people, the key conversation with Webb's science advisor took place. Less than eight months later, Golden completed his remarkable tour of the community of military/intelligence/technology experts thought relevant to the Bureau of the Budget's "detailed investigation."

Golden's Bureau of the Budget records and memoranda are available at the American Association for the Advancement of Science Internet site. His key BOB memoranda, covering most of his Bureau's field-work from September 1950 through April 1961, outline an extraordinary exploration of possible covert technological operations, with the Bureau of the Budget, the State Department, and the CIA closely consulted.[1]

Of the three "non-physicists" most interviewed by Golden, two were part of the larger BOB/intelligence context: Don K. Price, a political scientist who, predictably, had been with the Bureau of the Budget; the other was James Killian, president of MIT.

Over an eight-month period, Killian, in fact, was an important conversation topic in fifty phone calls from Killian to Golden, Golden to Killian, and Golden to a series of military, academic, and intelligence figures. As the BOB's field investigator, Golden was very interested in the management of "scientific intelligence," and Killian looked like the person for the job. Ultimately the MIT president, running for several years the "science" side of the White House's intelligence policy options, became President Eisenhower's Science Advisor.

Through Golden's eight month study crucial areas were examined, which helped to shape how American science took part in the Cold War, especially as a working ally of American intelligence.

October 27, 1950, signaled the beginning of the Bureau of the Budget/U.S. scientific intelligence "review." It quickly became apparent that key issues besides satellites and super-sonar were being explored." James E. Webb, Undersecretary of State, introduced as conversation topics with Golden the "U.S. Information Service and the Voice of America," "CIA intelligence activities in [undefined] scientific matters," a reference to the Troy Report (concerning Killian's Troy/Cenis operation at MIT), and the State Department's "Special Assistant-Intelligence": W. Park Armstrong, who was in fact the chief of the State Department's intelligence operations. Webb's implicit interest was, of course, psyops. BOB master scout Golden would have his attention called to this crucial area of "technological intelligence" throughout the entire eight months of his BOB review.

Webb directed Golden to W. Park Armstrong at State, who then fed Golden material in certain "scientific matters," recommended Golden consult the Director of Scientific Intelligence for the CIA, and observed that Webb's scientific assistant at State would be doing "scientific intelligence" work for the Agency.

James R. Killian

On December 19, 1950, Golden had an important telephone conversation with James R. Killian. The MIT president was running an "ad hoc group" examining the entire area of scientific advice to the president. Clearly Killian wished to convey to Golden that the topic of a scientific advisor (and an associated supporting committee) for the president had not been fully explored, a tactic promoting Killian as the soundest source for such an exploration, rather than a diverse group that was unable to define its discourse (as Killian had implied). At one point, Killian obligingly described his ideal candidate for the presidential scientific advisor slot, a description remarkably like a profile of Killian himself. Golden could not have missed the implication.

Finally, Killian asserted that his group had "a definite feeling that representation [on the advisory committee] should not be of the physical sciences exclusively; that is, there was a genuine recognition of the growing importance of the social sciences, particularly ... the interrelationship [of the two]...." Killian then cited "the Troy Report now under way ... at MIT."

Killian could not have been clearer: scientific technology in the 1950s had to include psychological warfare.

On December 21, 1950, Golden met with Lloyd Berkner, "a good friend of James Webb, Undersecretary of State," who was devoting half of his work time to the Troy Report under the "direction" of the MIT "Dean of Humanities," who answered, of course, to James Killian. By now Killian's man Berkner was being pushed as one of the leading candidates for the scientific advisor post.

That office finally went to Dr. Herman Spoehr, James Webb's scientific advisor, and the BOB/intelligence grip on "technological intelligence" seemed secure. Spoehr, however, left the office early, and Golden conferred with Dr. Lawrence Hafstad on February 6, 1951. The ideal person for the job sounded, again, remarkably like James Killian: "a younger, more enterprising, vigorous and idea-full man was necessary, and particularly one who knew his way around in the Government and especially in Washington."

Lawrence Hafsted, on cue, informed Golden he was "much interested in [Golden's] ... intelligence and overall studies of the Troy type...." Psyops was the major topic again.

On February 20, 1951, Golden met with the CIA'S Assistant Head of the Agency's Scientific Section: the Company delivered to Golden its "critical comments" on Killian's Research and Development Board, nothing less than a confirmation of the CIA'S "technological" intentions.

On March 6, 1951, near the end of Golden's review of scientific intelligence sponsored by the Bureau of the Budget, he had a crucial conversation with James R. Killian at Golden's home in New York. Killian let Golden believe he was in full agreement with whatever the BOB'S agent had discovered and concluded. But, Golden recorded in his memorandum, "as we were walking to his train at Grand Central, he spoke of his interest [in] ... unorthodox warfare matters, and we talked briefly about this [topic] with reference to the Troy report...."

Killian had again established the priority of psyops, and the Bureau of the Budget and U.S. Intelligence had established their agenda for the 1950s.

The relations between Percival Brundage and his associates fused intelligence and budget control issues that further defined the sources of U.S. power and profit. Brundage had a select circle of powerful elitist friends, and chief among them was fellow Unitarian James R. Killian, Jr.[2]

Because of the OSS/CIA links to the Unitarians, Killian's religious connections have remained relevant. At a local parish level, Killian was the chair of the Standing Committee of the Unitarian Church in Wellesley, Massachusetts; more importantly, he had been a member of the Board of Directors and the Moderator of the national American Unitarian Association. What the Unitarians did nationally and internationally would have been of particular interest to Killian, linked personally and professionally with both areas.

Killian & MIT: Technology and Intelligence

James Killian and MIT were united in the exploitation of technology for intelligence purposes beginning in World War II, when MIT cooperated with the U.S. military in communications and navigation research & development. The Cold War introduced the government-sponsored "Project Lincoln" that spawned MIT's Lincoln Laboratory." One of the laboratory's projects became "SAGE," the Semi-Automated Ground Environment tracking program." Ultimately "Mitre," a derivative of the Lincoln Lab, and SAGE were developed into prototype military and civilian space control systems. Throughout his tenure at the academic tech center, James Killian directed MIT's union with U.S. techno-intelligence.

Killian earned a degree in 'Management' at MIT, serving in his senior year as editor of *The Tech*, MIT's undergraduate newspaper. Invited to write a part-time column on MIT undergraduate education for *Technology Review*, Killian soon became the assistant managing editor, then managing editor, 1930-39. Killian also reportedly helped to establish MIT's Technology Press.

In 1939, Killian became executive assistant to MIT President Karl Taylor Compton, and when the National Defense Research Committee called on Compton to join in the war effort, Killian became the MIT president's surrogate manager in running the Cambridge technological center at precisely the same time MIT was deeply involved in development and research for the U.S. Government. Killian made himself so indispensable that on June 8, 1942 Compton requested a 3B draft deferment for Killian so he could continue to direct MIT's collaboration with the War Department. James Killian was certainly responsible for enlarging MIT's role as the "largest of the university military contractors."

By 1943, Killian had become executive vice president of MIT, and by 1945, he was vice president of MIT and an MIT Corporation member.

In 1949, Killian ascended to the presidency of the Massachusetts Institute of Technology. This began his career in the development of science, technology and the arts at MIT, his government service and his direct involvement in American intelligence. It was an unprecedented rise to academic/technological power. Killian reportedly registered his support for academic freedom immediately after his inauguration as MIT president, but within a year he accommodated Harvard's Project Troy for meetings on his MIT campus. Project Troy/CENIS became a think-tank dedicated to intelligence analyses of China, the Soviet Union, to nuclear weapons and their delivery systems.

Troy/CENIS' fusion of intellectual exploration, psychological warfare (sparked by C.D. Jackson), and practical defense applications must have been an exciting mix to James R. Killian, Jr., whose "vision ... gave a humanistic sensitivity to [MIT's] ... role as a foremost institution of science and technology." "The Center for International Studies [CENIS] at MIT ... was at its founding financed ... by the Central Intelligence Agency."

James Killian's secretly funded MIT programs were serendipitously monitored by Killian himself, whose "board" was "designed to provide ... surveillance of the CIA...." A comment from a close friend of U.S. Intelligence was kind: "It could be argued that MIT was ... providing 'cover' for [the] CIA." In fact, MIT provided bigtime cover for clandestine military and/or intelligence projects for fifty years.[3]

Killian's intelligence links were further developed in 1951, when MIT's Lincoln Laboratory was established, where the SAGE air defense system was researched and developed. In turn, Lincoln Lab was founded on the work of Killian's associate Edwin Land and a series of government-sponsored Cold War investigations. Land had a major "secret career as a military advisor" to President Eisenhower.

1954 was a key moment in the careers of Percival Brundage and James Killian. Topping off three years of dedicated work for U.S. technical Intelligence while at the helm of MIT, Killian accepted the chairmanship of President Eisenhower's Technological Capabilities Panel, commissioned to measure the nation's "security and intelligence capabilities following the Soviet Union's announcement in August of 1953 ... it had successfully tested a hydrogen bomb." From that moment on, Eisenhower relied heavily on Killian-approved scientists and technicians for advice on "arms control" and military questions.

The new panel was authorized to study both military and intelligence applications of "high-flight reconnaissance;" in effect technological snoopery by people like Edwin H. Land, inventor of the Polaroid Land camera, Richard Bissell and the magical U-2. Aerospace espionage was the top and bottom line.

Land was appointed by James Killian as chief of the top-secret intelligence section of the Air Force Technological Capabilities

Panel, giving him theoretical control of all high-flight reconnaissance operations, and establishing the R & D line that led to the U-2 and major U.S. satellite technology.

Land himself was responsible for Eisenhower's decision to give the U-2 program to the CIA.

Predictably and logically within the Cold War paradigm, the Killian Panel recommended increased reliance on science and technology in the collection of aerospace military intelligence, with continuing close cooperation between Killian, Land, Bissell, and Eisenhower's close White House associate, General Andrew Goodpaster.

In 1957, Killian was appointed President Eisenhower's Special Assistant for Science and Technology, holding a cabinet-level portfolio in everything except name. Killian's assignment from 1957 through 1959 was "evaluating national technological and intelligence capabilities."

Like Percival Brundage, Killian was a full-fledged member of the American elite, the "advisor, trustee, or director for ... organizations such as the Alfred P. Sloan Foundation ... the Boston Museum of Fine Arts, AT&T, Cabot Corporation, General Motors, IBM, Ingersoll-Rand, and Polaroid."

Obviously, Killian's organizational expertise was especially valued in the corporate sector of defense and aerospace.

While Killian served for a remarkable and productive number of years as MIT President and Chairman of the MIT Corporation from 1948 through 1971, he remained in intimate touch with U.S. Intelligence activities. Immediately after he stepped down from chairmanship of the Technological Capabilities Panel, Killian became Eisenhower's Special Assistant for Science and Technology. In 1956 Eisenhower appointed him first chairman of the U.S. Board of Consultants on Foreign Intelligence Activities, an oversight committee created on January 13, 1956, then reconstituted under Kennedy as the President's Foreign Intelligence Advisory Board. The board's official task was to oversee and "report to him [the president] periodically on the work of the intelligence organizations ... particularly the CIA...."

In establishing his Board of Consultants, Eisenhower closely followed the advice of the Hoover Commission on White House intelligence re-organization, heavily supported by the Bureau of the

Budget's Percival Brundage.[4] The Board served loyally as an effective cover for foreign covert intelligence programs, including the historic U-2 flights. Among the members in its first six months was Joseph Kennedy Sr., the upstart Irishman who made his fortune during prohibition, served as Ambassador to the Court of St. James, and fathered a tragic dynasty. Kennedy Sr. resigned prematurely when his son began his unsuccessful 1956 campaign to become the Democratic Party's Vice-Presidential candidate.

As the chair of the president's Board of Consultants, Killian asked David Bruce, an experienced U.S. foreign diplomat and former OSS officer, and attorney Robert Lovett to examine the CIA'S clandestine operations and report to the president: the "Bruce/Lovett" report is still secret. But enough of it has been leaked to researchers and writers to establish that the report attacked the incestuous political and covert ops relationship between Allen and John Foster Dulles, a poison pill for any foreign or domestic policy initiatives not friendly to the brothers' personal agenda.

Killian's 1956 strategy insured he would be called upon to instruct the president concerning crucial intelligence decisions in the future. Further, his support of the Bruce-Lovett report had no effect on his role as an intelligence team player, including control of the U-2 program.

The U-2, Allen Dulles & the CIA

The history of U.S. Intelligence oversight could rightly be called "Hen House watchers wanted... Foxes only need apply." When it became clear that the U-2 would revolutionize aerospace and high-flight intelligence surveillance, a dozen information-gathering units of both civilian and military intelligence put in their bids for operational control. Following the advice of his Board of Consultants, led by James Killian and Edwin Land, Eisenhower called on CIA Director Allen Dulles to organize and oversee the high-flight surveillance program. Dulles delegated the work to his deputy Richard Bissell. According to Bissell, the program was funded from the CIA'S "contingency reserve." The reserve was dedicated to covert operations, and "replenished periodically" by the U.S. Congress, in a rubber-stamp version of the Executive Branch's budget review process. This special Agency budget exemption was based on a rhetorical fiction: any outlay of funds "had to be authorized by the director of the BOB and approved by the president."

Apparently, no detailed cost-accounting was ever demanded for the high altitude surveillance operation, insuring "quickness and flexibility" as well as "greater secrecy," but the procedure "also created opportunities for misuse that the CIA would exploit in future years for questionable programs...."

Supported by the ever-present BOB, the project was "code-named Aquatone."

In the interest of advancing the White House's argument for what would become NASA, on February 7, 1958, the ever-present James Killian, Edwin Land and Andrew Goodpaster counseled President Eisenhower that the Air Force was a failure at developing "a photographic reconnaissance satellite." The Air Force program designated SENTRY, and then SAMOS, was turned over to the CIA, with Kelly Johnson and Richard Bissell appointed as the leaders of the program, renamed CORONA.[5]

Killian's small circle of elitists continued to control the U.S.' most advanced intelligence technology.

When Killian resigned from the president's intelligence Board of Consultants and left for Boston, the Board "went into hibernation and... ceased to be a functioning body...." No official document has explained why such an important presidential intelligence group would suddenly fold up its tent, making Killian's departure the logical trigger.

Responding to a signal from either the White House or a high-ranking official in U.S. Intelligence, the slumbering Board awoke briefly two weeks before John F. Kennedy was inaugurated, and officially "disbanded on January 7, 1961, when the entire membership resigned in anticipation of the new JFK administration." Some skewed accounts claim JFK disbanded the Eisenhower/Killian intelligence board, but the group conveniently cancelled itself just before the new broom swept in the door.[6]

After the Bay of Pigs disaster, JFK moved quickly to re-establish the White House's connection to foreign intelligence monitoring, and, following the advice of close associates, he offered the chair of his new President's Foreign Intelligence Advisory Board (PFIAB) to a trusted friend of U.S. Intelligence: James R. Killian, Jr.[7]

Killian's technological and intelligence credentials, especially in high-flight surveillance and aerospace, impressed the new president. From the day the NSC and CIA were created, control of the government's space policy became a path to immense power and profit. When the smoke cleared, that policy was "molded chiefly by the National Aeronautics and Space Administration, the nation's civilian space agency, and the Department of Defense, especially the U.S. Air Force."

Who Structured the Control of U.S. Space Policy?

After World War II, the "American military had decided to concentrate on the existing manned aircraft fleet to deliver its nuclear might and not actively pursue the development of an intercontinental ballistic missile (ICBM)." The Soviets could not compete with U.S. conventional air power and nuclear warhead technology, so they opted for developing "the enormous rocket boosters required to carry their heavy nuclear bombs over intercontinental ranges." The so-called "missile gap" had been born.

Edwin Land (according to MIT scholar Victor McElhney) was a secret military advisor to President Eisenhower on "photo-reconnaissance technology." Land participated in a series of "advisory committees and study panels, including Project Charles and Project Beacon Hill." And it was Project Charles, focusing on U.S. "air defense measures," that "provided a justification for ... MIT's Lincoln Laboratory...." For James Killian, the ultimate chief of Lincoln Lab, Land was a key intelligence asset.

In 1951, Killian's Lincoln Laboratory analyses on "U.S. air defense" had been initiated, and in January of 1951 the U.S. Air Force gave its first "funded ICBM study contract to Convair," inaugurating the ICBM program. Four years later, eclipsing both the Army and Navy in missile development, the Air Force and associated aerospace companies such as General Dynamics, which took over from Convair on ICBM development, Martin-Marietta and Douglas received the Eisenhower administration's official blessing. Friends in very high places, including James Killian, Percival Brundage, and Lyndon Baines Johnson, helped the process.[8]

In the fall of 1955, the American government had three possibilities for launching satellites; two were tested vehicles closely associated with the Pentagon. The third was "an entirely new launch vehicle based on the Viking sounding rocket technology." Despite the new and largely untested launcher having both military and intelligence support, and despite its primary advocate being Percival Brundage, a long-time advocate of the dominant military/intelligence/corporate mix, President Eisenhower apparently accepted the argument that the launcher should be a civilian operation. Given the strong psyops orientation of the White House, it would help "to present an image to the world of the United States fostering the peaceful uses of space...." That image was, of course, another fairy tale: Project Vanguard was always about satellite military surveillance.

For the next two years, Vanguard was a multi-million dollar failure. By the fall of 1957, aerospace/Air Force advocate Senator Stuart Symington was calling for "a full investigation," and Senator Lyndon Johnson announced he planned an immediate inquiry into the missile/satellite gap. Too little money, too little expertise: the U.S. space program, civilian and military, needed a white knight.

On November 7, 1957, only 48 hours after the second successful Soviet Sputnik launch, President Eisenhower announced that Dr. James R. Killian, the president of MIT, a powerful member of the Unitarian community, had accepted the position of his Science Advisor. When Eisenhower established the President's Science Advisory Committee (PSAC), he handed Killian still another technological baton as PSAC's head honcho. It was no coincidence that Edwin Land immediately became a powerful member of PSAC, co-authoring a policy paper that helped establish the National Reconnaissance Office (NRO), one of the most secret of U.S. secret intelligence programs. Killian was coordinator of the DOD and CIA organization of the NRO. His deputy Edwin Land continued to review "proposals and provide technical oversight for spy-plane and spy-satellite projects" until President Nixon closed down the group.

Edwin Land ultimately served five U.S. presidents and an equal number of CIA directors, steering a technological ship manned by Killian and Land's military, intelligence, corporate, and academic allies.

It seemed inevitable that Killian would gain control of the U.S. space program, but the institutional distribution of power, privilege and profit within that program was a major concern of the establishment, the Pentagon, American intelligence, and the aerospace corporate community. "NASA and the Pentagon's missile and high-flight surveillance operations were about to become airborne."

The Space Program as Psyops

Space historian Homer Newell, also a major participant in the development of U.S. aerospace, did not name C.D. Jackson as the chief source of Eisenhower's space psyops program, but the president was clearly following his recommendations on presenting the appearance of U.S. aerospace leadership, whatever the Soviets were doing. Beginning in the "formative months of late 1957 and the first half of 1958," the various U.S. academic, industrial, and political forces merged in a common conviction that the country must put its aerospace house in order. Next came a psyops campaign to convince the world that American leadership would be "open"; the theme of both Percival Brundage and C.D. Jackson's campaigns in support of Eisenhower's "Open Skies" initiative. Both men were well aware that the satellite program was really intended to give the United States unrivaled high-altitude surveillance.

"It was an important thesis for the U.S. public to continue to believe and to sell to the rest of the world and, therefore, in a matter as portentous as space seemed to be, special efforts were needed to present the proper image." The "proper image" of the U.S. space endeavor was to be "open, unclassified," "visibly peaceful," and "conducted ... to benefit, not harm, the peoples of the world."

Whether or not James Killian was fully aware of the major psyops dimension of Eisenhower's space proposal, Percival Brundage, in his advocacy of the Vanguard, certainly was.

The solution to the organizational control of U.S. aerospace development, both civilian and military, would have been to establish an independent agency with two subdivisions, one clearly scientific and research oriented, the other clearly combining the efforts of the Army, Navy, Air Force and any of the ongoing or planned aerospace programs.

But one big problem was the 13th Fairy: U.S. Intelligence got no invitation to Aerospace Beauty's birthday party. Where were the CIA, the NSC, the NCO, the DIA, the ONI, and all the other acronyms?

The cover story continued to be that, though the military had the most aerospace experience, "the program should be set up under civilian auspices." Newell's official history of the period simply falsifies several key factors, including Eisenhower being "distressed over the enormous power and unmanageability of ... the military-industrial complex ..." and the his concern about "adding still another very costly enterprise to the Pentagon's responsibilities." The growing Defense octopus only seems to have worried Ike as he went out the door, and nothing in the Bureau of the Budget's documents even hints at any anxiety about a red-ink problem at the Pentagon.

In reality, the reconstitution of the Eisenhower administration, with a new Secretary of Defense, establishment of the Advanced Research Projects Agency, and the Defense Reorganization Act with its Office of the Director of Defense and Research Engineering helped create a maze of defense and space research appointments, allowing the real national players like James Killian to take control.

As Eisenhower's top gun for science and technology, Killian led his associates on the President's Science Advisory Committee, the Rocket and Satellite Research Panel, the National Academy of Sciences, the Space Science Board, the American Rocket Society, and still other organizations and groups of concerned scientists and researchers in "pressing for a space program under civilian management with a strong scientific flavor."

Despite this heavy support for a "program under civilian auspices," a "deluge of proposals descended upon various congressional committees" that guaranteed the final decision would be made by a small group of powerful people.

Killian Hi-jacks the Space Program

Killian's solution was bizarre and yet absolutely perfect: he organized his argument in favor of the National Committee for Aeronautics (NACA), the least likely candidate to run the American Space program. "NACA would not have been the choice of most scientists. As a highly ingrown activity, the agency did not enjoy a particularly great esteem in scientific circles, being thought of more as an applied research activity serving primarily industry and the military." By the time Killian chose NACA, "many scientists ... as well as aircraft manufacturers and military officers ... [felt] that NACA had withered into a timid bureaucracy...."

At its best, beginning in March 1915, NACA had pursued "solid, aerodynamic research," first for the War Department and then the

Department of Defense and the successive department's collaborating corporations.

But NACA had at least one significant and authentic intelligence link that compromised all its future scientific goals, initiated by the Brundage/Killian/ Bissell network: "In early 1956, Bissell paid [a] … call on Hugh Dryden … head of the National Advisory Committee on Aeronautics [then] purely a domestic operation, furnishing information on air turbulence and other problems to military and commercial aircraft makers." Bissell informed Dryden about the U-2 and enlisted NACA in the cover story: "NACA would announce the existence of a plane called the U-2 to be used for a NACA weather program." Despite NACA's "nervous" response, Dryden signed it up as the CIA'S front man, announcing that the Lockheed U-2's were on loan from the Air Force, their civilian pilots on loan from Lockheed itself.[9]

Killian prepared his NACA proposal in close cooperation with Percival Brundage, enthusiastic friend of military and intelligence spending.

On March 5, 1958 Nelson Rockefeller, intelligence fan and chairman of the President's Advisory Committee on Government Organization, Percival Brundage and James Killian "jointly delivered" to the president their memorandum nominating NACA as the civilian wing of the U.S. space program. Though they admitted to a "number of liabilities" in promoting NACA, the triumvirate assured Eisenhower these problems would be "overcome by enacting appropriate legislation."

Rockefeller, Killian and Brundage had, in fact, structured a shell labeled "NACA," renamed it the "National Aeronautical and Space Agency," and argued for retaining NACA's seventeen-member "governing committee," assuring the president that committee "membership would be changed and its power reduced."

NACA ultimately turned over considerable assets to NASA, including eight thousand employees, three laboratories (renamed "research centers"), a flight station, a rocket facility, and a $100 million budget.

The president accepted the "civilian space agency" proposal on the same day he received it. The White House immediately commissioned Percival Brundage and his Bureau of the Budget to "draft [Congressional] legislation."

Preparing to submit his enabling bill to Congress, Brundage received "assistance" from NACA, now a lame duck agency, but most significantly from the office of James Killian. Thus Killian and Brundage, allies of the aerospace corporations, the Pentagon and U.S. Intelligence, controlled the administration's legislative proposal for a "civilian" space program.

On April 2, as the president offered his "NASA" legislation to Congress, Percival Brundage argued for "a single responsible head for the new agency," who would not be hampered by any "board of experts." Critical arguments piled up against the administration's legislative proposal, for example, that its "provisions" lacked key "congressional oversight" or "international cooperation" and that it was missing a score of fundamental elements crucial to drawing a bright line between civilian and military aerospace controls and goals, but Congress blinked and adopted the legislation. How could it have happened?

LBJ Gets His Way

Aerospace, U.S. Intelligence, and the Bureau of the Budget had a close friend in Congress. Adding to his multiple legislative hat collection, on February 13, 1958, Majority Leader Lyndon Johnson was elected chairman of the Senate's Special Committee on Space and Astronautics, and the body soon became a permanent committee overseeing the crucial U.S. space budget. LBJ's potent cooperation was vital to moving the Brundage/Killian legislation through the Senate, despite the bill's obvious defects.

On April 14, 1958, the Eisenhower administration's space bill was officially introduced in Congress. "NACA" was to become "NASA," and U.S. aerospace operations were to be administered in some undefined relationship between NASA and the Pentagon, "with no formal coordination dictated in the legislation." Some critics of the less than candid empowerment bill wanted to know who, in fact, would be in charge of the American aerospace effort. James Killian and his Scientific Advisory Committee rode to the rescue and sternly "advised that setting up a joint civilian-military space program would violate President Eisenhower's personal philosophy and jeopardize the U.S. initiative to reserve space for scientific and peaceful purposes. Though the Senate version of the Eisenhower space bill differentiated between NASA and the Department of Defense, the Congressional conference committee opted for the House version, which only established a "military liaison committee ... of personnel from the DOD." This liaison committee was then given the absolute power to coordinate NASA and Pentagon operations.

Ongoing Army and Navy space capabilities were folded into NASA, while the U.S. Air Force and the operations of the Advanced Research Projects Agency (ARPA) became major components of the Department of Defense's aerospace endeavors.

Following Senator Johnson's impressive lead, Congress failed to define "the specific content of the space program with which the NASA Act was concerned." The entire organization of the U.S. aerospace operation, including its research, military, and civilian dimensions, was placed in legislative outer space.

As Percival Brundage intended, the "lack of a specifically prescribed [aerospace] program gave the first administrator of NASA a wide degree of latitude ... a freedom of choice ... little curtailed by guidance ... James Killian supplied in the summer of 1958...." That lack of "guidance" by Killian as the president's science advisor meant that only the preferred people in both civilian space research and the more highly developed intelligence programs of the Department of Defense would wield actual power.

Theoretically, "an administration for space was established, including [1.] a mechanism for adjudicating possible conflicts between NASA and DOD via the Civilian-Military Liaison Committee and [2.] a method for forming total space policy via the National Aeronautics and Space Council with the President as the first Administrator."

By law, Eisenhower had indeed become both a working member of the Council and its chair. But the Council was a cumbersome organization based, though not by law, in the White House's Executive Office, its membership made up of the Director of NASA, the chairman of the Atomic Energy Commission, the Secretaries of Defense and State, and three presidentially-appointed members.

The president "made little use of the Aeronautics and Space Council," the legislated governing body of NASA. Killian, Brundage and Senator Johnson had fashioned a "civilian" aerospace control mechanism that was unworkable. Crucially, the president, impatient with the Council's complexity, had not provided the Council with its own permanent Executive Office staff. "So it was left to NASA and the Bureau of the Budget to do the [Council's] staff work." The BOB took charge of the administrative side of U.S. aeronautics, and thenceforth became its own watchdog.

By September 1960, NASA and the Pentagon had established an "Aeronautics and Astronautics Coordinating Board" that effectively "took over the functions of the Civilian-Military Liaison Committee."

Whatever non-military brake on the U.S. aerospace intelligence program that had been theoretically in place was thrown by the wayside.

But NASA registered a series of launch failures, the BOB and LBJ's Senate committees broadcast NASA's ineptitude, and in the 1960 presidential campaign John F. Kennedy, following the advice of fellow nominee LBJ, pressed the dangers of both missile and space "gaps."

LBJ: Space Commander

After defeating Richard Nixon, Kennedy immediately began to plan the elimination of the ubiquitous "missile gap," advancing his vision of manned space exploration and an eventual lunar landing. Responding to Johnson's urgent desire to command U.S. aerospace activities, Kennedy "decided in January 1961 that ... Johnson would have special responsibilities for coordinating and overseeing U.S. space efforts." The National Aeronautics and Space Council (NASC) was placed officially in the Executive Office, with the Vice President replacing the President as its chairman. The Council was decreased in size, and commissioned to coordinate cooperation "among all departments and agencies of the United States engaged in aeronautical and space activities."

LBJ had become the head of Kennedy's entire aerospace program.

Johnson's first assignment was to find a new chief for NASA. The Vice President immediately selected James E. Webb, though he had several candidates who were considered outstanding, and whose experience in space technology was considerably greater than Webb's.

Recall that Webb was closely associated with a Bureau of the Budget search that touched on psyops, the Troy project, James R.

Killian, Jr., and the CIA. With his earliest credentials in education and law, beginning in 1932 Webb worked in politics and public service. Between 1936 and 1944, he moved from personnel director to vice-president at Sperry Gyroscope, then left to serve as a Marine officer in World War II. After the war, Webb returned to Washington and joined the staff of an old friend, O. Max Gardner, then Undersecretary of the Treasury. A consummate Beltway insider, Webb was perceived to be a wizard of bureaucratic manipulation.

From 1946 through 1949, when the Bureau of the Budget capped its deconstruction of the OSS by supporting the establishment of the National Security Agency and the CIA, James E. Webb was the Director of the Bureau of the Budget.

The Bureau had surfaced again.

Nominated on LBJ's recommendation, Webb was endorsed by LBJ's old Space Committee and then gained the enthusiastic confirmation of the U.S. Senate. To hire his NASA chief, Vice President Johnson had gone directly to the trusty administrative water carrier for U.S. space intelligence: the BOB.[10]

The National Aeronautics and Space Council, reactivated by President Kennedy, was also turned over to the vice-president, making Johnson JFK's most powerful aerospace officer, in control of the contracts and connections that made Texas the mega-productive center of military and intelligence aerospace.

Whatever scientific or purely non-military goals the U.S. space program might have had, Percival Brundage, James Killian, and LBJ insured that the matrix of aerospace/corporate/intelligence interests would go into financial orbit along with the space program.

The fiction that NASA was ever the "civilian" side of U.S. space programs has become threadbare: from NASA's inception it was conceived as an intelligence and military operation. William E. Burrows, America's foremost historian of the Space Age, concluded in 1998: "Where international politics and the balance of power were concerned, the military and civilian space programs were not only interchangeable, they were fundamentally inseparable."

Following Alan Shepard's successful flight into space JFK assigned his aerospace commander LBJ "to study the matter in hand" and bring a bold proposal to eclipse the Soviets. Johnson assigned Secretary of Defense Robert McNamara and James E. Webb (the perfect union of corporate power, Pentagon, BOB and Intelligence) to write the proposal that would define NASA's epic goal of a trip to the Moon as "part of the battle along the fluid front of the cold war."

Given the military and intelligence interests of the team LBJ put together, President Kennedy must have known his inspirational project was supported by people with less exalted aspirations. For Lyndon Baines Johnson and his close military, intelligence and corporate friends, the lunar landscape was transformed from green cheese to a golden harvest.

In popular folklore, JFK's "personal and decisive participation in [aerospace] policymaking ... gave the nation a clear space policy with management by a strong civilian agency, with a firm goal, and with strong direction expected to continue [after his murder] from the top of the Government." Though somewhat romanticized, especially in regard to the "strong civilian agency," this assessment is actually close to the truth.

Shell Game: The BOB & the CIA

Throughout the Truman, Eisenhower, Kennedy and Johnson administrations, Defense budget monitoring was a successful sleight-of-hand trick. Contrary to accepted mythology, the expenditures of the DOD were seldom or never independently monitored and analyzed by the BOB or, after 1969, the Office of Management and Budget. Beginning with the Eisenhower administration, the chief representative of the Joint Chiefs of Staff conferred with the Director of the Budget or his Deputy Director, usually prior to a joint meeting with the Secretary of Defense and the current president. After the obligatory soft-shoe between Defense and the BOB the Pentagon's amorphous shopping list was invariably approved, with a few cosmetic cuts.

We then understand comments like: "During the Eisenhower years, the Bureau of the Budget ... played a ... relatively minor role in defense budgeting. [Later] ... BOB had virtually no independent role in the formulation of the defense budget...."

This rubber-stamp process insured that the "military-industrial complex" would be well-stocked with weapons, support systems, and both military and "civilian" black-budget packages hidden under the Pentagon's unsupervised national security umbrella.

After the NSC and CIA were established in 1947, the Bureau of the Budget was a working partner or, at worst, "a minor irritant" to the Agency. As late as 1974, the "International Affairs Division's intelligence branch" of BOB's successor, the Office of Management and Budget, had a staff of only five people to oversee the CIA, the NSA, the National Reconnaissance Office, the Defense Intelligence Agency, and all "the rest of military intelligence." Even with the best of intentions, the job was overwhelming.

When the National Security Council mapped out its military and intelligence goals and established its range of necessary funding, the NSC then released the BOB from any further responsibility for monitoring CIA spending, allowing the Agency to deal directly with Congress' various oversight committees and subcommittees, especially the CIA'S longtime Senate and House supporters.

What was true in the late 1940s and 1950s was still true in the late 60s: "the CIA has been granted certain privileges uncommon to government agencies. It is not required to publish personnel data in the Federal Register; it is exempted from certain congressional and Bureau of the Budget oversight requirements; and it can bring up to 100 aliens into the country annually outside the normal immigration channels. Finally, very few public officials even know what the CIA'S budget is [,] since it is effectively concealed within the budgets of a number of other agencies."

Over the years, almost everyone has simply had to guess at the Agency's actual spending power: "It was not until 1997 that the CIA finally disclosed the annual intelligence budget: $26.6 billion." But that figure was still not accurate. Though it included all "intelligence" outside of the Pentagon, it did not add the value of and income from various properties and proprietary businesses (probably including banks), which the CIA either owned or operated.

When Bureau accountants in the 1950's cut social service (but not military) expenditures, Eisenhower was "understandably reluctant" [as have all presidents] to overrule his own budgetary watchdog. The Director of the Bureau of the Budget was all-powerful, except, of course, for the double clout of the Department of Defense and the CIA. The 1958 fiscal budget was the largest "ever drawn up in peacetime" and dominated by defense and foreign aid: the latter two areas "accounting for close to 60 percent of all federal expenditures." Eisenhower had apparently wished for some reductions in funding projections; but the Joint Chiefs of Staff appeared at Congressional appropriations hearings and not only opposed any suggested expenditure cuts but begged for still more money. With no real control exerted by Brundage's BOB, and Congress eager to support defense programs located in their home states, the Pentagon got what it wanted.

Despite the 1947 enabling act that placed the CIA outside the legal and constitutional monitoring process, the fiction of budget overview was still thinly maintained; yet even then the CIA flaunted its extra-budgetary strength by refusing to allow the BOB examiner to enter its headquarters until his identity was "checked." The Agency finally eliminated even that minor annoyance by placing "former" CIA operatives as auditors in the BOB, assigned to examine the Agency's books. By this time, the foxes almost outnumbered the chickens.

The slightest accounting challenge to the CIA was met with Agency attitude: Its actions were regularly claimed to be "above normal bureaucratic restraints." President Eisenhower had worked closely with the BOB on the difficult 1958 fiscal budget, but he knew that control of Defense spending was, in fact, a two-step dance performed by the hungry Joint Chiefs and a compliant Congress.[11]

In terms of "Defense" spending, Eisenhower's time in office was one long accounting disaster for the federal government: "Lax and sloppy enforcement of government regulations and contractual provisions, preferential treatment of the giant [defense] contractors, unconcern with the economic consequences of military [and black budget operations] spending ... became the order of the day...." All the supposedly responsible divisions of the U.S. government so lost national accounting control that military and covert intelligence spending was simply set free from civilian (and constitutional) oversight.

While the Joint Chiefs and the BOB played the same self-serving shell game throughout the Eisenhower years, the Joint Chiefs of Staff regularly complained "that the Bureau of the Budget's conservative approach to government expenditures was impairing new programs such as those for intercontinental ballistic missiles, nuclear aircraft carriers, the B-70 bomber and the nuclear-powered airplane."

But the BOB never blocked such programs except in support of some other equally or more important project of the same intelligence/corporate/military cabal.

When LBJ became chair of the Committee on Aeronautical and Space Science, the Texas powerbroker had two significant military/ intelligence hats, chairing both the Senate Preparedness Subcommittee and Aeronautical and Space Science. In 1959 and then in 1960 during Senate hearings called "Missiles, Space, and Other Major Defense Matters," Johnson gave a splendid "I'm shocked" response to testimony from the Bureau of the Budget, the Joint Chiefs, and from a raft of "military experts." Even Eisenhower's Secretary of Defense cooperated with Senator Johnson in establishing the fictional but highly useful "missile gap."

A typical LBJ concern was: Is my missile bigger than the Russki's? With Johnson's enthusiastic support, it became a major political argument in the 1960 presidential campaign, an issue often mistakenly attributed to Kennedy himself.

LBJ: Funding the CIA & the Pentagon

Having gone in the tank for years at every encounter with the Pentagon, the BOB took another dive during the 1960 LBJ Senate hearings, as the Bureau wore the somber colors of Eisenhower's "administrative failures." Senator Johnson was able to generate "a litany of military requests" that became, in fact, a Defense Department "shopping list." Throughout the Eisenhower administration, Senator Johnson was the crucial ally of the military/intelligence coalition, especially after the heavily publicized threats of Soviet space and missile programs. The easiest pickings for U.S. Intelligence's black budget operations then became the hot areas of "air" and "space," specifically through the Air Force's programs in research and development, and then through NASA: hence Johnson's pressure in 1959-1960 on the Eisenhower White House, topped by his 1960 Senate hearings.[12]

What followed were the "research and analysis" contracts (with their significant intelligence dimensions) for aircraft and space companies and think tank/ development corporations funded by the Pentagon, all of them ostensibly working for the Air Force and the U.S. aerospace program. For LBJ and Texas, the payoff was staggering: "As President, [LBJ] ... helped engineer the greatest Pentagon raid on the treasury since World War II. Among other results was a gigantic Defense industry boom for his home state, Texas."

Johnson had elected to hop on the gravy train in the early 1950s, collecting Senatorial power and privilege. As Vice-president he acquired more potency for U.S. space and missile programs, the only areas that really mattered to him and Texas (besides oil subsidies), until he "rode the tiger of military spending into the White House ... [and] it rode him out."

After Defense Secretary McNamara was commissioned to manage the Pentagon budget, the BOB "lost whatever influence it once had over military spending to the National Security Council...." Thus, the Bureau completed its long-term clandestine mission: to explode the DOD budget and bury the funding of covert ops in the Executive Branch's back room. The Security State had effectively taken control of both defense spending and intelligence funding. Fifty years later, that iron grip has not yet loosened.

The Bureau not only protected the CIA for decades, it actively conspired with the Agency. In the mid-1960s, for example, the Bureau "discovered" that the "CIA budget for Vietnam provided for dollar expenditures at the legal exchange rate." But the Bureau also knew that the CIA was using the Vietnamese black market to buy piasters so the Agency had "two to three times" more buying power than the Agency's official budget indicated. In brief, the "Boys in the Back Room" were making a killing.

The Bureau of the Budget moved in, flashing its financial fangs and demanding "all figures be listed at the actual black-market rate." But the BOB also requested that the CIA purchase black-market Vietnamese piasters for the rest of U.S. operations in Vietnam to cut costs, a highly illegal action. The CIA managed to avoid this money-saving request, arguing that the Company did not want "the secrecy of its money-exchange operations disturbed." Ever the faithful lackey, the Bureau of the Budget backed off.

"The budget of the fiscal year 1959 was almost entirely the work of the old-fashioned budget-balancer, Percival Brundage...." On paper, Brundage's budget "called for expenditure of a smaller percentage of the estimated ... gross national product than the budget of the previous year." In reality, "spending for other than defense purposes had ... a smaller slice of what was available." The Bureau had simply robbed Peter (the Public), to pay Paul (guess Who). Defense spending in 1959 went up, not down.

In the 1959 Senate hearings on 'Major Defense Matters', and while Percival Brundage was still operating as the Bureau's key "consultant," two full days were dedicated to "The Role of the Bureau of the Budget in Formulation and Execution of [the] Defense Budget." LBJ, then chair of the powerful Senate Preparedness Committee, interrogated new BOB Director Maurice H. Stans on the BOB'S national funding "straightjacket" and the Bureau's "arbitrary limitations" on military preparedness.

Stans assured Senator Johnson and his committee that the Bureau of the Budget "did not even review the Pentagon's budget requests the way it did those of other agencies." According to Stans, the Bureau of the Budget only did a "joint" review of military funding proposals and *never* attempted to "eliminate" Pentagon monetary requests. Stans further testified to Johnson and his watchdog committee that, for the Department of Defense, the BOB did not "make [any] eliminations or [even] determine a budget figure."

According to official Senate Preparedness Committee records, Johnson seemed more than curious about how the Pentagon could even overrule what vestigial budgetary control the BOB allegedly still possessed. Stans assured LBJ and his fellow senators that several definitive reasons excluded the Budget watchdogs from prying into Defense Department matters. Though Director Stans' explanations lacked common sense, Johnson and his associates apparently swallowed them whole.

After JFK was assassinated, President Johnson's Defense Secretary Robert McNamara gave testimony before the House Armed Services Committee on U.S. military funding; the Committee's chair asked McNamara whether the BOB exercised any significant control over the Pentagon budget. McNamara confidently replied, "The Bureau of the Budget has absolutely no authority to determine in any way the budget of the Defense Department."

Challenges to the administration's military budget have been rebuffed for decades regardless of who sits in the Oval Office, with the lapdog "oversight" mechanism always there to help slam the door. Senator William Proxmire once attempted "to press Budget Director Robert May, asking questions about items in the defense requests...." Mayo "loftily replied" that "the president's flexibility is better served by not getting into a debate on what is and what is not in the Defense budget."

How did our elected representatives in Washington, D.C. lose control of both Pentagon funding and U.S. Intelligence? A joint effort of the Bureau of the Budget and the Intelligence "community," often the same people, laid down an official paper trail that quietly stripped U.S. presidents of any real authority in the matter.

Following World War II, the elitist officials of the BOB under President Harry Truman dissolved the dangerously independent Office of Strategic Services, and promoted a series of bureaucratic acts culminating in the creation of the National Security Council and the Central Intelligence Agency.

President Eisenhower had lived with intelligence operations from his 1942 North Africa campaign through the surrender of Nazi Germany, and "paid considerable attention to [intelligence] ... during his tenure in the White House." His major intelligence briefings came from meetings with Foster Dulles, his Secretary of State, and Allen Dulles, his Central Intelligence Director, but an intermediate source may have been the most relevant: the president "had [the bulk of] his intelligence information channeled primarily through his staff assistant Colonel ... Andrew Goodpaster."

Though the president might not have fully realized it, Goodpaster was the White House's direct line to the operational side of the CIA. Listed with a variety of titles, Goodpaster (by 1961 a brigadier general), was both Eisenhower's White House staff secretary and the president's Pentagon liaison. Colonel Goodpaster also collaborated with the Bureau of the Budget and Percival Brundage in 1957 on the funding of Project Vanguard, "the result of NSC 5520 and ... intended to establish [the high-sounding] 'Freedom of Space'– [but actually] the right to overfly foreign territory for future intelligence satellites."

Goodpaster was the perfect link between the BOB, Percival Brundage, the President and budgetary decisions affecting serious intelligence collection. When Gary Powers' U-2 spy plane was brought down, Allen Dulles convened a CIA task force to evaluate the event which he had probably helped instigate, and Goodpaster was in attendance, ostensibly representing the White House.

In 1959, Eisenhower especially needed vital intelligence information about Berlin.

Brundage and Eisenhower had worked on several successive national budgets, a process actually constituting a review of viable covert intelligence actions, and Eisenhower was energized: "As a result of the President's [heightened] interest, the Bureau of the Budget increased its review of the size and scope of the United States intelligence effort." The president apparently wanted to direct a major overhaul of U.S. Intelligence machinery. But the BOB inundated him with eighteen proposed budget surveys, and only two of them "concerned the work of the intelligence agencies." Robert Macy, the chief of the Bureau's International Division, had taken an intensely "active interest in the work of the intelligence agencies...." Macy, in fact, was crucial as the Bureau's intelligence expert. Choking in all the memoranda smoke, "the Bureau's proposal for ... intelligence studies could not seem to get moving. All discussions resulted in such complete disagreement that nothing happened." The friends of U.S. Intelligence in the Bureau of the Budget had accomplished their purpose.

In Eisenhower's farewell address cautioning America about the marriage of Pentagon and corporate power, he failed to mention his administration's complete cooperation with the BOB in walking the bride and groom down the aisle. Once the Bureau had helped build that colossal cash cow, it assisted in turning it over to the Pentagon and the CIA, freeing both from any effective Constitutional restraints, apparently until worldwide peace breaks out, or Hell freezes over.

Percival Brundage & America's Power Structure

Following a long line of establishment money managers in the Treasury and the Bureau of the Budget, Director Percival Flack Brundage was a valued participant in official Cabinet meetings. He sat with the powerbrokers of defense and intelligence as a regular member of Eisenhower's National Security Council, his presence reverently noted by *US News and World Report* in April 1956.

The Director of the BOB continued to attend National Security Council sessions: for example, the NSC met in April, 1960, to examine C.D. Jackson's anti-Castro radio broadcasts. Brundage was still a consultant at the BOB in May 1960, just after the U-2 disaster aborted the scheduled U.S.-Soviet peace talks, when the Bureau again "initiated a study of all U.S. Intelligence activities."[13]

Not officially a National Security Council operation, it was sponsored by the Bureau of the Budget and staffed by "a special task force headed by the Director of Central Intelligence and ... representatives from State, Defense, the White House, the Budget Bureau, and CIA ..."; the task force had been "charged with the responsibility of preparing a comprehensive report to outgoing President Eisenhower prior to the end of 1960." Those two final phrases were awkwardly symptomatic: the task force was made up of close and influential friends of the Pentagon, whose intent was to build a unified military intelligence operation. Its mission was to organize and consolidate the Department of Defense's covert operations before John F. Kennedy, the probable incoming president, took office.

Officially, of course, the "motivating force behind the desire of the [outgoing] President and the Budget Bureau ... was the need for consolidating various Pentagon intelligence activities." But note the triangulation: the White House, the Pentagon, and the BOB.

The recommendations of the BOB's intelligence task force of May 1960 have never been open to public scrutiny, but the outcome was readily apparent: the "creation of the Defense Intelligence Agency ... and a corresponding reorganization of the U.S. Intelligence Board." When it was over the individual military services had lost their voting rights on the Board, while the new DIA gained significant leverage. Army, Navy and Air Force intelligence units were unceremoniously relegated to the peanut gallery. Score one more for the foxes.

Despite his retirement from the Bureau business, Brundage was apparently still operating as an asset of the BOB in 1962. Serious anxieties about funding for U.S. covert operations, including several "much criticized public media projects," were aired at a meeting organized by a "former budget official" who had brought together officers of "the Bureau of the Budget, CIA, FIAB, and relevant Undersecretaries in consideration of budgetary modifications." This conference in the early 1960's, organized by a "former budget officer" (unnamed, but obviously Percival Brundage), was described and cited in the minutes recorded on January 8, 1968 at the Council on Foreign Relations' third meeting of the "Discussion Group on Intelligence and Foreign Policy. According to the rather cryptic record of that 1968 meeting, the "problem" faced by the earlier Bureau of the Budget conferees was two-fold: retaining successful intelligence programs, and cutting away failed actions in hidden-budget items, black ops, and psychological warfare; the latter delicately designated "public media projects."

That early 1960s Bureau of the Budget meeting (cited at length by former CIA Deputy Director Richard Bissell in 1968) had faced a watershed moment: how could the Bureau and the U.S. Intelligence community replace old, unsuccessful projects with new foreign (and illegal domestic) policy enterprises, and keep the cash-flow at its current level?

The Agency stalled, not wanting to lose covert funding for an unnamed allied "foundation." Precious time was lost; then, before any significant operational backing could be achieved for both old and new CIA programs, the scheduled "next big review" of the BOB, the CIA and allied departments was trumped and dumped, "as a consequence of the Cuban missile crisis." Richard Bissell's secular parable of an earlier Budget/intelligence/foreign policy "problem" illustrated how difficult it was in 1968 to achieve an agreement on funding new covert actions without cutting old and treasured operations and institutions.

One attendee of the 1968 meeting, who had worked with both U.S. Intelligence and "private industry," actively supported what he called the "combined cryptologic budget," and seconded Bissell's argument.

But Douglas Dillon moved to close off this apparently sensitive area of concern.

The BOB, the CIA, the Military, & P.F. Brundage

Though U.S. military and covert intelligence establishments knew the truth for some time, the average American citizen might have had some difficulty understanding that an historic transfer of budgetary power to the Executive Office of the President occurred after 1939, controlled "for the most part by the powerful Bureau of the Budget...." In turn, the Bureau was staffed at the top by solid business and banking figures out of the national establishment, including Brundage. The Appropriations committees in the House and the Senate might trim a program here or there (especially domestic social programs and foreign aid), but the Bureau would triumph, working under the guise of "budget proposals from the President." An unnamed "candid member of the [Senate] Appropriations Committee" during the Eisenhower years admitted that for Congress, the defense "budget" was, in fact, a large political pork barrel.

Brundage finally "left" the Bureau of the Budget in 1960, precisely when his accounting genius was no longer needed. Surprisingly, the most comprehensive and even-handed examination of the BOB was authored by Percival Flack Brundage.

The foreword, by Robert P. Mayo, Director of the BOB in 1970, established two major truths about Percival Brundage. The first was personal: "[Brundage was] remembered fondly by his many friends at the Bureau as a gentleman of great courtliness and generosity ... wise in the ways of raising the esprit of the staff to new heights." The second was political, involving the recommendations of the so-called "second Hoover Commission" in reconstructing the accounting procedures of the U.S. government: Percival Brundage "was not only deeply involved in the effort to pass appropriate legislation [to effect that reconstruction], he was also responsible for establishing the Office of Accounting within the Bureau of the Budget to take the lead in an accelerated program for improving the accounting function throughout the government."

That is, of course, except for defense and intelligence funding.

Brundage's historical examination of the spending procedures of the federal government, from 1780 through 1970, was supported by seven charts and seventeen tables, clearly demonstrating his absolute and confident understanding of the business of national budgeting.

But in Chapter VIII, devoted to the BOB and the Department of Defense, Brundage did not confess to any collaboration between himself, his Bureau, and the military establishment. Instead, he quietly commented that, long after *he* left the Bureau, "former Budget Director Schultze and Director Mayo in June 1969 [in their testimony to the Joint Economic Committee of Congress] ... indicated that for several years the Bureau had not been questioning military priorities to the same extent that it had those of the civilian programs."

For "several years," read 'dog-years'.

In his chapter on "Social, Economic, and Other Civilian Agency Programs" Brundage might have included some comments on the CIA and its protected budget, but, save for two inconsequential references, the book is silent on the subject. Further, except for one irrelevant FBI reference, Brundage covers none of the other intelligence-gathering or secret operations of the federal government.

Brundage did reveal, with a few scattered citations, that he regularly sat representing the BOB at meetings of both the National Security Council and the president's Cabinet, and that the Eisenhower administration relied on the National Security Council to establish all the goals and expenditures of both the Defense Department and the CIA. He registered some minor fragments of his inside knowledge of the OCB, the committee inside the National Security Council that ran the nation's most delicate covert operations.

Percival Brundage: Personal History

William Mifton Brundage, Percival's father, had given up his Methodist ministry and become a Unitarian. Percival absorbed his father's liberal Protestant consciousness and became an active and influential Unitarian, deeply involved in international youth movements and European refugee needs.

As early as 1938, with both religious relief organizations and American intelligence strongly interested in the flow of refugees from Spain into Portugal and France, Percival Brundage directed the American Christian Committee for Refugees. In 1942, he was appointed director of the American Unitarian Association (AUA), holding that position through 1948, a time when the AUA was committed to humanitarian refugee work and U.S. Intelligence was hungry for information being generated from those same refugees. Brundage was active throughout the war years with European refugee relief, the National War Fund, the International Rescue and Relief Committee, the Joint Anti-Fascist Refugee Committee, the War Refugee Board, and the Refugee Relief Trustees, a knowing participant in that government-supported and intelligence-linked tangle. Brundage held key meetings with Joy Gano, the Dexters, and others closely associated with the collaboration between OSS and the Unitarian Service Committee.

On February 4, 1942, Brundage met with Howard Brooks and Vanan Fry, a signal association of refugee work officials with clandestine connections; Brundage described the meeting in a letter to Robert C. Dexter, Allen Dulles' intelligence asset on the Unitarian Service Committee. Brooks and Fry urged that the Unitarians financially support what Brundage called Fry's "project." Though he did not discourage Brooks and Fry, Brundage pointed out that the USC was short of funds "without tapping new sources of contributions," assuming Fry would contact other offices of the USC.

Earlier, in September 1941, at the exact time Varian Fry was sent back to the United States, the USC held a meeting on financing of projects in France and to hear certain "confidential reports" from Joy and Brooks, both of whom had intelligence connections in Europe.

Primarily interested in refugee relief and USC funding, Brundage was in a unique position to collect European intelligence information.

In 1949, he became director of the USC, an office he occupied through 1954, marked by the USC's apparent continuing cooperation with U.S. Intelligence, principally with the CIA. From 1952 though 1955, Brundage was president of the International Association for Liberal Christianity and Religious Freedom, later shortened to 'International Association for Religious Freedom' (IARF), with key American Unitarians, including Percival Brundage, holding influential offices in its worldwide liberal Protestant communion. From 1959 through 1962, Brundage chaired the Unitarian Development Fund Campaign, supporting key Unitarian domestic and international programs.

Brundage held pivotal offices in the Unitarian Church movement both at home and abroad from at least 1942 through 1954, twelve years that saw the Unitarian Service Committee and officers of its parent organization working closely with the OSS in World War II, then hopping effortlessly into bed with the CIA. In turn, the Agency protected its Unitarian assets, heavily censoring OSS-related records before turning them over to the USC.

Brundage & Southern Air Transport

After leaving the Bureau of the Budget, Percival Brundage and an associate, E. Perkins McGuire, a former Assistant Secretary of Defense, were asked in 1960 to hold the majority of a new airline's stock "in name only." Agreeing to do so, the two former federal officials assisted in establishing a major wing of the CIA's vast air transport system that included the legendary Air America. Specifically, with Pentagon-friendly Perkins McGuire, Brundage became a registered stockholder of Southern Air Transport (SAT), incorporated in Miami to fly major missions in both the Caribbean and Southeast Asia.

E. Perkins McGuire was the right man to call on for coordinating the massive efforts of U.S. business and the nation's military machine. McGuire's dedication to meeting the material needs of America's fighting forces and their undercover allies was coupled with his willingness to serve the U.S. power structure. By 1945, already familiar with the loci of critical decision-making, McGuire had become a member of Naval Secretary James Forrestal's Executive Office. Appropriately, McGuire was the Deputy Assistant Chief in charge of Industrial Readjustment.

In 1952, the Pentagon's combined Armed Services Support Center was the key to the united supply and logistics strategies. With his post-war transition experience, Perkins, now the Assistant Secretary of Defense for Supply and Logistics, became the crucial link between defense contractors, the national shippers of military common supplies, and the Armed Forces procurement divisions.

By 1955, Perkins had drawn close to the Joint Chiefs of Staff, testifying before the Senate Committee on Foreign Relations on American support of Batista's Cuba and colonial control of Cambodia. His identity badge now read "Deputy Assistant Secretary of Defense for Mutual Assistance."

McGuire's Pentagon associates in the 50's, including Deputy Undersecretary of Defense Robert B. Anderson, Deputy Secretary of Defense Donald Quarles, and Deputy Secretary of Defense Thomas S. Gates, were all at one time or another members of the select Operations Coordinating Board (by July 1, 1957, a part of the National Security Council). It was made up of CIA Director Allen Dulles, C.D. Jackson, Special Assistant to the President in Psychological Warfare, and McGuire's close friend from the Bureau of the Budget, Percival Flack Brundage.

When not a formal government employee, Perkins McGuire remained close to military and intelligence activities dependent on profitable industrial and business support. Listed as a "corporate executive," McGuire was chair of the U.S. Commission on Government Procurement from 1969 through December 1972, exhaustively examining and making recommendations on "legal remedies," "negotiation and subcontracting," "research and development," and "pre-contract planning." In 1985-86, McGuire was the Chair of the "President's Blue Ribbon Commission on Defense Management."

With Percy Brundage, E. Perkins McGuire was a perfect fit as one of the two stockholders of the CIA'S Southern Air Transport.

Wings Over The World

The history of McGuire's and Brundage's Southern Air Transport began with Paul Helliwell, "the CIA'S original overseas paymaster and Mister Black Bag." Throughout World War II, Helliwell headed U.S. special intelligence in China for the OSS, afterward creating a maze of banking operations that handled funding of major CIA clandestine actions in East Asia and the Pacific.

Helliwell bridged the gap between the demise of the OSS and the creation of the CIA as the "chief of the Far East Division of the War Department's Strategic Service Unit."

In 1950, while an officer of Wisner's Office of Policy Coordination, Helliwell initiated the take-off of our fledgling undercover air force by helping to "negotiate the sale of General Claire Chennault's airline, Civil Air Transport, to the CIA." By 1959, Air America, veiled behind its "parent" company, the Pacific Corporation, had evolved from Chennault's Civil Air Transport. Wholly owned and operated by the CIA, the company was subdivided into smaller units (including Southern Air Transport).

Helliwell established Sea Supply and Air America using "the Philippines and Thailand as staging bases for secret operations throughout Southeast Asia." For example, Helliwell's "black money" supported the Lansdale/Kaplan CIA/Catherwood psyops and covert operations in the Philippines. Helliwell's Sea Supply "ran guns and dope for the CIA in Thailand." His Castle Bank and Trust "was involved in fraud and political money movement in the Bahamas."

Castle Bank's reach was extensive: "One client company of Castle Bank was tied ... to the laundering of $5 million for the CIA'S use.... The client company was run by Wallace Groves ..." Groves was an Agency asset, a convicted stock swindler, and a close partner of Organized Crime leader Meyer Lansky.

Helliwell's sponsoring of narcotics trafficking and his "series of banks through which both CIA funds and drug profits were laundered" resulted in "a nationally protected drug traffic."

Helliwell was anointed by the upper reaches of CIA command as an unqualified success in the Pacific and Asia. Richard Bissell, the Agency's director of dirty tricks, "brought Helliwell back from the Far East to set up a Western Hemisphere version of Sea Supply and Air America out of Miami called Southern Air Transport, [together with] a new chain of black-money banks to pay for the Bay of Pigs operation that Bissell was planning."

Southern Air Transport was the Caribbean wing of operations, carrying with it all of Helliwell's dark baggage of drugs and guns, and was directly linked to the support of the Bay of Pigs invasion, channeled through the Double-Chek Corporation.

Double-Chek, a CIA front founded in Miami on May 14, 1959, recruited U.S. pilots for the Bay of Pigs. Its principle Florida attorney and officially listed president was Alex E. Carlson. In 1962, Carlson was also the registered legal representative "for [the] CIA proprietary, Southern Air Transport." Under Carlson as chief operating officer, Southern Air Transport was described by the Pentagon as "a civilian operation holding a $3.7 million contract to move mixed [unidentified] cargo and passenger loads on Far Eastern routes."

With Percival Brundage listed as one of the airline's two owners, SAT carried shipments of weapons, heavy supplies and narcotics in support of covert operations in Vietnam, Laos and Cambodia.

Southern Air Transport reportedly "operated out of offices in Miami and Taiwan." SAT's primary Asian address was "a post office box [#121241] in Taipei, Formosa...." Given its two main stockholders (Brundage and a former Department of Defense assistant secretary), it was understandable that "Southern's role in the Far East was ... flying profitable routes for the Defense Department."[14]

As late as 1972, SAT was financed in part by a "$2 million AID contract to fly [unidentified] relief supplies to ... Bangladesh." The intentionally tangled CIA airline financial controls meant, for example, that one of the Agency's key operations, CAT, leased a Southern Air Transport jet in 1968 that later crashed on Taiwan. In 1968 and again in 1972, the CIA supported SAT, hoping to assist in obtaining jet aircraft to continue to "live its [clandestine] cover." In 1968, the Agency was still exploring "Southern's capabilities for future interventions in Latin America...."

As a confirmed supporter and enabler of black-budget operations bypassing Constitutional controls, Percival Brundage allowed his name to be used as a "brass plate" in support of covert air operations in both Southeast Asia and Latin America. After several national investigations, this connection was confirmed by both the *Washington Post* and *Newsweek* in 1975.

Even Brundage's apparently selfless acts of support for humanitarian causes had a shadowy side. He served as the treasurer and director of Project HOPE, "the People-to-People Health Foundation," a seaborne medical aid program touring the poverty and disease-ridden ports around the Pacific Ocean and Southeast Asia for many years.

The biggest booster of the humanitarian project was C. D. Jackson, whose main interests were, naturally, the psyops possibilities. Conveniently, Project HOPE extended its healing largesse by shipping its materials aboard Southern Air Transport.[15]

Casparis, Brundage, & Schweitzer College

From 1950 through 1954, as Percival Brundage rose to power in both the Bureau of the Budget and the Unitarian Church, Swiss cleric Hans Casparis, together with his English wife and a group of liberal Protestant ministers, developed Schweitzer College. The American Friends of Albert Schweitzer College gave the institution significant moral, spiritual, and monetary support from the mid-1950's through the 1960's.

The College's curious history, the dubious academic record of Hans Casparis, and the anxieties of J. Edgar Hoover during the investigation into Lee Harvey Oswald's non-appearance at ASC, all demand a closer look at the college's supporters and their backgrounds.

Reviewing Percival Flack Brundage's career: [1] major Unitarian Church officer from 1942 through 1954 when the Unitarian Church was actively cooperating with the OSS and the CIA. [2] Deputy Director, Director, then key consultant of the Budget Bureau, 1954-1960, working in the interests of the Pentagon and CIA. [3] signatory of the incorporation papers of Southern Air Transport, a notorious CIA proprietary. [4] President of the IARF 1952-1955, when Schweitzer College was developed and proudly supported by the IARF as its "crown jewel."

On April 17, 1953, the Certificate of Incorporation of Friends of Albert Schweitzer College, Inc., was filed by the Law Offices of

Francis T. Christy at 30 Rockefeller Plaza in New York City, with the New York State Secretary of State. Though the direction, energy, and monetary support for the college would come from Boston and Cambridge, the "principal office of the Corporation [was] ... to be located in the Borough of Manhattan, City, County and State of New York."

"The number of its Directors shall be not less than three and not more than fifty." Three directors were listed: John H. Lathrop, John Ritzenthaler, and Percival Flack Brundage." Ritzenthaler was a close friend of Percival Brundage, both residing in Monclair, New Jersey. John Lathrop, a perfect director for the Friends of Albert Schweitzer College, was listed as one of the "subscribers" to the college's New York State incorporation along with Ritzenthaler, Brundage, Edward A. Cahill and Frederick May Eliot.

In 1938, John H. Lathrop worked with the Dexters (Allen Dulles' OSS connection to the Unitarians) and with Frederick Eliot and Seth Gano (both linked to the OSS). Lathrop, of course, may not have been aware of his associates' U.S. Intelligence operations.

The connection was, of course, Percival Flack Brundage, with his American intelligence connections. U.S. support for the strange Swiss institution flowed through the organization established by him and his fellow directors.

Oswald, Schweitzer College & Providence

On December 5, 1963, less than two weeks after the assassination of John F. Kennedy, Dr. Robert Schacht, pastor of the historic First Unitarian Church in Providence and the U.S. Director of Admissions for Albert Schweitzer College, was interviewed by FBI agents. Schacht had called the Bureau immediately following the murder of the president in Dealey Plaza, having recognized Oswald's name.

Dr. Schacht: "Oswald had filled out an application ... in the spring of 1959 while still in the Marine Corps.... Because the Oswald application was approved, I am sure that he must have given three references and their reports must have appeared satisfactory. But I cannot recall now who they were."

As stated earlier, Schacht's information has called for careful examination. Did Oswald ever write a letter of inquiry to Schacht? The Unitarian pastor referred only to Oswald's March 1959 college application. Did Schacht receive the shorter or longer application form from Oswald? Only the longer form would have had the necessary three references (all of which, as we have seen, were fictitious). Did Schacht, in fact, ever receive supporting letters from those fanciful references? If so, where are those letters? Schacht reported that Oswald's "application was approved...." How did Schacht receive this information? Did he get it from the Swiss college, the FBI, or his own Benevolent Street file that was permanently appropriated by the FBI?

When Schweitzer College's board of directors met in Switzerland just after the Kennedy assassination, its chief concern was the nature of Oswald's references. The board could not account for Oswald's acceptance by the American branch of the college's screening process. In his statement to the FBI, Schacht used a time-honored bureaucratic dodge, "the Oswald application was approved," begging the question, *who,* specifically, approved it?

For Pastor Schacht, December 5, 1963, was, at the very least, stressful. He was questioned by FBI agents about Oswald and gave up his Schweitzer College application files, never to see them again. Now he had to deal with a serious economic issue: literally, the continued life of the American Friends of Albert Schweitzer College, Inc.

An Urgent Message for Percival Brundage

From Switzerland, Ernest Cassara contacted the American Friends of Albert Schweitzer College on November 20th, and again in the first week of December, to say the college's American "Committee" was in economic trouble, so Robert Schacht wrote to the one person in the Unitarian community most qualified to help. On the morning of December 5th, before the FBI visit, Schacht called Percy Brundage in Washington, D.C., failed to make contact, then called him at his "home in [Pompano Beach,] Florida but could obtain no answer." Schacht needed Brundage's opinion on the relationship between the American Friends of Albert Schweitzer College and the "Bureau of Internal Revenue." In a letter to Brundage, Schacht's last paragraph summed up the problem: "Perhaps you have learned the bizarre news that Lee Oswald actually registered in the spring of 1959 for study in the third term of '60 at A.S.C. His application was processed and references sent to the College in Switzerland. However, he never showed up. What a strange world!"

Again the telling use by Schacht of the passive voice: Oswald's "application was processed and references [were] sent to the College in Switzerland."

Who else but Schacht would have "processed" and then sent the Oswald application to Switzerland? Who else but Schacht would have sent those references?

A strange world indeed: Robert Schacht had somehow allowed the future accused assassin of President John F. Kennedy to attach himself to Albert Schweitzer College. On the same day the FBI interviewed Schacht about Oswald's relationship to the college, the Providence Unitarian minister had written to one of the closest friends of the U.S. military and intelligence communities. Brundage was President of the American Friends of Albert Schweitzer College from 1953 through 1958: crucial developmental years, when the institution attracted students from the United States and around the world, and eventually U.S. Marine Lee Harvey Oswald.

In 1958, when Lee Harvey Oswald 'discovered' and applied to the relatively unknown Albert Schweitzer College, Percival Flack Brundage was Director of the Bureau of the Budget; he was one of the three incorporating officers of the Friends of Albert Schweitzer College, and President of the American Friends of Albert Schweitzer College. Oswald's application was officially approved by a mysteriously unspecified officer of the College, but when the school bell rang in 1959, he was nowhere to be found.

Lee Harvey Oswald
Passport Photo

Essay Eight

The Oil-Intelligence-Unitarian Universe of Lee Harvey Oswald

After the assassination, "[Allen Dulles] joked in private that the JFK conspiracy buffs would have had a field day if they had known ... he had actually been in Dallas three weeks before the murder ... that one of his mistress Mary Bancroft's childhood friends had turned out to be a landlady for Marina Oswald ... and that [the] landlady was a well-known leftist with distant ties to the family of Alger Hiss."

The spymaster's post-assassination jocularity was not only revealing of his black and twisted soul, it was seriously inaccurate. Mary Bancroft's so-called childhood attachment was to the mother-in-law of Marina's close friend Ruth Paine. Marina and her children were living with Ruth as friends in need, not renters The alleged Alger Hiss relationship to Ruth Paine's family, however, suggested how sensitive Allen Dulles was to the dangerously *reticulate* context of the John F. Kennedy murder.

Oswald & the Unitarians

From 1958 through 1963 and beyond, Lee Harvey Oswald's life and death were embedded in the Unitarian Church movement and its liberal religious associations; in turn, that same Unitarian network was infused with major domestic and foreign intelligence connections, a Unitarian/intelligence matrix that defined the JFK assassination. US Intelligence's misuse of religious institutions could not have been better illustrated. ASC was cooperatively created by European and American Unitarians and their liberal allies.

Frederick May Eliot and Percival Flack Brundage, two powerful American Unitarians closely linked to US Intelligence, were significant leaders of the Unitarian coalition establishing and then supporting Schweitzer College.

As a False Identity candidate, Lee Harvey Oswald fit the profile of a US counter-intelligence asset; part of a 40 year-old network run by Allen Dulles, using religious individuals and groups, including Quakers and Unitarians. John Foster Dulles, with his own history of misusing liberal religious groups, worked hand-in-glove with his brother.

Following the JFK assassination and Oswald's death, Unitarian minister Robert Schacht in Providence, Rhode Island, program chairperson for US citizens applying to Schweitzer College, was visited by FBI agents who confiscated his Oswald file, never returning it. Later, the Warren Commission examined Lee Harvey Oswald's visit (or visits) to Los Angeles and his possible attendance at the First Unitarian Church of L.A. where he may have received information about Unitarian-supported ASC from Stephen Fritchman, a radical Los Angeles Unitarian minister whose activities were investigated by an American intelligence officer tracking both the L.A. minister and Lee Harvey Oswald. Oswald had been enmeshed in US intelligence-monitored Unitarianism in Europe and the US. But did Oswald have an even closer and more personal Unitarian connection in Texas?

Oswald & the Paines

When Marina and Lee Harvey Oswald settled in Dallas, Michael Paine and his wife Ruth Hyde Paine ("the kindly Quaker woman") were already residents of the area. No other household in the United States supplied the Dallas Police, FBI, and Warren Commission with more "evidence" of Lee Harvey Oswald's alleged guilt than the Paines: the Paine garage in Irving, Texas, was an incriminatory storehouse. According to Galeton Fonzi, a Congressional investigator, "One glaring example of the quality of the [House Select] Committee's investigation was ... Ruth Paine was never called as a witness."

Who, then, were Ruth and Michael Paine?[1]

Ruth Paine's father and mother, William Avery Hyde and Carol Hyde, were prominent Unitarians in Ohio. The Unitarian Service

Committee, a significant supporter of Schweitzer College, had collaborated with the OSS in World War II and, later, with the CIA-penetrated US Agency for International Development (USAID). During World War II, Hyde was an agent of the OSS. Later, he worked for USAID as it cooperated closely with the CIA. In addition, Ruth's brother-in-law John Hoke worked for the Communications Resource Division of USAID.

According to John Gilligan, President Jimmy Carter's USAID director, many offices of the USAID were populated "from top to bottom" by CIA agents or assets. According to Gilligan, "The idea was to plant operatives in every kind of activity we had overseas-government, volunteer, religious, every kind." Ruth Hyde Paine's familial Intelligence connections were close. Ruth's sister, Sylvia Hyde Hoke, worked either for the Air Force, the CIA, or both. In 1957, William Avery Hyde (Ruth's father) was evaluated for a CIA assignment in Vietnam but (at least officially) was not used by the Agency. Hyde toured Latin America from October 1964 to August 1967, covering Peru, Bolivia, Ecuador, and Panama, afterward composing a report sent to both the State Department and the CIA. William Avery Hyde and George De Mohrenschildt had both worked for the International Cooperative Alliance (ICA).

A post-assassination intelligence report on Ruth Paine and her father recorded that William Avery Hyde and his wife Carol had closely associated with known CIA operatives, but the report contained an additional and important notation: "Sam Papich" had been given the information. Papich was the partner of William Sullivan in the FBI's counter-intelligence operations, cooperating with James Jesus Angleton of the CIA's corresponding unit; Papich was the Bureau's CIA counter-intelligence contact reporting directly to Angleton; and both he and Sullivan were longtime Bureau investigators of False Identity and Illegals espionage cases. One such case concerned Lee Harvey Oswald.

William Avery Hyde

Baron George De Mohrenschildt, Oswald's closest friend in the Russian community of Dallas/Fort Worth and a world traveler with close links to at least four spy agencies, had a working relationship with J. Walton Moore, the chief of the CIA's Domestic Contacts Division in Dallas. Joseph Dryer, an asset of the CIA, friend of

De Mohrenschildt and witness for the House Select Committee on Assassinations was supplied with a list for possible identification "of names of a number of people who may have had some connection or association with George De Mohrenschildt." Dryer recognized two names: one was "Dorothe Matlack." Ms. Matlack was the US Army's Assistant Director of the Office of Intelligence and the Office's contact with the CIA. In effect, Dorothe Matlack was the Pentagon's liaison to the Agency. In turn, Director Matlack and De Mohrenschildt met on May 7, 1963, just prior to the Baron and his wife leaving for Haiti on an intelligence-related mission.

The meeting between Army intelligence and Oswald's reputed "sitter" was, in fact, a densely populated thicket. Present were: Clemard Charles, a Haitian banker who dealt in arms sales, acted as a CIA funding conduit, and functioned as a top advisor to the president of Haiti; Army intelligence officer Sam Kail, close associate of anti-Castro Cubans at the Miami JM/WAVE station and responsible for key elements of the Army/Agency plots against Fidel; CIA officer Tony Czaikowski, an Agency staff officer representing the CIA's interest in Haiti as a launching platform for another invasion of Cuba.

Clemard Charles pleaded for the overthrow of President Duvalier (at least one plot reportedly including De Mohrenschildt) as the Haitian banker who apparently toted large sums of money around Washington for investment and gifts to D.C. politicos just short of bribery. There were at least two cover stories for the Baron: a Haitian-approved "geological survey" and a contemplated exploration of sisal and hemp plantation purchases or leases.

The second name Joseph Dryer recognized was "William Avery Hyde." Everything about Hyde and De Mohrenschildt suggests their foreign travels would have been valuable to the CIA'S Domestic Contacts Division both in Washington and in Dallas. Certainly William Avery Hyde's OSS/CIA links, given Hyde's closeness to his daughter Ruth Paine, ought to have troubled any government investigator of the JFK assassination.

Ruth Hyde Paine's family was apparently dysfunctional. William Avery Hyde consigned his wife of over thirty years to an Ohio mental institution before divorcing in her in 1961. Carol Hyde was "treated for paranoia and delusions," but her daughter Ruth was apparently doubtful about the grounds for her mother's commitment.

She herself felt partly responsible for her mother's behavior. After the divorce, Carol Hyde was released from the Ohio sanitarium, entered Oberlin College and pursued ministerial studies to become a hospital chaplain. She was ordained a Unitarian minister.

Michael & George Lyman Paine

Michael Paine's father was George Lyman Paine, called Lyman Paine by his son and those who knew him well. Lyman Paine was a Harvard graduate, a New York architect, and, after the Great Depression, a serious explorer of Marxist alternatives. Moving to Los Angeles, Lyman Paine married Freddie Drake and joined a "socialist splinter group," becoming a key figure in the anti-Stalinist Trotskyite movement in the United States. The Socialist Workers Party, chief organ of the Trotskyites in the United States, was closely monitored and even infiltrated by US Intelligence, becoming a path for American counter-intelligence to run operations against the Communist Party and keep a close watch on the Fair Play for Cuba Committee, heavily supported by Trotskyites.

Lyman Paine was suspected (by some) of being a double agent tasked to penetrate and permanently cripple Trotskyism as an independent Socialist entity. Oddly enough, Michael Paine, apparently knowledgeable about nuances of Marxist/Leninist anti-Stalinism, once characterized his friend Lee Harvey Oswald as a Trotskyite, and FBI Agent Hosty testified to the Warren Commission that on November 5, less than two weeks before the murder in Dealey Plaza, Ruth Paine told Hosty that Oswald "admitted to her being a Trotskyite Communist."

According to a Dallas FBI agent, "George Lyman Paine, Jr., had telephoned [his son Michael] ... the night of the assassination. A long-distance operator ... illegally listened in on the conversation [why?] and later reported what she had heard to the FBI." The Paines' telephone lines were obviously being monitored by US Intelligence. According to that same Bureau agent, "George Paine was a well-known Trotskyite, and during his telephone call to his son ... said, 'We all know who did this....'" The FBI had, in fact, been monitoring George Lyman Paine for some time as a Bureau "security-index subject." From no later than 1953 through as late as October 2, 1963, the FBI submitted regular reports on Lyman Paine: one in 1953, another in 1955, three in 1956, two in 1957, one in 1958, three in 1959, three in 1960, and the last in 1963, just before the assassination. All the Bureau's reports are preserved in the Warren Commission's documents (CD 600-615).

Apparently the FBI found the coincidence not at all remarkable: that the Paines, with their liberal/anti-Communist orientation and with a major anti-Communist/Trotskyite link in their family, should befriend the family of an admitted Trotskyite (who had re-defected from the Soviet Union), at least according to Michael and Ruth Paine. Despite the clear contradictions in Oswald's left-wing resume´, including his closeness to the son of a major anti-Stalinist socialist being tracked by the FBI, the Bureau apparently took no further notice after November 22, 1963.

The Warren Commission did pay some attention to the odd confluence, closely questioning Michael Paine about his father, about Lyman Paine's political interests, and whether Michael was aware that his father had used at least two pseudonyms: "Thomas L. Brown" and "Lyman Pierce," the latter probably a pun on that which caused pain, a pierce; or the surname of Charles Pierce, a philosopher Lyman Paine admired; or both.

Ruth Forbes Paine Young

Michael Paine's mother was Ruth Forbes, who had an impor-tant intelligence connection: she and Mary Bancroft, Allen Dulles' OSS lover and fellow agent, were lifelong friends. In Mary Bancroft's careful rendition of her life as an OSS agent, she identi-fied George Lyman Paine and Ruth Forbes Paine as her close friends both in Boston and New York; but they disappeared from Bancroft's narrative after 1933, though Ruth Forbes Paine remained a part of Bancroft's life. After her divorce Ruth and her second husband, Ar-thur Young, were intimates of Mary Bancroft for years.

Ruth Young, or Ruth Forbes Young, or Ruth Forbes Paine Young be-came a World Federalist, founded the International Peace Academy, and, together with her husband Arthur, created the Institute for the Study of Consciousness, Berkeley, California.

Arthur Young, Michael Paine's stepfather, was an inventor, and deeply interested in what would later be called general systems theory, includ-ing its para-psychological and spiritual dimensions. He "had a serious interest in both extrasensory perception and astrology," an oversimpli-fied tag for Young's belief in a pervading cosmic synergy. Young was one of the creators of the Bell Helicopter and was responsible for obtaining a high-tech/high security clearance job for his stepson Michael Paine at Bell's operation near Dallas. Michael had earlier worked for the Franklin Institute, a CIA "conduit."

Michael's wife Ruth apparently considered Arthur and Ruth Young important elder mentors. She periodically consulted the Philadelphia-area Youngs about undisclosed topics, especially in the summer of 1963. Michael and Ruth were originally from the Philadelphia area, where they were reportedly active Quakers. How had it all begun?

Ruth Avery Hyde

Ruth Avery Hyde established her earliest liberal, philosophical and political credentials at Antioch College in Yellow Springs, Ohio. By 1951, she had become a member of the Quakers, the Society of Friends. Ruth instructed senior Russian Jews at the YMCA in Philadelphia and taught physical education to schoolchildren in a Friends program; her post-graduation years were lived in "Quakerism's great American stronghold, southeastern Pennsylvania...." Ruth met Michael Paine in 1955 at a Quaker service, and they sang together in the madrigal group. They were married in December, 1957.

For a short time Ruth and Michael lived in a barn on the estate of Arthur Young, Michael's stepfather. It was here, reportedly working with Arthur Young on "aeronautical designs," that Michael picked up sufficient expertise to land an engineering job at Bell Helicopter in Fort Worth. It may have helped that Arthur's patent, sold to Larry Bell in 1941, made the Bell Helicopter possible.

The Paines moved to Irving, Texas, and by 1958, sparked by Ruth's Russophilia, became active in the Dallas/Fort Worth area's expatriate Russian community. This was a highly conservative, anti-Soviet and Orthodox Christian community whose hierarchy was compromised by both the CIA and the KGB. Prominent among the White Russians was Paul M. Raigorodsky, at one time employed by the NATO Special Representative to Europe, probably an intelligence-related office. In 1963, Raigorodsky was a member of the Board of Directors of the CIA-funded Tolstoy Foundation. The relationship between the ostensibly liberal Philadelphia Quaker couple and the reactionary Russian expatriates was a curious fit.

The Oswalds Meet Ruth Paine

In February 1963 Lee and Marina Oswald were brought by George De Mohrenschildt and his wife to a social gathering in the Dallas-Fort Worth area. There the Oswalds met Ruth Paine, and an intimate relationship between Ruth and Marina began. Though the Paines had recently separated, the couple remained close. Marina and her first child lived with Ruth while Michael and Lee visited periodically. The circumstances surrounding the initial meeting of Ruth Paine and Oswald resonate with special intelligence dimensions, suggesting he was already being evaluated (or even prepared) as a possible patsy.[2]

Volkmar Schmidt

In the 1950s, both George De Mohrenschildt and his wife had major connections to the CIA; and though the Baron played with a variety of political ideas, he was ultimately an anti-Communist elitist involved in petrochemical intelligence. Among De Mohrenschildt's many conservative and reactionary friends with oil interests and suspected intelligence links was a young man named Volkmar Schmidt. An émigré from Germany, Schmidt had resided in the United States for less than two years, becoming a research chemist at the Mobile (Socony-Vacuum) Magnolia Research Laboratories in Duncanville, Texas. The Baron reportedly decided that the German reactionary Schmidt and the anti-Soviet Marxist Oswald should meet.[3]

Mrs. de Mohrenschildt prepared a buffet-style dinner, with the Oswald's and Volkmar Schmidt invited. When Schmidt made his appearance, Marina and the de Mohrenschildts withdrew to another room, conversing in Russian, while Lee and Schmidt talked in the kitchen for over three hours. According to Edward Epstein, Schmidt found Oswald "articulate" but "emotionally detached" in his impressive political commentary contrasting the Soviet Union and the United States.

Oswald must have intended to provoke Schmidt, who reportedly did not rise to the bait, or Schmidt deliberately falsified the conversation. According to Schmidt (as reported by Epstein), Oswald virulently attacked President Kennedy's foreign policy, specifically pinpointing the Bay of Pigs and the Cuban Missile Crisis, citing them as instances of US "interventions" and "imperialism." But every assassination witness who knew anything of Oswald's political feelings testified that Lee admired John F. Kennedy. Lee's alleged outburst against JFK should therefore be considered either a deliberate provocation or it never really happened, and was fabricated to fit the government line.

Schmidt told Epstein he feigned sympathy for Oswald's positions, employing a psychological strategy he learned in Germany. Schmidt baited Oswald with a negative analysis of right-wing General Edwin A. Walker and the impending American Fascist state. According to Schmidt (again as reported to Epstein), Oswald became increasingly agitated.[4]

After the dinner, George and Jeanne drove the Oswalds home in the Baron's car. They characterized Volkmar Schmidt as a neo-Nazi fascist whose ideas were embodied in the John Birch Society, but Lee was silent. Musing over his new acquaintance, Schmidt decided he had closely read Oswald's distorted psyche, concluding that he was completely alienated, self-destructive, and suicidal. Schmidt decided to do something about poor Lee's mental health: he would organize a party for this character out of Dostoevsky so Lee "could meet and talk to other people interested in political ideas."

The Magnolia Party

Volkmar Schmidt shared his living space with three other men: Everett Glover, the owner of the house and a research chemist at Magnolia Research Laboratories, who apparently worked in Dallas; geologist Richard Pierce, also at Magnolia; and Michael Paine, separated from his wife. Glover had met Lee and Marina earlier at the De Mohrenschildts, and he thought it would be entertaining to have Oswald air his views on the Soviet Union. But after joining Glover in planning the party and sharing in its costs, Schmidt left for Germany "on business" and reportedly never saw the Oswalds again.

Both Michael and Ruth Paine were invited to the party, but for some reason Michael did not attend, despite Schmidt's reported intention to link up Oswald and Paine because they shared an interest in politics. Present were Magnolia employee Richard Pierce and his "girlfriend" Betty "Mooney" MacDonald, onetime Jack Ruby employee, and Magnolia's librarian. Also attending was another Magnolia research employee, Norman Fredricksen, with his wife Elke.

The separation of Lee and Marina Oswald began on February 22, 1963, at the Glover party. Seated in the kitchen were Ruth Paine, Marina Oswald, and the De Mohrenschildts. Though Ruth Paine was a student of Russian, she spoke in English, with the De Mohrenschildts translating into Russian for Marina. Marina's isolation had begun. In the living room, Elke Fredricksen, Norman Fredricksen, Betty MacDonald, Richard Pierce, and Everett Glover, the entire Magnolia party group, "pulled their chairs ... in a circle around Oswald and began asking questions about what life was like in the Soviet Union."

The Sun Oil Company

The most inclusive frame of reference for the "party" was not Mobile Oil, Socony/Vacuum Oil, or even the Magnolia Research Labs, but rather Ilya Mamantov's Dallas employment by the Sun Oil Company (Sunoco). Sun Oil was owned and operated by multi-millionaire J. Howard Pew and his family, among the richest and most powerful financial supporters of the Republican Party in the 1950s and 60s, major funders for extreme right-wing political groups in the United States, and enthusiastic backers of key anti-Communist Christian revivalists.[5]

Though the Pew Memorial Fund was one of the thirteen most heavily-endowed of US philanthropism, its operations were carefully cloaked: Texas Congressman Wright Patman, for example, complained about the Pew Fund's "defiance" of his Congressional investigation. Like Arthur Young, Ruth Forbes Paine Young, and the Catherwood family, the Pews were a prominent part of the Philadelphia elite: twenty-one Pew family members were listed in the Philadelphia Social Register.

Among the many Sun Oil/Pew Memorial Trust activities linked to both political and petroleum intelligence was the Pew/Rockefeller operation supporting Wycliffe Bible/Summer Institute of Linguistics evangelism in Brazil's Amazon forests, a part of the Rockefellers' long history of using religion for the family's political and economic ends. The fusion of bible-thumping and oil exploration in the dense Brazilian rain forest called for a futuristic sky vehicle capable of taking off from postage stamp airstrips, able to make fast getaways under fire, yet capable of hovering at very slow speeds over an area targeted for religious pamphlet bombings and/or the collection of intelligence on hostile Amazon natives. The Helio Courier was precisely that kind of aircraft. A Miami Cuban-American, reportedly a CIA contact, had a Helio Courier plane available, purchased from him and presented to the Wycliffe Bible/Pew/Rockefeller operations in Brazil.

The Cuban-American received a payment split between Sam Milbank, a Rockefeller agent, and the Pew Memorial Fund. The Helio in the Amazon concretely illustrated the manipulation of religion by invasive oil companies (Pew/Sun Oil and Rockefeller) and the CIA. In the 1960s, Pew/Sun Oil operative Ilya Mamantov was a solid indication that reactionary oil operations had serious US intelligence connections in Dallas. His influence was pervasive: in the Russian-speaking Dallas/Fort Worth community; in establishing the Russian Orthodox Church parish; in his teaching of scientific Russian to Magnolia technology experts; and in his translation of Marina Oswald's first post-assassination statements.

After the JFK murder, neither the Dallas Police, the Dallas County Sheriffs Office, the Secret Service, nor the FBI initially gained control of Marina Oswald's earliest statements on key evidence: Jack Alston Crichton, a "petroleum independent operator," a member of the Army Reserve's Intelligence Service, and the chief of "a local Army Intelligence Unit" was quickly at Marina Oswald's side. Crichton then called Sun Oil agent Ilya Mamantov to assist in interpreting Marina.

Mamantov and Crichton shared a right-wing orientation centered in the Republican Party: Ilya Mamantov was a precinct boss for the GOP, and Jack Crichton became the party's candidate for governor in 1964. Beginning in 1955, Mamantov was a Dallas Sun Oil research geologist; in 1960 he taught technical Russian "in the Dallas area" to "scientific personnel" pursuing "scientific research" at the Magnolia Research Lab in Duncanville, Texas. Mary Ferrell recalled that the majority of research people at Magnolia Labs, including French and Russian technicians, held "doctorates."

Why, after all the corporate decisions that transformed Vacuum Oil, Socony Oil, Socony-Vacuum, and Mobile, did Magnolia (though primarily its laboratories) remain Magnolia? The Mobile/Socony-Vacuum decision was obvious: it kept its oil exploration, research, and intelligence focus in the Magnolia Labs as a single Cold War entity, opening it up to expatriate French,

German, and Russian oil experts. Among those experts was Ilya Mamantov.

Mamantov was well known in Dallas: James Herbert Martin, local lawyer with connections to Jack Ruby and, after the assassination, to Marina Oswald and Time, Inc. He was asked during his Warren Commission testimony about Mamantov; Martin replied: "I think he works for Sun Oil Company...." Ilya Mamantov was not only well known; he knew everyone who came to the Feb. 22 ambush party for Lee and Marina Oswald.

The Magnolia Party's Connections

Everett Glover and Volkmar Schmidt were members of a madrigal ensemble along with Michael and Ruth Paine. Glover's Magnolia group studied Russian under Ilya Mamantov. Peter Gregory, a Dallas-area "consulting petroleum engineer," and Mamantov were both involved in translating, interpreting, and finally manipulating Marina Oswald's post-assassination statements and testimony. Volkmar Schmidt and Norman Fredricksen had psychological warfare connections: Schmidt admitted to being "fascinated with the techniques of hypnosis," and, in Germany, "Fredricksen's father had been director of (C.D. Jackson's) Radio Free Europe," a communication program utilizing pysops methods.

Thus, the intervention party for the Oswald's included people with CIA-supported ultra-conservative religious ties, psyops and right-wing links in petrochemical intelligence, and military/industrial connections. In this context, Quaker/Unitarian Ruth Hyde Paine's presence gives rise to some questions.[6]

Ruth Paine Inserts Herself

Two months after Ruth Paine and Marina Oswald met, Lee announced he was moving to New Orleans to seek employment, and Ruth asked Marina to bring her infant daughter and live with Ruth in her home. In May 1963, Oswald informed Marina and Ruth he had found work. Ruth Paine then drove Marina and her child to New Orleans. On September 23, 1963, Ruth returned to New Orleans, packed up Marina, pregnant with her second child, and drove them back to her home in Irving, Texas, where her second daughter was born. Marina and the two children resided there until just after the assassination and subsequent murder of her husband.

Prior to leaving New Orleans, Oswald had told Ruth and Marina he would be looking for work in Houston or Philadelphia. Houston made sense, since Dallas/Fort Worth, Houston and New Orleans constituted a kind of tri-city employment area; but why Philadelphia? Both Michael and Ruth Paine had been residents of the area, and his parents were still there, so Ruth herself may have suggested the city to Oswald. Even this possible benevolence on Ruth's part had a darker side: the Russian-speaking community of the Dallas area's St. Nicholas Parish had received substantial support from an important source of CIA money, the Catherwood Foundation, founded in Bryn Mawr, Pennsylvania, ten miles outside of Philadelphia.

After Oswald returned to the Dallas area, he visited Marina and the girls on weekends. "The Pain," as Lee sardonically nicknamed her, successfully kept the Oswalds from re-uniting during the run-up to Dealey Plaza. It was she who helped Lee get his job at the Texas School Book Depository in October, 1963, moving him into place as the designated fall-guy. The contents of her garage and household, combined with her Warren Commission testimony, provided the most damning hard evidence against the dead man. Only her confused, monoglot and highly suggestible ward Marina did more damage to her husband's character. In both Ruth's and her husband's family background were humanitarian, religious, and government-related/intelligence activity. Was this woman Marina's covert handler in the deadly murder game.

Ruth Paine & the US-Soviet East-West Exchanges

Beginning in 1957, Ruth Paine began an intensive study of Russian, starting with Berlitz books and records, then at the University of Pennsylvania, and finally Middlebury College as late as the summer of 1959. The Paine's then moved to Irving and quickly hooked up with the disgruntled right-wing Russian émigrés, as if it had all been pre-ordained.

In Philadelphia in 1958, Ruth was an active member of the Young Friends Committee of North America, acting, according to her own Warren Commission testimony, as the primary liaison between its East-West Contacts Committee and the US State Department. Earlier, Ruth and Friends had promoted correspondence between young American and Soviet citizens, then actual visits by

Russians to the United States. The committee eventually brought over a grand total of three: "a journalist, a factory worker, and an economics student," with Ruth assisting in "preparations for their tour" and later meeting them at a Philadelphia party.[7]

This apparent good-will gesture had a particularly, multi-layered dimension. In January 1958, Ambassadors William Sterling Byrd Lacy and Georgi N. Zaroubin signed an agreement to establish technical, cultural and educational exchanges between the feuding superpowers. On February 21, 1958, the US Council on Student Travel in New York and the Soviet Youth Committee in Moscow jointly announced that the commencement of the program. With Lacy's official signature, Ruth Paine's plans could move forward.

William S. B. Lacy

Born in Grand Junction, Colorado in 1910, Lacy attended the elitist Morey Preparatory School in Denver and received his bachelor's degree from the University of Colorado in 1932. In World War II, Lacy was appointed chief of the division of controls and analysis in the Foreign Economic Administration (FEA); its mission was overseeing America's "foreign economic affairs." Created on September 25, 1943, by presidential decree, the FEA incorporated six already-existing relief and rehabilitation organizations and operations, including the Office of Economic Warfare. In addition, the FEA became the political/economic cover for the Export-Import Bank of Washington, the Petroleum Reserves Corporation, the Rubber Development Corporation, and the US Commercial Company.

William S. B. Lacy brought with him his Foreign Economic Administration experience in political and economic intelligence when he moved to the United Nations Relief and Rehabilitation Administration (UNRRA). UNRRA was actually a function of the US government, its "United Nations" label adopted before the UN was established. Lacy was appointed assistant deputy director of UNRRA handling major supplies and procurement for the "liberated areas" and "planning for the control of occupied territories." A flood of political, military, economic, industrial, and displaced persons information flowed through the Foreign Economic Administration and UNRRA while William S.B. Lacy held key positions in both wartime institutions. Much of the actions and decisions of the two agencies were strongly influenced by the US Department of

State, and in 1945 Lacy joined the Department and was assigned to its Division of Philippines and Southeast Asian Affairs, headquartered in Washington, D.C.

Lacy, Southeast Asia & Ed Lansdale

In the federal archives, the Division's "Confidential U.S. State Department Special Files" on Southeast Asia (1944-1966), contain a huge body of information and intelligence on Indochina, Thailand, China and Taiwan, Hong Kong, Indonesia, Japan, Macao, Malaya, South Vietnam, Laos, Cambodia, South and North Korea, and the Philippines. The largest file in this collection is the "Records of the Philippine and Southeast Asian Division, 1944-1952," which includes the available papers and documents on "the plans and overall policies of the State Department for the Philippines" as well as the occupied islands of the Pacific Ocean and the "European colonies in Southeast Asia." The documents cover US policies governing the "political, economic, commercial, and military matters" of the entire Pacific/Southeast Asian area. From 1945 through 1950, William S.B. Lacy helped to create and maintain these State Department records, laboring at the Office of the Philippine and Southeast Asian Affairs. In 1950, he was appointed Director of the crucial division.

John F. Melby was an associate of Lacy's in his southeast Asia bailiwick. A career US Foreign Service Officer from 1937 through 1955, Melby gave an "Oral Interview" for the Truman Presidential Museum and Library in November 1986, in which Robert Accinelli questioned him about William S.B. Lacy and the activities of the division. During his tenure there, Melby was in close contact with the CIA'S Ed Lansdale in the Philippines. Melby believed Lansdale's anti-Huk operations had nothing to do with "Communist groups outside the Philippines"; rather, the Huk group was a populist "radical movement ... [that] came out of the rice situation in Luzon." In 1950, Lacy became Melby's "immediate supervisor." Melby described his director as flamboyant, dressed in funereal black with bright red hair and a theatrically curled "guardsman" mustache. According to his division associate, Lacy was a "great poseur," desperately interested in establishing a Lacy family link to British nobility, "a sort of Louis XIV reactionary."

Melby, however, may have been deflecting any real examination of Lacy's serious side. He noted that Lacy had "strange people" with

French Indochina and OSS backgrounds occupying critical division desks. Strange people, that is, with relevant intelligence experience. Melby was the most knowledgeable person about the Philippines at the division: he was "in charge of the Philippines," and had headed a mission out of the Pentagon to the Pacific in late 1950. The mission's tour included Indochina and the Philippines, assessing anti-Communist military needs and checking crucial arms traffic for the Defense Department. The Philippines and Thailand, in fact, were the only Asian allies of the US with troops in Korea after the "Police Action" broke out in 1950. Melby united major intelligence and military concerns of the US government.

William Lacy had predicted that "we" would eliminate all the "Commies," and then, "by God," all "the goddamn liberals." He was moved to the Philippines in 1952 to join a crucial military/intelligence operation. Lacy followed a flood of US military, intelligence, and economic missions that began in 1950. From 1952 through 1955, Lacy, "a brilliant and aggressive diplomat," was Counselor and Deputy Chief of Mission at the US Embassy in Manila, first working with the Philippine military and with Ed Lansdale's anti-Huk CIA program of psychological warfare in support of Ramon Magsaysay, the Agency's choice of Filipino defense minister/general. Magsaysay was ultimately elected president of the Philippines in 1953, a psyops-driven victory. Lacy and Lansdale, representing the US State Department, the military, and the CIA, effectively ran President Magsaysay and his government. Lansdale, Magsaysay's closest advisor, linked up the CIA, the Joint US Military Advisory Group and the US Embassy, through William S.B. Lacy.

Time magazine, on November 23, 1953, took note, citing Lansdale's crucial roles in Magsaysay's anti-Huk campaign, presidential victory, and subsequent elevation to anti-Communist sainthood. *Time* also noted that, "Polished, precise William Lacy, Councilor of the US Embassy, became the man to whom Magsaysay turned daily for counsel." Flushed with counterinsurgency success in the Philippines, Lansdale left in 1953 to supervise two Southeast Asian narcotics investigations before he was deployed to Vietnam. William Lacy was awarded the Filipino Legion of Honor, the fifth highest "military and security" decoration of the Philippines, established in 1947 and carrying its highest rank of "Commander."

Yearning to be a full-fledged ambassador, Lacy was posted in 1955 to the Republic of Korea as an "envoy," a "minister/counselor." After less than a year, Lacy was booted out of Korea. His antipathy to non-Caucasians, not to mention other abrasive qualities, resulted in President Syngman Rhee declaring Lacy persona non grata.

When Lacy died on December 11, 1978, the victim of a ravaged stomach already three-quarters removed, his State Department obituary listed him as "Ambassador (Ret.)." He had been a member of the Board of Examiners for the Foreign Service and the Deputy Commandant of the National War College, whose curriculum always emphasized "the politico-military aspects of Defense policies and programs," a perfect focus for the politico-military elitist Lacy.

Before retiring in 1961, William Sterling Byrd Lacy, a frustrated anti-liberal racist, was appointed by Secretary of State John Foster Dulles as Dulles' Special Assistant for East-West Exchanges. The year was 1956. Lacy would oversee the key State Department program of student exchange between the Soviet Union and the United States following a formal agreement. In early October 1957, Frederick T. Merrill, Director of the East-West Contacts Staff at the State Department and, through Lacy, separated by only one degree from Foster Dulles, announced that State was "making plans to actively facilitate such exchange."

By November 1957, the Office of East-West Contacts was focusing on Soviet/US youth group exchanges. The compact between the two nations was formalized in January 1958, between Soviet Ambassador Zaroubin and Ambassador William S. B. Lacy, the State Department's Special Assistant for East-West Exchanges, his resumé stuffed with political, economic, and military intelligence.

In their testimony before the Warren Commission, both Michael and Ruth Paine reportedly could not recall the State Department official with whom Ruth Paine had communicated to effect her Soviet-US student exchange, but that person was most likely the Director of the East-West Contacts Staff who worked under William S. B. Lacy : "The entire [student exchange] project had the official encouragement of the US Department of State and received approbation from Frederick T. Merrill."

Who Was Frederick T. Merrill?

In the late 1920s, Merrill was already participating in a national behavior modification program focusing on the negative effects of illegal substances. Merrill and his associates argued (with questionable evidence) that available narcotics were traceable to the Far East. Merrill published papers in 1927, 1928, 1938, and 1950 supporting this Fu Manchu narcotics argument. Merrill co-wrote articles on illegal drugs with Harry J. Anslinger, Commissioner of the Bureau of Narcotics, and appeared as a presenter on panels organized and chaired by Anslinger.

At a Marijuana conference on December 12, 1938, for example, Merrill presented a paper at the gathering under the auspices of the Bureau of Internal Revenue and the Treasury's Bureau of Narcotics. Frederick Merrill was identified at that 1938 conference as a member of the Foreign Policy Association, the Establishment's middle-octave equivalent to its Council on Foreign Relations. FPA member Frederick T. Merrill joined the US Foreign Service in 1940 in the midst of his intense anti-drug activities. A participant in the FPA's persuasion programs targeting the educated US middle-class, Merrill was active on the FPA's Narcotics Committee. In turn, Bureau of Narcotics Director Harry Anslinger had a long history of interest in drugs capable of inducing behavior modification and had cooperated closely with the CIA in its search for the key to mind control.

Before retiring in 1965, Anslinger's long-time associate Frederick Merrill was a member of the UN Office on Drugs and Crime team that visited Thailand in 1964 investigating Thai narcotics production. Merrill was listed as a "specialist in opium problems in the Far East." C.D. Jackson's Free Europe Committee (ultimately the Committee for a Free Europe) distributed covert CIA funding to a series of anti-Communist exile groups, especially the Assembly of Captive European Nations (ACEN). Frederick Merrill, Foreign Policy Association member, State Department Foreign Service officer, and anti-Communist narcotics expert, helped transfer the Free Europe Committee's CIA funds to the ACEN in 1955-1957. When Ruth Paine's Quakers were organizing their youth exchange, Ruth dealt directly with Merrill in his capacity as East-West Contacts Director.

Ruth Paine's Exchange: The KGB Component

Ruth Paine's East-West exchange program had another dark layer. On August 2nd, 1957, Eugeni Alekseevich Zaostrovtsev "became Cultural Attaché for Cinema and Education at the Soviet Embassy in Washington, D.C." Five months later the major cultural/educational agreement was signed between the Soviet Union and the United States.[8]

In April 1958, the Quaker East-West Contacts Committee (including Ruth Paine) met to plan a US trip for the three reputedly young Soviets, all between 26 and 32 years old; that same spring, Soviet Cultural Attaché Zaostrovtsev assisted Ruth Paine's Friends Committee to bring those three Soviets to the United States. Any of the three Soviets, of course, could have been a KGB asset or agent. Zaostrovtsev, in fact, had a major clandestine link. After assisting Ruth Paine's American Friends Committee, Zaostrovtsev continued to pursue his Quaker connection that ultimately resulted in a double-agent spy sting run against Zaostrovtsev that was directed by the FBI.

On May 15th, 1959, Eugeni Zaostrovtsev, Second Secretary of the Soviet Embassy, the cultural attaché who had made Ruth Paine's Quaker/Soviet exchange possible, was expelled from the United States. According to the FBI, he was a KGB agent.[9]

Ruth Paine's Quakerism had involved the US State Department, State's East-West Contacts Staff run by two Foreign Service officers with extensive ties to American intelligence, the Soviet KGB, and the FBI.

The Quaker Paines Join the Unitarians

Testifying under oath before the Warren Commission, Ruth Paine affirmed that she and her husband were indeed Quakers when they settled in Irving, Texas. Michael, however, said they found no substantial Quaker group in the Dallas area, so he joined the local Unitarians, later worrying about not meeting his pledged promise to the Dallas Unitarian Church. The couple sang in the madrigal group and Ruth was perceived to be a member of the congregation, though she did not attend with any regularity.

The Warren Commission staff was curious about Ruth's religious practices and her Soviet friendship activities: they had discovered that Unitarianism ran in the family. Carol Hyde, Ruth's mother, was a recently ordained Unitarian minister. Though the Commission established Ruth Paine's questionable Soviet interests and her odd Unitarian/Quaker orientation, it finally backed off from any further exploration of these important but inconvenient leads.[10]

After the Kennedy assassination, the FBI asked a few timid questions about Ruth Paine. She had delivered Marina Oswald to New Orleans and contacted Ruth Kloepfer, a Quaker who was the clerk of the Orleans area Friends Meeting. Paine had informed Kloepfer that Lee Harvey Oswald was in New Orleans, asking the Quaker to assist the Oswald family. Kloepfer and her two daughters, both coincidentally studying Russian, then visited Lee and Marina. What assistance they offered to the Oswalds has not been recorded. The Bureau did take some note, however: it was concerned that a possible connection had been made between Oswald and the New Orleans Council for Peaceful Alternatives, a Friends organization embodying Ruth Paine's reported pacifist outlook. The FBI had begun exploring the murky links between Ruth Paine, the Quakers, Mexico City and Lee Harvey Oswald.

"Oswald" in Mexico & the Quakers

Though it seems highly unlikely that Lee Harvey Oswald actually visited Mexico City and the Soviet and Cuban embassies there prior to the JFK assassination, someone certainly did show up in Mexico who represented himself as Oswald and displayed convincing identity documents. For the FBI and the CIA, this series of events conjured up unpleasant possibilities of a Soviet KGB or Communist Cuban involvement with Oswald. Real or fake, an Oswald in Mexico City who had contacted Soviet or Cuban intelligence was ominous.

For the FBI, a Quaker-intelligence connection to Oswald with a Mexico City locale was one more unwanted complication, primarily because of Ruth Paine and her closeness to the Oswald family. The locus of that Quaker complication was the Friends House, the Casa del Los Amigos, in Mexico City. In September 1963, Homobono Amo Alcaraz, himself a Quaker, had reportedly met an "Oswald" in the company of several Quakers at Sanborn's Restaurant located (according to researcher Mary Ferrell) next to the American Embassy in Mexico City. All the Quakers were either staying at the Casa del Los Amigos or were connected to it. Alcaraz asserted that "Oswald," riding on the back of the motorbike of an unidentified US citizen, had left the restaurant for a trip to the Cuban Embassy, ostensibly in an attempt to get "Oswald" (or both of them) a Cuban visa.

Interviewed by the FBI, Von Peacock, the Acting Director of the Quaker's Casa del Los Amigos, suggested the motor biking American could have been Robert Kaffke, a San Francisco Quaker who, along with fifty-seven other students, visited Cuba illegally in the summer of 1963, but the Kaffke story sounded too much like a botched attempt to implicate "Oswald" in a Cuban-sponsored murder of JFK. This "Oswald" had left the Quaker House before Kaffke registered; Kaffke reported that Casa residents "were still talking about Oswald's visit." He also stated that "Oswald" was in possession of a sizable amount of money and the Casa residents "were really scared when the name of Oswald [was] mentioned," presumably after November 22nd, 1963. Beyond the confused calendar, what made the Kaffke revelations suspicious was his intelligence link; he was an undercover informant for the FBI's San Francisco office. Helpfully, the FBI reported it did not believe Kaffke was the motorbike companion of "Oswald."

Ms. Barrie Milliman, a Berkeley undergraduate, visited Homobono Amo Alcaraz in Mexico City and heard about Oswald's alleged Quaker connections there. Milliman then reportedly told another student, Judith Gordon, and on January 15, 1964, Gordon notified the FBI office in San Francisco. Like Kaffke, Gordon was an undercover Bureau informant. The Quaker Good Samaritan who wanted to go to Cuba with "Oswald" was later reportedly identified as Steve (or Larry) Kennan. Homobono Alcaraz, interviewed in 1994 by researcher/writer Tony Summers, stated that the Quaker on a motorbike in Mexico City was from Philadelphia. He was, indeed, Steve/Larry Kennan, and Kennan was most probably "LICOZY-3," a double (if not a triple) agent run by the CIA operating in Mexico City. Kennan was a Quaker from Philadelphia "recruited by the Soviets while a student in Mexico City ... [who then] reported [his] ... recruitment [to the CIA] and [afterward] worked for the Mexico City station." And when he returned to the United States, double agent Kennan became, of course, an FBI under-cover informant.

The Oswald-among-the-Quakers in Mexico City story is obviously rich with CIA/FBI ramifications, not the least of which was the Philadelphia/Quaker identity of the motor-biking friend of "Oswald." Ruth Paine's influential in-laws, Ruth Forbes Paine Young and Arthur

Young, were powerful Quakers in the Philadelphia area. Philadelphia was the international center of the Quakers; the American Friends Service Committee (AFSC) was headquartered in Philadelphia and was responsible for Casa del Los Amigos, the Mexico City Friends' hostel/camp for US students. Like its Unitarian (USC) counterpart, the Quakers' service operation had cooperated with US Intelligence through two wars and into the anti-communist era.

The CIA, the Catherwoods, the Youngs & Ed Lansdale

Both the CIA and the Catherwood Foundation had been established in 1947; both supported the Russian Orthodox Church in the United States, including St. Nicholas Parish in the Dallas/ Fort Worth area.[11]

Ruth and Michael Paine were part of that curious Texas community of Russians. Throughout the Cold War, the Catherwood Foundation operated as a CIA front and conduit for funding covert Agency operations, with its offices in Bryn Mawr, Pennsylvania, just ten miles outside of Philadelphia. Cummins Catherwood, born in Philadelphia, was the founder of the Catherwood Foundation and "a financier, philanthropist, banker, oilman, patron of the arts, [and] avid yachtsman ... a pillar of the Philadelphia establishment."

The Catherwood Foundation had been a major presence in the Philippines in the 1950s, the period when Colonel (later General) Edward Lansdale ran the country for the CIA, using psychological warfare techniques remarkably similar to C.D. Jackson and CIA agents E. Howard Hunt and David Phillips. "Lansdale had found a niche in psychological warfare with the OSS during World War II as an intelligence officer on MacArthur's staff, working for General Willoughby. By the war's end, he was their chief of intelligence in the Philippines."

Lansdale's "alter ego" was "Gabe Kaplan, New York lawyer, politician, and public relations man ... [whose] first operational cover [as a CIA agent] was the Asia Foundation, later the Committee for Free Asia, and then the Catherwood Foundation...." The Catherwood family and the Youngs (Ruth Paine's in-laws) were members of the same Philadelphia elitist circle, and both had significant ties to the Central Intelligence Agency; further, Ruth Paine considered the Youngs her mentors, visiting them frequently in Philadelphia.

Were Ruth Paine's Religious Ties Other Than Spiritual?

Could Ruth Paine have been a Quaker by convenience, given the Quaker/Soviet spy incident involving her American Friends and the "Philadelphia" Quaker incidents in Mexico City? Did Ruth bend the truth in her Warren Commission testimony concerning her Texas switch from Quakerism to Unitarianism? The Dallas/Fort Worth area had, in fact, a strong Quaker presence; Ruth and Michael Paine could have easily resumed their American Friends identity immediately after arriving in Texas. Why, then, would Ruth return to her family's Unitarian orientation, rich with intelligence intrigue, after moving to the Dallas area? Were Ruth and Michael Paine willing participants in the destruction of Lee Harvey Oswald, or were they, like Oswald, manipulated?

Michael Paine: Another "Oswald"?

Michael Paine, a physical double of Lee Harvey Oswald, extended his interests in Oswald's contradictory politics by participating in a questionable action that mimed Lee Harvey Oswald's often provocative posturing. In the spring of 1963 at the edge of Dallas's Southern Methodist University, Michael Paine lounged at Luby's, eating lunch and holding "conversations or debates" with SMU students who dropped in for a Sunday afternoon lunch.

According to the FBI, Paine argued for "peaceful coexistence" in Eastern Europe and supported Castro's Cuba against ongoing US policy, maintaining Fidel Castro had only responded to major American provocations. Both opinions were consonant with positions held by the Socialist Workers Party, the Fair Play for Cuba Committee, and Lee Harvey Oswald. Michael Paine had set up these SMU political confrontations after being a Sunday communicant at a "nearby" Unitarian Church.

Oswald, The Unitarian Church, & the FBI Investigation

From 1958 through 1963, Lee Harvey Oswald's extensive Unitarian connections were focused on and made local in Ruth and Michael Paine, who had defined Oswald's fate.

For more than fifty years, Mary Ferrell, the matriarchal presence in JFK research, lived just blocks away from Dallas' First Unitarian Church on Preston Road. After the JFK murder, Mary learned that Ruth and Michael Paine had attended that same First Unitarian Church. She asked a young friend of her oldest son if he knew anyone from the church to whom she might be introduced.[12]

Mary Ferrell met Rev. Byrd Helligas, the assistant pastor of the First Unitarian Church, who told Mary "the government" had visited his Dallas church and examined its records, looking for anything about Lee Oswald. Byrd Helligas also recalled that federal agents "didn't just do that in Dallas …[;] they went all over the country picking up [Unitarian] records." What had happened in Providence and Dallas, according to Reverend Helligas, occurred throughout the United States. Unitarian individuals and groups connected to the accused assassin were linked to significant US Intelligence actions throughout the Cold War.

After the JFK murder, a persistent and honest inquiry by the FBI, the CIA, the Warren Commission, and subsequent investigations would have discovered all of them. But an honest inquiry would also have exposed US Intelligence's manipulation of religious individuals and groups, including the Quakers, the Unitarians, and especially Albert Schweitzer College. An honest inquiry would also have asked whether Lee Oswald was deliberately steered toward a Swiss college that had such significant US Intelligence ties, and why. Nothing of the sort was ever initiated in the official investigations involving assassination of John F. Kennedy.

Character Witnesses for the Paines: From the Dark Side

If an electronic search is made with the word "Unitarian" in the NARA online database covering all the official investigations of the JFK assassinations, only *one* (apparently irrelevant) document will be found. A search of the name "'Ruth Paine" will produce a mountain of material, but nothing about Unitarianism. Since the Unitarian churches of Providence, Los Angeles, and Dallas (at least) were investigated by federal officers before and after November 22, 1963, the absence of official JFK assassination documents relating to Unitarianism is profoundly disturbing.

Beyond the FBI checks of Ruth and Michael Paine's several families, the Bureau apparently needed character references for the Paines, given their closeness to Lee Harvey Oswald and his wife Marina. Support for Michael and Ruth was offered by their friends Nancy and Frederick Osborn, Jr., and recorded by the Bureau. But there is no evidence that the FBI asked why members of the internationally prominent Osborn family should feel the Paines needed their personal support.

What the Bureau declined to explore, or found but suppressed, was a history of elitist/right-wing social and political positions held by the Osborn family that tracked back to 1902. Those often extreme positions were consonant with political and social values espoused by Allen Dulles and John Foster Dulles, by Caucasian/ Protestant eugenics activists, by CIA-supported psychological war enthusiasts (including C.D. Jackson), and by US military behavior modification ("mind-control") researchers.

Henry Fairfield Osborn

In 1902, Professor Henry Fairfield Osborn, director of the New York Zoological Society and the American Museum of Natural History, joined a growing eugenics movement that already included leading eugenics researchers and scientists, the Carnegie Institute, the Brooklyn Institute of Arts and Science (with its Long Island Cold Harbor laboratory), and enthusiastic eugenics supporters throughout Europe. For twelve years, Osborn was a key figure in establishing and directing a series of organizations sponsoring national and international meetings on eugenics.

The onset of WWI in 1914 halted international eugenics cooperation in Europe, but "America continued its eugenic program and held its place as the world leader in eugenic research, theory and activism." After the war, the United States commanded the world's eugenics troops, with Henry Fairfield Osborn as the president of the Second International Congress of Eugenics, scheduled for 1921 in New York. "The second congress was rich with typical raceological dogma and dominated by American biological [racist] precepts." In his speech opening the congress, Osborn left no doubt that the most intellectual of eugenicists could also be a racist.

The International Committee on Eugenics, the governing body supported by Osborn and his associates, became the Permanent International Commission on eugenics, again dominated by the United States. That American dominance insured that the most racist aspects of the worldwide eugenics movement were enforced for over fifty years.

Through World War II (and even after), "hundreds of thousands of Americans and untold numbers of others [throughout the world] were not permitted to continue their families by reproducing. Selected because of their undesirable ancestry, national origin, race or religion, they were forcibly sterilized, wrongly committed to mental institutions where they died in great numbers, prohibited from marrying, and sometimes even unmarried by state bureaucrats." The entire process was intended to "create a superior Nordic race," whatever the careful, seemingly high-minded pronouncements of its elitist collaborators. In fact, "this pernicious white-gloved war was prosecuted by esteemed professors, elite universities, wealthy industrialists and government officials colluding in a racist, pseudo-scientific movement called eugenics."

Before Henry Fairfield Osborn died on November 6, 1935, he lived to see Nazi Germany take the lead in its pursuit of an "Aryan master race," heavily influenced by the work of Osborn and his fellow American eugenics advocates. The racial purification programs both in the United States and in Europe always contained key elements of propaganda, persuasion, and coercion, psychological warfare against the weak: behavior modification in support of a better life through bio-chemistry.

Frederick Henry Osborn, Sr.

By 1937, the leadership of the American push for racial purity passed to the Pioneer Fund and its secretary, Frederick Henry Osborn, Sr., the nephew of Henry Fairfield Osborn and the father of the character witness for Michael and Ruth Paine: Osborn was a "leading proponent of racial eugenics." "Although virtually unknown to the American public, Osborn was one of the most influential men of his generation." Osborn numbered the Roosevelts and the Rockefellers among his top-drawer friends, was a trustee of Princeton University, and held influential positions with the Carnegie Corporation, the Population Association of America, the American Society of Human Genetics, and was a founder and the first administrator of a key Rockefeller enterprise, the Population Council.

The Pioneer Fund

The Pioneer Fund, created in 1937, was funded by "a group of wealthy Northeastern conservatives," led by Frederick Osborn and Wickliffe Preston Draper, "heir to a Massachusetts [textile] manufacturing fortune'" and well-known for his "support of southern segregationists."[13]

Draper asked Osborn and Harry Laughlin, who contributed to Nazi Germany's race purification programs, to "organize research projects and distribute pro-eugenic propaganda." Osborn's partner Harry Laughlin was Director of Carnegie Institute's Eugenics Record Office; one year before Draper tapped both Laughlin and Osborn as the Pioneer Fund's chief research contributors, Laughlin had received a signal honor from Germany for his "contributions to Nazi eugenics." His acceptance statement noted that America and the German nation had a "common understanding" regarding the future of "racial health."

In 1937, Frederick Henry Osborn announced that the racial sterilization program adopted by Nazi Germany could be "the most important social program which has ever been tried." The Pioneer Fund had just begun in 1937 when its directors developed a plan to improve the breeding stock of America, focusing on the US Army Air Corps. For many, the Corps was a company of heroic aviators following in the slipstreams of the brave wingmen of World War I.

Frederick Osborn held at least two meetings with Harry H. Woodring, President Roosevelt's Secretary of War, pitching the Pioneer Fund's eugenics proposal. Impressed with the Pioneer project, Woodring connected Draper, Laughlin, and Osborn with "top military leaders," including Air Corps General "Hap" Arnold. In the late summer of 1937, Arnold gave his approval. The Pioneer Fund had organized a "pilot procreation plan," singling out top US (Caucasian) airmen who had sired at least three children but were reluctant to have more. The Fund offered the Air Corps families the contemporary equivalent of $60,000 for the education of any child born in 1940.

Behavioral psychologist John C. Flanagan ran the project: an especially telling choice, since it involved behavior modification bolstered by a monetary reward. The children chosen by the Pioneer Fund ultimately became decent but ordinary US citizens. The racial strengthening experiment of Laughlin, Draper, and Frederick Henry Osborn was a failure, but its underlying dark intention spoke to the fears and prejudices of elitists who largely approved of Nazi Germany's eugenic experiments.

Frederick Henry Osborn had begun to move away from some of the more obviously racist arguments and intentions of the eugenics movement as early as 1933. Though he remained a dedicated eugenicist until his death, the behavior modification aspects of the Pioneer Fund's airmen experiment loomed large in Osborn's mind. With the US moving closer to actual participation in the war in Europe, "Osborn eased into government service, chairing a joint Army-Navy committee on potential morale issues in wartime."

Frederick Osborn & Behavior Modification

Soon after, bolstered by his boyhood friendship with President Franklin Delano Roosevelt, Frederick Osborn was offered a general's rank and the command of "a new branch of the service focused on issues of morale, training, and education." Osborn enlisted Army Chief of Staff George Marshall in his plan, "bringing social science techniques to bear on the analysis of morale." Given a green light, Osborn and his social scientists tested, evaluated, and stored data on tens of thousands of US military personnel, resulting in a massive behavior modification program utilizing "tools of social manipulation" not yet fully analyzed.

Osborn's wartime pysops program began in October 1941, as the Army's "Morale Branch." It then became the "Morale Services Branch" in June of 1942, "Special Services Branch" in November 1942, and finally "Information and Education Division" in February 1944. Osborn's program extended through 1947, but the written records, including its subsequent application to Korea, Vietnam and other Cold War conflicts, have remained unexplored.

Frederick Henry Osborn was the key rescuer of the post-war eugenics movement. Adopting the less controversial tag of 'Genetics', the eugenics advocates quietly pursued their elitist and racial purification agenda, while Osborn argued for a more enlightened approach to improving the human gene pool. But eugenics was not Osborn's only elitist interest. Graduating from Princeton in 1910 between John Foster Dulles (1909) and Allen Dulles (1911), Osborn maintained a friendly and productive letter exchange with the brothers. In 1949, still attempting to reorganize American eugenics by applying a more acceptable social scientific movement, Osborn joined Allen Dulles and Arthur W. Page as organizing founders of the National Committee for a Free Europe (NCFE), incorporated on May 11, 1949.

The National Committee for a Free Europe

George Kennan, creator of the Office of Policy Coordination (OPC), first suggested gathering together elite US citizens in a major anti-Communist effort. The idea was taken up by Allen Dulles and his pal Frank Wisner, his pick to run the OPC. Dulles and his intelligence-connected associates established the National Committee for a Free Europe in 1949, assigning its undercover direction to Wisner's OPC. The OPC was absorbed by the CIA in 1950 as its International Organizations Division (IOD), which took over responsibility for the NCFE.

In 1949, the NCFE created the Crusade for Freedom (CFF); by the early 1950s, the Crusade was the NCFE's "highly visible [public] presence." Three long-time CFF supporters, often sitting together at fund-raising dinners, were high-ranking spiritual warriors in Allen Dulles' campaign against the Reds: Cardinal Spellman, Bishop Henry Knox Sherrill, and Rabbi David de Sola Pool. Spellman was a long-time enthusiastic collaborator with the CIA. Bishop Sherrill was elitist, liberal, and anti-Communist, the leader of the Episcopal Church in the United States and later head of the World Council of Churches (WCC): Dulles and his OSS had counted on the Council's information-gathering during World War II.

Orthodox Rabbi David de Sola Pool was the spiritual director of the Sephardic Shearith Israel in New York, and his wife was a passionate Zionist. This theological triad more than adequately illustrates Allen Dulles' post-war manipulation of religious groups and individuals for elitist political and intelligence purposes.

The Crusade quickly developed Radio Free Europe and Radio Liberty. All these entities were covert psychological warfare operations of the CIA, but where did the funding come from? Open financing of any politically motivated Agency action was illegal. So the Crusade for Freedom functioned as the NCFE's major money-laundering operation. Publicly, it created the fiction of enthusiastic US citizen support. Covertly, it funneled untraced funds into the CIA's psychological warfare and other covert operations.

Osborn, Dulles, & Arthur W. Page

Frederick Henry Osborn, Sr., Allen Dulles, and Arthur W. Page helped establish the National Committee for a Free Europe, Inc. Its massive committee list was stuffed with elitist power, including Dulles, Osborn, and Page. In turn, the CIA's allies appointed Frederick Osborn Chairman of the Crusade for Freedom (CFF), establishing its headquarters in New York City and enlisting Mayor Vincent R. Impellitteri as its honorary chairman.

On October 4, 1950, one week before the Agency initiated its domestic propaganda operation that eventually covered twenty-six states, Chairman Osborn wrote a careful letter to CIA consultant Allen Dulles. It concerned the funding of the Crusade, its Freedom Bell (installed in Berlin on October 24, 1950), and implicitly its support of the rest of the CIA's covert operations agenda, including Radio Free Europe and Radio Liberty. Indeed, the Hoover Institute's RFE/RL site had recently announced the Crusade "was incorporated to raise funds [for] and promote Radio Free Europe." Osborn pointed out the obvious: that the Manhattan-based Crusade campaign was intent "on getting [as many] signatures to the [Freedom Bell] Scrolls and as many small subscriptions as possible," since the overt campaign was, in fact, pure psyops. Osborn continued: "The whole setup is directed to this end and we are not in a position to go out for large subscriptions. The reasons are quite obvious in our organization...."

Osborn wrote that the actual funding for the National Committee for a Free Europe (and therefore its overt operations) would have to come from "another group." He knew what he was saying: despite the massive nation-wide psyops campaign, the CFF actually raised only $1,317,000 in "small subscriptions" in its first year, totally inadequate for financing the anticipated covert actions of the NCFE/CIA. So, Osborn recorded, "if you [Allen Dulles] and Arthur [Page] can do anything towards getting large subscriptions ... there is more likelihood of success...." Osborn's last line was telling: "I am writing a similar letter to Arthur." Two letters: one to Allen Dulles, the other to Arthur Page, both on funding the National Committee for a Free Europe through "large subscriptions" developed by "Allen" and "Arthur." Allen Dulles' source for "large subscriptions" was, of course, Frank Wisner and the Office of Policy Coordination in the CIA.[14]

Arthur W. Page: Power Player & Psyops Master

What about Arthur W. Page, the recipient of Osborn's second letter? Page had lived an exemplary elitist life: AT&T,

Chase Bank, Westinghouse, Kennecott Copper, a trustee of both Bennington College and Columbia University's Teachers' College, the Carnegie Corporation, the Metropolitan Museum of Art, the Morgan Library, a member of the overseers of Harvard University; consultant to presidents Roosevelt, Truman and Eisenhower, cabinet secretaries, and the powerful military/intelligence community. Page began his covert career in World War I on General John "Black Jack" Pershing's AEF G2-D staff, a propaganda/psyops intelligence unit.

Page's influence in the American power structure can be traced back to the Coolidge administration, but especially to his close friendship and political association with the legendary Henry L. Stimson, no later than 1930. An early and enthusiastic student of psychological warfare, Arthur Page exchanged letters with Frederick Osborn on military morale while Osborn was the chair of the Joint Army Navy Committee on Welfare and Recreation UANC) in 1941.

After Osborn left that committee to take on other psyops duties, Page joined the JANC and headed a subcommittee on radio communication and propaganda, targeting the US military. Page was named "a special consultant to the Secretary of War, a title he held for the duration [of World War II]." One of Page's key wartime jobs was to craft the official proclamation to American troops preparing for the invasion of Hitler's Europe. Page finally became the major psyops consultant for the US Army's public relations program in World War II. In that capacity, Page worked as a troubleshooter for General Frederick Osborn in 1945 when he was chief of the US Army's Information and Education Division. In that same year, Page was a key participant in the guarding of information about the Manhattan Project.

At the end of the war, Page prepared President Truman's momentous announcement that America had just obliterated an entire Japanese city with one demonic bomb. In 1949, Page was a key founder of the National Committee for a Free Europe that in turn "created" Radio Free Europe. As early as 1951, C.D. Jackson joined Osborn, Arthur Page, and Allen Dulles on the Committee. By 1953, Page had become chairman of the Executive Committee of the Free Europe Committee, the major Cold War manifestation of the National Committee for a Free Europe run by the CIA.

Arthur Page, Frederick Osborn, C.D. Jackson, and the Dulles brothers all worked vigorously to propel Dwight David Eisenhower into the presidency. After his victory, Ike invited twenty-two leading government and business celebrities to a special thank-you dinner: among them were John J. McCloy, Arthur Page, Abbott Washburn, and C. D. Jackson. Osborn, Page, and Jackson played key roles in the psyops justifications for America's atomic weapons and atomic energy policies. Clearly, when Frederick Osborn wrote to Arthur Page and Allen Dulles about major financial support for the NCFFE, Arthur Page's "large subscriptions" would be exactly the same as those of Allen Dulles: the CIA. Abbott Washburn, a former OSS agent, managed the fund laundering for Page's Crusade for Freedom.

Washburn's secretary made regular trips to the Wall Street offices of Henry Sears & Co., where a member of the investment firm, World War II veteran (General) Charles Saltzman would pass on the CIA'S laundered beneficence. Saltzman was a former N.Y. Stock Exchange officer, former Assistant Secretary of State, confidant of General George C. Marshall, and active Eisenhower supporter. Arthur Page worked with psychological warfare expert C. D. Jackson. He often cooperated directly with the CIA, including key Agency officers involved in psyops, especially Cord Meyer, and was in constant communication with Allen Dulles. Page, a close associate of John Foster Dulles, Allen Dulles, and Frederick Osborn throughout his career, was the father of corporate public relations and a consummate psyops master for US Intelligence.

Arthur Page died in New York on September 5, 1960, but the psychological warfare infrastructures he helped shape for the military, intelligence, and business in the interests of behavior modification continued without pause.

The Osborn Matrix & the Paines

Any reference to Frederick Henry Osborn after the assassination of John F. Kennedy ought to have elicited a flood of material linking the Osborn family to sixty years of elitist and sometimes racist military, intelligence, and behavior modification records. Yet key references to these leads, especially to Frederick Henry Osborn fronting for the National Committee for a Free Europe, were apparently edited out of Osborn's several biographies and obituaries at some time after the JFK assassination. Only through Arthur W. Page can Osborn's complete intelligence operations and connections be discovered.

Immediately following the killing in Dealey Plaza, the appropriate references linking Frederick Osborn, Arthur Page, Allen Dulles, and the CIA must still have been available. In 1956, Nancy Osborn and her husband Frederick Osborn, Jr., son of Frederick Henry Osborn, were still members of the leading American "genetics" organization supporting the senior Osborn's eugenics orientation. Just eight years later, the same Nancy and Frederick Osborn were FBI character witnesses for Michael and Ruth Paine.

The FBI and the Warren Commission were both silent about the Osborn family's extraordinary connections, just as they were silent about Ruth and Michael Paines' Unitarian-US intelligence links.

Don't Go There

The patterns of elitist and intelligence power in the Osborn and Paine families should now tell us where we will discover the real killers of JFK. The Osborns were enmeshed in a National Security State complex devoted to anti-communism, including the powerful Stimson Committee on the Marshall Plan, the Council on Foreign Relations (an Ivy League complex of Harvard, Columbia, Yale, and Princeton), US Intelligence, the Committee for a Free Europe, and the Crusade for Freedom with its bully pulpits, Radio Free Europe and Radio Liberty.[15]

The oil/intelligence/Unitarian universe of Lee Harvey Oswald was a perfect multiple nexus. The Big Oil-Intelligence sector in which he was embedded would allow Oswald to be routed in any of several directions: left or right, CIA or KGB, domestic or foreign. The Unitarian-Intelligence link, especially with the participation of the Paines, would also allow Oswald to be routed in any of those same directions. But the added Osborn family "character references" for Ruth and Michael Paine sent a major signal to any post-assassination Federal investigator who ventured into the Osborn family's rich elitist past: "Don't go there."

Kennedy and Dulles

Epilogue

A Summary & Some Conclusions

One religious individual, Noel Field (American Quaker, Unitarian, and Marxist) was used by Allen Dulles to manipulate religious relief organizations in World War II and in the post-war period. Dulles finally utilized Field to help destabilize Communist Eastern Europe. Dulles apparently collaborated in this plan with Jozef Swiatlo, a Communist/CIA double agent, who later surfaced in the Warren Commission's Kennedy assassination investigation of Lee Harvey Oswald.

ASC, the Unitarians, & US Intelligence

Schweitzer College had major religious origins that were both social and political. Post-war liberal Protestant movements in Europe, including the International Association for Religious Freedom, helped to create the college in Switzerland, the country at the center of Allen Dulles' nearly fifty-year spy program. In the United States, the college was supported by a powerful coalition of American religious liberalism, primarily the Unitarian Church, the Unitarian Service Committee, and the American Friends of Albert Schweitzer College.

Albert Schweitzer College's history strongly suggests that American espionage assets helped establish the college and then used it, probably with the knowledge and even cooperation of some of its religious supporters in the Unitarian Church movement and those who worked for the college in Switzerland.

One leading Unitarian who worked closely with both US Intelligence and the military in the '40s and '50s was President of the

American Friends of Albert Schweitzer College when Lee Harvey Oswald applied. That same intelligence-connected Unitarian worked with a second influential Unitarian to help control US space programs, including the U-2 over-flights, and in the 1960s fronted for a major CIA proprietary. Those who set policy for ASC were, therefore, elite members of the establishment and allies of the CIA.

In 1959, Lee Harvey Oswald registered to attend ASC and therefore became a direct link between the college and American intelligence.

Whoever masterminded the Oswald college action was knowledgeable about both the OSS and the CIA'S use of Quakers, officials of the World Council of Churches, and Unitarians as contacts, assets, and informants (often as double agents). They were also aware of the FBI's responsibility in tracking down and identifying Soviet Illegals and double agents. Oswald was, therefore, a creature of someone in American counter-intelligence who possessed precisely that double body of knowledge.

The Flawed Candidate

At the same time Albert Schweitzer College was extending its international recruiting effort, both the Soviet and American Illegals and False Identity programs were operating. For those espionage groups, Lee Harvey Oswald initially looked like a candidate. But Oswald was a stunningly imperfect False Identity/Illegals prospect. A faulty False Identity operation had apparently been carried out using Lee and run by a branch of American intelligence.

Oswald's imperfections were certain to trip counter-espionage alarm wires. The context of the Oswald "legend" game was Switzerland, earlier the center of massive spy operations run by Allen Dulles.

Oswald had called maximum attention to his strange exit from the Marines, his dubious trip to Europe, his suspicious registration at Schweitzer College, his failure to arrive at the college, and his so-called defection to the Soviet Union.

In a very short time, Oswald piled up obviously faulty documents and suspect postal communications. What followed was a major FBI inquiry in 1959 and 1960 that apparently attempted to find the missing enigma. Oswald's Marine Corps record, including his Pacific duty experience and U-2 service, made him a prime candidate for Soviet civilian and military intelligence, and both American and Soviet intelligence groups were aware of his candidacy.

Oswald's espionage activities most probably included informing the Soviets of scheduled U-2 flights, leading to the shoot-down of Gary Powers and the collapse of imminent Soviet/American peace talks. He was also apparently scheduled to play a part in exposing Soviet intelligence moles in activist student movements and liberal Protestant institutions in both Europe and the United States.

From the moment Oswald registered at Schweitzer College, and without ever setting foot in Switzerland, he moved (or was moved) to the center of a complex and dangerous double-agent operation.

Lee Harvey Oswald possibly looked too much like a false defector. When he returned to the United States as a re-defector he was suspect: at least five intelligence agencies (the GRU, KGB, CIA, FBI and ONI) found his curious false-identity profile highly suspicious. But that same profile was extremely well suited to those who ultimately planned to murder President John F. Kennedy. Oswald could be manipulated in a half-dozen ways and in a half-dozen ongoing espionage games.

The Perfect Patsy

Why, and how, did Lee Harvey Oswald become the designated patsy in the JFK murder?

Six years (or more) of complex and questionable US Intelligence espionage activities, along with their initiators, sponsors and handlers ranging from the very top of the American Establishment down to the 'boots on the ground', would have been threatened by a real investigation of Oswald's past.

A real inquiry would have closely covered, for example, his probable Marine Intelligence activities, his Cuban contacts, his mail coverage by the CIA'S HTLINGUAL program, the Agency's multiple "mole" inquiries, the real origins of Albert Schweitzer College, Oswald's Fair Play For Cuba Committee connections, and the plots against President Eisenhower.

An open process would have closely examined the persuasive but circumstantial evidence that, upon returning from the USSR, he was employed by a yet-to-be discovered "private investigative agency doing industrial-security work" funded by either US Intelligence or the US military. Peter Dale Scott has called attention to the "numerous signs that Oswald's employment recurrently coincided with opportunities for surveillance of FBI subversive targets." But Oswald apparently was the field asset of "other investigative agencies as well ... [including] the Alcohol, Tobacco, and Firearms unit ... of the US Treasury." Though Oswald's targets were or seemed to be those of the FBI, he was more likely to have been "an employee not of the FBI but of a private agency with contracts to more than one federal government agency." Therefore, any examination of Oswald's real work history after returning from the Soviet Union would have been a disaster for both government intelligence and those private-sector "industrial security" entities.

Each node of any real post-assassination investigation would have registered multiple extensions and been recognized as a psychological warfare operation. Examining HTLINGUAL in depth would have required a close look at US Illegals and False Identity programs; examining the CIA'S mole investigation would have led to HTLINGUAL, to US counter-intelligence Illegals and False Identities operations, to US intelligence's misuse of domestic and foreign postal systems, the abuse of liberal Protestant institutions in the US and Europe, and the grey history of Albert Schweitzer College. Finally, examining the oil-intelligence-Unitarian complex in Dallas would have meant exposing the Osborn family, character witnesses for Ruth and Michael Paine, as intimate associates of the US elite Establishment, the military, US Intelligence, government psychological warfare and behavior modification programs, and key Cold War covert operations.

At the end of each of those potential investigative extensions was the enigmatic Lee Oswald and the long, winding road he walked down to his final destination in "the deadliest game": Dallas, Texas, on November 22, 1963.

Editor's Note: This edition of *A Certain Arrogance* has been revised with the informed general reader in mind.

End notes have been reduced to essential additions to the text and a general bibliography. Those engaged in scholarly research may consult the heavily annotated 1st edition, published in 2006 by Xlibris Corporation.

End Notes

PROLOGUE:

[1] p. 11 To help demystify the Warren Commission and its materials, consult "Researching and Writing in the JFK Assassination and Related Topics" in The Assassination Chronicles, Volume 2, Issue 1, March 1966.

ESSAY ONE:

[1] p. 19 John Newman is the only author (other than I) calling attention to what he dubs Mr. "Fannan: FBI Mystery Man" 134). Newman points out "confusing" and "curious" aspects of the "Fannan" story, originally a small part of a lengthy interview conducted by a U.S. Secret Service agent on 12/25/63. The Secret Service interviewer recorded "Fan nan (phonetic)" twice during his questioning of Mrs. Oswald. I have made an extensive and thorough internet search for three versions of the alleged FBI man's name: Fannan, Fannen, and Fannin. Fannan and Fannen elicited nothing; Fannin yielded up two individuals: one a former FEMA official, John Fannin, the other Walter C. Fannin, Captain, Burglary and Theft Bureau, Dallas Police. He was involved in the JFK investigation.

[2] p. 20 Mrs. Oswald voiced that disturbing possibility several times in her letters and statements, My portrait (above) of Lee's mother was developed within a framework assuming her innocence. But what if Mrs. Oswald was not at all innocent? For example: 1. Why did she agree to what can only be called a fake workplace accident? 2. What about her extraordinary series of address changes? Changes of address were an important way for a peripatetic agent :) maintain contact with American intelligence: see Lee Harvey Oswald's own record of residence changes. 3. What about the stream of apparently confused information she supplied official government and police agencies both before and after the assassination? 4. What about the "agent" noise ("Fannan" and "Fain") she injected into her son's disappearance? Were there, in fact, two FBI agents (Fannan and Fain) or only one? Was she interviewed twice or only once? If once, by whom? 5. What about all her curious omissions, hesitations and lapses?

[3] p. 20 How to lose a College: to search for Albert Schweitzer College both at NARA and on the web, enter the correct spelling; but also enter: Schweitzr; Sechweitzer; Schweitzer; Scweizer; Schwetzer; Scweizer; and Switzer.

[4] p. 28 Given the mail-opening program then operating at Holabird, Oswald's Marine postal record should have been available to government assassination investigators, but it was not.

[5] p. 31 Following the developing but tangled history of Soviet intelligence and espionage agencies can be daunting. To simplify: the NKVD operated from 1922 through 1946; the NKGB operated only in 1946; the MGR operated from 1946 through 1953 (in that same period, the KI operated from 1947-51). In 1953, Beria's MVD operated; and from

1953-1954 through the demise of the Soviet Union, the KGB was the Soviet's major intelligence/espionage operator.

The Soviets' military intelligence operation, the GRU, ran from the spring of 1920 on, including its Illegals operations through World War II, but it was infiltrated by both British MI-6 and the CIA. To block this significant penetration, the Soviet's military espionage wing was put under the control of the KGB no later than the early 1970s.

[6] p. 33 See also Joseph J. Trento, *The Secret History of the CIA*: "While he was being processed out of the Marines in Los Angeles, the FBI photographed him meeting with Lieutenant Colonel Pavel T. Voloshin, a top KGB recruiter who was in L.A. with a Soviet dance troupe. The FBI placed the picture in a counterintelligence file on KGB 'watchers' of cultural organizations visiting the United States. The FBI also took another picture of Oswald … visiting the Cuban consulate in Los Angeles."

Trento's personal sources were the files and persons of James Jesus Angleton and William R. Corson. According to Trento, the FBI did not know who Oswald was or why he was visiting with Voloshin and the Cubans. Since FBI counterintelligence, run by Branigan, Sullivan and Papich, was always in close touch with Angleton and his Agency counter-intelligence group, it seems highly unlikely some exchange did not occur between the FBI and the CIA concerning those alleged visits. And why has Trento now been able to reveal this "Oswald" KGB/Cuban material so long after all of it was withheld from the Warren Commission? Trento (and therefore Angleton and Corson?) missed the Schweitzer College connection. Or did they? Epstein, whose source was Angleton himself, reported the Voloshin ASC link.

[7] p. 35 Beyond Nelson Delgado, Kerry Thornley was probably the chief source of the "Red Marine" image created for Oswald. Thornley could very well have been an important source of disinformation concerning Oswald.

[8] p. 36 I have queried the present pastor of the First Unitarian Church of Los Angeles, but she has been unable to sort through the material Stephen Fritchman left behind. Valuable Schweitzer College papers may well be lurking among these disorganized documents in L.A.

[9] p. 37 Nagell's intelligence records may bring some light to the darkest part of the JFK assassination conspiracy. Though the Warren Commission apparently never interviewed Nagell, the Assassinations Records Review Board did mail a letter dated October 31st, 1995, to Nagell, inquiring about his possible possession of JFK assassination records. Nagell then promptly died of "heart disease" the next day, November 1, 1995. Though the Warren Commission apparently never interviewed Nagell, the Assassinations Records Review Board did mail a letter to Nagell dated October 31, 1995, inquiring about his possible possession of JFK assassination records. Nagell then promptly died of "heart disease" the next day, November 1st, 1995.

[10] p. 37 Fritchman's earlier association with Noel Field and the establishing of the Unitarian Service Committee with its significant OSS/Allen Dulles links cannot be ignored.

[11] p. 37 Did Soviet and American hawks in civilian, financial, military, and intelligence institutions, motivated by the will to power and greed, collaborate after World War II to create the so-called Cold War? The history of that collaboration would, of course, include Lee Harvey Oswald and John F. Kennedy.

[12] p. 38 According to Dmitiry Bilibin, the chancellor of the People's Friendship University of Russia (the institutional successor to Lumumba University), Nikita Khrushchev had visited Indonesia in February, 1960. Informed that Indonesia intended to establish a university for foreign students, Khrushchev responded that the Soviet Union already had one in existence. Within twenty-four hours, "Patrice Lumumba University" had been organized and was operational.

[13] p. 41 A particularly potent context for these espionage collaborations was Cold War Berlin: a special source of tantalizing hints can be found in Murphy. Kondrashev and Bai-

ley, *Battleground Berlin: CIA vs. KGB in the Cold War*, rich with exhausting detail but ultimately a major venting vehicle for former Soviet and American intelligence officers: see especially 267-281 and 440-446. Note the off-handed definition of illegals as "intelligence officers [rather than assets or agents] documented as foreign citizens and sent abroad…"

[14] p. 43 Oswald's spelling and punctuation, his grammar and sentence structure, his rhetoric, and his logic varied so considerably throughout his reported communications and writing as to raise serious questions about what he might have personally written, what was dictated to him or copied by him verbatim, and what was fabricated, imitating either closely or very broadly his handwriting and 'style.' Anything relatively well-written and largely free from error might therefore be suspect as an intelligence invention; unless its anomalous literacy was an intentional red light, to raise questions about a false-identity Oswald.

[15] p. 51 Did the series "Ana" misspelled as "Anna" replaced by the incorrect "Barbara" anticipate the subtle 'mistake in Oswald's mailing addresses once he came home to Texas and New Orleans?

]16] p. 55 The gaming aspects of intelligence and espionage have been explored most extensively in so-called "spy" fiction, primarily in the United Kingdom and the United States. Gaming phenomena can be observed in detective fiction, in popular romance, in the history of "comic books," in the development of action cinema, including the serials of the 1930s and 40s, and in the confluence of these popular cultural strands in video games. Some well-known JFK assassination figures are also available as game pieces, but others, including Noel Field (discussed later), obviously qualify.

[17] p. 57 My experience has suggested that both the FBI and CIA are uninterested in supporting historical research in the JFK assassination. Arguing that a number of non-government archives, files, and documents be designated "JFK Assassination Records," to be preserved at NARA, might be more productive.

Essay Two

[1] p. 61 See the CIA Inspector General's Report on Cubela. In fact, the Kostikov-Cubela connection might have dangerous for the Bureau to pursue vigorously. If the FBI knew of Cubela and knew that the CIA was running Cubela, he then constituted a potential conspiratorial link between the CIA and the FBI. A distorted version of this hypothesis may be seen in FBI agent James Hosty's "bombshell" story about the suppressed evidence reportedly not available to the Warren Commission about an alleged meeting between Oswald and Kostikov in Mexico City: see James P. Hosty. Jr., Assignment: Oswald, on Oswald and his alleged contacts with Cubans and the Soviets.

[2] p. 65 American intelligence, the Warren Commission, and all subsequent investigations ignored the direct links between Cubela's patron, Carlos Prio and Jack Ruby, the killer of Lee Harvey Oswald. The CIA continued to nudge forward if not actively push the Cubela/Kostikov connection. Epstein, relying on Angleton, pressed the Cubela question, suggesting that Cubela's contacts with Kostikov were, in fact, a Cuban "provocation." But a provocation for what? To provoke a counterattack on Castro? To establish a motive for attacking JFK (or someone else)? And what did the Agency really make of the Cubela/Kostikov connection, unless it was, in fact, one CIA asset (Cubela) contacting another CIA asset (Kostikov)? But are they, then, both suspect? As part of the ongoing larger espionage game, this possibility is, at least, intriguing.

[3] p. 67 "As liberal religion affirmed and refined theological ideas about God's universal love, the perfectibility of humankind, the applicability of reason to religious questions and freedom of conscience, it inevitably applied those ideas to the social order." In that sense, given the life of Albert Schweitzer in that liberal religious tradition, the

establishing of Albert Schweitzer College in Switzerland was all but inevitable. As early as 1917, the Unitarian Fellowship of Social Justice moved "to institutionalize Unitarian social activism."

[4] p. 77 Obviously I suspect Oleg Kalugin of running an operation for the CIA inside the KGB and collecting agents both double and doubled.

[5] p. 78 In 1994, Kalugin implicitly minimized the RFK link, most probably because the back channels stories were then circulating.

[6] p. 79 A major Soviet (GRU) illegal's network operated in Switzerland during World War II that included an extraordinary false identity agent, Alexander Foote, who may have been a British Communist, was a Spanish Civil War veteran, and was finally a Soviet spy-ring radio operator. After the collapse of the GRU's Swiss espionage network, Moscow blamed Foote. In 1947, apparently fearing for his life, he defected to the British. Unless Foote simply went home to his actual handlers.

Essay Three:

[1] p. 86 My search for religious liberal youth files at the headquarters of the Unitarian/Universalist Service Committee in Cambridge elicited nothing about Albert Schweitzer College.

[2] p. 89 The Central Intelligence Agency refused to declassify the purloined Schweitzer letters; "Schweitzer believed that people ... were tampering with his personal mail at the Lambarene post office."

[3] p. 92 My associate Charles Drago believes the FBI agents were from Providence rather than Boston: logically, they should have been.

[4] p. 96 For example, from Zurich: an email to me dated 9/04/2001: "I inform you that Hans Casparis did not receive a degree at Zurich University and that he was not a student at this university 1919-1934." *Universitaet Zuerich, Archiv*, Dr. Heinzpeter Stucki. I received personal communications by email from all the universities confirming Casparis did not receive degrees or diplomas from any of them.

Essay Four

[1] p. 107 An important source for the negative Herbert Field story was Robert Murphy, a powerful Foreign Service officer. But Murphy's account was carefully edited: Allen Dulles as a spymaster played no part in Murphy's account of both World Wars, though Switzerland was an important Murphy site. Further, the Lenin role in the McNally/field narrative was altogether missing. How knowledgeable (or deliberately unwitting) Murphy was of intelligence activities can be gained through one important paragraph of commentary, its OSS/CIA spin quite apparent: "Incidentally, I have followed with interest the career of Herbert Field's son, Noel, who entered the foreign service after World War I and eventually defected to the Communists.

He was last heard from in Budapest, but defectors live in danger and apparently the Communists suspected Noel Field of being a double agent. At any rate, he vanished. Perhaps some day we may learn what happened to this too-bright young man who worked secretly for the Communist side in the Spanish Civil War, using a League of Nations job as cover for his activities."

[2] p. 108 Rex A. Wade, The Bolshevik Revolution and Russian Civil War. "Lenin became one of the most extreme antiwar spokesmen, calling for transformation of the world war into [worldwide] civil war and arguing that Russia's defeat was the lesser evil."

[3] p. 109 Was there ever an "evacuation train" from Vienna to Bern? Certainly such a train could have run from Vienna to Zurich (the residence of both Herbert Field and Lenin), but apparently only local transportation existed between Zurich and Bern.

[4] p. 111 This version of the story is hopeless: it includes a call from Lenin on "a Friday afternoon" (80) and Dulles instructing him to "call back the next day." That was, of course, Good Friday, Easter weekend.

This, however, is not the most noteworthy tale. On June 21, 2004., James L. Pavitt reported the following version, possibly heard from Dulles but more likely a variant transmitted to Pavitt in a faulty oral tradition. "Indeed, some of our best officers have learned from their mistakes. In the previous century, a junior intelligence officer in Switzerland received word on Sunday evening that a disturbed Russian sought to speak to an American official. Not wanting to spoil his weekend tennis outing, our officer told the duty officer to direct the disturbed Russian to return the next day-Monday-during duty hours. Unfortunately, Vladimir Lenin chose not to return to the mission. Allen Dulles ... was the junior intelligence officer. He recovered admirably from this early stumble and learned a lesson he imparted to future generations of operations officers." This version adds the fascinating possibility that Lenin had actually visited the "mission" in person. The address to the Foreign Policy Association was delivered by James L Pavitt, in 2004 the Deputy Director for Operations, Central Intelligence Agency.

[5] p. 114 Ambrose had a remarkable opportunity to explore the dark infrastructure of the international elite network that used and supported Allen Dulles, the OSS, and the CIA and, when that network could, manipulated Eisenhower, but Ambrose opted out. The book promised much (see, for example, the back flyleaf): "It is an account of the transformation of – the wartime OSS into the CIA...." But Ambrose's Ike's Spies is no such thing, ignoring, for example, the important story of Arbenz in Switzerland, giving the reader only a photograph of the exiled couple; ignoring the Atsugi U-2 Air Base except for a single reference; ignoring Allen Dulles in "Berne" except for a single reference; ignoring the FBI except for two pages. Its fullest and most relevant discussion – on the U-2 – was apparently controlled by CIA agents and assets. See also Richard H. Immerman, Ambroses "Research Associate," and his background connections and interviews.

[6] p. 115 The immoral decision to accomplish good ends through evil means was also made by Allen Dulles' brother, John Foster Dulles, and also included the manipulation of religious individuals and institutions for personal and political goals. Political decisions fundamentally immoral, unethical, and evil have been at the heart of American intelligence's misuse of religious individuals and institutions. But Robert N. Bellah has concluded that fighting perceived evil with evil is central to the American ethos. Planted early on by exclusionist Puritan Protestants, this became a significant part of the American Establishment's deep structure: Robert N. Bellah, "Evil and the American Ethos."

[7] p. 117 Fry's own account of his astounding rescue work is heavily sanitized (possibly by Fry himself). In a long and fairly informative "Afterward" attributed to the "United States Holocaust Memorial Museum," Paul Hagen is identified as "Karl Frank," but the index simply gives "Frank, Karl, see Hagen, Paul." The "Afterward" is apparently a careful instance of damage control, possibly with the assistance of Israeli intelligence in cooperation with the CIA. And Fry's close connections to religious organizations, specifically the Quakers and the Unitarians, are also cloaked. The links between the religious humanitarian groups and American intelligence would be reasons enough for Fry's editorial care.

[8] p. 117 According to Chester, "Karl Frank was instrumental in recruiting Fry for the post of European representative of the Emergency Rescue Committee."

[9] p. 124 For how extensive was the success of the COI and then the OSS in recruiting and organizing anti-Nazi liberal and radical circles, see the "Memorandum by Willy Brandt ([from] Stockholm): Opposition Movements in Germany." Brandt named Paul Hagen as a key leader of one of the "oppositional socialistic groups ... based upon democratic principles."

[10] p. 124 Despite several negative comments circulated about Dulles and his Swiss intelligence-gathering, some knowledgeable sources have verified the value of Dulles' work;

for example: "An exceedingly small staff of agents ... produced some of the best OSS intelligence of the war." That information included "early intelligence on atomic and bacteriological research, location of the V-I and V-2 development and testing sites, the ... attempt on Hitler's life, and negotiations ... for the surrender of Axis forces in northern Italy...."

[11] p. 125 Von Schroeder later held an SS rank equivalent to a general. He was also the leader of a secret operation that pressed funding from Ruhr business leaders to support Heinrich Himmler.

[12] p. 125 Former OSS and CIA hands (as well as faithful biographers) have praised Dulles' Second World War espionage activities in Switzerland. But many British intelligence sources have minimized and even trivialized Dulles' trumpeted accomplishments. One relatively disinterested, well-informed and conservative commentator on Dulles has been Angelo M. Codevilla in his *Between the Alps and a Hard Place*. Codevilla served as a U.S. Naval Officer, a Foreign Service officer, a senior staff member of the Senate Select Committee on Intelligence, and a Stanford University Hoover Institution senior research fellow. He concluded that "Swiss intelligence enjoys a mythic [that is, a largely fictional] reputation, as does the role of intelligence gathered [in World War II] in Switzerland." On American intelligence, he added that the information and intrigue that flowed through ... [Switzerland] played [little] more than a marginal role in the outcome of World War II." Codevilla did note that "America's Office of Strategic Services (OSS) began as an extension of Colonel William Donovan's private contacts...." But the reality was that Dulles' Swiss OSS operations were also based on rancor "private contacts" with American/German industrial and financial individuals and groups, religious ..." institutions and human service activists, and with liberal/radical resistance organizations.

Allen Dulles' two overarching goals were to defeat Germany while saving the German industrial power-elite. Codevilla ignored the overwhelming evidence, relegating the output of Allen Dulles to a dependent clause: "The pressure of events – rather than anything that Swiss intelligence or America's spymaster in Switzerland, Allen Dulles, did – was what increased the flow of intelligence [leaked from German sources into Allied operations]."

[13] p. 126 Waller asserted that Field was ... a member of the Communist party" and an avowed ... Communist and Soviet apologist ... but offered no evidence or proof for the party membership except to cite the standard anti-Hiss sources.

[14] p. 126 Field's adventures and complexities deserve a tragic epic; see, for example, Hede Massing's *This Deception* on Field and Marxism, and on Field as an intellectual, on psychoanalysis, and on Field at the Lincoln Memorial. For a physical description that was valid until his arrest in Prague.

[15] p. 133 Breindel: "Shipped from Czechoslovakia to Hungary, the hapless Field ... was used as a 'witness' in the show trial of Hungarian Foreign Minister Lazlo Rajk. Subsequently, Field ... also provided a confession, that served as evidence in the 1952 Slansky trial, an ugly anti-Semitic affair that sent Rudolf Slansky, the General Secretary of the Czechoslovakia Communist Party to the gallows." Given the trumped-up charges based on Field's dubious testimony, why should his specific statements about Alger Hiss be accepted as truthful'?

[16] p. 134 "[Random House president] Alberto Vitale ... negotiated an agreement with the KGB's retired agents' group, as a result of which the Russian Foreign Intelligence Service; a KGB successor agency, allowed a small group of Western and Russian scholars ... access to previously unavailable Soviet intelligence files." (xi) Weinstein and Vassilie also were supported by the CIA and the National Security Agency. (xii) Left unexplored by at least the American co-author Allen Weinstein, with a distinguished professional resume, was to what extent he was manipulated by both former Soviet and present Russian intelligence agents as well as cooperating American intelligence.

[17] p. 140 Though Katz in Foreign Intelligence gave no indication OSS Research and Analysis had any interest in examining and exploiting religious and church contacts, the available OSS documents indicate extensive contacts and manipulation.

[18] p. 140 The irony of having "only" psyops intelligence value must be remembered when the reader reviews the psychological warfare actions of Allen Dulles, John Foster Dunes, Dwight David Eisenhower and C. D. Jackson.

[19] p. 140 J.S. Conway, *The Nazi Persecution of the Churches*. See also Conway 289: "it was never proved that any of this circle of high-minded men were actually engaged in the plot...."

[20] p. 141 Two of the seven Circle members charged with plotting Hitler's assassination were hanged: Father Augustin Rosch and Dr. Theodor Haubach.

[21] p. 142 Niemoeller was much more negative about the post-war future of the "German church" than the OSS, primarily because American intelligence (and the Dulles brothers),viewed the institution as a social and political instrument, while the German theologian thought it should have been measured by the (less pragmatic) canons of religious morality: "He was pessimistic about the revival of the German church and personally thought that 'the spirit of the Nazis' had never been stronger in Germany [after the war!] meaning not just the Nazis' political concepts but the whole evil, totalitarian, godless attitude that oversimplified everything and chose violence to achieve its ends."

[22] p. 147 "Jo Tempi came to the United States on a speaking tour, and because of her previous membership in the German Communist Party, the FBI followed her." The Bureau claimed Tempi was "sexually involved with ... Dr. Charles Joy." Denying all accusations, Joy was still fired by the Unitarian board in August. 1946.

[23] p. 147 Alexander and Helene Rado are, of course, not Allen Dulles' Emmy Rado and her husband: "Rado" is a not-uncommon Hungarian family name, and the husbands may have been related.

[24] p. 149 Steven is the primary and most reliable source for Operation Splinter Factor. Though he has cited Flora Lewis as his initial"springboard," it is more likely he was first alerted to the Field/Swiatlo story by at least one member of British intelligence. Though referred to throughout his text. British/English intelligence and its Secret Intelligence Service (SIS) are NOT indexed; SIS Captain Michael Sullivan IS indexed (249): see 34-39 and 49-56. Steven identified "four distinct categories of sources· (229) for his Operation Splinter Factor history: former CIA members (229-230); former operatives of East European and "Current employees of government and governmental organizations in the West." (230) This last "source" is curious, because it is made up mainly of British intelligence, as a close reading of Steven throughout verifies.

Because of its British intelligence sources, Steven's account is accurate but also marked by disinformation. For the disinformation side: British intelligence's negative attitude toward Allen Dulles; for accuracy, Frank Wisner's (and possibly Kim Philby's) connection to the Field/Swiatlo story.

Jozef Swiatlo, who initially established a British counterintelligence link but was sent to American intelligence by British SIS, was contacted by Steven (230) and apparently agreed (at least initially) with Steven's Operation Splinter Factor analysis. (280) But Swiatlo "corrected my original information-that this [Splinter Factor operation] was a British rather than an American operation." (230) Though Steven apparently accepted Swiatlo's statement, the story still strongly suggests that a British/American counterintelligence cabal was responsible. Steven gave one extremely significant clue, admitting that "the [British SIS officer] Sullivan material [actually) came from a former employee of the CIA who was on the inside track of Operation Splinter Factor from its very beginnings and who personally knew Sullivan," (234) Josef Swiatlo's biography, reasonably detailed in Steven (40-46), might by absolutely accurate (that is, well recounted from Steven's sources) and still be a work of "illegal" fiction, constructed on the early record of a Jozef Swiatlo who died and whose identity was then constructed and given to an intelligence agent (American or Soviet) who became "Swiatlo."

[25] p. 151 One murky source reported that Anna Duracz, Berman's secretary, who coincidentally had been Field's secretary in Switzerland, "agreed to transmit a letter from Field to Berman asking him to facilitate contacts with Russians...." Swiatlo gained possession of a copy of the letter, and was able to compromise both Berman and Field. In Wilfred Burchett, *At the Barricades.* The letter may have been an intelligence invention: Duracz was probably working for either Dulles, Swiatlo, or both.

[26] p. 153 Dulles' biographers have attempted to minimize the spymaster's counterintelligence and political duplicity, but Allen was agreeable to Glaser working with the OSS's labor movement operatives in Germany, despite the high probability that he learned from Field about Erika's Swiss Communist connections.

[27] p. 153 Before Herta Field herself went to Europe to find her husband Noel, she had asked his brother Hermann to investigate Noel's disappearance (4 and 19), citing: "complexities" and the Hiss trial for not going to American authorities for assistance. (19) Though scattered throughout the book, Kate and Hermann's commentary on their own work, their disbelief in Noel's substantive spying for Dulles, and their minimization of Hermann's curious history all suggested the strong possibility Hermann Field was also involved, no matter how minimal, in intelligence activity. Kate Field had been working in British refugee work in 1938 (122) when she met Hermann. Though he had no experience in refugee service, he agreed to become involved at Kate's request (122-123) and was remarkably successful (123), assisting displaced and threatened people to enter Great Britain. (418) Hermann's possible intelligence connections can be reviewed on 4. 167-169. 69-72, and 157, for example. Though Hermann asserted he did not believe Noel's intelligence links to the OSS (109), he allowed that Noel could very well have been a spy. (171) Kate and Hermann Field dismissed Operation Splinter Factor (that is, the plot using Swiatlo and Noel Field to destabilize Communist Eastern Europe), but their conclusion concerning the functions of the purge trials is precisely the same as mine. (See 415-417) The curious "Afterward" written by Stanford professor Norman M. Naimark (who was apparently responsible for getting Stanford University Press to publish the book), cited Flora Lewis's Red Pawn and The Haunted Wood for information on Noel Field, but nothing else, yet Naimark went beyond Kate and Hermann Field in examining Hermann's refugee work (420) and the "similarities" between Hermann and Noel. (420) Professor Naimark descended into absurdity by asserting that Noel Field used Allen Dulles. (421) While rejecting the Swiatlo story (423-24) and Field's involvement in a plot to destabilize Eastern Europe, the professor did at least admit that Noel Field "was friendly with the likes of Allen Dulles ..." (423), a considerable understatement.

[28] p. 153 Hungarian intelligence had intercepted and reviewed Allen Dulles' radio communications that probably included reports on his meetings with Max Egon von Hohenlohe in an attempt to establish a peace separate from the Soviets; since the Soviets had penetrated Allied intelligence and were aware that Dulles was negotiating with the Nazis (Simpson 122-124,124-125, and 347-348 note #23), the Hungarians and Soviets may indeed have believed Dulles was a traitor to the Allied/Soviet war effort. It was no secret among international cognoscenti that Allen and John Foster Dulles were "two of the more influential advocates of separate peace tactics in elite U.S. circles." (Simpson 121)

[29] p. 154 Whiting 228. Hermann and Kate Field (Noel Field's brother and sister-in-law) did not accept the argument that the CIA, through Swiatlo and Noel Field, catalyzed the Eastern Europe purges, but their conclusions as to the trials' intent and outcome were identical to those here presented: see Field Trapped 110-11.

[30] p. 163 The United States Agency for International Development (AID) and AID's "police advisory program," has been widely suspected of collusion with the CIA; see A. J. Langguth, *Hidden Terrors*. 120, 138, 232. "In the late 60s the U.S. Agency for International Development {AID) contracted with the UUSC [the Unitarian Universalist Service Committee] to run a social work education project in Vietnam. Reports that the Central Intelligence Agency was infiltrating private agencies working in Vietnam on AID contracts alarmed opponents. In May 1969 a group of divinity students staged a sit-in at UUSC for five days, protesting.... When the contract with AID ended in 1971 [,] the UUSC withdrew from the controversial project." Roger Fritts, sermon on February 9, 1997, on website.

Eliot is one of two most likely candidates for the protected OSS/CIA asset or agent among the Unitarians; Essay Eight reviews the second. It is not impossible, of course, that both candidates were, in fact, being protected: one dead, one still alive at the time of the transmission of the sanitized OSS records.

[31] p. 164 See also Hughes 93: Catchpool spent more than two years attempting to book a lecture tour for Colin Ross, a German writer and traveler and the brother of a German Quaker whom Catchpool had aided. But Ross was also "an ardent Nazi ... who believed that Sir Oswald Mosley was destined to be the British Fuhrer...." As Hughes dryly commented: "a series of lectures given by him in England would certainly not have served the [Catchpool] cause of reconciliation."

[32] p. 165 See also the splendid historical and analytical study: J.S. Conway, *The Nazi Persecution of the Churches*. Though beyond the focus of my own study, Conway's work is both precise and moving; anyone interested in the complexity of the terrible time in Germany must see Conway on the following topics: documents xi; Nazi subversion of the German churches xiii; the struggle of the churches xiii-xviii; the destruction of the churches 328; faith and conspiracy 329; the fatal weakening 329; the stressful mixed record of the Nazis and the Germans 329-332; the "four factors" helping to explain the German Christian failure to oppose Hitler 332-337; the reawakening (as of 1968) 337; and the Christian anti-Nazi heroes 338. I realize this full citation repeats an earlier full citation: the Conway text deserves the duplication.

[33] p. 165 "Just how and why Albert and Anne Martin ... were chosen, remains a mystery." But Albert Martin himself is a special mystery, suggesting he may have been involved in Allied intelligence activities: see Schmitt 111-114.

[34] p. 166 This Catchpool peace-making, however, had its bizarre aspect; with the world about to discover the breadth and depth of the crimes against humanity committed by the Nazis, Catchpool wrote and spoke "to remind people of the 'forgotten Germany,' the Germany of romantic idealism, love of nature, simple piety, philosophy, poetry and music." (Hughes 185) All of this nostalgia for an earlier Germany was, like John Foster Dulles' concern for moral righteousness and German industry, "to show how inconsistent with the Christian way a retributive peace would be." {Hughes 185)

[35] p. 166 According to Schmitt (216), Catchpool had a change of heart, realizing he ought not to take sides in what was essentially a German "civil war." (Schmitt 216) Of course, Catchpool's apparent reversal might well have been dictated by a branch of Allied intelligence.

[36] p. 167 Catchpool's humanitarian dedication, his persistence in peace-making, his Quaker spirituality, have all been movingly attested to by William R. Hughes, his close friend. (Hughes 187-233)

ESSAY FIVE:

[1] p. 171 See Antony C. Sutton, *America's Secret Establishment*. Though occasionally marked by conservative bias, Sutton's work is more relevant to an extended close study

of the American Establishment and the National Security State than the Silks. See especially Sutton. 36-46, where Sutton places the Council on Foreign Relations, the Trilateral Commission, and several other important Establishment organizations in their proper relationship to what Sutton has called "The Order." See also Sutton's excellent summary of the major influence of the Bundy family (Yale and Skull & Bones) 47-52, and contrast it with the Silks deliberate minimizing of both McGeorge and William Bundy's Yale connections: Silks 49 and 205-206.

[2] p. 184 Dulles was the U.S's major negotiator of a 1951 treaty that "sought to eliminate any possibility of Japanese war reparations." Steven C. Clemons, "Recovering Japan's Wartime Past – and Ours," *New York Times*, September 4, 2001, A23: Dulles was able to establish "a deliberate forgetfulness whose consequences haunt us today."

[3] p. 186 For a brilliant commentary and analysis on Foster Dulles' "religiosity," consult Joel Kovel, *Red Hunting in the Promised Land.* Kovel's judgment of Foster Dulles' ranting (65), moralizing (65), clamor (65), madness (66), cunning (66), craft (66), bombast (66), threat (66), compromise (66), and nuance (66), is accurate. See Kovel's sharp and cogent examination of Dulles' Old Testament posture, his argument for Christianity and Western imperialism, his so-called morality, his Aristotelian-Augustinian splitting of absolute good and evil, and Dulles' Revelations-based Apocalyptic view of the world (76, 85).

[4] p. 187 Hoopes 487-491. The American nation finally united with John Foster Dulles in his pragmatic and spiritually empty religiosity: see, for example, Charles C. Alexander, Holding the Line 135-137. But Alexander also pointed out the parallel and directly-related explosion of"radical sectarianism" (137), an evangelistic expansion that by 1958 counted more than six million converts in the United States alone. (137) Ironically, the collector of Dulles' moral musings, Henry Van Dusen, commented that "Peter and Barnabas and Paul might find themselves more at home in a Holiness service or a Pentecostal revival than in the formalized and sophisticated worship of other churches, Catholic or Protestant." Indeed, so might have Jesus of Nazareth.

[5] p. 188 Given that the manipulators of the so-called Cold War had operated in bad faith, revisionist historical examinations have rightly called our attention to "the strategy of deterrence [that] prolonged rather than ended the {Cold War] conflict," Richard Ned Lebow and Janice Gross Stein, We All Lost the Cold War. This otherwise excellent analysis of Cold War fictions ignored Allen Dulles and John Foster Dulles as the major creative collaborators in that monstrous political deception.

Essay Six:

[1] p.195 Though intelligence agent Richard Case Nagell argued persuasively that his Soviet handlers directed him to kill Oswald, because they suspected the re-defector of being a major player in a JFK assassination plot, Nagell did not (of course) complete his assignment, and Nagell was, at the same time, allegedly in touch with or taking orders from American intelligence. If Nagell was indeed a legitimate double or doubled (or even tripled) agent, who, then, wished Oswald dead and who wished him alive?

[2] p. 196 The RAND/Rand Development story is tangled: see Epstein, Legend 312; HR 207-209; 12 HH 463-465; and, ultimately, Peter Dale Scott. Dallas Conspiracy, Chapter Two. p. 2.

[3] p.199 See Summers 178-179 for information about a most provocative defector from 1958-59 who spent months in Minsk but whose identity was protected by the CIA.

[4] p. 200 Gary Hill, "Webster and MKULTRA: the Smoking Gun," The Fourth Decade, Volume 5, Number 6, September. 1998, has been the most productive researcher in enlarging our understanding of Robert Webster. According to Hill, Dick Russell reported Webster had told him he knew Marina in the Soviet Union (13). Hill has concluded that

Oswald and Webster were both "part of the same 'false defector' program." (13) Hill also concluded that both "were also subjects in the MKULTRA project which may have been used to create dual personalities ..." (13) Hill has made an excellent case for Webster being monitored and maintained by the CIA's MKULTRA program and then abandoned, left in a vegetative state. (14) See also Joseph J. Trento, The Secret History of the CIA, 217, for the Snyder/CIA confirmation.

[5] p. 201 Either Oswald was the lone assassin or he was not. If he was, then all the agencies still have to answer a fundamental question: why was so suspect an individual allowed the freedom of movement Oswald obviously enjoyed, both before his trip to the Soviet Union and especially after? But if he was not the lone assassin, why did they not acknowledge that fact? Or is the answer too obvious?

[6] p. 202 Charles Douglas Jackson preferred "C.D." He died on September 18th, 1964, at the age of 62: see "C.D. Jackson Dies; Time, Inc., Official," New York Times, September 20th, 1964. The Times story on Jackson, like much else that can be found (with some difficulty) about him is both incomplete and inaccurate. For example, the obituary identifies Jackson as an official of the "Allied Air Force Headquarters" in North Africa, 1943. Actually, he was an official at General Dwight David Eisenhower's Allied Force Headquarters (AFHQ) in Algiers. Both the error and omission are significant, since the 1943 North African collaboration between Jackson and Eisenhower probably marked at least one of the earliest between Eisenhower and "the confidant of the former President ..." Jackson has also been misidentified in some sources as "Charles David."

[7] p. 211 Despite the largely unexamined premise that North Korea invaded South Korea, the opposite is most probably true: see I.F. Stone, The Hidden History of the Korean War. The Stone book is precisely (as the author indicates) a study of "war propaganda" (xvi): that is, psyops.

[8] p. 213 The author was Music Editor, Sound Effects Editor, and Story Recording Director at Hearst-Metrotone News in New York in the 1950s with no control over content: the subtle yet clearly anti-Soviet scripting of the news and documentary programs produced for the U.S. government, ironically, most of the script voice-over readers (in dozens of languages and dialects) were political liberals and radicals, passionately committed to democratic reforms in their home countries and suspicious of what they perceived were American neocolonial goals.

[9] p. 219 In the New York Times, Stephen Kinzer introduced eleven "previously classified" State Department documents illustrating in detail the CIA's role in PBSUCCESS. All of them, but especially "Memorandum for the record, Oct. 29, 1953," "Memorandum from PBSUCCESS headquarters to C.I.A. station in Guatemala, Apr. 28. 1954," and "Dispatch from PBSUCCESS headquarters to all PBSUCCESS stations, June 13, 1954," could have been written by C.D. Jackson, and probably were.

[10] p. 219 After Kennedy's victory, a major modification in CIA plans, intending the Bay of Pigs operation to fail, may have occurred: several historians, including this author, have called the Bay of Pigs a "perfect failure."

[11] p. 221 Michael Beschloss in May-Day made his first reference (of only two references) to C.D. Jackson, quoting at length from Jackson's personal records on John Foster Dulles' concerns about Eisenhower's "Vienna" conference vulnerability (97). The Dulles message to Jackson was delivered in December 1954, when the Secretary of State might still have felt it was politic to call C.D. Jackson a "friend": but Beschloss should certainly have known better. Beschloss wrote that Jackson had been on "the [Eisenhower] White House staff" before he returned to his Life/Time/Fortune position, certainly a major understatement.

[12] p. 222 Eisenhower's absolute faith in psychological warfare has been 'reported' so many times without definitive documentation that it itself reads like a psyops action.

[13] p. 225 Jackson was an innovator in using youth and student exchanges and visits for psyops goals.

[14] p. 226 Kai Bird is absolutely correct in identifying John J. McCloy as the elite establishment's "chairman": Bird Chairman 11. Though the McCloy family was originally Philadelphian working-class and shared the area's Quaker values, John J. McCloy became a Episcopalian (like many of the Philadelphian Quakers) operating within the highest elitist circle of Episcopal power rather than as a devout church member. See Bird Cm 23-36, 57-58,190.

[15] p. 226 Steinem's communications to C.D. Jackson can be found in the C.D. Jackson papers at the Eisenhower Presidential Library in Abilene, Kansas. Steinem wrote to Jackson, for example, on March 19th, 1959: see Bird Chairman 727 note # 145. Years later, Steinem approved of the covert funding she received from the Central Intelligence Agency: Bird '72'7 note # 143.

[16] p. 233 Edward K. Thompson was the Life magazine editor who accepted responsibility for altering the shape of the rifle in the "Oswald" backyard photos: see 21 H 450-453 and Lane 358-59. Hinckle 165.

[17] p. 235 To be perfectly clear: I am not accusing C.D. Jackson of plotting the assassination of John F. Kennedy. But the individual or individuals who designed the suspicious false identity/defector/redefector called "Oswald" must have had extensive psyops experience. For example: C.D. Jackson practiced psyops in publishing, advertising, fund-raising, public opinion shaping, and propaganda and political pysops in magazine editing and publishing in military black propaganda and covert intelligence operations for OWI, OSS, and PSR; in political campaigns and administrative propaganda operations; in economic/global and elitist/establishment actions; and working with or influencing psyops experts Allen Dulles, Frank Wisner, David Atlee Phillips, E. H. Hunt, and possibly James Jesus Angleton.

Here is the masterfully obscured covert career of C.D. Jackson:

*Organizer of General Eisenhower's wartime Psychological Strategy Board in North Africa and Europe.

*A major manipulator of U.S. World War II "public opinion."

*The first "Cold War" advisor and director of national psyops for Eisenhower; the model for all future holders of that appointive office (under a variety of titles).

*Directed President Eisenhower's nuclear weapons/atomic energy initiative threatened by Albert Schweitzer and Patrice Lumumba.

*Ran major U.S. psyops through the NSC and the CIA in the 1950s

*Directed psychological warfare for the CIA, its fronts, and CIA-supported propaganda/public relations organizations, 1951-1959.

*Joined with Henry Luce and Time, Inc., to sponsor and support American psyops programs and to protect the CIA.

*Worked with American intelligence psyops experts, including David Atlee Phillips, to destabilize foreign governments and in CIA assassination attempts on foreign leaders.

*Recommended, helped organize, and supported U.S. government and CIA psyops funding of student/youth organizations and individuals to attend European youth programs in Europe, 1959-1962, whose American intelligence goals were always anti-Communist and anti-Soviet.

*Organized and established the U.S. branch of the international Bilderberg Conference; was an active and influential member of the Council on Foreign Relations; and a regular, enthusiastic attendee at all Bohemian Grove events.

*Assisted major corporations and the government, working together to create a new economic order, anticipating globalization.

*Worked for the CIA and the Luce media empire in Dallas immediately after the JFK assassination; isolated and manipulated Marina Oswald; used an "Oswald" backyard rifle photo for major media propaganda; withheld the Zapruder film from public viewing. In addition, C.D. Jackson:

*May have teamed with Allen Dulles after World War II to run anti-Soviet psyops (including Illegals and false defectors).

*May have worked with Allen Dunes and John Foster Dulles manipulating religious individuals and groups through 'World War II and the Cold War in pursuit of political and economic goals.

ESSAY SEVEN:

[1] p. 243 October 19, 1950: actually the memorandum from Bureau of the Budget Director F. J. Lawton to President Truman, in effect informing the president that the Bureau was already running what it called an "informal review" through William T. Golden for which it had not yet gotten presidential approval; Truman "approved" the Lawton memo on October 20, 1950), in Selected; October 27.1950, in Memoranda; November 1. 1950, in Memoranda; December 19. 1950, in Selected; December 21,1950, in Memoranda; February 6,1951, in Selected; February 20.1951, in Selected; and March 6.1951, in Selected.

[2] p. 245 According to Killian: "I find in Unitarianism the freedom and stimulus to seek a lofty sense of the meaning of life. The important thing is to build a faith in a divine power or principle larger and beyond oneself. For me, Unitarianism contributes most effectively toward this objective." The statement, with its defective syntax, clichés, and ethical dodges, effectively defines James Killian.

[3] p. 247 MIT cooperated with the U.S. military and more secretly with the CIA from the years following World War II through the Clinton Administration: American military and intelligence received immeasurable benefits and the MIT administration and faculty reaped superior rewards. See, for example, the excellent analysis, Bob Feldman, "MIT: Still Collaborating with the 'Pentagon'?" posted as of March 25th, 2001, at cndyorks. gn.apc.org/news/articles/mit.htm.

[4] p. 248 Brundage had sent his analysis and recommendations to President Eisenhower on April 23,1956; Eisenhower took note and approved of Brundage's "plans to have the Bureau of the Budget give greater emphasis in its work to the evaluation and advancement of administration in the executive agencies,as a means of more rapidly bringing about improvement in organization and management ... throughout the executive branch." (Eisenhower's response to Brundage, April 29th, 1956) Brundage's analysis was reviewed by the Subcommittee of the Committee on Appropriations. House of Representatives, where the Hoover-Brundage proposals began their successful march through the existing Federal budget controls.

[5] p. 250 When Allen Dulles left as the Director of the CIA, JFK again accepted expert advice and appointed engineer and former chairman of the AEC John Alex McCone. The friends of the CIA then pressed McCone to develop the scientific and technological aspects of intelligence," led by Edwin Land of Polaroid. William Baker of Bell Laboratories and James Killian of MIT. All were members of the President's Foreign Intelligence Advisory Board: (Kirkpatrick 243)

[6] p. 250 Another crucial spy/space decision was made just days before JFK became president: in March 1960 the Secretary of Defense recommended to President Eisenhower that the U.S.'s huge conglomerate of covert intelligence be closely reviewed. On May 6, 1960, after the U-2 shoot-down, Killan's board of Consultants, Thomas Gates, the DOD Secretary, Gordon Gray, Allen Dulles, Maurice Stans and the president met, resulting in a Joint Study Group being tasked to examine closely the U.S.'s "foreign intelligence

effort"; the board's recommendations and three subsequent United States Intelligence Board meetings led to a National Security Council debate on January 12, 1961. Allen Dulles argued that the National Photographic Interpretation Center, whose program was already being run by the CIA, should continue to be administered by the Agency, since the material generated had "tremendous political significance" beyond its military intelligence value Richelson *Wizards* 30-31). Allen Dulles won the argument for the CIA (Richelson *Wizards* 31): but with Killian, Gray, the Bureau of the Budget, and Dulles all on the same team, how could the outcome have been otherwise? Given Richelson's deep interest in high-flight spy operations and the Langley "wizards," it is more than surprising that, except for a handful of passing references to NASA, neither the wizards' major responsibility for NASA nor NASA's connection to military and civilian intelligence goals was examined by Richelson.

[7] p. 250 Though the received history of the Board is that President Kennedy "reorganized the panel" (Deutch), the Eisenhower "Consultants" board had voluntarily ended its existence on January 7, 1961. (Wise and Ross, *Invisible* 187)

Given Kennedy's interest in getting the very best people regardless of party or privilege for key positions in his new government, and knowing that he took advice from key members of the U.S. elite community, identifying the specific person who recommended Killian would be instructive.

[8] p. 251 Naming the three most important actors, of course, simplifies a series of complicated historical actions. From 1947 through 1961, the three sides of the powerful and profitable triangle were 1. Killian and Brundage, 2. Killian (with his associates) and LBJ, and 3. Brundage's Bureau of the Budget and LBJ.

[9] p. 255 Beschloss May-Day II. Beschloss expanded on NACA nervousness, raising an interesting but unexplored issue: "In 1956, Congress was by no means resolved to spend vast sums to send men into space. If something went wrong with the U-2 and NACA was exposed as the CIA's servant, the space program might never get off the ground." But why would Dryden worry about the space program: it was highly unlikely that NACA (dedicated to terrestrial "weather problems") anticipated being involved with space. Unless, of course. Bissel had already suggested just that future for NACA as a payment for its clandestine cover of U-2 spying.

[10] p. 259 The official postings on James E. Webb have trumpeted his praises, giving him full credit for completing JFK's lunar initiative. But President Kennedy announced his space vision on May 25, 1961, and Webb did not achieve JFK's goal until 1968, when the lunar landing operated as an heroic diversion from LBJ's failed domestic and foreign policy programs.

[11] p. 262 As late as 1971, CIA Director Richard Helms lied to the American Society of Newspaper Editors when he implied that the CIA budget was audited "line for line by the Office of Management and Budget." (Marchetti 320) Anyone can read a so-called budget "line for line."

[12] p. 263 "Every year [through the 1970s] the budget of the National Aeronautics and Space Administration had some CIA money hidden within it." John Ehrlichman, Washington: Behind Closed Doors.

[13] p. 267 Whether Gary Powers' ill-fated U-2 flight crashed due to a "malfunction" or because the Soviets shot it down, the American officials who scheduled it may have been the same people with interests in dooming the up-coming U.S.-Soviet peace talks. In fact, Richard Bissell, the CIA's director of dirty tricks, sent Powers and his U-2 into Soviet skies with the approval of Colonel Goodpaster, Eisenhower's Pentagon/CIA liaison: Beschloss May-Day 131.

[14] p. 275 The titles "Assistant Secretary of Defense" and "Deputy Secretary of Defense" have been frequently confused in popular sources. If Brundage's associate in underwrit-

ing Southern Air Transport for the CIA was, rather than an "assistant secretary," a former "Deputy Secretary of Defense," then both he and Brundage would have served together with C.D. Jackson and Allen Dulles on the five-member OCR committee monitoring U.S. intelligence's covert operations, an even closer fit for the CIA's Southern Air Transport.

[15] p. 275 Southern Air Transport was reportedly founded by arch-conservative Fred Bachelor. Among SAT's notable officers has been Hugh Fred Grundy, who worked in Africa with Pan American Airlines, a military/intelligence partner inside the U.S. economic establishment, to build a supply route for the Allies in World War II. After serving in the Army Air Corps (most probably in an intelligence capacity), Grundy signed on with the China National Corporation (CNAC) in Shanghai, becoming CNAC's Chief Engineer, where he helped develop General Chennault's Civil Air Transport (CAT). For twenty years, Grundy was president of CAT, managing the CIA's Air America operations in Greater Asia directing the Pacific actions of Southern Air Transport. Grundy eventually commanded over 10,000 employees and operatives (open and covert) in Southeast Asia. Thailand, Japan and Korea for U.S. intelligence. He retired from his Asian duties in 1976 and became senior vice president and then director of Southern Air Transport, which had a long history of association with the members of the "retired U.S. intelligence community that congregated in Southern Florida. Among SAT's Miami Dade County operatives who served as the airline's legal counsel was attorney Thomas R. Spencer. Jr., who was General Counsel in the Department of Defense during the Nixon and Ford administrations. Though his various biographical sources do not specifically identify Spencer as a former agent of the CIA (or as a retired member of any other intelligence group), he has proudly announced himself a longtime working associate of Theodore Shackley, the notorious Agency operator who commanded assassination hitmen and death squads out of JMWAVE in Florida and in Vietnam; who was an active participant in the Bay of Pigs operation and the CIA's multiple assassination attempts against Fidel Castro; who worked closely with psyops master David Phillips; and who directed such dark CIA figures as the admitted assassin David Sanchez Morales. When Ted Shackley died, Spencer delivered the funeral oration celebrating Shackley's covert intelligence career. Shackley's close associate Thomas Spencer has been a member of the Board of Directors of the powerful Miami-Dade chapter of the Association of Former Intelligence Officers (AFIO), serving there, for example, with the grandson of the CIA's James Jesus Angleton. Spencer remains a life-time member of AFIO and has been an active member of the AFIO's national board of directors (2003), directing programs and forums for the national ex-spooks' conventions and symposia. Spencer's intelligence links include the American Security Council Foundation Intelligence Officers; the National Business Intelligence Symposium (as chair for several years); the Overseas Security Advisory Council, U.S. Department of State, Bureau of Diplomatic Security, Infragard, Federal Bureau of Investigations (civilian status); and (but not limited to) Operation On Guard, Department of Homeland Security, U.S. Coast Guard Auxiliary, District 7, Miami Station 1. Finally, Spencer's resume includes his extensive and impressive Florida Republican Party connections, including his role as the Republican Party Executive Committee's chief poll watcher and recount witness after the disputed Florida vote in the 2000 national election.

ESSAY EIGHT:
[1] p. 282 What has been called the "Paine Project," led by researchers and writers Carol Hewett, Steven Jones, Barbara LaMonica, and William Kelly has meticulously documented the extraordinary participation of Ruth and Michael Paine in the lives of Lee and Marina Oswald

The Paine/Hyde/Hoke familial network to which Michael and Ruth Paine belonged exhibited a complexity of U.S. intelligence connections either withheld from or ignored by the Warren Commission.

William Avery Hyde, Ruth Paine's father, was the subject of several CIA file documents that referred to his family's support of Norman Thomas' anti-communist Socialist Party, which was being funded by the Agency. Hyde and his wife Carol were associated with Talbot Bielfeldt, an agent of the Foreign Documents Division of the CIA; yet Carol Hyde (Ruth Paine's mother) was characterized as a "radical" by U.S. double-agent Herbert Philbrick, who cited her activity in the Woman's International League for Peace and Justice: according to Philbrick, a communist "front."

Sylvia Ludlow Hyde, Ruth (Hyde) Paine's sister, also called both Sylvia Hyde Hoke and Sylvia Hoke (after marrying John Hoke), was employed by the U.S. Labor Department from 1949 through 1953. During World War II and the Cold War, the OSS and the CIA recruited anti-Nazi and then anti-Communist labor activists and union leaders. The U.S. Labor Department was, therefore, a long-time center of U.S. intelligence/anti-Communist activity and the site of U.S. covert penetration of both the domestic and foreign labor movements.

Sylvia Hyde was employed by the CIA as early as 1954; her "cover" was as a Personnel Research Technician, Placement and Employee Relations Division, Director of Civilian Personnel, HQ, Department of the Air Force, Washington, D.C. The Air Force had, in fact, provided sanctuary for both intelligence "black" budget items and covert intelligence personnel in the 1950s and '60s.

Sylvia Hoke's Security File 348 201 was inside the CIA's Office of Security, Security Analysis Group. Sylvia's contacts included her mother-in-law, Mrs. Helen Hoke, who had a close relationship with Dorothy Wilson, allegedly a member of the North Beach, California branch of the Communist Party, in the early 1940s. Sylvia Hoke also worked at *Time* magazine when she gave Gerritt E. Fielstra as a reference, reputedly a communist sympathizer and labor organizer. But Fielstra may have himself been a U.S. double agent. On April 17, 1956, Sylvia Hoke was granted a Top Secret security clearance by the Agency for International Development (USAID), a long-time collaborator with the CIA. Because of her labor and left-wing associations (and those of her mother-in-law), Sylvia Hoke's clearance was questioned by the FBI. Yet her clearance with USAID was revalidated on January 17, 1962.

As late as November 11, 1963, the CIA's Office of Security was queried internally about Sylvia Hoke. The 1961 Falls Church, Virginia Directory listed Sylvia Hoke as an "emp CIA": that is, employed by the Central Intelligence Agency. Evidence also indicated that Sylvia Hoke either worked for Naval intelligence at the same time or had an active file there because of her husband's intelligence-related activity.

Sylvia Hoke's husband was John Lindsey Hoke (Ruth Paine's brother-in-law). On February 4, 1956, John Hoke was appointed an audio-visual consultant with the International Cooperation Administration (predecessor of USAID, U.S. Operations Mission in Panama City. John Hoke admitted to the Deputy Director of Communications, ICA, that he did "intelligence type work for the American Embassy." In Surinam and later in Washington, D.C., John Hoke worked for ICA and then USAID, but ran into trouble with the House Subcommittee on Government Operations when it was discovered his solar-powered boat project in Surinam was also intended to generate "personal profit." On June 30, 1963, John Hoke left USAID, yet on August 22, 1963, the CIA granted a second and indefinite "Approval for Liaison" with John Hoke. Hoke remained in the good graces of both the U.S. Military and U.S. Intelligence through at least 1965, employed by the military-industrial partner Atlantic Research where he was the subject of a positive U.S. Naval intelligence check. The Hyde/Paine/Hoke network of intelligence and intelligence-related activities strongly suggests a liberal familial complex whose members were willing double-agents in support of anti-Communist goals. Ruth Hyde Paine was at the center of that Hyde/Paine/ Hoke counter-intelligence complexity.

[2] p. 288 Edward Epstein, the confidante of both the CIA's James Jesus Angleton and FBI's William Sullivan and their counterintelligence associates interviewed six (or more) people present at the Oswald/Ruth Paine party meeting (see Epstein 317, end note for Chapter XII: the party is covered on 203-206). Epstein apparently considered the party's ambiance a necessary factor in Oswald's motives for allegedly shooting at General Edwin Walker and, subsequently, John F. Kennedy. The reader must therefore keep Epstein's major anti-Oswald intelligence connections in mind when evaluating statements ostensibly made by the party's participants and subsequently 'reported' by Epstein.

[3] p. 288 The maze of oil company names associated with the Magnolia Research Labs can be mystifying and maddening. Texas oil explorations, oil company foundings, mergers and name changes are Byzantine, but the ones associated with Magnolia Labs can be sorted out. In 1866, the Vacuum Oil Company (Texas) was incorporated. In 1879, John D. Rockefeller's Standard Oil Company of Ohio purchased a 75% interest in Vacuum Oil. In 1882, Rockefeller consolidated his oil holdings in the Standard Oil Trust, which was established and headquartered in New York. In 1911, with the breakup of the Standard Oil Trust, Socony (Standard Oil Company of New York) was founded. That same year, Magnolia Petroleum Company (Texas) was organized, its pre-consolidation history dating back to 1898. Though Vacuum Oil was originally a Texas operation, it was controlled by Yankee Rockefellers.

Magnolia Oil was perceived to be authentic Texas oil and, in particular, Dallas oil. In 1922, the Magnolia Oil Building in Dallas was opened, crowned by the rotating, neon-bright Flying Red Horse symbolizing Magnolia Oil. Dallas proudly pointed out the Magnolia Building at 1401 Commerce Street as the tallest man-made structure west of the Mississippi River. But Magnolia gained in importance in Texas and the Southwest, and Standard Oil took a special interest, purchasing Magnolia stock. Late in 1925, all Magnolia stock was exchanged for Standard Oil of New York stock, with Magnolia Oil properties consolidated and Socony the actual financial entity. In 1931, Socony Oil and Vacuum Oil were consolidated, becoming the Socony-Vacuum Oil Company; Magnolia became an "affiliate." By 1949, Magnolia was, in effect, owned by Socony-Vacuum. In 1955, Socony-Vacuum became the Socony Mobil Oil Company. In 1959-1960, the Socony Mobil Petroleum Company and its Magnolia affiliates were separated, at least on paper, and the Magnolia Building in downtown Dallas became the Mobile Building. The Magnolia Labs, still part of the mega-corporate structure of Mobile/Socony-Vacuum, were designated the home of the company's oil research (and Russian language instruction), Through the 1960s, Mobil Oil, Mobile Chemical, Mobile Petroleum and Socony Mobil were titles of the company's various operations. Possibly because of its "affiliate" designation or because the Magnolia Labs had a special corporate objective (or both), "Magnolia" was therefore reserved for the research side of the mega-corporation.

[4] p. 289 Schmidt had "studied and lived with 'Dr. Willhelm Keutemeyer, professor of psychosomatic medicine and religious philosophy at ... Heidelberg." (204) According to Schmidt as reported by Epstein, "Keutemeyer had been experimenting ... on a group of schizoids during World War II. The experiments had been interrupted in 1944, when Keutemeyer had become involved in the plot to assassinate Hitler and had been forced into hiding from the Nazis." (353) The network of double-agent intelligence activity surrounding the family and relatives of Ruth Hyde Paine was, therefore, enriched by this same plot against Adolph Hitler (July, 20, 1944), involving Dr. Keutemeyer, Dr. Hans Gisevius, Mary Bancroft (a close friend and companion of Ruth Paine's mother, an OSS spy, and the lover of Allen Dulles), and Allen Dulles himself (never examined by the Warren Commission). Dr. Keutemeyer's son was a close friend of the doctor's psychology student, Volkmar Schmidt. Keutemeyer was also reputedly a colleague of Carl Jung, who had his own close associations with Mary Bancroft, Allen Dulles, David Bruce, OSS officer and

future distinguished U.S. diplomat, and the psychological intelligence activities directed against Adolph Hitler: see Diedre Bair, Jung 482-492.

[5] p. 290 Walter C. Pew, the grandson of Sun Oil's Joseph Newton Pew, was listed in 1979 as the ninth-richest Philadelphian: E. Digby Baltzell, Puritan Boston and Quaker Philadelphia 210. Joseph Newton Pew, always given credit for building the Pew Sun Oil fortune, in fact married into oil through Mary Anderson, "whose family had been pioneers in the oil business." (Baltzell 229)

[6] p. 292 Larrie Schmidt was one of the instigators of the anti-JFK advertisement that appeared in the *Dallas Morning News* on November 22nd, 1963. Larrie's brother Rob was the driver for General Edwin Walker; and Walker later suspected the Schmidt brothers, with Lee Harvey Oswald, were complicit in the alleged assassination attempt against him on April 10, 1963. (Benson 410.) No familial relation between the Schmidt brothers (both right-wingers) and Volkmar Schmidt has so far been discovered. Despite Ruth and Michael Paine's apparent liberal (if not left-wing) orientation, Peter Dale Scott characterized Michael Paine as "an extreme right-winger..." (Scott Deep 277) Though Scott offered no supporting evidence for Michael's Paine's rightist orientation, the label is provocative given Paine's Trotskyite family background, his Bell Helicopter employment, and his living with the Magnolia men's association.

[7] p. 294 On January 9,1964, the FBI questioned Wilmer Stratton and Paul Lacey concerning Ruth Paine, but not about the East-West Exchange program thick with intelligence meanings. Rather, both Quakers were queried about Ruth's initial relationship with Marina Oswald: both of Ruth's Friends associates had specific information about Ruth and Marina: see FBI interview IP 105-3441 Pettijohn/McDonald (1/15/64). The "105" prefix on the Bureau document indicates the interviews were part of a counterintelligence investigation.

[8] p. 299 The Zaostrovtsev story is given by Carpozi in detail on 79-87: fAA Washington Spy Courts the Quakers." Carpozi's espionage revelations had a short but important run in the late 60s, based primarily on his access to FBI files and documents. Reasonably objective, moderately liberal and rational, Carpozi pointed out that Elizabeth Bentley and her friends had brought dubious testimony and charges against innocent U.S. career government workers who may have cooperated with representatives of the government of the Soviet Union; but that alleged cooperation was never documented by Carpoz. Included in Carpozi's photo album (after 96) is a picture (according to Carpozi) of President Truman greeting Alger Hiss at the San Francisco United Nations meeting: but Alger Hiss would have needed a very long right arm with its hand reversed (at birth). Obviously. Truman's right hand is about to be grasped by an unidentified person at the meeting who was not Hiss. Carpozi gave a fanciful 'description' of "illegals" who were being trained at the Soviet Marx-Engels Institute in Gorki (12-13), strongly suggesting his primary source was the FBI. See also Carpozi's commentary on "illegals" and "legals," again suggesting Carpozi's source, and ultimately all his spy "sources" was J. Edgar Hoover.

[9] p. 299 The East-West Exchange history is apparently still being protected by U.S. Intelligence. One of the few documents covering that history: Guy E. Godden, "The Intelligence Hand in East-West Exchange Visits," written sometime in the late 1950s for the IAC Ad Hoc Committee on Exchanges, is a bland review of "the possibilities of a gain to the United States from a technical and intelligence point of view." The IAC was dissolved on September 15, 1958. Coriden's paper, as late as "2 July 96" still heavily "sanitized" after a "CIA Historical Review Program Release," can be recovered at http://cia.gov/csi/docs/v02i3a09p_0001.htm.

[10] p. 300 The Warren Commission at least began an inquiry; the House Select Committee on Assassinations never called either Ruth Paine or her husband to testify. Before the

HSCA had finished its deliberations, a set of important questions to be put to Ruth Paine had been delivered to the committee.

[11] p. 302 With the Quaker connection, there seems to be an underlying thread of detached financial and administrative assistance from a number of 'non-profit' religious oriented charity organizations" in the Oswald story. Kelly Philadelphia.

[12] p. 304 Priscilla Johnson McMillan reported (without elaboration) that Ruth and Michael Paine "belonged to a Unitarian congregation ..." (386) As did other Warren Report supporters, McMillan ignored relevant and readily available Paine/Unitarian/Oswald materials. For example, Bell Helicopter research engineer Raymond Krystinik met his friend and co-worker Michael Paine at an American Civil Liberties Union meeting on the campus of Southern Methodist University, held the night of October 25, 1963. Paine had invited Lee Harvey Oswald to the meeting and introduced him to Krystinik. Michael Paine had an earlier conversation with Krystinik concerning Michael's fear he would not be able to fulfill his Unitarian tithe pledge; and just before the ACLU meeting, Michael Paine briefed his friend Krystinik on Oswald's politics. Rev. Byrd Helligas, the assistant pastor at Michael and Ruth Paine's first Unitarian Church in Dallas, was in charge of monitoring the ACLU's coffee supply and running the slide projector at the meeting. Krystinik, Paine, Oswald, and Helligas were involved in at least one reported conversation during the ACLU meeting. On December 1, 1963, ten days after the JFK assassination, a national newspaper quoted Helligas concerning that conversation with Oswald: the Unitarian cleric characterized Lee as "erudite" and "an intellectual." Rev. Helligas elaborated: "He had a good vocabulary. No dangling participles or split infinitives." But when interrogated by the FBI on December 19, 1963, Helligas maintained he could supply nothing about either Oswald or the other ACLU meeting attendees at SMU. A Bureau sweep of Unitarian sites in search of Oswald connections had apparently taken place between December 1 and December 19. Sources: 9 H 461 and 464; Washington Post, December 1, 1963; CE 1388 (CD 206); and Helligas' statement to Mary Ferrell.

[13] p. 307 Frederick Henry Osborn. Sr., whose son was a character witness for Michael and Ruth Paine, was Wickliffe Preston Draper's ideological and financial partner in establishing the eugenics-driven Pioneer Fund in 1937. The web of Osborn/Draper family associations included William Draper, Jr., a cousin of Wickliffe Draper, who shared the military /industrial/ eugenics mix of the Osborn/Draper right-wing alliance.

In the late 1920s and early 1930s, the investment house of Dillon-Read included James Forrestal, Paul Nitze, C. Douglas Dillon (who would run the Treasury Department and the Secret Service under President John F. Kennedy). Ferdinand Eberstadt (who would become a "central figure in the creation of the CIA"), and William Draper,Jr. With Sullivan & Cromwell (including Foster Dulles) acting as investment agent for American companies in Europe, especially in Germany, the money transfers through the banks and investment houses of the U.S. establishment were phenomenal; Draper, Dillon-Read, and the Dulles' brothers cooperated in generating enormous wealth for the elite establishment Dillon-Read's V.P. William Draper "emerged as one of the most prosperous traders in these markets." Christopher Simpson, The Splendid Blond Beast (64)

Wickliffe Draper's wealth was based on his immediate family's ownership of "textile mills, patents on textile equipment, and a substantial share of the international trade in fibers." (249) His cousin, William Henry Draper, Jr., had similar textile origins. Noah Draper, an early 19th-century textile worker in England, had five sons; each of them went into textiles. One of those sons established the Massachusetts Draper line that included Wickliffe Draper. Another of the sons, Noah Draper Jr., had one son, William H. Draper (Sr.), who was five years old when has father moved to the United States. William's father first worked in textiles – in Hebronville, Mass., but began to accumulate real estate, and in 1883 moved to Pawtucket, Rhode Island, now a relatively wealthy Republican and Methodist Episcopalian. William H. Draper (Sr.) was first a mill worker, later a traveling jewelry salesman, then a retail jewelry store owner on North Main St. in Providence and, finally following his father's lead, a real estate investment figure. His wealth grew appreciably, and he became one of the leaders of Rhode Island society. In 1914, for example, he was the "Commodore" of the Edgewood Yacht Club. Cranston. RI, on Narragansett Bay.

His son, William H. Draper,Jr. would achieve prestige and power in the upper divisions of the National Security State, sharing conservative and even reactionary interests with his Draper cousin's family and the Osborn family.

In 1932, William H. Draper, Jr. had already financed the International Eugenics Congress, a long-standing Draper /Osborn interest. At the end of World War II, associates of Draper in the War Department and the Navy (Secretary Forrestal, former president of Draper's old firm Dillon-Reed) "engineered Draper's appointment as chief of the economic division of the joint Allied Control Council for Germany (the central occupation government at the time) and as director of economic policy for the German territories administered by the U.S." (248) In brief, Draper became the most powerful individual determining both the future financial and industrial power of Germany and the director of "denazification programs aimed at German bankers and businessmen." (248) Loyal to his class and financial interests, William H. Draper, Jr. destroyed the denazification programs and turned back Germany to the very banking and investment leaders who had supported Adolph Hitler.(249-253; 262-263) After Draper, of course, came John J. McCloy. General William H. Draper, Jr. became a member of the Army's General Staff, 1945-47; Under Secretary of War,1947; and Undersecretary of the Army, 1947-1949. Draper was also called upon to cooperate with the Bureau of the Budget in shaping President Truman's 1947-48 budgets.

Draper was a key figure in the population control/eugenics movement in the United States (joining the Draper/Osborn family fusion in behavior modification), holding leading positions in a half-dozen highly influential population control organizations. At the direction of President Eisenhower in 1958. Draper, a four-star general and Chair of the U.S. Committee on Foreign, Military and Economic Aid produced the "Draper Report," advocating eugenics for the poorer nations of the world, an obvious population (and nation) control strategy. (Tobin)

[14] p. 311 The Hoover site noted without comment that "the Crusade for Freedom never raised enough money to actually fund RFE-the CIA subsidized both radios [RFE and RL] until 1972 ..."

[15] p. 313 To sort out the major elements of this mix of the elite establishment primarily from the perspective of Arthur Page's several careers with reference to both Allen Dulles and Frederick Osborn, see Griese, 2001. For a splendid study of psyops experience, theory, and practice, see Christopher Simpson, Science of Coercion, where a single reference to Frederick Osborn (60) is imbedded in discussions of Osborn's Morale Research Branch, 26-29, 34-35, and 58-60; General McClure 26, 35-36; the Army's Psychological Warfare Division, 25-27,29, and 35; the Carnegie Corporation, 58, 59-60,102, 112; the OPC and Wisner. 39-40. 45. 49; the Philippines and Lansdale 74-75; C.D. Jackson. 27.75; the OSS and the OWI. 24-29. 32-34; DeWitte Poole. 25-26. 50.131; and the National Committee for a Free Europe, Radio Free Europe, and Radio Liberty, 50,126,131. See also Simpson's irreplaceable "Bibliographic Essay." Finally, with a shift in focus, see Simpson, *Blowback*, for the reticulate complexities of the NCFE, CFF, RFE, RL, CIA funding and control, the International Rescue Committee, and the employment of Nazis, 125. 126, 127, 128,128-129,200,205,217,219,227,228-229,293 note #3, 317 note #1.

Bibliography

PROLOGUE:

The Kennedy Assassination Chronicles, Vol. 1, Summer 1995, #2; and Vol. 2, Issue 2, March, 1996.

Warren Commission, Report of the President's Commission on the Assassination of John F. Kennedy (Washington Government Printing Office, 1964)

Warren Commission, Hearings Before the President's Commission on the Assassination of President Kennedy (Washington Printing Office, 1964)

U.S. National Archives, Warren Commission Documents.

ESSAY ONE:

John Newman, *Oswald and the CIA* (New York: Carroll & Graff, 1995).

Jean Stafford, *A Mother in History* (New York: Farrar, Strauss & Giroux, 1966).

John Ranelagh, *The Agency: The Rise and Decline of the CIA* (New York: Simon and Schuster, 1986).

Lyman B. Kirkpatrick, *The Real CIA* (New York: Macmillan Co., 1968).

Christopher Simpson, *Blowback* (New York: Weidenfeld & Nicholson, 1988).

Leonard Mosley, Dulles [:] *A Biography of Eleanor, Allen, and John Foster Dulles and Their Family Network* (The Dial Press/James Wade: New York, 1978).

Robin W. Winks, *Cloak and Gown* (William Morrow & Co.: New York, 1987).

Nigel West, *Games of Intelligence* (Crown Publishers, Inc.: New York, 1989).

William R. Corson, *Armies of Ignorance* (Dial Press: New York, 1977)

Rhodri Jeffrey-Jones, *The CIA and American Democracy* (New Haven: Yale University Press, 1989).

Barry M. Katz, *Foreign Intelligence [:] Research and Analysis in the Office of Strategic Services[,] 1942-1945* (Cambridge, Mass.: 1989)

Ed. Leo Schelbert, *Switzerland Under Siege* (Rockport, Maine: Picton Press).

Allen Dulles, *The Secret Surrender* (New York: Harper & Row, 1966)

Ray & Mary La Fontaine, *Oswald Talked[:] The New Evidence in the JFK Assassination* (Gretna, La: Pelican Publishing Co., 1996).

Jerry D. Rose, "On Getting Too Excited," *The Fourth Decade*, Sept. 2000, Vol. 7, no. 6.

Edward J. Epstein, *Legend: The Secret World of Lee Harvey Oswald* (New York: Reader's Digest Press, McGraw-Hill Book Co., 1978).

Jim Garrison, *On The Trail of the Assassins* (New York: Warner Books, 1988).

Paul L. Hoch, "CIA Activities and the Warren Commission Investigation," unpublished manuscript, 1975.

Peter Dale Scott, Paul L. Hoch, & Russell Stetler, editors, *A Guide to Coverups and Investigations* (New York: Vintage Books, 1976).

Jerry D. Rose, "Double Agent Unmasked: A Reconstruction," The Third Decade, Vol. 3, #6, Sept., 1987.

Jim Marrs, *Crossfire* (New York: Carroll & Graff, 1989).

John Barron, *KGB, The Secret Works of Soviet Secret Agents* (New York: Reader's Digest Press, 1974).

Also: *KGB Today: The Hidden Hand* (New York: Reader's Digest Press, 1983. New York: Berkley Books, 1985).

Gordon Thomas, *Journey Into Madness* (New York: Bantam Books, 1989).

Joseph L. Trento, *The Secret History of the CIA* (New York: Carroll & Graff, 2005).

Southern California Library of Social Studies and Research, Selected Collections on Los Angeles: First Unitarian Church Collection, 1938-1981. (archives @socallib.org).

Biographical Material on Linus Pauling: Unitarian/Universalist Assn. website.

Dick Russell, *The Man Who Knew Too Much* (New York: Carroll & Graf, 1992).

John H. Clarke, "The Passing of Patrice Lumumba," 1961.

Linda Slattery, "The Congo: How and Why the West Organized Lumumba's Assassination,"

Alex D. Smith, "Eisenhower ordered Congo killing"

Brian Carnell, "Did Eisenhower order Lumumba killing?"

Ludo de Witte, *The Murder of Lumumba* (Verso Books, 2001).

Richard D. Mahoney, *JFK: Ordeal in Africa* (New York: Oxford University Press, 1983).

U.S. Congress Activities, Book 2, Intelligence Activities and the Rights of Americans, 94th Congress, 2nd Session, Senate Report #94-755 (Washington: Government Printing Office, 1976).

Lumumba, a film by Raul Peck.

Craig Roberts, *The Medusa File* (Tulsa: Consolidated Press International, 1997).

William Blum, *The CIA: A Forgotten History* (London & New Jersey: Zed Books Ltd., 1986).

Andrew Tully, *CIA[:] The Inside Story* (New York: William Morrow & Co., 1962).

Adam Hochschild, *King Leopold's Ghost* (Boston, New York: 1998).

Roger Anstey, *King Leopold's Legacy* (London: Oxford University Press, 1966).

Robert B. Edgerton, *The Troubled Heart of Africa*: A History of the Congo (New York: St. Martin's Press, 2002/2003.

Madeleine G. Gelb, *The Congo Cables*, 1982.

Murphy, Kondrashev, and Bailey, *Battleground Berlin: CIA vs KGB in the Cold War* (New Haven: Yale University Press, 1997).

Oleg Kalugin, *The First Directorate* (New York: St. martin's Press, 1994).

Flora Lewis, *Pawn: The Story of Noel Field* (Garden City, New York: Doubleday & Co., Inc., 1965).

Essay Two:
Melissa B. Robinson, Associated Press Summary.

Peter Dale Scott, *Deep Politics and the Death of JFK* (Berkeley: U of California Press, 1993).

CIA Inspector General's Report on Rolando Cubela.

James P. Hosty, Jr., *Assignment: Oswald* (New York: Arcade Publishing, 1996).

Hugh Thomas, *The Cuban Revolution* (New York: Harper & Row, 1977).

Tad Szulc, *Fidel: A Critical Portrait* (New York: William Morrow & Co., 1986).

Inspector General's Report on Plots to Assassinate Fidel Castro, 1967 (Prevailing Winds Research, August 4th 1994).

Boake, "Personal memories of the IARF," IARF-religiousfreedom.net

David Wise & Thomas B. Ross, *The Espionage Establishment* (New York: Random House, 1967).

William Corso, Susan B. Trento & Joseph J. Trento, *Widows* (New York: Crown Publishers, Inc., 1979).

Christopher Andrew & Vasili Mitrokhin, *The Sword and the Shield* (New York: Basic Books, 1999).

Sanford J. Ungar, *FBI* (Boston: Little, Brown & Company, 1976).

David Wise, *Molehunt* (New York: Random House, 1992).

Michael R. Beschloss, *May-Day* (New York: Harper & Row 1986).

Walter Laquer, *A World of Secrets: The Uses and Limits of Intelligence* (New York: Basic Books, Inc., 1985).

Peter Deriabin & Frank Gibney, *The Secret World* (New York: Ballantine Books, 1959 & 1987).

Steven Lee Myers, "In Treason Trial, Echoes of Soviet Past and KGB Secrets," *New York Times*, June 11, 2002, and "Russia Convicts a Former KGB General Now Living in U.S.," June 27, 2002.

David Stout, "Once A Top Russian Spy, Now a Proud American," *New York Times*, August 24, 2003.

Ladislav Bittman, *The KGB and Soviet Disinformation* (Washington [etc.]: Pergammon-Brasseys' International Defense Publishers, 1985).

James Srodes, *Allen Dulles: Master of Spies* (Washington, D.C.: Regnery Publishing, Inc., 1999).

John H. Waller, *The Unseen War in Europe* (New York: Random House, 1996).

Joseph Persico, *Piercing the Third Reich* (New York: Viking, 1979).

Essay Three:
Richard Boeke: Recorded statement on IARF web site.

Harvard Divinity School, Andover-Harvard Theological Library , Correspondence and Memoranda of the officers of the Friends of Albert Schweitzer College in the United States, 1953-1972.

Lawrence S. Wittner, "Blacklisting Schweitzer," The Bulletin of the Atomic Scientists, May/June 1995, Vol. 51, #3.

Edward L. Schapsmeier, "Paul H. Douglas: United States Senator," Notable American   Unitarians biographical archive.

"Congressional Bio: Douglas, Paul Howard, 1892-1976."

Eric Thomas Chester, *Covert Network* (Armonk, New York: M.E. Sharp, 1995).

Van Eric Fox & Alice Blair Wesley, "James Luther Adams," Dictionary of Unitarian and Universalist Biography.

Louis Budenz, *The Techniques of Communism*, (1954).

George W. Pickering, *American Journal of Theology and Philosophy*, May, 2000, Vol. 21, #2.

James Luther Adams, *Not Without Dust and Heat: A Memoir* (Exploration Press, 1995).

David Little, "Liberalism and World Order: The Thought of James Luther Adams," Harvard Divinity Bulletin, Vol. 31, #3, Summer 2003.

Lawrence S. Wittner, "Blacklisting Schweitzer," The Bulletin of the Atomic Scientists, May/June 1995, Vol. 51, #3.

Essay Four:

Penny Lernoux, *Cry of the People* (Penguin Books, 1982).

Owen Chadwick, *The Christian Church in the Cold War* (London: Allen Lane, Penguin Press, 1992).

Anthony Cave Brown, ed., *The Secret War Report of the OSS* (Berkley Medallion Books, 1976).

John D. Marks, "The CIA's Church Connection: Missionaries as Informants," National Catholic News Service, July 18, 1975.

Frances Stonor Saunders, *The Cultural Cold War* (New York, New York Press, 1999).

Reinhold Niebuhr, "The Moral World of Foster Dulles," *The New Republic* CXXXIX, Dec. 1, 1958.

Hilton Kramer, *The Twilight of the Intellectuals: Culture and Politics in the Era of the Cold War* (Ivan R. Dee, 1999).

Stephen J. Whitfield, *The Culture of the Cold War* (Johns Hopkins U. Press, 1991).

Mark Silk, *Spiritual Politics: Religion and America Since World War* II (Simon & Schuster, 1988).

Christopher Simpson, *The Splendid Blond Beast* (Common Courage Press, 1995).

Herman Field and Kate Field, *Trapped in the Cold War* (Stanford U. Press, 1999).

Robert Murphy, *Diplomat Among Warriors* (Doubleday & Co., 1964).

Rex A. Wade, *The Bolshevik Revolution and Russian Civil War* (Greenwood Press, 2001).

H.W. Brands, Jr., *Cold Warriors* (New York: Columbia University Press, 1988).

Peter Grose, *Gentleman Spy* (Houghton Mifflin, 1994).

Wade, *Greenwood Press Guide to Historic Events of the 20th Century.*

Michael Pearson, *The Sealed Train* (G.P. Putnam's Sons, 1975).

Hans A. Schmidt, *Quakers and Nazis: Inner Light in Outer Darkness* (U of Missouri Press, 1997).

Roger C. Wilson, *Quaker Relief* (George Allen & Unwen Ltd., 1952).

Stephen Ambrose, *Ike's Spies: Eisenhower and the Espionage Establishment* (Doubleday, 1981).

Heideking & Mauch, eds., *American Intelligence and the German Resistance to Hitler: A Documentary History* (Westview Press, 1996).

Robert N. Bellah, "Evil and the American Ethos," Sanctions for Evil (Beacon Press, 1971).

Varian Fry, *Surrender on Demand* (Johnson Books, 1997).

Andy Marino, *A Quiet American: The Secret War of Varian Fry* (St. Martin's Press, 1999).

Stewart Alsop and Thomas Braden *Sub Rosa: The OSS and American Espionage* (Harcourt Brace, 1946, 1964).

Burton Hersh, *The Old Boys* (Charles Scribner's Sons, 1992).

Charles Whiting, *The Spymasters* (E.P. Dutton & Co., 1976).

Angelo M. Cordevilla, *Between the Alps and a Hard Place: Switzerland in World War II and Moral Blackmail Today* (Regnery Publishing, 2000).

Adam Le Bor, *Hitler's Secret Bankers* (Carol Publishing Group, 1997).

Hede Massing, *This Deception* (Duel Sloan & Pierce, 1951).

Jeremy Taylor, "UU Roots – The Founding of the Unitarian Service Committee, jeremytaylor.com.

Joseph E. Persico, *Casey: From the OSS to the CIA* (Viking Penguin, 1990).

John Chabot Smith, *Alger Hiss: The True Story* (Penguin, 1997)

Herbert Romerstein, "Soviet Archives Confirm Hiss Guilt," *Human Events* 1/21/94, Vol. 50 Issue 2.

Eric Breindel & H. Romerstein, "Hiss: Still Guilty," New Republic 12/30/96 Vol. 215 Issue 53, Alger Hiss, *In the Court of Public Opinion* (Alfred A. Knopf, 1997)

J.S. Conway, *The Nazi Persecution of the Churches* (Basic Books, Inc., 1968).

Peter Dale Scott, *The Dallas Conspiracy.*

Mary Bancroft, *Autobiography of a Spy* (William Morrow & Co., 1983).

David F. Rudgers, *Creating the Secret State: The Origins of the Central Intelligence Agency, 1943-1947* (University Press of Kansas, 2000).

David J. Dallin, *Soviet Espionage* (Yale University Press, 1955).

Robert J. Lamphere & Tom Schactman, *The FBI-KGB War* (Random House, 1987).

Douglas Martin, obituary, *New York Times*, 2/11/02.

Stewart Steven, *Operation Splinter Factor* (J.B. Lippincott Co., 1974).

Wilfred Burchett, *At the Barricades* (Times Books, 1981).

Bobby R. Inman, "Spying for a Long, Hot War," *New York Times*, Oct. 9, 2001.

UUSC History Archives, Drawer 3, Row 1.

A.J. Langguth, *Hidden Terrors* (Pantheon Books, 1978).

David Chidester, *Christianity: A Global History* (Harper San Francisco, 2000).

Jonathan Glover, Humanity: A Moral History of the Twentieth Century (Yale University Press, 2000).

Essay Five:

Antony Sutton, *America's Secret Establishment* (Liberty House Press, 1986, TrineDay Books, 2009).

Townsend Hoopes, *The Devil and John Foster Dulles* (Little, Brown & Co., 1973).

Ronald W. Pruesson, *John Foster Dulles* (The Free Press, 1982).

Michael A. Gulin, *John Foster Dulles: A Statesman and His Time* (Columbia U. Press, 1972).

James Goold-Adams, *John Foster Dulles: A Reappraisal* (Greenwood Press).

Lorenzo Albacete, "Divine Promotion," *New York Times Magazine*, 2/11/01.

Herbert S. Parmet, *Eisenhower and the American Crusades* (Macmillan Co., 1972).

Andrew H. Berding, *Dulles on Diplomacy* (D. Van Nostrand Co., Inc., 1965).

John Robinson Beal, *John Foster Dulles* (Harper & Brothers, 1957).

Gerald Colby [with Charlotte Dennett] *Thy Will Be Done: The Conquest of the Amazon; Nelson Rockefeller and Evangelism in the Age of Oil* (Harper Collins, 1995).

Myer Kutz, *Rockefeller Power* (Simon & Schuster, 1974).

Louis L. Gerson, *John Foster Dulles* (Cooper Square Publishers, 1967).

Henry Van Dusen, ed., *The Spiritual Legacy of John Foster Dulles* (Westminster Press, 1960).

I.F. Stone, *The Haunted Fifties* (Random House, 1963).

Ferdinand Lundberg, *The Rockefeller Syndrome* (Lyle Stuart, Inc., 1975).

F.W. Sollmann, *Religion and Politics* (Pendle Hill Pamphlets, 1941).

Walter La Feber, *America, Russia and the Cold War, 1945-1990* (McGraw-Hill, 1991).

I.F. Stone, *The Truman Era* (Monthly Review Press, 1953)

John L. Gaddis, *Strategies of Containment* (Oxford U. Press, 1982)

John Foster Dulles, *War or Peace* (Macmillan Co., 1950).

Joel Kovel, *Red Hunting in the Promised Land* (Basic Books, 1994).

Justin Lewis, *Constructing Public Opinion* (Columbia U. Press, 2001).

Medhurst, Ivie, Wander, & Scott, eds., *Cold War Rhetoric: Strategy, Metaphor, and Ideology* (Greenwood Press, 1990).

Charles C. Alexander, *Holding the Line: The Eisenhower Era, 1952-1961* (Indiana University Press, 1975).

James Munves, *The FBI and the CIA: Secret Agents and American Democracy* (Harcourt Brace Jovanovich, 1975).

Richard N. Lebow & Janice G. Stein, *We All Lost the Cold War* (Princeton U. Press, 1994).

Essay Six:

Michael Canfield & Alan J. Weberman, *Coup d'etat in America* (The Third Press, 1975).

G. William Domhoff, *Who Rules America?* (Prentice-Hall, Inc., 1967).

L. Fletcher Prouty, *The Secret Team* (Prentice-Hall, Inc.).

David Wise & Thomas B. Ross, *The Invisible Government* (Vintage Books, 1964).

Anthony Samson, *The Arms Bazaar* (Viking Press, 1977).

Philip H. Melanson, *Spy Saga* (Praeger Publishers, 1990).

Michael Benson, *Who's Who in the JFK Assassination* (Citadel Press Book, 1993).

Joseph J. Trento, *The Secret History of the CIA* (Carroll & Graf, 2005).

Blanche Wiesen Cook, *The Declassified Eisenhower* (Doubleday, 1981). Also, "First Comes the Lie: C.D. Jackson and Political Warfare," *Radical History Review* 31, 1984.

James L. Baughman, *Henry Luce and the Rise of the American News Media* (Twayne Publishers, 1987).

Elizabeth Mcintosh, *Sisterhood of Spies: The Women of the OSS* (Naval Institute Press, 1998).

Lawrence C. Stoley, *Radio Warfare* (Praeger, 1989).

Christopher Simpson, *Blowback* (Weidenfeld & Nicollson, 1988).

Eliot Harris, *The 'un-American Weapon: Psychological Warfare* (M.W. Lads Publishing, 1967).

I.F. Stone, *The Hidden History of the Korean War* (Monthly Review Press, 1952).

Robert Bowie & Richard H. Immerman, *Waging Peace* (Oxford U. Press, 1998).

Robert J. Donovan, *Eisenhower* (Harper & Bros., 1956).

Stephen Schlesinger & Stephen Kinzer, *Bitter Fruit* (Doubleday, 1982).

Jon Elliston, ed., *Psywar on Cuba: The Declassified History of U.S. Anti-Castro Propaganda* (Ocean Press, 1999).

McGeorge Bundy, *Danger and Survival* (Random House, 1988).

Martin J. Medhurst, *Armed Forces & Society* Summer 1997.

Stephen E. Ambrose, *Eisenhower, Volume Two, The President* (Simon & Schuster, 1984).

Kai Bird, *The Chairman* (Simon & Schuster,1992).

Webster Tarpley & Anton Chaitkin, *George Bush* (Executive Intelligence Review, 1992).

Robert Sam Anson, *"They've Killed the President!"* (Bantam Books, 1975).

Warren Hinckle & William Turner, *The Fish is Red* (Harper & Row, 1981).

ESSAY SEVEN:
Dwight David Eisenhower, *Mandate for Change: 1953-1956* (Doubleday, 1963).

Percival F. Brundage, *The Bureau of the Budget* (Praeger, 1970).

Francis E. Rourke, *Bureaucracy, Politics, and Public Policy* (HarperCollins, 1984).

David M. Barrett, *The CIA and Congress* (University Press of Kansas, 2005).

Richard F. Kaufman, *The War Profiteers* (Bobbs-Merrill, 1970).

Joseph E. Kallenbach, *The American Chief Executive* (Harper & Row, 1966).

William Stevens, *A Man Called Intrepid* (Ballantine, 1977).

Peter Woll, *American Bureaucracy* (Norton & Company, 1963).

Louis Fisher, *Presidential Spending Power* (Princeton U. Press, 1975).

Howard E. Shuman, *Politics and the Budget: the Struggle Between the President and the Congress* (Prentice-Hall, 1984).

Tim Weiner, "[obituary] W.L. Pforzheimer, 88, Dies; Helped to Shape the C.I.A.," *New York Times*, 2/16/03.

William T. Golden, "Memoranda of William T. Golden," American Assn. for the Advancement of Science: Oct. 1950-April 1951.

Henry Howe Ransom, *The Intelligence Establishment* (Harvard U. Press, 1970).

Philip Taubman, *Secret Empire* (Simon & Schuster, 2003).

Andrew Tully, *CIA: The Inside Story* (William Morrow & Co., 1962).

Col. Cass Schichtle, *The National Space Program: from the fifties into the Eighties* (National Defense University Press, 1983).

Glen Asner, "Edwin Land and Restraint by Reconnaissance," 2/12/99.

Homer E. Newell, Jr., *Beyond the Atmosphere: Early Years of Space Science*.

Arthur L. Levine, "United States Aeronautic Research Policy, 1915-1958," doctoral dissertation, Columbia U.

Richard J. Barnett, *The Economy of Death* (Atheneum, 1972).

Arnold Kantner, *Defense Politics* (U of Chicago Press, 1979).

Victor Marchetti & John D. Marks, *The CIA and the Cult of Intelligence* (Dell Publishing, 1975).

Charles E. Jacobs, *Policy and Bureaucracy* (D. Van Nostrand Co., 1966).

William E. Burrows, *The New Ocean* (Random House, 1998).

Richard A. Caro, *Master of the Senate* (Knopf, 2002).

Chester J. Pach, Jr. & Elmo Richardson, *The Presidency of Dwight D. Eisenhower* (University Press of Kansas, 1991).

John Ehrlichman, *Washington: Behind Closed Doors* (Kangaroo Book/Pocket Books).

Marquis Childs, *Eisenhower: Captive Hero* (Harcourt Brace, 1958).

Mark green, James M. Fallows, & David R. Zwick, *Who Rules Congress* (Bantam Books, 1972).

William Corson, *The Armies of Ignorance* (Dial Press/James Wade, 1977).

Michael Warner, "The Creation of the Central Intelligence Group," Studies in Intelligence, Fall, 1995.

Percival Brundage, [on] "Project Vanguard," April 30, 1957. BOB files, Eisenhower Library.

Tristram Coffin, *Passion of the Hawks, The Armed Society* (Penguin Books, 1964).

G. William Domhoff, *The Higher Circles* (Vintage Books, 1971).

Seymour Melman, *Pentagon Capitalism* (McGraw-Hill, 1970).

Alpern, Marro, Clark, & McGee, "How the CIA Does Business." *Newsweek*, 5/19/75.

Jonathan Kwitny, *The Crimes of Patriots* (Touchstone, Simon & Schuster, 1987).

Penny Lernoux, *In Banks We Trust* (Viking Penguin Books, 1986).

Darrell Garwood, *Undercover: The Thirty-five Years of CIA Deception* (Grove Press, 1985).

Alfred W. McCoy, *The politics of Heroin in Southeast Asia* (Harper Colophon Books, 1972).
Robert Schacht, Letter to Percival Brundage dated 12/5/63, Harvard Divinity School Library.

Essay Eight:
Gaeton Fonzi, *The Last Investigation* (Thunder's Mouth Press, 1993).
Thomas Mallon, *Mrs. Paine's Garage* (Pantheon Books, 2002).
Nancy Wertz, "Michael Paine – A Life of Unanswered Paradoxes," Kennedy Assassination Chronicles, Vol. 4, Issue 4, Winter 1998.
Mary Bancroft, *Autobiography of a Spy* (William Morrow & Co., 1983).
Diedre Bair, *Jung* (Little, Brown, 2003).
E. Digby Baltzell, *Puritan Boston and Quaker Philadelphia* (New York: 1979).
Arnold Forster & Benjamin Epstein, *Danger on the Right* (Random House, 1964).
Carlos P. Romulo & Marvin M. Gray, *The Magsaysay Story* (John Day Co., 1956).
William J. Pomeroy, *An American Made Tragedy* (International Publishers, 1974).
George Carpozi, Jr., *Red Spies in Washington* (Trident Press, 1968).
Anthony Summers, *Not in Your Lifetime* (Marlowe & Co., 1998).
Philip Agee, *Inside the Company* (Stonehill, 1975).
David Wise, *Nightmover* (HarperCollins, 1995).
Sterling Seagrave, *The Marcos Dynasty* (Harper & Row, 1988).
Edwin Black, *War Against the Weak* (Four Walls Eight Windows, 2003).
Douglas A. Blackmon, "A Breed Apart ..." *Wall Street Journal*, 8/17/99.
Mary Meehan, Meehan Reports, "Eugenics and the Power Elite," *Social Justice Review*, Nov.-Dec., 1997.
Barry Mehler, "In Genes We Trust"
"Constructing A Postwar World: The G.I. Roundtable in Context
Larry Collins, "The Free Europe Committee: American Weapon of the Cold War" (Carlton U on microfiche, 1975).
Noel L. Griese, *Arthur W. Page: Publisher, Public Relations Pioneer*, Patriot (Anvil Publishers, 2001).
Michael Nelson, *War of the Black heavens* (Syracuse U. Press, 1997).
Christopher Simpson, *Science of Coercion* (Oxford U. Press, 1994).

Epilogue:
George Michael Evica, "Perfect Cover," The Assassination Chronicles Vol. 1, Issue 4, December 1995.

Index

Frank, Richard A. 59
Frederick May Eliot as I Knew Him. 158
Fredricksen, Norman 289, 290, 292
Fritchman, Stephen 34-37, 84, 86, 87, 128, 159, 282
Fry, Varian 116-123, 129, 230, 271, 325, 345

G

Gaebler, Maas ("Max") D. 83
Gano, Joy 271
Gano, Seth 128, 145, 159, 160, 271, 276
Gardner, O. Max 258
Gates, Thomas S. 273
Gehlen, Reinhard 151, 152, 224
Gilligan, John 283
Glaser, Erika 137, 152-154
Glover, Everett 289-292
Goldberg, Arthur 114, 115, 123, 137
Golden, William T. 242-245
Golitsin, Anatoly 75
Goodpaster, Andrew 90, 248, 250, 266
Gordon, Judith 301
Graf, Allen D. 27
Graham, Billy 106, 176
Gray, Gordon 215, 216, 334
Greeley, Dana McLean 91
Green, James 90
Gregory, Peter 233, 292
Grimm, Kurt 125
Grose, Peter 108-111, 113
GRU (*Glavnoye Razvedyvatel'noye Upravleniye*) 75, 78, 79, 135, 192, 317

H

Hafstad, Lawrence 244
Harriman, Averell 135, 140, 240
Harrington, Donald 146, 159
Harvard Divinity School 41, 51, 85, 88, 91, 95, 98, 102, 158
Harvey, William King Jr. 61, 149
Harwell, Helen 229
Heindel, John Rene 27
Helligas, Byrd 304

Helliwell, Paul 273, 274
Herman, Stewart W. 137, 138
Hersh, Berton 151
Herter, Christian 42, 45, 55-57, 191, 203
Herzog, Helene 111
Hickey, Edward J. 70, 71
"Hidell, A.J. 22, 23
Hiss, Alger 132-136, 148, 151, 281
Hitler, Adolph 311
Hoch, Paul L. 28
Hoegner, Wilhelm 139
Hoke, Sylvia Hyde 283, 336
Hooft, W.A.V. 139, 140
Hoover, J. Edgar 11, 13, 17, 25, 26, 57-61, 64, 66, 69-71, 75, 135, 142, 276, 280
Hopkins, Harry 134, 135, 203, 223, 240
Hopper, Leon 86, 87, 91
House Select Committee on Assassinations (HSCA) 16, 28, 63, 199, 232, 284
HT/LINGUAL 44, 194, 317, 318
Huks 295, 296
Hunt, E. Howard 64, 219, 302
Hyde, Carol 282-285, 299, 336
Hyde, William Avery 282-284, 336

I

I.G. Farben 125
Institute for the Study of Consciousness 286
International Association for Religious Freedom (IARF) 83, 272, 276, 315
International Peace Academy 286
International Relief and Rescue Committee (IRRC) 129, 130
International Rescue Committee (IRC) 98, 119, 120, 129, 212, 228-231
InterPol 93

J

Jackson, C.D. 144, 155, 202-228, 231-235, 247, 252, 253, 267, 273, 275, 292, 298, 302, 305, 311, 312, 327,

Martin, Douglas 345
Martin, James Herbert 232, 233, 292
Martin-Marietta 196, 197, 251
Massachusetts Institute of Technology
(MIT) 243-248, 251, 252
Massing, Hede 133, 148
Matlack, Dorothe 284
Mayo, Robert P. 265, 269, 270
McCarthy, Joseph 106, 135, 151, 154
McCloy, John J. 11, 13-16, 225, 312
McClure, R.A. 206-208, 211-213, 219,
221
McCone, John 17
McCord, James 64
McCormick, Vance 173
McDonough, Sue 22
McElhney, Victor 251
McGuire, E Perkins 272, 273
McNally, James C. 107, 108, 112
McNamara, Robert 259, 263, 265
Meagher, Sylvia 16, 229
Medhurst, Martin J. 186, 220
Melanson, Philip H. 199
Melby, John F. 295, 296
Merrill, Frederick T. 297, 298
Metropole Hotel 20
Mexico City 192, 300-303
Meyer, Cord 225, 312
MI-6 79
Milliman, Barrie 301
Moore, Don 75
Moore, J. Walton 142, 283
Morale Services Branch 308
Mosley, Leonard 107-109, 111, 152

N

Nagell, Richard Case 37
National Aeronautics and Space Admin-
istration (NASA) 250-252, 255-
259, 263
National Archives and Records Admin-
istration (NARA) 22, 35, 41, 59,
63, 66, 71, 143, 155, 304
National Committee for Aeronautics
(NACA) 254-256
National Committee for a Free Europe

(NCFE) 154, 210, 212, 213, 308-
310
National Council of Churches (NCC)
187, 188
National Security Agency (NSA) 25,
213, 259, 260
National Security Council (NSC) 143,
208, 214-218, 238, 241, 250, 253,
260, 261, 263-267, 270, 273
Nechiporenko, Oleg 76
Newell, Homer 252, 253
Newman, John 43, 53, 55, 193
New Orleans Council for Peaceful Al-
ternatives 300
Newsweek 220, 275
New York Daily News 89
New York Herald Tribune 220
New York Times 89, 132, 147, 174
Nicolai, Colonel Walther 112
Niebuhr, Reinhold 106, 115, 116, 184
Niederer, Werner 95
Niemöller, Martin 141
Nixon, Richard 135, 194, 227, 230, 252,
258

O

Office of Management and Budget 260
Office of Naval Intelligence 22, 27-29,
33, 55, 72, 174, 195, 196
Office of Policy Coordination (OPC)
143, 151, 152, 218, 309, 310
Office of Strategic Services (OSS) 21, 25,
60, 70, 72, 80, 99, 100, 105, 106,
114-116, 118-125, 128-132, 134-
139, 141-146, 150, 152, 154, 156,
157, 159-163, 197, 201, 203, 204,
208, 212, 219, 228, 230, 233, 239,
241, 245, 246, 249, 259, 269, 271-
274, 276, 282-284, 286, 295, 302,
309, 312, 316
Office of the Coordinator of Information (OCI) 114, 116, 123, 124,
239, 240
Office of War Information (OWI) 204,
205, 206, 219
Operation AMLASH 63-65

TrineDay's FEATURED TITLES

The True Story of the Bilderberg Group
NORTH AMERICAN UNION EDITION
BY DANIEL ESTULIN

More than a center of influence, the Bilderberg Group is a shadow world government, hatching plans of domination at annual meetings ... and under a cone of media silence.

THE TRUE STORY OF THE BILDERBERG GROUP goes inside the secret meetings and sheds light on why a group of politicians, businessmen, bankers and other mighty individuals formed the world's most powerful society. As Benjamin Disraeli, one of England's greatest Prime Ministers, noted, "The world is governed by very different personages from what is imagined by those who are not behind the scenes."

Included are unpublished and never-before-seen photographs and other documentation of meetings, as this riveting account exposes the past, present and future plans of the Bilderberg elite.

Softcover: **$24.95** (ISBN: 9780979988622) • 432 pages • Size: 6 x 9

ShadowMasters
BY DANIEL ESTULIN

AN INTERNATIONAL NETWORK OF GOVERNMENTS AND SECRET-SERVICE AGENCIES WORKING TOGETHER WITH DRUG DEALERS AND TERRORISTS FOR MUTUAL BENEFIT AND PROFIT

THIS INVESTIGATION EXAMINES HOW behind-the-scenes collaboration between governments, intelligence services and drug traffickers has lined the pockets of big business and Western banks. Beginning with a last-minute request from ex-governor Jesse Ventura, the narrative winds between the author's own story of covering "deep politics" and the facts he has uncovered. The ongoing campaign against Victor Bout, the "Merchant of Death," is revealed as "move/countermove" in a game of geopolitics, set against the background of a crumbling Soviet Union, a nascent Russia, bizarre assassinations, wars and smuggling. DANIEL ESTULIN is an award-winning investigative journalist and author of *The True Story of the Bilderberg Group*.

Softcover: **$24.95** (ISBN: 9780979988615) • 432 pages • Size: 6 x 9

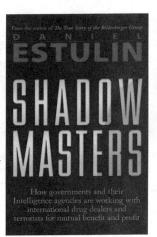

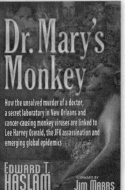

Dr. Mary's Monkey
How the Unsolved Murder of a Doctor, a Secret Laboratory in New Orleans and Cancer-Causing Monkey Viruses are Linked to Lee Harvey Oswald, the JFK Assassination and Emerging Global Epidemics
BY EDWARD T. HASLAM, FOREWORD BY JIM MARRS

Evidence of top-secret medical experiments and cover-ups of clinical blunders
The 1964 murder of a nationally known cancer researcher sets the stage for this gripping exposé of medical professionals enmeshed in covert government operations over the course of three decades. Following a trail of police records, FBI files, cancer statistics, and medical journals, this revealing book presents evidence of a web of medical secret-keeping that began with the handling of evidence in the JFK assassination and continued apace, sweeping doctors into cover-ups of cancer outbreaks, contaminated polio vaccine, the genesis of the AIDS virus, and biological weapon research using infected monkeys.

Softcover: **$19.95** (ISBN: 0977795306) • 320 pages • Size: 5 1/2 x 8 1/2

The Oil Card
Global Economic Warfare in the 21st Century
BY JAMES NORMAN

Challenging the conventional wisdom surrounding high oil prices, this compelling argument sheds an entirely new light on free-market industry fundamentals.

By deciphering past, present, and future geopolitical events, it makes the case that oil pricing and availability have a long history of being employed as economic weapons by the United States. Softcover **$14.95** (ISBN 0977795390) • 288 Pages

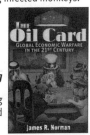

THE 9/11 MYSTERY PLANE
AND THE VANISHING OF AMERICA

BY MARK GAFFNEY

FOREWORD BY

DR. DAVID RAY GRIFFIN

Unlike other accounts of the historic attacks on 9/11, this discussion surveys the role of the world's most advanced military command and control plane, the E-4B, in the day's events and proposes that the horrific incidents were the work of a covert operation staged within elements of the U.S. military and the intelligence community. Presenting hard evidence, the account places the world's most advanced electronics platform circling over the White House at approximately the time of the Pentagon attack. The argument offers an analysis of the new evidence within the context of the events and shows that it is irreconcilable with the official 9/11 narrative.

Mark H. Gaffney is an environmentalist, a peace activist, a researcher, and the author of *Dimona, the Third Temple?*; and *Gnostic Secrets of the Naassenes*. He lives in Chiloquin, Oregon. Dr. David Ray Griffin is a professor emeritus at the Claremont School of Theology, and the author of *The 9/11 Commission Report: Omissions and Distortions*, and *The New Pearl Harbor*. He lives in Santa Barbara, California.

Softcover • **$19.95** • 9780979988608 • 336 Pages

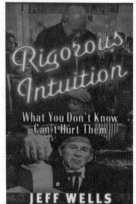

Rigorous Intuition
What You Don't Know, Can't Hurt Them
BY JEFF WELLS

"In Jeff's hands, tinfoil hats become crowns and helmets of the purest gold. I strongly suggest that you all pay attention to what he has to say." —Arthur Gilroy, Booman Tribune

A welcome source of analysis and commentary for those prepared to go deeper—and darker—than even most alternative media permit, this collection from one of the most popular conspiracy theory arguments on the internet will assist readers in clarifying their own arguments and recognizing disinformation. Tackling many of the most difficult subjects that define our time—including 9/11, the JonBenet Ramsey case, and "High Weirdness"—these studies, containing the best of the Rigorous Intuition blog as well as original content, make connections that both describe the current, alarming predicament and suggest a strategy for taking back the world. Following the maxim "What you don't know can't hurt them," this assortment of essays and tools, including the updated and expanded "Coincidence Theorists' Guide to 9/11," guides the intellectually curious down further avenues of study and scrutiny and helps readers feel empowered rather than vulnerable.

Jeff Wells is the author of the novel *Anxious Gravity*. He lives in Toronto, Ontario.

Softcover • **$19.95** • 978-0-9777953-2-1 • 505 Pages

PERFECTIBILISTS
The 18th Century Bavarian Illuminati
BY TERRY MELANSON

The shadowy Illuminati grace many pages of fiction as the sinister all-powerful group pulling the strings behind the scenes, but very little has been printed in English about the actual Enlightenment-era secret society, its activities, its members, and its legacy ... until now.

First choosing the name Perfectibilists, their enigmatic leader Adam Weishaupt soon thought that sounded too bizarre and changed it to the Order of the Illuminati.

Presenting an authoritative perspective, this definitive study chronicles the rise and fall of the fabled Illuminati, revealing their methods of infiltrating governments and education systems, and their blueprint for a successful cabal, which echoes directly forward through groups like the Order of Skull & Bones to our own era.

Featuring biographies of more than 400 confirmed members and copiously illustrated, this book brings light to a 200-year-old mystery.

Softcover: **$19.95** • 9780977795381 • 530 pages • Size: 6 x 9

The King of Nepal
Life Before the Drug Wars
BY JOSEPH PIETRI

From the halcyon days of easily accessible drugs to years of government intervention and a surging black market, this tale chronicles a former drug smuggler's 50-year career in the drug trade, its evolution into a multibillion-dollar business, and the characters he met along the way. The journey begins with the infamous Hippie Hash trail that led from London and Amsterdam overland to Nepal where, prior to the early 1970s, hashish was legal and smoked freely; marijuana and opium were sold openly in Hindu temples in India and much of Asia; and cannabis was widely cultivated for use in food, medicine, and cloth. In documenting the stark contrasts of the ensuing years, the narrative examines the impact of the financial incentives awarded by international institutions such as the U.S. government to outlaw the cultivation of cannabis in Nepal and Afghanistan and to make hashish and opium illegal in Turkey—the demise of the U.S. "good old boy" dope network, the eruption of a violent criminal society, and the birth of a global black market for hard drugs—as well as the schemes smugglers employed to get around customs agents and various regulations.

Softcover • **$19.95** • 9780979988660 • 240 Pages

Expendable Elite
One Soldier's Journey into Covert Warfare
BY DANIEL MARVIN , FOREWORD BY MARTHA RAYE

A special operations perspective on the Viet Nam War and the truth about a White House concerned with popular opinion

This true story of a special forces officer in Viet Nam in the mid-1960s exposes the unique nature of the elite fighting force and how covert operations are developed and often masked to permit — and even sponsor — assassination, outright purposeful killing of innocents, illegal use of force, and bizarre methods in combat operations. *Expendable Elite* reveals the fear that these warriors share with no other military person: not fear of the enemy they have been trained to fight in battle, but fear of the wrath of the US government should they find themselves classified as "expendable." This book centers on the CIA mission to assassinate Cambodian Crown Prince Nordum Sihanouk, the author's unilateral aborting of the mission, the CIA's dispatch of an ARVN regiment to attack and destroy the camp and kill every person in it as retribution for defying the agency, and the dramatic rescue of eight American Green Berets and hundreds of South Viet Namese.

DANIEL MARVIN is a retired Lieutenant Colonel in the US Army Special Forces and former Green Beret.

Softcover: **$19.95** (ISBN 0977795314) • 420 pages • 150+ photos & maps

Fighting For G.O.D.
(Gold, Oil, Drugs)
BY JEREMY BEGIN, ART BY LAUREEN SALK

This racehorse tour of American history and current affairs scrutinizes key events transcending the commonly accepted liberal/conservative political ideologies — in a large-size comic-book format.

This analysis delves into aspects of the larger framework into which 9/11 fits and scrutinizes the ancestry of the players who transcend commonly accepted liberal/conservative political ideologies. This comic-book format analysis examines the Neo Con agenda and its relationship to "The New World Order. This book discusses key issues confronting America's citizenry and steps the populace can take to not only halt but reverse the march towards totalitarianism.

Jeremy Begin is a long-time activist/organizer currently residing in California's Bay Area. Lauren Salk is an illustrator living in Boston.

Softcover: **$9.95**, (ISBN 0977795330) 64 Pages, 8.5 x 11

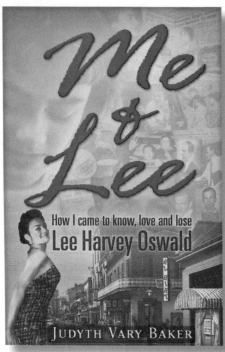

Me & Lee
How I Came to Know, Love and Lose Lee Harvey Oswald
BY JUDYTH VARY BAKER

FOREWORD BY

EDWARD T. HASLAM

JUDYTH VARY WAS ONCE A PROMISING science student who dreamed of finding a cure for cancer; this exposé is her account of how she strayed from a path of mainstream scholarship at the University of Florida to a life of espionage in New Orleans with Lee Harvey Oswald. In her narrative she offers extensive documentation on how she came to be a cancer expert at such a young age, the personalities who urged her to relocate to New Orleans, and what lead to her involvement in the development of a biological weapon that Oswald was to smuggle into Cuba to eliminate Fidel Castro. Details on what she knew of Kennedy's impending assassination, her conversations with Oswald as late as two days before the killing, and her belief that Oswald was a deep-cover intelligence agent who was framed for an assassination he was actually trying to prevent, are also revealed.

JUDYTH VARY BAKER is a teacher, and artist. Edward T. Haslam is the author of *Dr. Mary's Monkey*. Hardcover • **$24.95** • ISBN 9780979988677 • 580 Pages

ORDER BY ONLINE OR BY PHONE:
TrineDay.com

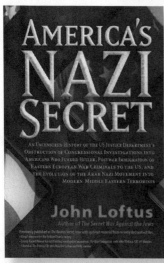

America's Nazi Secret
AN UNCENSORED HISTORY OF THE US JUSTICE DEPARTMENT'S OBSTRUCTION OF CONGRESSIONAL INVESTIGATIONS INTO AMERICANS WHO FUNDED HITLER, POSTWAR IMMIGRATION OF EASTERN EUROPEAN WAR CRIMINALS TO THE US, AND THE EVOLUTION OF THE ARAB NAZI MOVEMENT INTO MODERN MIDDLE EASTERN TERRORISTS
BY JOHN LOFTUS

Fully revised and expanded, this stirring account reveals how the U.S. government permitted the illegal entry of Nazis into North America in the years following World War II. This extraordinary investigation exposes the secret section of the State Department that began, starting in 1948 and unbeknownst to Congress and the public until recently, to hire members of the puppet wartime government of Byelorussia—a region of the Soviet Union occupied by Nazi Germany. A former Justice Department investigator uncovered this stunning story in the files of several government agencies, and it is now available with a chapter previously banned from release by authorities and a foreword and afterword with recently declassified materials.

John Loftus is a former U.S. government prosecutor, a former Army intelligence officer, and the author of numerous books, including *The Belarus Secret, The Secret War Against the Jews, Unholy Trinity: How the Vatican's Nazi Networks Betrayed Western Intelligence to the Soviets,* and *Unholy Trinity: The Vatican, the Nazis, and the Swiss Banks.* He has appeared regularly as a media commentator on ABC National Radio and Fox News. He lives in St. Petersburg, Florida.

Softcover • **$24.95** • ISBN 978-1-936296-04-0 • 288 Pages

The Hunt for Kuhn Sa
DRUG LORD OF THE GOLDEN TRIANGLE
BY RON FELDER

FOR TWO DECADES, the Burmese warlord Khun Sa controlled nearly 70 percent of the world's heroin supply, yet there has been little written about the legend the U.S. State Department branded the "most evil man in the world"—until now. Through exhaustive investigative journalism, this examination of one of the world's major drug lords from the 1970s to the 1990s goes behind the scenes into the lives of the DEA specialists assigned the seemingly impossible task of capturing or killing him. Known as Group 41, these men would fight for years in order to stop a man who, in fact, had the CIA to thank for his rise to power. Featuring interviews with DEA, CIA, Mafia, and Asian gang members, this meticulously researched and well-documented investigation reaches far beyond the expected and delves into the thrilling and shocking world of the CIA-backed heroin trade.

Ron Felber is the CEO of Chemetell, North America, and the author of eight books, including *Il Dottore: The Double Life of a Mafia Doctor*, *Presidential Lessons in Leadership*, and *Searchers: A True Story of Alien Abduction*. He lives in New Jersey.

Softover • **$19.95** • ISBN 9781936296156 • 240 Pages

1-800-556-2012

Mary's Mosaic
MARY PINCHOT MEYER & JOHN F. KENNEDY AND THEIR VISION FOR WORLD PEACE
BY PETER JANNEY
FOREWORD BY DICK RUSSELL

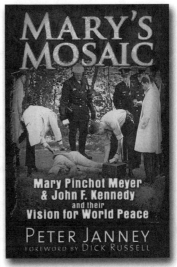

CHALLENGING THE CONVENTIONAL WISDOM surrounding the murder of Mary Pinchot Meyer, this exposé offers new information and evidence that individuals within the upper echelons of the CIA were not only involved in the assassination of President John F. Kennedy, but her demise as well. Written by the son of a CIA lifer and a college classmate of Mary Pinchot Meyer, this insider's story examines how Mary used events and circumstances in her personal life to become an acolyte for world peace. The most famous convert to her philosophy was reportedly President John F. Kennedy, with whom she was said to have begun a serious love relationship in January 1962. Offering an insightful look into the era and its culture, the narrative sheds light on how in the wake of the Cuban Missile Crisis, she helped the president realize that a Cold War mentality was of no use and that the province of world peace was the only worthwhile calling. Details on her experiences with LSD, its influences on her and Kennedy's thinking, his attempts to negotiate a limited nuclear test ban treaty with Soviet Premier Nikita Khrushchev, and to find lasting peace with Fidel Castro are also included.

Peter Janney is a former psychologist and naturopathic healer and a cofounder of the American Mental Health Alliance. He was one of the first graduates of the MIT Sloan School of Management's Entrepreneurship Skills Transfer Program. He lives in Beverly, Massachusetts. Dick Russell is the author of *Black Genius: And the American Experience*, *Eye of the Whale*, *The Man Who Knew Too Much*, and *Striper Wars: An American Fish Story*. He is a former staff writer for *TV Guide* magazine, a staff reporter for *Sports Illustrated*, and has contributed numerous articles to publications ranging from *Family Health* to the *Village Voice*. He lives in Boston, Massachusetts and Los Angeles.

Hardcover • **$29.95** • ISBN 978-1-936296-49-1 • 576 Pages

The Franklin Scandal
A Story of Powerbrokers, Child Abuse & Betrayal
BY NICK BRYANT

A chilling exposé of corporate corruption and government cover-ups, this account of a nationwide child-trafficking and pedophilia ring tells a sordid tale of corruption in high places. The scandal originally surfaced during an investigation into Omaha, Nebraska's failed Franklin Federal Credit Union and took the author beyond the Midwest and ultimately to Washington, DC. Implicating businessmen, senators, major media corporations, the CIA, and even the venerable Boys Town organization, this extensively researched report includes firsthand interviews with key witnesses and explores a controversy that has received scant media attention.

 The Franklin Scandal is the story of a underground ring that pandered children to a cabal of the rich and powerful. The ring's pimps were a pair of Republican powerbrokers who used Boys Town as a pedophiliac reservoir, and had access to the highest levels of our government and connections to the CIA.

Nick Bryant is a journalist whose work largely focuses on the plight of disadvantaged children in the United States. His mainstream and investigative journalism has been featured in Gear, Playboy, The Reader, and on Salon.com. He is the coauthor of America's Children: Triumph of Tragedy. He lives in New York City.

Hardcover: **$24.95** (ISBN: 0977795357) • 480 pages • Size: 6 x 9

Strength of the Pack
The Personalities, Politics and Intrigues that Shaped the DEA
BY DOUG VALENTINE

Through interviews with former narcotics agents, politicians, and bureaucrats, this exposé documents previously unknown aspects of the history of federal drug law enforcement from the formation of the Bureau of Narcotics and Dangerous Drugs and the creation of the Drug Enforcement Administration (DEA) up until the present day. Written in an easily accessible style, the narrative examines how successive administrations expanded federal drug law enforcement operations at home and abroad; investigates how the CIA comprised the war on drugs; analyzes the Reagan, Bush, and Clinton administrations' failed attempts to alter the DEA's course; and traces the agency's evolution into its final and current stage of "narco-terrorism."

Douglas Valentine is a former private investigator and consultant and the author of *The Hotel Tacloban, The Phoenix Program, The Strength of the Wolf*, and *TDY*.

Hardcover: **$24.95** (ISBN: 9780979988653) Softcover **$19.95** (ISBN 9781936296095) • 480 pages • Size: 6 x 9

A TERRIBLE MISTAKE
THE MURDER OF FRANK OLSON AND THE CIA'S SECRET COLD WAR EXPERIMENTS
BY H.P. ALBARELLI JR.

In his nearly 10 years of research into the death of Dr. Frank Olson, writer and investigative journalist H.P. Albarelli Jr. gained unique and unprecedented access to many former CIA, FBI, and Federal Narcotics Bureau officials, including several who actually oversaw the CIA's mind-control programs from the 1950s to the early 1970s.

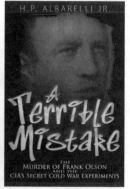

 A Terrible Mistake takes readers into a frequently bizarre and always frightening world, colored and dominated by Cold War concerns and fears. For the past 30 years the death of biochemist Frank Olson has ranked high on the nation's list of unsolved and perplexing mysteries. *A Terrible Mistake* solves the mystery and reveals in shocking detail the identities of Olson's murderers. The book also takes readers into the strange world of government mind-control programs and close collaboration with the Mafia.

H. P. Albarelli Jr. is an investigative journalist whose work has appeared in numerous publications and newspapers across the nation and is the author of the novel The Heap. He lives in Tampa, Florida.

Hardcover $**34.95** (ISBN 978-0977795376) • 852 pages • Size: 6 x 9

Softcover **$29.95** (ISBN 978-1936296088)

ORDER BY ONLINE OR BY PHONE:
TrineDay.com

P.O. Box 577
WALTERVILLE, OR 97489

1-800-556-2012